Believers Church
Bible Commentary

Elmer A. Martens and Willard M. Swartley, Editors

BELIEVERS CHURCH BIBLE COMMENTARY

Old Testament
Genesis, by Eugene F. Roop
Exodus, by Waldemar Janzen
Judges, by Terry L. Brensinger
Ruth, Jonah, Esther, by Eugene F. Roop
Jeremiah, by Elmer A. Martens
Ezekiel, by Millard C. Lind
Daniel, by Paul M. Lederach
Hosea, Amos, by Allen R. Guenther

New Testament
Matthew, by Richard B. Gardner
Mark, by Timothy J. Geddert
Acts, by Chalmer E. Faw
2 Corinthians, by V. George Shillington
Ephesians, by Thomas R. Yoder Neufeld
Colossians, Philemon, by Ernest D. Martin
1–2 Thessalonians, by Jacob W. Elias
1–2 Peter, Jude, by Erland Waltner and J. Daryl Charles
Revelation, by John Yeatts

Believers Church Bible Commentary

Mark

Timothy J. Geddert

HERALD PRESS
Scottdale, Pennsylvania
Waterloo, Ontario

Library of Congress Cataloging-in-Publication Information
Geddert, Timothy J.
 Mark / Timothy J. Geddert
  p. cm.— (Believers church Bible commentary)
 Includes bibliographical references (p.) and indexes.
 ISBN 0-8361-9140-4 (alk. paper)
  1. Bible. N.T. Mark—Commentaries. I. Title. II. Series.
 BS2585.53 .G43 2001
 226.3'077—dc21   00-063232

The paper used in this publication is recycled and meets the minimum requirements of American National Standard for Information Sciences— Permanence of Paper for Printed Library Materials, ANSI Z39.48-1984.

Bible text is used by permission, with all rights reserved, and unless otherwise noted is from NRSV: *New Revised Standard Version Bible,* copyright 1989 by the Division of Christian Education of the National Council of the Churches of Christ (DCENCCC) in the USA. GNB: *Good News Bible;* KJV: *King James Version;* NIV: *New International Version ®,* copyright © 1973, 1978, 1984 by International Bible Society, Zondervan Publishing House; NLT, *New Living Translation,* © 1996-2000 Tyndale House Publishers, Inc., Wheaton, IL 60189; RSV: *Revised Standard Version Bible,* © 1946, 1952, 1971 by DCENCCC in the USA; TJG, by author.

BELIEVERS CHURCH BIBLE COMMENTARY: MARK
Copyright © 2001 by Herald Press, Scottdale, Pa. 15683
 Released simultaneously in Canada by Herald Press,
 Waterloo, Ont. N2L 6H7. All rights reserved
Library of Congress Catalog Card Number: 00-063232
International Standard Book Number: 0-8361-9140-4
Printed in the United States of America
Cover and charts by Merrill R. Miller

10 09 08 07 06 05 04 03 02 01 10 9 8 7 6 5 4 3 2 1

To order or request information, please call 1-800-759-4447 (individuals); 1-800-245-7894 (trade). Website: www.mph.org

To Gertrud,
my loving wife and companion in ministry,
whose encouragement and support
while I was writing this commentary
were truly amazing

Abbreviations

The copyright page names and credits Bible versions. For other abbreviations in capital letters, see the Bibliography.

*	Text in Biblical Context (as flagged in Contents)
+	Text in Life of the Church (as flagged in Contents)
//	parallel to
=	parallel to, equal
adj.	adjective
ca.	circa, about
cf.	compare
chap./chaps.	chapter, chapters
[Messianic Secret]	typical reference to Essays preceding Bibliography
e.g.	for example(s)
esp.	especially
Heb.	Hebrew text, unless obviously for the NT book
lit.	literally
LXX	Septuagint, Greek translation of OT
n.	note
notes	Explanatory Notes
np.	no place of publication shown
NT	New Testament
par.	parallel to, parallels
OT	Old Testament
sing.	singular
TBC	The Text in Biblical Context
TLC	The Text in the Life of the Church
trans.	translation/translated by
v./vv.	verse/verses

Contents

Series Foreword

The Believers Church Bible Commentary Series makes available a new tool for basic Bible study. It is published for all who seek more fully to understand the original message of Scripture and its meaning for today—Sunday school teachers, members of Bible study groups, students, pastors, and others. The series is based on the conviction that God is still speaking to all who will listen, and that the Holy Spirit makes the Word a living and authoritative guide for all who want to know and do God's will.

The desire to help as wide a range of readers as possible has determined the approach of the writers. Since no blocks of biblical text are provided, readers may continue to use the translation with which they are most familiar. The writers of the series use the *New Revised Standard Version*, the *Revised Standard Version*, the *New International Version*, and the *New American Standard Bible* on a comparative basis. They indicate which text they follow most closely, as well as where they make their own translations. The writers have not worked alone, but in consultation with select counselors, the series' editors, and the Editorial Council.

Every volume illuminates the Scriptures; provides necessary theological, sociological, and ethical meanings; and, in general, makes "the rough places plain." Critical issues are not avoided, but neither are they moved into the foreground as debates among scholars. Each section offers explanatory notes, followed by focused articles, "The Text in Biblical Context" and "The Text in the Life of the Church."

The writers have done the basic work for each commentary, but not operating alone, since "no . . . scripture is a matter of one's own

11

interpretation" (2 Pet. 1:20; cf. 1 Cor. 14:29). They have consulted with select counselors during the writing process, worked with the editors for the series, and received feedback from another biblical scholar. In addition, the Editorial Council, representing six believers church denominations, reads the manuscripts carefully, gives churchly responses, and makes suggestions for changes. The writer considers all this counsel and processes it into the manuscript, which the Editorial Council finally approves for publication. Thus these commentaries combine the individual writers' own good work and the church's voice. As such, they represent a hermeneutical community's efforts in interpreting the biblical text, as led by the Spirit.

The term *believers church* has often been used in the history of the church. Since the sixteenth century, it has frequently been applied to the Anabaptists and later the Mennonites, as well as to the Church of the Brethren and similar groups. As a descriptive term, it includes more than Mennonites and Brethren. *Believers church* now represents specific theological understandings, such as believers baptism, commitment to the Rule of Christ in Matthew 18:15-20 as crucial for church membership, belief in the power of love in all relationships, and willingness to follow Christ in the way of the cross. The writers chosen for the series stand in this tradition.

Believers church people have always been known for their emphasis on obedience to the simple meaning of Scripture. Because of this, they do not have a long history of deep historical-critical biblical scholarship. This series attempts to be faithful to the Scriptures while also taking archaeology and current biblical studies seriously. Doing this means that at many points the writers will not differ greatly from interpretations which can be found in many other good commentaries. Yet these writers share basic convictions about Christ, the church and its mission, God and history, human nature, the Christian life, and other doctrines. These presuppositions do shape a writer's interpretation of Scripture. Thus this series, like all other commentaries, stands within a specific historical church tradition.

Many in this stream of the church have expressed a need for help in Bible study. This is justification enough to produce the Believers Church Bible Commentary. Nevertheless, the Holy Spirit is not bound to any tradition. May this series be an instrument in breaking down walls between Christians in North America and around the world, bringing new joy in obedience through a fuller understanding of the Word.

—The Editorial Council

Author's Preface

Mark has been my special companion for many years. The relationship began when I decided to take on the challenge of memorizing a Gospel. I chose Mark because it was the shortest. Over the next months, I worked hard to master Mark's text; gradually I realized that it was mastering me.

Thus my first intense involvement with Mark did not include complex arguments about Synoptic relations, historical-critical methods, grammatical anomalies in the Greek text, variants in the manuscript tradition, and so on. Instead, I paid careful attention to the exact wording of sentences, the geographical markers, the similarities and differences between incidents, the arrangement of episodes within larger units. That was the only way I could memorize the text. In the process, I discovered fascinating patterns, allusions, nuances, and recurring themes. During my doctoral studies, I studied Mark in depth. That was when I learned that most of the discoveries I had made in Mark had actually been found by others before me. Learning from Markan scholars only deepened my desire to learn from Mark.

My doctoral dissertation was published under the title Watchwords: Mark 13 in Markan Eschatology; it was for specialists, those who read the text in Greek and keep abreast of developments in Markan scholarship. Even before that book was released, I knew that my real dream was to write a commentary on Mark.

I have prepared this commentary for all who want to understand Mark's Gospel, perhaps particularly for those who have the privilege, as I do, of teaching and preaching it. I have aimed to share in a nontechnical way what I have learned from Mark and from the interpreters of Mark who preceded me.

I am grateful for the many opportunities I have had to teach seminary courses on Mark. Often I have used Mark's Gospel to help my students apply their growing abilities in Greek to the task of interpreting Scripture. Other times I have taught Mark from the English Bible. My students have motivated me to dig deeper and have helped me uncover new gems in the Gospel of Mark.

The introduction to this commentary alludes to numerous scholarly writers who have contributed to my understanding of Mark. Yet I recognize others who have contributed to this commentary. They have read rough drafts of the manuscript, offered critical suggestions, and often helped me avoid bad arguments, clumsy wording, and boring sentences. These include present and former students, various family members and friends, theological colleagues and, not least, the editors and Editorial Council of the Believers Church Bible Commentary series and at Herald Press.

I know I would omit some significant contributors if I tried to name them all. Nevertheless, I will mention two people by name and offer them special thanks. Sue Nylander gave me the gifts of countless hours and of her ability as a theologian and writer; without her help, the final draft would have merited far more critical feedback than it received from the Editorial Council. In addition, Willard Swartley gave me the gifts of excellent advice and feedback, important literature suggestions, and not least, the opportunity to write this commentary in the first place. Most readers know that Willard himself could have written a masterful commentary on Mark.

This has been a long process. I wrote an original test section in Tübingen in 1992, while my family lived with me in Germany. I slowly chipped away at the task alongside busy teaching years at the Mennonite Brethren Biblical Seminary in Fresno, California. In Fall 1997, I enjoyed a sabbatical semester and hid away in my prophet's chamber (cf. 2 Kings 4:8-37) at my parents-in-law's house in Deutschhof, Germany; most of the first draft was written there. Finally, I spent many early mornings and late nights since then, completing the project.

That I was able to write this commentary during busy years in which three active sons were born into our family is testimony to the incredible support of my faithful wife, Gertrud, to whom this commentary is dedicated.

I pray that something of the joy and blessing I have received in writing this, will also be the experience of those who read it.

—*Timothy J. Geddert*
Mennonite Brethren Biblical Seminary, Fresno, California

Introduction

As you embark with me on this voyage of discovery, I need to state my own personal convictions about Mark and my goals in writing this commentary.

The Kind of Gospel Mark Wrote

Mark's Gospel looks back, it looks around, and it looks forward. It is about what God did through Jesus of Nazareth, continues to do (or still desires to do) among those who follow Jesus, and will yet do until Jesus comes again.

Looking backward is one of the most obvious things Mark does. From a vantage point about four decades later, Mark reports and interprets key events surrounding the life, ministry, death, and resurrection of Jesus. Among these are the following:

- Events preceding and preparing for Jesus' announcement that God's reign has arrived (1:1-15).
- The call of disciples (1:16-20).
- Effective ministry and growing popularity (1:21-45).
- Conflict with religious leaders (2:1—3:6; 3:22-30; 7:1-23).
- The creation of a new spiritual family (3:7-35).
- Mysterious words about the secret kingdom of God (4:1-34).
- Mighty deeds revealing the presence of God's reign (much of 4:35—8:26).

As Mark's Gospel approaches its midpoint, the focus narrows and concentrates on a journey to Jerusalem:

- Jesus teaches about discipleship on the way (8:27—10:52).
- Jesus confronts the religious leaders and is rejected by them in Jerusalem (most of 11:1—14:26).
- Jesus submits to God's will, allowing himself to be tried, mocked, crucified, and killed (14:47—15:47).
- Jesus is raised from the dead and goes before his followers into Galilee (16:1-8).

Mark also looks around at the followers of Jesus in his own day and at those who still need to hear and respond to the message of the Gospel. Mark teaches his fellow believers to look again to Jesus, to learn from him to think divine thoughts (8:33), to follow Jesus with courage even in tough times, and to proclaim the gospel with conviction. Jesus' first disciples are occasionally presented as positive models to be followed; more often they are foils. As we observe them, we learn what it means to misunderstand Jesus, to hold wrong priorities, and to fail in the crisis. For Mark, Jesus is the one who models faithfulness. By learning from Jesus' teaching and example, believers in Mark's day are drawn into the discipleship journey.

Mark also looks forward. Mark lives in the end time (chap. 13). It is a period Jesus said would be filled with crises of many kinds, with persecution for his followers, and with opportunities for gospel proclamation. Mark reminds his readers of Jesus' promise that he will some day return as the Son of Man in power and glory. Like Jesus before him, Mark teaches believers what it means to discern the times and serve the Master faithfully until he comes back.

Mark betrays great interest in what the historical Jesus actually said and did, what he suffered, and how he was vindicated by God. It is fair for us to assume that Mark had faithful traditions to rely on and that he preserved them with care. Yet Mark is much more than a historian; he is also a great storyteller. Taking up reliable traditions, Mark has creatively shaped them into a gripping short story, a mini-historical novel, a closet drama, a sermon, a crafted proclamation. Mark's Gospel tells God's good news (1:14-15). It does so with vividly portrayed characters, a fascinating plot, artfully employed literary devices (such as deliberate ambiguity, irony, foreshadowing, and paradox), and a powerful life-challenging message.

Mark has many priorities: he recounts the historical origins of Christian faith, interprets these events theologically, and provides encouragement and challenge to his readers. But his highest priority is to proclaim a message of good news. What he wrote was designed not only to inform readers but also to challenge them; not only to enlighten them concerning other people's responses to Jesus, but also to urge them to make life-changing responses themselves.

The Nature of This Commentary

In this commentary, my goal is to help the reader listen carefully to Mark. I will be following the NRSV translation most of the time, though at places I will compare it to the NIV or occasionally other translations. Sometimes I will indicate where a rather literal reading (or my own translation) is different from these.

This commentary reminds or informs the reader of details that Mark presumed his audience would know. I highlight OT background texts, explain the meaning of words, briefly describe first-century customs and movements, and discuss Greek grammar. In all this, there is only one goal, that we may listen to Mark more carefully.

Some, if not most, of the people in Mark's original audience were aware of these things. Many knew the OT well, and all of them understood Greek. Furthermore, they lived in the first century and knew the customs of the day. Where Mark thought they might not know important background information, he supplied it (7:3-4). However, since we live in a different time and place, we lack much of the information needed to understand Mark as well as his contemporaries; hence, we need commentaries. Our goal is to understand correctly what the author has written, not to critique his writing or stand in judgment over the Gospel's reliability.

On a personal note, my earliest training in biblical interpretation emphasized listening to the divine author, with the human author considered relatively unimportant. Today I do not see these two as being in tension with each other. The references to "what Mark is saying" can be understood as "what God's Spirit is saying through Mark." My reason for focusing on Mark's meaning is to pay careful attention on this exploring voyage to one of the voices through which God's Spirit speaks. When we try to listen simultaneously to all the voices through which God's Spirit speaks, the message becomes less clear, not more clear.

Sometimes it is helpful for us to make sideward glances at the way Matthew and Luke present similar material, or how they understood Mark. Often, however, such sideways glances at Matthew and Luke will be deliberately avoided; it is too easy to read Matthew's meaning or Luke's meaning into Mark, thus masking Mark's unique contribution to God's Word.

Mark wrote primarily for people already sharing his conviction that the Gospel traditions are reliable. Mark interprets Jesus, rather than trying to verify traditions about him. And I will interpret Mark, not try to verify the accuracy of what he proclaims. This commentary is thus not first and foremost about the Jesus of history. It will not often make statements about "what Jesus actually said" or "what probably really happened." It will not label Mark's claims as "historically problematic."

Please do not misunderstand me. I believe that attempts to reconstruct the actual words and deeds of the historical Jesus are important. If that were my goal, I would use Mark alongside other sources. But then I would not be looking at the Gospel of Mark itself to understand what Mark wrote; I would be looking through his Gospel to find evidence for something else.

When I speak of Jesus, I really mean Jesus as portrayed by Mark. I believe Mark's portrait is a clearly recognizable portrait of the historical Jesus. Those who knew Jesus and later read Mark would say, "Yes, that's the Jesus we knew." Yet it is still a portrait, for it includes only what Mark chose to include, it highlights what Mark chose to highlight, and it is interpreted as Mark chose to interpret it.

Similar comments apply to other characters. When I speak of Pharisees, I really mean Pharisees as portrayed by Mark (judgmental, narrow, legalistic, opposed to Jesus). Mark has characterized the group of Pharisees as many of them really were. He does not claim, however, that there were no other kinds of Pharisees in the historical situation.

When I refer to Jesus' disciples, I mean the disciples as they are portrayed by Mark. This Gospel portrays them far more negatively than do the other Gospels. Mark has no vendetta against them; he has chosen to teach discipleship by contrasting Jesus' faithfulness with the disciples' frequent unfaithfulness. Sensitivity to Mark's characterization will help us understand Mark's text.

I am trying hard to read Mark as literature, being as sensitive as I can to the reading experience. Nevertheless, I avoid the technical vocabulary of literary and reader-response criticism, except for common terms such as narrator, story, and (occasionally) discourse.

A narrative involves various levels of communication. Characters are talking to each other within the story; through this discourse, the author is speaking to the reader. Sometimes the narrator gives the reader information unknown to the characters in the story. This happens frequently in Mark. Readers then have a privileged vantage point as they evaluate what is going on within the narrative. The formerly unknown information also creates a situation in which irony can flourish, as it does in Mark's Gospel.

Mark designed his Gospel to have a particular impact as readers work through it from beginning to end. He also designed it to have additional impact on those who begin again and read each part in the light of the whole. In my commentary, I aim to be sensitive to what Mark's reader is expected to know at any given point in the story, and also sensitive to what they can be expected to understand through later readings. This is the way we intuitively treat any good historical novel, film, sermon, or drama; we need to learn to do this also to biblical literature, especially biblical books with a narrative form.

We cannot fairly interpret Mark without sometimes referring to OT backgrounds, aspects of Greek grammar and vocabulary, features of first-century politics, religion, culture, and so on. I will try to use these resources when necessary, without becoming bogged down in them. Detailed background information is sometimes interesting but not always helpful. For example, we know that the Sea of Galilee is deep enough to drown people if their boat sinks (Mark 4:38). Otherwise, its exact depth may interest some people but has no bearing on the meaning of Mark's text. Neither does the location of Arimathea (15:43), the kind of millstone mentioned in 9:42, or the identity of Rufus (15:21). Nevertheless, seemingly minor details in Mark's text sometimes turn out to be quite important. I do my best to include whatever helps us understand Mark and leave out whatever does not.

In terms of its format, this commentary follows the others in this series. A Preview locates each section within the larger framework of Mark's Gospel and shows how the section is structured. Explanatory Notes are not simply notes, isolated facts, background clues, but rather invitations to see Mark's Gospel come alive as we read the text with care. The Text in Biblical Context (TBC) picks up several themes from the section just studied and comments on how OT and/or other NT material contributes to its understanding (or vice versa).

The Text in the Life of the Church (TLC) focuses on one or two issues from each larger section and explores either how they have been or how they ought to be understood in the Christian church. This TLC section runs the risk of being narrowly focused, since no commentator can effectively speak out of or into the situation of the whole church worldwide. My comments reflect my own background in the believers church tradition (see Series Foreword). My own personal church experiences, in congregations of Western Canada, California, Eastern Scotland, and Southern Germany, will sometimes show through.

Finally, most commentaries on Mark are considerably less interesting than Mark's Gospel itself; some of them even give the impression that Mark's Gospel is not interesting. I hope to persuade the reader that Mark's book is both important and fascinating.

Who Is Mark? Where and When Did He Write?

Mark's Gospel was written anonymously. No early church leader ever claimed that the author was an eyewitness to the events recorded. Thus to argue for any one particular author is not necessary. Early church tradition attributes this Gospel to John Mark, companion (at different times) of both Paul and Peter (Acts 12:12, 25; 13:5, 13; 15:37-39; Col. 4:10; Philem. 24; 2 Tim. 4:11; 1 Pet. 5:13). There is much to be said for the viewpoint that John Mark was the writer (see below).

More important than the name of the author is the author's relationship to the historical facts. Did Mark have access to early traditions about Jesus? Did he care whether they were reliable and have ways of verifying his information? Two different theories were held by second- and third-century church leaders. The first theory is that Mark relied on information he gained by hearing the apostle Peter preach and teach; in fact, he was trained by Peter to narrate the stories of Jesus. The second theory is that Mark's main source was the Gospel of Matthew, and that Mark therefore relied on the traditions preserved by Matthew, himself an apostolic eyewitness (as they believed).

There are several reasons why the first theory is to be preferred. Peter and Mark both experienced significant discipleship failure (Mark 14:66-72; Acts 13:13; 15:37-41). In his Gospel, Mark pictures Peter (and maybe also himself; see notes on 14:51-52) in uncomplimentary terms. He also highlights the theme of second chances for disciples who fail. These facts are well explained if Mark and Peter both had life themes emphasizing the amazing fact that the resurrected Jesus offers forgiveness and renewal for disciples who fail (16:7, notes). The Greek text also reveals some traces of a Peter tradition lying behind the wording of Mark (1:29, 36-37).

I hold (along with almost all modern scholars) that Matthew and Luke both wrote their Gospels after the Gospel of Mark and used Mark as a source, rather than vice versa. If this is correct, then careful observation of the differences between Mark and the other Gospels is of some importance in interpreting Matthew and Luke, but is of almost no value in interpreting Mark. In this commentary, I will omit such observations except in a few cases where it seems important to help readers notice what Mark does not say. Our goal is to avoid reading into Mark meanings (and even content) from Matthew and Luke, which we know so well.

Where and when did Mark write? Early church traditions claimed that Mark wrote in Rome. The text provides some clues that Mark's readers were suffering persecution, and that the Gospel was not written in Palestine. There is no reason to doubt that Rome is the location, but also little to be gained by insisting on it.

Regarding when the Gospel was written, there is more at stake. Some scholars argue for an early date (A.D. 55-65) based on the assumptions that Luke used Mark and that Luke wrote both his Gospel and Acts before Paul died. Others argue for a date after 70 either because they believe Mark wrote after Matthew (e.g., C. S. Mann; see Bibliography) or because of a particular interpretation of Mark 13. My own view is that Mark wrote no later than the time of the temple's destruction (perhaps 65-70).

When I write "Mark," I sometimes refer to the Gospel by that name and sometimes to the person who wrote it (whoever that was). If at times it is not clear whether my reference is to the book or the person, that is because it sometimes does not matter. For example, when I say, "Mark is teaching us," I mean that the text teaches us and does so because the author designed it to do that. When I attribute motives and goals and even desires to "Mark," I am attributing them to the so-called implied author, as this can be discerned from the text. But it is too cumbersome to say that all the time. I assume that the real author consciously intended virtually all the important insights revealed through the text that the author produced.

How Has Mark's Gospel Been Received?

Mark's Gospel is arguably the most influential book ever written. If Matthew and Luke both used Mark as a source (as is likely), then Mark contributed immeasurably to the development of Christianity, and thus also to the course of history in the Western world and increasingly in the rest of the world as well.

Yet because ancient scholars settled on the unlikely conclusion that Mark wrote after Matthew, they began to view Mark as a crude, abbreviated, non-apostolic version of the more illustrious Gospel written by the apostle Matthew. For many centuries, Mark was the least read and least valued of the four Gospels. As far as we know, only two or three commentaries on Mark were written in a period of over a thousand years (through the twelfth century). Thereafter, only about four were written until the Reformation.

The rehabilitation of Mark began in the nineteenth century, when the conviction grew that Mark was the earliest of the Gospels. Scholars then gave Mark renewed attention because it was considered an artless retelling of historical traditions, and therefore useful in reconstructing the "historical Jesus." At the beginning of the twentieth century, Mark was studied because it was considered a valuable source of insight into the theological struggles of the early church. Just after the middle of the twentieth century, attention shifted to the question of where Mark agreed and disagreed with the emphases in the traditions he inherited.

Only recently has Mark been truly valued as the work of a serious Christian theologian preserving history by interpreting it theologically in the form of a narrative. Today Mark enjoys the glory and suffers the fate of being considered a literary masterpiece, in the esteem of many readers. Various different interpretive methods are used to probe the meaning of Mark's text, and they often bear a rich harvest of insight, though not all scholarly fruit is edible! Mark's message confronts readers and challenges them to make life-changing decisions about following Jesus. The more carefully we listen to Mark's unique message, the more effectively it can do that.

Reading Mark as Historical and Theological Literature

Scholars use a wide variety of critical methods. Some readers of this commentary may want to learn more about some of these methods and how they influence the interpretation of Mark. I encourage them to examine such books as *Hearing the New Testament: Strategies for Interpretation* (edited by J. Green) and *Mark and Method* (edited by J. C. Anderson and S. D. Moore; see Bibliography). I also recommend commentaries and studies of Mark that use various critical disciplines, such as the following:

- Historical criticism and source criticism: V. Taylor, S. Johnson.
- Form criticism: D. Nineham.
- Redaction criticism: R. Pesch.
- Literary criticism: E. Schweizer, N. Perrin, W. Kelber.
- Reader-response criticism: R. Fowler.

Many commentators draw on a combination of different methods. Of these, I recommend M. Hooker and R. Guelich (for Mark 1-8) as well-balanced studies that interact judiciously with many different disciplines. R. Gundry's recent commentary is comprehensive in its references to other scholars (though his own conclusions are not always persuasive). In seminary classes I have often used the studies of W. Swartley, D. Senior, J. D. Kingsbury, and D. H. Juel. Finally, R. H. Lightfoot's study, first published in 1950 and far ahead of its time, is a good model of the kind of interpretation for which I aim.

I have tried to learn from many methodologies, but this commentary will not focus on historical-critical, source-critical, form-critical, or redaction-critical matters. I find that the tools of literary criticism and reader-response criticism contribute most directly in helping readers interpret the message of Mark. Yet no critical method should be used alone. I have no interest in discovering how much can be accomplished while using one tool. I would much rather see what tools are helpful in interpreting the Gospel of Mark, and they will not be the same in every text.

Yet all the critical methodologies combined are not as important for the task of interpreting Mark as reading the text over and over again (in English if necessary; in Greek if possible), studying it in the context of a Christian community, and seeking to live what Mark teaches and to follow the One he proclaims.

The Theology of Mark's Gospel

Since Mark's theology is presented in the form of a narrative, summarizing that theology really means previewing Mark's story line and highlighting some of its key themes.

Jesus' coming marks the arrival of God's kingdom, God's dynamic reign. His mighty works are the works of God. His authoritative teaching interprets God's ways. His mysterious parables separate those with spiritual discernment from those who have already rejected Jesus. Those with eyes to see, discern that in all Jesus does, the secret kingdom is being established.

When Peter confesses Jesus as Messiah, Jesus turns his attention to the inseparable themes of the Messiah's destiny and the way of God's kingdom. Accepting God's reign by following this Messiah means self-sacrifice, servanthood, humility, standing with the weak, and rejecting the power-hungry and glory-seeking ways of the world. It means allegiance to a Messiah who will suffer and die. It means living by the values of the coming kingdom, where God's thoughts, not human thoughts, determine what is right.

In Jerusalem, Jesus and his message are proclaimed (sometimes ironically)—by festival crowds, by Jesus himself, by Scripture, and by a woman expressing her devotion to Jesus and unwittingly anointing him as the Messiah. In Jerusalem, Jesus is also rejected—by Judas, by religious leaders, by nationalistic crowds, and by Pilate, who gives in to pressure and authorizes the execution of Israel's true King.

In Jesus' unjust death, his true identity is revealed: he is God's Son and Messiah, who gave his life to redeem others. After three days, the crucified one becomes the resurrected one. Jesus offers new beginnings to those who have failed him; they are invited back to a life of faithful discipleship and mission.

At 16:8, Mark's narrative ends (see "Preview" for 16:1-8 and essay [Textual Criticism of Mark]) with a provocative resurrection message offering second chances to disciples who have failed to follow and who are afraid to proclaim the good news. But Mark's story includes guidance for the post-resurrection period of waiting for the Son of Man to return with great power and glory. In the end time, watching has nothing to do with seeking signs or sketching out God's timetable (chap. 13). Those who keep alert discern appropriate responses to crises of all kinds, courageously proclaim the Gospel, and serve and follow Jesus right up to the end.

As the narrative unfolds, certain themes emerge as central. The most important of these is Christology: Who is Jesus? Mark's main titles for Jesus are Christ and Son of God. Secrecy surrounds both titles, because their true significance can only be understood by those who accept the way of the cross.

We also find other key themes in Mark:

• God's reign is being established as Jesus proclaims, interprets, and enacts God's secret kingdom.

• Authentic discipleship involves following Jesus on the way of the cross (understood as the way of submission to God's reign and its principles, even if it involves suffering).

• Discernment in the context of discipleship is the way to understand the teaching of Jesus. One gains insight, not through signs and objective evidences, but by having seeing eyes and hearing ears.

• Jesus breaks through barriers of religion, piety, tradition, and ethnicity to bring God's good news to those formerly excluded.

Part 1

Ministry in and Around Galilee

Mark 1:1—8:26

OVERVIEW

The first half of Mark describes (after a brief prologue) the main ministry of Jesus within Galilee and occasionally in neighboring regions. It is a ministry of announcing and demonstrating the arrival of God's reign in deeds of power, in authoritative teaching, and in the formation of a disciple community.

Mark's Gospel has often been described as action-packed. Jesus (at least in the first half) seems always to be on the move. The dramatic action appears in many different scenes (synagogue, house, open spaces, boat trips, mountain retreats, and so on). Jesus is engaged in many kinds of activities (calling and training disciples, teaching, driving out demons, prayer, miracles of many kinds, conflict with enemies, and more). Often Jesus' plans change quickly, as the crowds throng around him or his disciples misunderstand him.

Some have compared Mark's narrative technique to a slide show. A picture flashed on the screen is replaced with another, almost before the first can be studied. Scholars have pointed out that almost half of the NT occurrences of the Greek word for *immediately* occur in Mark, and almost all of these in the first half. The pace is quick.

However, that does not mean that Mark discourages careful reflection. On the contrary, he almost teases the reader with riddles and puzzles, forcing the reader to watch for hidden clues, study the relationship between episodes, and discern larger patterns. Readers are challenged, along with Jesus' disciples, to have "hearing ears" and "seeing eyes." Only with such ears and eyes will they discern Jesus' true identity and the nature and presence of God's kingdom.

At Mark's midpoint, the disciples (in the person of Peter) declare their conviction that Jesus is the Messiah (8:27-30). Mark's Gospel then takes a dramatic turn in a new direction (cf. "Overview" to Part 2, for 8:27—16:8). (For outline of Part 1, see table of contents.)

Mark 1:1-15

Preparing the Way

PREVIEW

Mark's Gospel is much more than a historical report of the life, death, and resurrection of Jesus. It is a proclamation of *good news*, an interpretation of Jesus and his message, a challenge to faithful discipleship, a theological and a literary masterpiece.

On the surface of the text is a clear and simple message. It has led many to faith and has challenged believers to know Jesus and follow him more closely. Yet there is much more here as well. Mark's Gospel is loaded with subtle hints that more is going on than meets the eye.

The recurring calls to see and to hear are not only Jesus' challenges to his disciples *within the story;* they are also Mark's challenges *to his readers.* At times Mark's readers are told things that the disciples in the narrative do not know. At times we learn that Jesus has explained things to *them,* but the explanations are not reported to *us.* So we learn with the disciples, sometimes going ahead, sometimes trying to catch up. We learn from Jesus as we listen to his teaching. And we learn from Mark as he guides the narrative.

The main subject of the book is *Jesus.* The opening verse of Mark's narrative makes that clear. The following narrative confirms that central focus. At the outset the reader is told that Jesus is both *Christ* and *Son of God* (1:1). We begin with an advantage over those within the narrative whom Jesus will call to follow him. They will only gradually come to understand who Jesus is.

Mark's Gospel contains no birth narratives and no reports of Jesus' childhood. There are only a few hints about his human origins

(6:3). Mark moves quickly to Jesus' ministry. In only seven verses, Mark reports how the way for Jesus was prepared by prophets of old (1:2-3) and by John the Baptizer (1:4-8). In another seven verses, Mark shows how the adult Jesus is inaugurated into his ministry. He is baptized by John (1:9), affirmed and commissioned by God (1:10-11), and tempted by the devil (1:12-13). Then Jesus steps onto the Galilean stage to announce the arrival of God's kingdom and to call people to repentance and faith (1:14-15).

These first 15 verses, Mark's prologue, are about "Preparing the Way." The OT prophets, John the Baptist (Jesus' forerunner), Jesus himself, the Galilean population, *and the reader* all participate in various ways as the way is prepared for the arrival of God's reign.

The word *euangelion* (*gospel/good news*, RSV/NRSV) marks off this section. Mark's announcement of good news to the readers (1:1) and Jesus' announcement of good news to the Galileans (1:15) form a bracket around the preparatory events. Other commentators make the first major break after verse 8, verse 13, or verse 20. The NRSV makes at least minor breaks at all those places.

All major breaks, however, are mixed blessings. They are created to make commentary writing (and reading) more manageable. Mark did not create these breaks. He carefully constructed a unified narrative, with transitions holding major units together. Thus, as the comments below reflect, verses 14-15 are transitional, closing off the prologue and leading directly into the next unit.

OUTLINE

The Beginning of the Good News, 1:1

Preparing the Way in the Wilderness, 1:2-3

John's Baptism and Message, 1:4-8

Jesus' Baptism and Commissioning, 1:9-11

The Temptation of Jesus, 1:12-13

Announcing the Kingdom, 1:14-15

EXPLANATORY NOTES
The Beginning of the Good News 1:1

The beginning of the good news of Jesus Christ, the Son of God.

The opening seven (Greek) words of Mark's Gospel are loaded with significance, ambiguity, and difficulty.

Beginning (archē) is the first word. Mark's Gospel opens just as the Hebrew Scriptures do: "In the beginning" God created (Gen. 1:1). Now Mark announces a new beginning.

It is *good news* that begins here. This word *euangelion,* usually translated *gospel,* is not a title for the book; *Gospel* is not yet a label for a type of literature (Gospel of Mark, of Matthew, of Luke, of John). Instead, Mark is telling us that the material to follow should be understood as good news. At times in the story, dark clouds loom; Mark wants his readers to remember that God's sunshine beyond all tragedy creates silver linings, keeping hope alive. A persecuted church needs to remember that. So also do commentators who are sometimes tempted to call Mark's Gospel depressing.

Many have commented that the "shadow of the cross" hangs over the whole book; that the Gospel paints a "negative portrait of discipleship"; or that "fear and failure" characterize the Gospel's ending. But Mark views his own work as a declaration of *good news.* Interpretations of Mark that do not preserve that attitude are suspect. As we work our way through this amazing book, we often need to remind ourselves that *the secret of the kingdom* (4:11) is the key to the optimism Mark asks us to share with him. On the surface, things may look dark; but we are asked to look deeper.

Good news of Jesus brings us to the first of many expressions in Mark with double meanings. We might take this phrase to mean the good news (the arrival of God's reign) that *Jesus* is proclaiming (as subjective genitive in Greek). Or the phrase might be taken to mean the good news about Jesus that *Mark* is proclaiming (as objective genitive). In the first option, Jesus is the *proclaimer,* Mark's role is to preserve the original words and works of the historical Jesus, and Mark's book is primarily a historical record. In the second option, Jesus is the *proclaimed one,* Mark's role is to interpret the meaning of Jesus' advent for his readers, and the book is primarily a theological and literary work.

Some interpreters defend one of these options and reject the other. However, the path of wisdom is to recognize an intentional double meaning: Mark presents Jesus as the proclaimer *and* the proclaimed one. Mark often creates such double meanings. They function to prevent oversimplification, to provoke deeper reflection, and to create irony. Mark is a subtle writer, and he provides frequent hints that not all the meaning is on the surface (6:52).

The NRSV's ambiguous *of Jesus* is a good translation (1:1).

Translations that choose one of the two options (e.g., *the good news about Jesus*, or *the good news that Jesus proclaimed*) impoverish the text. Mark is preserving Jesus' traditions for a later generation (subjective genitive); Mark is also interpreting and proclaiming Jesus (objective genitive). He is challenging readers to respond to the good news that can be theirs not only because Jesus came, but also because he is still calling people to respond to the gospel of the kingdom.

Appended to the name *Jesus* are two titles, *Christ* and *Son of God*, the two most important titles for Jesus in Mark's Gospel. Some early manuscripts do not include the second title, probably from a copying oversight: in Greek, each of the last six words of this verse ends with *-ou,* and one could easily miss a few similar words *[Textual Criticism of Mark].* Both titles for Jesus were likely part of Mark's original text.

Our familiarity with the phrase *Jesus Christ* often obscures the fact that *Jesus* is the *name* and *Christ* is the *title* (at least for Mark). In this opening verse, readers are told who Jesus is, something the characters within the story will be struggling to discover. These two key titles help us understand Jesus' identity and mission.

For the average first-century Jew, the title *Christ* (Messiah) meant a great political ruler, the expected coming king from the line of David. These associations triggered thoughts of political liberation from Rome, with freedom and prosperity for national Israel. Suffering and death would not fit into the picture. *Son of God*, especially for Gentile readers, would raise expectations of a great miracle-worker, a link between heaven and earth, one who appears human but is really one with God (or the gods). Again, the idea of suffering and death would be absent.

Mark's first verse uses both titles to tell us who Jesus is. The rest of the Gospel will clarify what it means to be *Christ* and *Son of God*. For Mark, both titles are tightly linked to Jesus' passion and death. When Jesus' disciples first confess that he is *Christ* (8:29, RSV; *Messiah,* NRSV), Jesus begins to teach about the coming passion, about the road of discipleship that leads to Golgotha (8:31). When Jesus completes his own journey from popularity and success to rejection and suffering (15:37), we hear the first human in this Gospel proclaim: *Truly this man was God's Son!* (15:39). Jesus is sentenced to death for confessing that he is the Messiah and God's Son (14:61-62). For Mark, there is no true confession of Jesus that is not interpreted in the light of the cross (8:29-34).

Mark's Gospel gives readers an interpretive key with the first verse: Jesus is the Messiah; Jesus is God's Son. That is something the disciples of Jesus (according to Mark) do not know at the beginning. But readers of the Gospel dare not glory in their superior knowledge; just like Jesus' disciples, we need to learn the meaning of truly confessing Christ as the divine Son. According to Mark's Gospel, that insight is hidden from those who do not walk the way of the cross.

One major question must still occupy us as we consider Mark's opening verse: To what does *the beginning of the good news* refer? Many possibilities come to mind:

1. The beginning is narrated in verses 2 and 3: "It all began when the prophets of old announced in advance that a messenger would prepare the way for God to come."

2. The beginning is narrated in verses 2-8: "It all began with the ministry of John, the forerunner (just as the prophets had said it would)."

3. The beginning is narrated in verses 9-13: "It all began with Jesus' baptism, commissioning, and temptation." That is where the time of preparation (1:2-8) shifts into the time of fulfillment (1:14f.).

4. The beginning is narrated in verses 14-15: "It all began when Jesus announced the arrival of God's kingdom." Verses 2-13 reveal how this came about.

5. The beginning is narrated in verses 1-20: "It all began when Jesus first recruited followers to join him as people of the kingdom (having himself gone through the stages of preparation for this ultimate mission)."

Each of these options is possible, but Mark likely intended something broader than all of them. For Mark, the *whole Gospel narrative* is the beginning of the good news. Mark writes a narrative so that the Christians in his day will know how it all began. It all began with Jesus' life and ministry, death and resurrection. That is what makes discipleship and mission possible.

The meaning of Mark's opening line influences how we understand his closing lines (16:7-8). The resurrection call to meet Jesus in *Galilee* is an invitation to go back once more to the *beginning*. It is an invitation to begin again, to experience insight after blindness, victory after defeat, renewed discipleship after failure. It is an invitation to recognize the true nature of the *Christ*, the *Son of God*, in the light of the passion and resurrection. On this reading, Mark 1:1 is not only a way of getting the narrative started. It is a way of summarizing its message and its impact (16:7-8, notes).

Preparing the Way in the Wilderness 1:2-3

Long before the advent of Jesus, God's people were taught to look forward to a coming one who would usher in the age of salvation. Malachi 3:1 and Isaiah 40:3 (the two main sources of the quotation Mark here attributes to Isaiah) both speak of a messenger who will prepare for God's coming. Mark modifies the prophetic texts slightly but significantly. In Malachi, the "LORD of hosts" announces that a messenger will precede the Lord's own coming to purify the temple. In Isaiah, the voice prepares a highway for *God*.

Slight modifications to both texts make it possible for Mark's text to be a prediction of *Jesus'* forerunner. Thus Jesus is the one bringing salvation. *Jesus* accomplishes what the prophets said *God* would do. This is the first of many hints that Mark considers Jesus to be truly one with God (4:41; 6:50; 14:62).

Moreover the reference to *wilderness* is transposed. In Isaiah, the voice spoke of a *"way in the wilderness."* In Mark, *the voice* (of John) is *in the wilderness*, but *the way of the Lord* is not only there. For Mark, *the way* will symbolize much more than simply what *John* prepares. It will ultimately become the way of the cross (see TBC, below).

John's Baptism and Message 1:4-8

John's baptizing begins the fulfillment of prophecies by Malachi and Isaiah. Those waiting for God's Messiah are called into the desert to prepare their hearts for his arrival. Baptism, usually reserved for proselytes to Judaism, is here administered to Jews, who consider themselves already members of the covenant people. John is inviting them to reenter the covenant, to rejoin the people of God. They are to come as repentant sinners and prepare their hearts for what is to come.

John's ministry seems incredibly successful. *The whole Judean countryside and all the people of Jerusalem* come to be baptized. This hyperbole highlights the eagerness of the Jews to welcome the coming one (1:7-8; cf. 3:8, notes); it serves as a contrast to the later overwhelming rejection of Jesus, when people discover who he is, how he comes, and what it will cost to follow him.

John is portrayed as one who lives the nomadic life of a desert wanderer. He eats locusts and wild honey, is dressed in camel's hair clothing, and wears a leather belt. On a deeper level, he is portrayed as Elijah (cf. 2 Kings 1:8; Zech. 13:4), whose coming is to precede "the great and terrible day of the LORD" (Mal. 4:5). Jesus later identifies John as the *Elijah* who *must come first* (9:12-13).

Here it is John's *voice* that Mark wants to stress. Thus emphasis falls on John's message in 1:7-8. John's task is to announce the coming of Jesus, the more powerful one, the more worthy one, the one who baptizes with a greater baptism. John's baptism is with water (a repentance baptism and only preparatory). Jesus' baptism will be with the Spirit; he is the one endowed with the Spirit, the one who does the work of God's Spirit in bringing end-time salvation.

If R. Gundry is correct, then the Spirit-baptism John predicts is not a Pentecost-type event in which Jesus gives the Spirit to others. Instead, John is referring to what Jesus will be doing from now on: acting in the power of the Spirit on behalf of others (Gundry: 45; see Bibliography). If Mark is thinking about Jesus giving the Spirit to others, there is no further reference to this event in Mark's Gospel (except a possible allusion in 13:11).

John's baptism and his preaching take place in the wilderness. *Wilderness* (or *desert*) has two kinds of associations in the Scriptures:

• Because of the very nature of a desert and because Israel experienced hard times in the desert before reaching the Promised Land, the desert is a place associated with barrenness, temptation, testing, hardship, danger, and evil (cf. Deut. 8:2; 1 Kings 19:4).

• Because God called Israel from Egypt into the wilderness/desert and there established a covenant with them, wilderness also came to be associated with election and call, intimacy with God, a place where God's people were prepared for renewal and for God's final deliverance and salvation (cf. Exod. 3:18; Isa. 35;1-10; 43:19; Hos. 2:14). In fact, some of Jesus' contemporaries had established religious communities in the desert (as at Qumran), where they sought to live pure lives as they awaited the fulfillment of God's end-time promises.

Mark plays on both themes: Jesus is tempted by Satan in the desert (1:12-13), and John's baptism in the desert is a preparation for God's salvation (1:4-8).

Jesus' Baptism and Commissioning 1:9-11

Through repentance and baptism *all the people of Jerusalem* and *people from the whole Judean countryside* have declared themselves ready for God's salvation (1:5). In contrast, only *one* comes from Galilee. The irony is that Jesus will be immensely popular in Galilee (though not in his hometown, 6:3-6) and rejected in Jerusalem. People *from Jerusalem* even become synonymous with

Jesus' enemies (3:22; 7:1). The baptism of the many will not be the beginning of a great renewal. Only Jesus' baptism will have a lasting impact. Yet Jesus' baptism does not symbolize cleansing from sin; instead, it sets him apart as the one whose faithfulness provides salvation *for many* (10:45; 14:24).

As Jesus emerges from the baptismal waters, the heavens are torn open (1:10). This is not a public event. It is something Jesus sees and something shared by the narrator with us, the readers. The prophet Isaiah longed for the day when God would "tear open the heavens and come down" (Isa. 64:1). That day has now arrived! Mark's Gospel uses the word *tear apart* (*schizomai*) only twice. Here it symbolizes the incarnation: God has come down to dwell among God's people. In 15:38 it symbolizes atonement: in response to the death of Jesus, the temple curtain is torn apart from top to bottom, signaling that the barriers between God and people have been removed (Lightfoot: 56).

The opening of the heavens is followed by the Spirit descending like a dove *into Jesus* (1:10, TJG; not *on* or *onto*, as in most English versions). Mark presents Jesus as having the driving force of the Spirit *within himself* (1:12). Obviously, this is *God's* Spirit; Mark makes this explicit in 3:22-30, after Jesus' critics have claimed that he operates in the power of a demonic spirit.

Here *dove* symbolizes the Spirit of God, and it is not clear what other associations are attached. Is it the promise of hope, the gentle voice of God, and/or the creative power of God? All these can be supported from OT texts and other Jewish literature. With the coming of the Spirit on God's chosen Messiah, the end time is inaugurated (Isa. 61:1). The one who has now received the Spirit begins his ministry of Spirit-baptism upon "all flesh" (Mark 1:8; Joel 2:28-32).

Next comes a voice from heaven: *You are my Son, the Beloved; with you I am well pleased* (1:11). "A loving father first expresses deep affection for his son and then gives him a ringing personal affirmation" (Boomershine: 48). Yet below the surface, much more is going on. God's "ringing affirmation" contains allusions to three OT texts:

You are my Son. (Ps. 2:7)
Take your son, your only son . . . whom you love. (Gen. 22:2)
Here is . . . my chosen, in whom my soul delights.
    I have put my spirit upon him. (Isa. 42:1)

The first text speaks clearly of God's anointed one, the Messiah (Ps. 2:2). The second introduces the story of Abraham sacrificing

Isaac, though in the end God provides a ram to take the place of the son. The third identifies Jesus with the Servant of the LORD in Isaiah, the one who is "led as a lamb to the slaughter," who "bore the sins of many" (Isa. 53:7, 12; *Abba*, in Mark 14:36, notes). Jesus is being assured of his Father's love, and is also being inaugurated into a Messianic ministry, characterized by the way of the cross. This time a ram will not take the place of "the Son." Instead, his death will forever end the sacrifice of animals for the atonement of human sin. Yes, Jesus is God's chosen Servant and Son, but chosen for a path of suffering and death, chosen for the way of the cross.

The Temptation of Jesus 1:12-13

Mark includes a brief narrative of Jesus' temptation by Satan. The Spirit drives Jesus to the place of testing, showing that the testing itself is part of his preparation for ministry. The desert symbolizes temptation, hardship, and danger, but also intimacy with God (1:4-8, notes); Jesus experiences both. The wild beasts are there (TBC, below), and of course Satan. Angels attend to him. The forty days recall Israel's forty years of temptation and wandering in the wilderness. They emerged to inherit the Promised Land. Jesus will emerge to announce the arrival of God's final victory.

Announcing the Kingdom 1:14-15

With verse 14, Mark begins a transition to the next section. The work of the forerunner is complete. John is *handed over* (TJG; *paradidōmi*). The translations *arrested* (NRSV) and *put in prison* (NIV) are poor. John was indeed arrested and put into prison (6:17), but the word used in 1:14 does not mean either of these. It means *handed over* (*delivered up, betrayed*). Mark has carefully chosen this word. Here John is *handed over*; later Jesus will be *handed over* (14 times *paradidōmi* refers to Jesus' passion; e.g., 3:19; 10:33); still later the disciples will be *handed over* (three times *paradidōmi* refers to their passion; e.g., 13:9-13).

Each time someone is *handed over*, a new stage in the proclamation of the good news is reached. The handing over of one leads directly into the ministry of another. For Mark, this is *the way;* it is the way of the cross (8:34). The passion of a faithful messenger of God is never a defeat for the secret kingdom (4:11); it is always a doorway through which the kingdom advances and grows (T. Geddert, 1989:155-8).

Mark has presented John as Jesus' forerunner. John has prepared *the way* by preaching and baptizing (1:3). Now he is preparing Jesus' way by going that way himself. *The way* is the way of obedience even in the face of rejection and death. Commentators often say that a cloud of suffering and death hangs over Mark's Gospel: If this is what happens to the forerunner, can the Messiah expect anything better? That view focuses on the dark cloud and not on God's silver lining. Mark would rather have his readers see things the other way around. The passion of John opens the door to the expanded kingdom ministry of the Messiah; the passion of Jesus will open the door to the expanded kingdom ministry of his followers; their ministry in turn will lead to the evangelization of the whole world (13:9-13).

Jesus' message is called *the good news **of** God* (1:14b). It is good news *from* God and also *about* God. God's reign *has drawn near* through God's own initiative (1:15, TJG) *[Kingdom of God in Mark]*.

The word for *has come near* can refer to nearness in time or in space. It can also mean either being almost here (but not quite) or having arrived. The verb (perfect) tense suggests something decisive has happened already, and the effects go on into the future. Thus Jesus announces not only the kingdom's *imminence* (nearness), but also the beginning of its *arrival.* Some events marking the kingdom's arrival are still future (Jesus' death and resurrection, and the return of the Son of Man). Yet Jesus is announcing that God's reign is already actively present for those who *repent and believe the good news* (1:15b). Repenting and believing are necessary preparations for a still future kingdom experience; they are also the means by which God's kingdom becomes a present experience.

Mark 1:14b-15 seems to indicate the content of Jesus' Galilean proclamation. Yet amazingly, not one of its elements is ever explicitly repeated throughout the entire Galilean ministry of Jesus! Never again does Jesus clearly say that the time of waiting is over. Never again does Jesus explicitly call people to either repentance or belief in the good news. Yet *implicitly,* that is what the entire ministry of Jesus is all about. Jesus will be demonstrating the arrival of the kingdom and calling people to respond to its offer and its demands (Hare: 20). The primary function of these two verses (and the entire prologue) is to give the reader advance information as to what this Gospel is all about (Fowler, 1991:17-20).

Readers know who Jesus is (Christ, Son of God); they know that he is infused with God's Spirit and will operate in the power of this Spirit; they know what God the Father says about the divine Son; they know that Jesus won an initial victory over Satan. By concluding his prologue as he does, Mark in effect tells his readers, "Everything that follows constitutes a proclamation (often veiled) that God's kingdom has arrived. Every time Jesus encounters people (potential disciples, those who hear him teach in the synagogue, those coming for healing, and critics), he gives an implicit call to repent and believe." That call is just as implicit for every reader of Mark. Jesus' announcement of the advent of God's reign "is the master symbol that controls the whole narrative" (Freyne: 51). How does Jesus demonstrate the arrival of God's kingdom? His first act will be calling disciples (1:16-20). He will ask them to leave their past behind and follow Jesus. Calling disciples, however, is not preparation for ministry; it is the very *heart* of Jesus' ministry and therefore belongs to the next section.

THE TEXT IN BIBLICAL CONTEXT

Jesus Fulfills OT Expectations

The first 15 verses of Mark contain numerous connections with the OT. Mark opens his Gospel with a composite quotation from the OT prophets. The voice of God at Jesus' baptism alludes to three OT texts. Numerous additional themes and motifs in this section build on OT precedents (e.g., allusions to Elijah, the torn heavens, the descending dove, and so on). These references appear in the notes (above) since they are necessary for understanding the text.

The following comments draw attention to still other OT (and intertestamental) background information and textual allusions.

Gospel/Good News

Two important NT words are *euangelion* (good news/gospel), and the related verb *euangelizomai* (to proclaim the good news/ gospel). Almost without exception, Matthew and Mark use the first of these (often with a verb for preach or teach), Luke uses the second, John uses neither, and Paul uses both. In Mark's first verse, the word *euangelion* refers to the *content* of the story Mark is about to tell. It was a small step for later commentators to apply the word to the four books we now call Gospels.

Prior to Mark's writing, Jesus used the word *gospel* (or its Hebrew/Aramaic counterpart) to speak of the good news that God's reign was being established; Paul was using it to refer to the benefits of salvation resulting from Jesus' death and resurrection (Rom. 1:1, 16; 1 Cor. 15:1-4).

The term *euangelion* is not found in the Greek translation of the OT, although similar terms are occasionally used. The Hebrew counterpart (bes̆orah) is used rarely and never in a clearly religious sense; it refers to any good news and/or the reward for bearing it.

Still, we must not underemphasize the influence of the OT on the NT concept carried by the term *gospel*. The Hebrew verb *bis̆s̆ar* (proclaim/publish) is significant. In Psalms and Isaiah, *bis̆s̆ar* is used to announce God's present victory and reign and to promise an even greater era of salvation in the future (Isa. 40:9; 52:7; 61:1). The OT usage holds together the *proclaimer* of good news, the *good news itself*, and the *effects* of proclaiming it (acts of creation or salvation). Indeed, a messenger who speaks with divine authority causes God's will to be done *by the proclaiming of the word;* how much more certain it is that God's purposes come about when *God* speaks directly (Gen. 1:3; Ps. 33:6). The OT thus supplies the background of the NT concept *gospel* (*euangelion*), even if not the exact vocabulary.

The Roman imperial cult popularized the Greek vocabulary. The words *euangelion/euangelizomai were* regularly used to describe announcements of a future emperor's birth, and especially his inauguration into imperial office.

NT usage of *euangelion* ties together the Roman associations (a monarch's birth and accession to the throne) and the OT associations (God creating and saving by the effective spoken word). Gospel is being proclaimed when angels announce Jesus' birth (Luke 2:10), Jesus announces that God's reign has drawn near (Mark 1:14-15), Jesus proclaims the era of salvation in his inaugural address (Luke 4:18), and apostles and missionaries proclaim the good news of salvation through Jesus' death and resurrection (1 Cor. 15).

Mark makes some distinctive contributions to the larger NT picture. For him, the whole Jesus story is the Gospel (*euangelion*), or more precisely, the *beginning* of the Gospel (1:1). For Mark, the Gospel demands a new orientation to life, and it creates a new kingdom community (1:14-20). Those who identify with God's good news (1:14) become themselves proclaimers of it (13:10); in so doing, they sacrifice much, perhaps even their lives (8:35; 13:9-13). But for their sacrifices, Jesus' followers experience immeasurable rewards already in this life and salvation in the next (10:28-30).

The Way

Israel of old traveled forty years in the wilderness. Their desert journey from Egypt to the land they would possess becomes a metaphor for the journey from bondage to victory. God is the one who helps them along the way through the desert (Exod. 23:20). The

OT preference for a movable tent over a stationary temple builds on this motif. God will not be contained in one sacred place; instead, God leads Israel on a journey from slavery into the Promised Land. The prophetic call to prepare a road through the desert picks up this theme (Isa. 40:3). Israel has lost the Promised Land to foreigners, but God will lead the chosen people home again, making a way through the desert and protecting them on their journey. Yet Israel's return to its land, and especially to Zion, would not only restore a glorious past; God would establish new things, never before seen (Isa. 43:18-19; cf. Marcus: 19, 28). God would come to live among the Israelites, setting up the divine throne on Mount Zion and giving Israel everlasting joy (Isa. 51:9-11). Metaphorically, Israel is perpetually on a journey from bondage to salvation. The journey will finally lead Israel, not to a mere earthly homeland, but to the fulfillment of all God's promises in the age to come.

The early church understood itself to be on a journey. Jesus had not promised to inhabit one holy place; he had promised to accompany his disciples as they went about the mission to which he had commissioned them (Matt. 28:18-20; Acts 1:8). The early church was called "people of *the way*" (Acts 9:2).

The Way (*hē hodos*) is an important motif in Mark's Gospel. John prepares the way for Jesus (1:2, 14). Jesus teaches his disciples *on the way* (8:27; 9:33-34; 10:32, 35). Jesus models faithful discipleship by going the way marked out for him (9:12-13). As stated (notes on 1:2), Mark breaks the link between *way* and *wilderness*. Jesus' way may *begin* in the desert, but it winds through synagogues and homes, in and out of villages, across the Sea of Galilee and back, into the Decapolis, and back into Galilee.

This way often includes excursions into the desert. Yet the way itself is not a way through the dangers of the physical desert; it is through the dangers of enemy territory, most significantly in Jerusalem. The way will not lead to a magnificent political conquest; it will lead to a cross. Beyond the cross, the journey continues as disciples are led to Galilee to meet the risen Jesus and experience the fulfillment of all he promised (14:27-28; 16:7; 13:27).

Jesus is the way-preparer. As he walks the way that he is defining, he blazes a trail of faithful obedience. As disciples are recruited, they are called to walk the same way after him. Jesus' way is the way of faithfulness, of obedient following, of servant ministry. It is the way that risks rejection for the sake of truth, the way of cross-carrying (living according to divine priorities, 8:33-34), the way that leads to life and final glory (TLC, below).

The way in Mark's Gospel builds on OT motifs, but it transforms them. *The way* is not the way of conquest, as God's people rid the land of foreign invaders; it is not a highway for exiles to travel in style back to the Jewish homeland. Instead, *the way* leads away from earthly securities into the unpredictable challenges and adventures of following Jesus. It defines a journey where self-sacrifice is richly rewarded in this life and the next (10:28-30).

The Wild Beasts and the Angels

The reference to wild beasts and angels in Mark's temptation narrative has puzzled commentators. Is the reference only to protection? The psalmist speaks of the guarding presence of God's angels when dangerous beasts threaten (Ps. 91:11-13). Or is there more? A close parallel to Mark 1:13 is found in an early Jewish writing (Test. of Naph. 8:4): "And the devil shall flee from you, and the wild beasts shall fear you; . . . and the angels shall cleave to you." Here the reference to wild beasts serves to emphasize danger and also God's ultimate protection for those who, though tested, are "blameless" (cf. Dan. 6:22; Mark 16:18; Acts 28:3-6). It foreshadows the day when humans and formerly dangerous beasts will live peaceably together (Isa. 11:6-9).

Jesus emerges from the desert after experiencing God's help in his time of temptation and danger. This will not be the final temptation of Jesus (14:32-42). Yet his decisive victory here, though not explicitly narrated, is presupposed by his emergence on the Galilean stage as the one announcing the arrival of God's kingdom (1:14-15).

Jesus' victory over Satan here also represents the tying up of the *strong man* that allows Jesus to *plunder* Satan's *house* (cast out demons) and deliver his captives (restore people to wholeness; 3:27). Jesus' victory over Satan in the desert both foreshadows and inaugurates God's final victory over Satan and all that Satan represents.

THE TEXT IN THE LIFE OF THE CHURCH

The Way of Glory and the Way of the Cross

Christians are a *people of the resurrection*. They celebrate Easter, Jesus' exaltation, and his glorious future coming. In so doing, they emphasize the victory Jesus won over sin and death. But Christians are also a *people of the cross*. The resurrection does not nullify the cross; instead, it demonstrates that the cross is the means by which God's glory is attained. When the emphasis on victory and celebration drains the cross of all its significance (except perhaps its necessity in atoning for sin), we seriously misunderstand the gospel, and especially Mark's Gospel.

The way of the cross is presented in the NT not only as a divine necessity in salvation history, but as a central symbol for Christian living. Jesus' death was a consequence of his self-giving life. The way of the cross becomes a metaphor for the self-giving life of Christian discipleship (notes on 8:34; TBC for 8:27—9:1; the essay [The Meaning of Cross-Carrying]). Peter's combined proclamation of the substitutionary and the modeling aspects of Christ's suffering is particularly striking: "Christ suffered for you, leaving you an example, that you should follow in his steps" (1 Pet. 2:21).

Saying yes to Jesus does not guarantee a life of unmitigated blessings. To follow Jesus is to begin a life of costly discipleship; there are rewards and also costs (Mark 10:28-30, mentioning both the hundredfold reward *and* persecutions).

Mark calls his readers (as Jesus did his disciples) to recognize Jesus as Messiah and Son of God. To do so, however, is not the goal of the discipleship journey; it is its beginning point. On the road of discipleship, key roles and titles for Jesus are clarified. The Messiah is one who reigns from a cross. The Son of God is one who reveals God's heart by giving himself fully even in death. From the very beginning of his Gospel (notes on 1:1, 11), Mark alludes to the unbreakable link between Christology and the cross of Jesus.

By connecting his two main titles (*Messiah* and *Son of God*) to the cross, Mark may have been countering a Christology and an understanding of the Christian life that focused on glory and victory but had no room for suffering and the cross. Mark's message is that no glorious messiahship or wonder-working divine sonship is possible, except by way of the cross. Jesus' followers do not seek a life of ease and earthly glory; they seek to follow faithfully the one who promised that true glory is found on the other side of *the cross*.

Seldom has this emphasis been more sorely needed than in a pampered Western society, where even Christians often expect that social, political, and economic systems, as well as the gospel of Jesus Christ, will foster our self-indulgence and guarantee success in our "pursuit of happiness." Mark's Gospel promises great rewards, but they are rewards for taking seriously the way of the cross (notes on 8:34—9:1; books by Bonhoeffer; Hershberger, 1958; Kraybill).

The Kingdom of God

The beginning of the twentieth century represented a significant turning point in studies of the Gospels and of the historical Jesus. The

central theme of Jesus' preaching, *the kingdom of God*, was rediscovered. Throughout the twentieth century, as never before, that
theme has been taken seriously; yet a century of study has failed to
bring about a consensus on exactly what Jesus and/or the Gospel
writers *meant* when they spoke of God's kingdom (cf. Perrin, 1976).

Many Christians assume that God's kingdom is to be equated with
the believers' heavenly destiny. It has become clear, however, that
many of Jesus' references to God's kingdom are about God powerfully breaking into the present earthly order to establish God's reign.
Major disagreement has persisted on this question: *When* does God
establish the kingdom? Three views have dominated the discussion:

• Some interpreters insist that Jesus expected the imminent arrival
of God's kingdom, but that he viewed himself as its proclaimer and
preparer, not its bringer (*consequent eschatology:* A. Schweitzer).

• Others insist that Jesus viewed his own coming and his ministry
as in some sense equivalent to the arrival of God's (long-awaited) kingdom (*realized eschatology:* C. H. Dodd).

• Still others adopt a paradoxical already/not yet view of the kingdom. Jesus inaugurates but does not consummate the kingdom. With
Jesus' arrival, the kingdom is initiated and makes its presence felt, but
a future glorious inbreaking of God's reign is still anticipated (*eschatology in the process of being realized:* W. Kümmel, G. Ladd).

Scholars are also divided on whether the Gospel writers have
faithfully preserved the original view of the historical Jesus. Many
scholars are willing to attribute the third view to the Gospel writers,
but not to the historical Jesus.

Clearly Mark holds to the third view. In his Gospel, the kingdom
is already secretly coming; someday it will be fully manifest. It is like
a seed already growing, holding promise of a great harvest (esp. 4:1-
34). It arrives in weakness, suffering abuse and rejection, or even
being completely overlooked; it is destined someday to be gloriously
revealed (13:24-27). It comes for those who take up their cross and
follow Jesus; yet they await the glory beyond the cross. In my opinion, there is a simple explanation for the fact that all four Gospel writers represent some form of the paradoxical already/not yet kingdom:
Jesus himself represented that view *[Kingdom of God in Mark]*.

The NT clearly portrays the kingdom as something *God* establishes. Jesus' followers participate in it, they proclaim it, they do its
works. But they cannot establish it or force God to do so. Repeatedly
throughout history, the church has tried to establish God's reign,
sometimes by political action (setting up a "Christian state," such as

the so-called Holy Roman Empire), and sometimes by military action (attacking "God's enemies" with the sword, as in the Crusades). Even among predominantly peaceful (and peacemaking) groups like the sixteenth-century Anabaptists, there were tragic aberrations. One group sought to establish God's reign by military might, taking and holding Münster (Germany) as the "holy city" of God's millennial kingdom. Jesus rejected all political and military methods of establishing God's reign. His way is the way of selfless serving, bold proclamation, and willingness to suffer for truth and righteousness. Those who would experience the kingdom that Jesus announced, must choose the way Jesus chose. In Mark, that choice is called repenting and believing the good news (1:15). The next section of Mark's Gospel shows what is involved in making that choice and joining Jesus as he proclaims the kingdom in word and deed.

Mark 1:16-45

Jesus' Ministry Begins

PREVIEW

Mark's prologue (1:1-15) has introduced Jesus to the reader. He is the Christ, the Son of God, two titles that Mark links inseparably to the cross. Mark's prologue has also presented a series of stages in the preparation for Jesus' ministry (prophecy, John's ministry, Jesus' own baptism, commissioning, and temptation). It has ended with a programmatic statement. With John being *handed over*, Jesus emerges on the Galilean stage, proclaiming the arrival of God's kingdom (1:14-15).

This section (1:16-45) shows *how* Jesus proclaims God's reign and ministers its presence. Jesus carries out kingdom ministries in word and deed. The range of ministries featured in the remainder of chapter 1 is broad (teaching, driving out demons, healing, praying, preaching, cleansing). Alongside all of these, and perhaps more basic than all of them, is the ministry of calling and training disciples.

Jesus begins by calling two sets of brothers to follow him. Later Jesus will call others (as in 2:13-14) and still later clarify the true nature of his kingdom community/family (3:31-35). Joining this community will seem to cost a great deal (1:16-20; 8:34-38), but we learn that there is also great reward (10:28-31).

The prologue has ended with Jesus' announcement that God's reign is arriving. As this section opens, we see that the first order of business in establishing God's reign is the creation of a kingdom people. We also recognize that the call to repentance and faith (1:15) is not answered in private. It is answered as individuals join the kingdom

44

community, the family of Jesus' followers.

Right from the start, Jesus' followers follow and observe and learn as Jesus models kingdom ministries. They later are commissioned to carry out similar ministries (6:7, 12-13). Mark 1:35-39 contains reflections on Jesus' priorities and projections for future ministry. These verses also reveal that the disciples who start so well are having trouble accepting the priorities of their master.

Embedded in this section are hints that controversy with the religious establishment is on the horizon. This becomes particularly clear in the final episode of the section, making this final episode an appropriate transition to the controversy section that follows (2:1—3:6).

OUTLINE

Fishing for People, 1:16-20

The Authoritative Teacher, 1:21-28
1:21-22	Teaching with Greater Authority Than the Scribes
1:23-26	Silencing and Expelling an Unclean Spirit
1:27-28	The Astonished Reaction of the Crowd

Jesus Heals Simon's Mother-in-Law, 1:29-31

Jesus Heals and Drives Out Demons, 1:32-34

Jesus and His Priorities, 1:35-39
1:35	Jesus Prays
1:36-37	Jesus' Followers Object
1:38-39	Jesus' Priorities

Jesus Cleanses a Leper, 1:40-45

EXPLANATORY NOTES
Fishing for People 1:16-20

Jesus walks along a lake. He sees four fishermen and announces that he has new plans for them. They are to give up everything and follow him. Their response is immediate: No questions asked, no preparations made. They simply leave everything and follow him. Readers are left shaking their heads. Just like that? No persuasive arguments given? No preparations for the journey? No clarification of where Jesus will lead them? No backup plans in case it turns out to be a bad choice?

From Mark's narrative alone, we would never infer that these men had ever been with John the Baptist or experienced his ministry of preparation (cf. John 1:35-42). Nor would we suspect that Jesus might have first done a miracle for them and then called them to follow (cf. Luke 5:4-11).

This text focuses on Jesus' authoritative call and their radical response. These first four disciples are responding to *Jesus*, not to sound arguments or to an amazing miracle or to persuasive sales tactics. Questions of cost and benefit will be dealt with later (8:34-38; 10:28-31). One minute these men are fishing and mending nets; the next they are following Jesus. One minute they are running a fishing business; the next they have left it all behind to follow a man they hardly know.

The TLC (below) develops more fully four aspects of their call and response that are worth mentioning:

1. The call to discipleship in 1:17 is threefold: to follow, to be changed (a literal translation is *I will make you* **to become**), and to engage in a ministry (*fishing for people*).

2. The primary ministry of the kingdom is to draw others into an experience of the reality of God's reign (*fish for people*).

3. Leaving does not always mean permanently abandoning. Here Simon does not cut all ties with home or family or boat, as we see in 1:29-31; 3:9; and so on.

4. The cost of discipleship is not experienced in the same way by everyone. The first two brothers are said to *leave their nets* and the second set to *leave their father*. The wording may well suggest what seems like the greatest cost to each of these sets of brothers.

With his four new recruits, Jesus enters the local synagogue and his public ministry begins.

The Authoritative Teacher 1:21-28

The next four episodes are linked by time references. We might view 1:21-38 as "A Day of Ministry": Jesus teaches and drives out an unclean spirit during a Sabbath gathering at a synagogue (1:21); just after the meeting, he heals Simon's mother-in-law (1:29); he heals many others that same evening after sundown (1:32); early the next morning, he prays and explains his priorities (1:35).

1:21-22 Teaching with Greater Authority Than the Scribes

Jesus enters a synagogue in Capernaum and begins to teach. The astonished reaction of his audience serves to highlight the main point of the text: He teaches with authority (1:22). According to Mark, the scribes appeal to traditions from the past (7:6-9). Jesus announces new things on the horizon (1:14-15; 2:21-22). They appeal to other scribes who have gone before. Jesus speaks as one commissioned by God, endowed with the Spirit, and ready to challenge the status quo (1:10-15).

At the earliest stages of Jesus' ministry, he regularly attends Galilean synagogues and uses them as platforms for his kingdom proclamation (1:39). One result is that his fame spreads quickly (1:28, 45). Another result is that the scribes, here unfavorably contrasted to this new teacher, will begin to challenge the authority that he claims and exhibits (e.g., 2:6-7).

But what was the content of Jesus' teaching? The reader is not told. Indeed, apart from two discourses (chaps. 4 and 13), the reader is hardly ever told what Jesus taught.

1:23-26 Silencing and Expelling an Unclean Spirit

Jesus' teaching is interrupted by a sudden outburst. A man in the synagogue has an unclean spirit. Such spirits (demons) are unclean or evil because (1) they make a person incapable of and unfit for true divine worship, and (2) they often lead to many other unclean or inappropriate associations and actions (cf. 5:1-20, notes).

Verse 24 suggests that this man (or the unclean spirit within him) speaks for all the spirits, shouting out the identity of the authoritative teacher, *Jesus of Nazareth, . . . the Holy One of God*. Jesus regularly silences demons for attempting to reveal his identity (1:34; 3:12). As readers, we have been told from the beginning who Jesus is (1:1, 11). Now we discover that the demons also know who Jesus is (1:24; cf. 3:11). The human characters of the story, however, are not to learn about Jesus' identity from the demons. For Mark, discernment leading to true insight into Jesus' identity comes in the context of discipleship, not as revelations from the divine or demonic world.

The spirit's first question, *What have you to do with us?* is difficult to translate (1:24). It might mean, *What do we have in common here?* The second question, *Have you come to destroy us?* might not be a question at all. It could as well be translated, *You have come to destroy us;* some commentators take it this way. The spirit(s) are apparently trying to ward off the negative effects Jesus' authority might have on it/them. But the authority of the spirit(s) is no match for Jesus' authority. With a rebuking command, Jesus silences and expels the demon(s).

1:27-28 The Astonished Reaction of the Crowd

Once more Mark records the reaction of the people. This second reference to their astonishment at Jesus' authority confirms that this is the main point of the text (1:22). The issues here are Jesus' identity (which the demons are forbidden to reveal) and Jesus' authority (greater than that of scribes or demons). Jesus' authoritative teaching provokes the demon's reaction. The demon's expulsion is interpreted as evidence of Jesus' authority.

Jesus Heals Simon's Mother-in-Law   1:29-31

A more-dramatic-than-usual synagogue service comes to an end. What follows is the first healing story Mark records. The story is told simply and directly: Jesus is brought into contact with Simon's ill mother-in-law; with an outstretched hand, he lifts her up, and the fever departs. She demonstrates that she is well by ministering to them (no doubt helping serve the Sabbath meal).

We learn later that some take offense at Jesus' Sabbath healings (3:2). Later still, we observe healings that are much more dramatic, complete with odd healing rituals and groans (7:31-37; 8:22-26). Moreover, these other healings sometimes serve to convey symbolic meanings above and beyond their immediate reference to healed ears and eyes. None of that seems present here. Jesus simply heals a woman with a fever.

This story, however, is not only about Jesus and a woman with a fever. It is also about the first four disciples Jesus recruited. They are literally *following* Jesus, going where he goes, being trained by observing their teacher. Later they will be commissioned to do as he does (6:6b-13, 30). They are also being shown that *fishing for people* involves more than recruitment (1:17); it includes teaching, healing, driving out demons. Jesus' multifaceted ministry here prefigures the disciples' ministry later (6:7, 12-13, 30).

Two more points are worth noting. First, Simon and the others have left everything to follow Jesus (1:18, 20; 10:28). Yet here they are again, in their hometown and their own home. Later we see them in the boats they left behind. Leaving everything to follow Jesus is thus about priorities more than about actually abandoning people and things. It is about putting kingdom matters first. It is about a readiness to drop everything that stands in the way of faithful discipleship.

Sometimes that will mean literally leaving people and things behind; sometimes it will not (TLC, below).

Second, this text may give an unintended hint that Simon (the apostle Peter) is the source Mark drew on for this episode (Introduction, above). The evidence is in the awkwardness of Mark's sentence. *They entered the house of Simon and Andrew, with James and John.* Who are they? In the context, *they* must refer to Simon, Andrew, and Jesus. These three went *with James and John.* But what an awkward expression: Why would Mark say that three of them went with the other two, unless Peter is the one telling the story? In Peter's mouth, the story reads smoothly: "We went with James and John to our house." Mark apparently didn't fully edit the account when he turned it into a third-person narrative. Thus we have an accidental confirmation that the early traditions of the church are correct: Mark's source was the apostle Peter himself.

Jesus Heals and Drives Out Demons 1:32-34

At sundown (when the Sabbath officially ends) the quickly spreading fame of this authoritative teacher (1:28) becomes evident. A crowd of people gathers at the house where Jesus is staying. Some are sick, some have demons, some are bringing others who suffer in mind or body. The sick are healed; the demons are silenced so they won't reveal Jesus' identity, and then they are thrown out.

The translation *possessed with demons* (1:32) is not accurate. Nowhere in Scripture is it ever said that demons *possess* people. People are said to have demons, but it is never reported that demons have people. The language of demonization (the usual word is *daimonizomai*) is varied, and so is the language of deliverance. Sometimes demons are driven away, sometimes thrown out, sometimes they simply leave. Mark does not seem interested in developing an elaborate demonology. Instead, his interest in the topic is twofold: he highlights various ways in which Jesus' presence brings people to wholeness; he portrays Jesus robbing Satan's house, thus bringing Satan's dominion to an end while establishing the reign of God (on demonization: TBC, below; 3:23-27; TLC for 9:2—10:16).

Jesus and His Priorities 1:35-39

Thus far Jesus' ministry has included kingdom proclamation (1:14-15), the recruitment and training of followers (1:16-20; 1:29, notes), teaching (1:21), driving out demons (1:25-26, 34), and multiple healings (1:31, 34). Jesus now demonstrates that his priorities also

include prayer (1:35), escaping popularity (1:38), and crossing boundaries (1:40-45).

1:35 Jesus Prays

Public preaching and teaching, though sometimes exhilarating,
can also be exhausting. When that public ministry is complicated by
extra spiritual battles, as during Jesus' Sabbath ministry in
Capernaum, the last thing desired is more people, more demands,
more ministry. Jesus must have gone to bed that evening exhausted.
Yet he rises before dawn to pray. It is one of his priorities.

Jesus seeks out a *desert-ed* place (in Greek, as in English, the
word is derived from *desert*). He wants a place for intimacy with God
and renewal of strength. Again he is modeling for his disciples aspects
of ministry they must learn if they are to become effective *fishers for
people* (TLC, below).

1:36-37 Jesus' Followers Object

The first four disciples are here called *Simon and his companions*. This may reveal that Simon is already emerging as a leader.
More likely, it betrays once more an earlier version of this story (1:29,
notes). If Peter is Mark's source, then of course Peter's version of the
story would simply have said "we." Mark's way of translating this into
the third person (Simon and his companions) is understandable, even
if not elegant.

We must read Mark 1:36 carefully: the disciples *hunted for* Jesus.
Their action is not dedicated following; the Greek word *katadiōkō*
really implies *hunting down* or *tracking down,* as one might pursue
an exhausted quarry (Lightfoot: 23). We must pay attention to Mark
1:37: the crowds from Capernaum are *searching for* Jesus. This
does not report a positive response; in Mark's Gospel the word *zēteō*
regularly implies either evil intent or misguided priorities (cf. 8:11-12).
The disciples do not want Jesus to get away, nor do the crowds in
Capernaum. They are more eager to marvel at his authority and benefit from his miraculous healing ministry than to respond appropriately to his kingdom message. "Why is he away praying when there
are so many to be healed in Capernaum!" (Dowd: 120).

These verses contain the first hints that Jesus' followers, the future
ministers he is mentoring, are not quite on the same wavelength he
is. They emerge here as interpreters of the wishes of the crowd, not
as disciples eager to learn of Jesus' own priorities. By implication,
they are opposed to Jesus taking time for private prayer when he

could be fostering public popularity. They certainly want him to return to Capernaum and its eager crowds. Jesus has other priorities.

1:38-39 Jesus' Priorities

Jesus has already moved from the clamoring crowds to the privacy of his desert retreat. Now instead of returning, he moves on to other villages. He has come to proclaim the message and do the works of the kingdom, not to expand his popularity as a miracle-worker.

This passage contains another of Mark's double meanings (1:1, notes). Jesus moves on to proclaim in other villages, informing his disciples, *That is what I came out to do.* Does Jesus mean he is moving *out of Capernaum* or *into the world*? Does he refer to his own that morning, or to God's priorities in sending him with the message of the kingdom? If Mark intends 1:10 as an allusion to the incarnation (1:10, notes), then he may want to affirm both possibilities here. Something similar is found in 2:17, when Jesus says *I have come to call not the righteous, but sinners* (2:17). Did he come only to Levi's party for that purpose, or did he also come into the world proclaiming the good news for that purpose? Mark says both.

If Mark intends a double meaning in 1:38, perhaps he intends one already in 1:37. *Everyone is seeking you* refers to the clamoring crowds in Capernaum. But Mark may want his readers to hear what Jesus hears, a reference to the broad and deep longing in all Israel and all humankind for the era of fulfillment to arrive. *That* is why he has come out. Indeed, precisely because of that universal longing, Jesus does *not* cater to the clamoring crowds in Capernaum. Everyone must hear the message; Jesus moves on to other villages.

The day of ministry ends (1:21-38), and Mark closes this section with a summary statement of Jesus' activities (1:39). He proclaims the message of the kingdom in synagogues throughout Galilee; where demonic opposition arises, he drives out demons as well.

Jesus Cleanses a Leper 1:40-45

Jesus has demonstrated a wide range of priorities. He did not want to be distracted by a popular healing ministry (notes, above), but he readily heals when opportunities and needs arise. A leper comes to Jesus and begs for cleansing ("Leprosy and Cleansing," TBC). The narrative highlights the imploring actions of the leper and the emotional responses of Jesus. The leper begs on his knees (though *kneeling* is absent from some manuscripts). Jesus is *moved with pity* (unless the original reading is *moved with anger;* the manuscripts differ). Later Jesus *sternly warns* the man.

The leper expresses great faith. He knows Jesus *can* heal; he wonders if Jesus is *willing* (1:41). Jesus exhibits not only his willingness and power to heal, but also his willingness to risk ceremonial uncleanness himself by touching the man ("Leprosy and Cleansing," TBC).

In this text, commentators have seen sprouting seeds of the conflict that will soon erupt. Jesus sends the man to the priest. He is to bring the appropriate sacrifice and will receive from the priest the legal pronouncement of cleansing. Surely this does not represent Jesus' own concern to stay within religious boundaries. After all, he has just conventionally defiled himself by touching the leper. Jesus might be showing his concern for the cleansed man by sending him to the priest, thus encouraging him to be certified clean so that future social contact is officially authorized. But the added comment *as a testimony to them* (1:44) suggests that there is more going on here.

The man's healing will vividly demonstrate the difference between Jesus and the custodians of official religion: they can only *pronounce* people clean; Jesus can *make* them clean. Indeed, the grammar of the phrase permits us to translate it *as a testimony **against** them.* Whether we translate it *to them* or *against them,* any testimony of Jesus' effective ministry will function as a witness against those who reject him and his message. That is what virtually all the religious leaders will do. This last episode in chapter 1 is not only a healing narrative but also an appropriate transition into the controversy section that follows.

We do not know whether the cleansed leper follows Jesus' counsel to go to the priest. What is clear is that he disobeys Jesus' strict warning not to report his healing (unless he has been forbidden to report it *only until* he has seen the priest). As a result of the man's open proclamation, Jesus' movement into towns is inhibited by the clamoring crowds. He moves (temporarily) away from towns and synagogues (2:1; 3:1).

Chapter 1 opens with the Judean crowds flocking to John in the desert. It closes with the Galilean crowds flocking to Jesus in the desert. Major transitions have taken place from John's preparatory ministry to Jesus' own multifaceted work of the kingdom. But what about the crowds? How sincere are the Jerusalem crowds? And how sincere are these from Galilee? At this point Mark leaves his readers wondering.

THE TEXT IN BIBLICAL CONTEXT
Driving Out Demons

The OT does not often refer to demons or to demonization. In the Synoptic Gospels and in Acts, there are numerous references to Jesus and later the early missionaries driving out demons or unclean spirits. John's Gospel refers to the "judgment of this world," as Satan is "driven out" (12:31). Revelation further develops this theme: Satan is first cast out of heaven to earth (12:10-12), then from earth into the abyss (20:3), and finally into the lake of burning sulfur (20:10).

As indicated in the notes above, Mark's interest in the topic of driving out demons seems twofold: he highlights the wholeness Jesus brings to individuals when Satan's influence in their lives is replaced with God's (esp. 5:1-20); and he sees in Jesus' successful victories over the demons a sign that Satan's kingdom is falling apart as God's reign is being established (3:23-27).

In Mark, Jesus never seeks opportunities to cast out demons; he simply responds to needs when they present themselves. Mark narrates four incidents where Jesus drives out demons (1:23-26; 5:1-20; 7:24-30; 9:14-29; cf. also 9:38-41) and in addition refers to such incidents in ministry summaries (e.g., 1:39). Besides the topic of driving out demons successfully, these texts highlight other important issues, such as the authority of Jesus (1:27), the need for secrecy about Jesus' identity (1:34; 3:11), Jesus' willingness to transgress social boundaries to be (and to make) a faithful missionary (5:1-20), the fact that God's grace is available even to a Gentile (7:25-30), and the importance of faith and prayer (9:23, 29).

Luke's Gospel has a significantly greater emphasis on Jesus' victories over Satan and Satan's hosts than does Mark's. Luke strategically places accounts of Jesus casting out demons, so as to provide evidence that Jesus truly is God's authorized "divine warrior" (e.g., Luke 7:18-22). Similar stories in Acts surround both the Pauline mission and the entire non-Palestinian mission (Swartley, 1994:85). Luke seems to make a connection between victories over demonic powers and Israel's conquest of Canaan. Moreover, Luke and Matthew explicitly link the casting out of demons with the arrival of the reign of God (Luke 11:20; Matt. 12:28). God's reign comes as enemies are driven out of the land. The NT, of course, makes it clear that the enemies are the demonic forces, not the humans who are their victims. Where humans are in fact enemies, they are to be loved, not conquered (Luke 6:35).

Seen from the larger NT perspective, Jesus successfully conquers

Satan and Satan's kingdom through various strategies. Jesus is the stronger one who ties up Satan and delivers Satan's victims (Mark 3:27). Jesus speaks God's word with such authority that he both provokes demonic reaction and subsequently also dispels it (Luke 4:32-36). Jesus is the one who creates *shalom* by conquering shalom's destroyer; thus he brings safety to those in danger (Mark 4:39), peace to those tormented (5:15), wholeness to those whose minds and bodies are being destroyed (9:29-27; Luke 13:16), and salvation to those who need forgiveness and new life (2 Cor. 4:4-6).

Jesus' ultimate conquest is not by a final show of force, but by sacrificing his own life and trusting God to vindicate him. Thus he destroys the power of evil through the greater power of good (Matt. 20:25-28; John 10:10 11; Rom. 12:21; see TLC after 10:16).

Jesus defeated Satan and Satan's hosts by his own superior authority and strength. But Jesus never overpowered Satan's victims; instead, he freed, healed, and restored them to life. He never used force against those who were deceived by (or even inhabited by) Satan (Luke 22:3). Instead, he allowed them to put him to death, and *by his willing sacrifice of himself*, defeated Satan, the real enemy (Heb. 2:14-15). What a contrast to many of Jesus' contemporaries who thought Satan could be defeated and demons expelled by oaths, spells, and incantations!

Those who follow Jesus participate in God's victory over evil. They do not take up weapons of destruction to fight against flesh and blood; they participate in Christ's victory against the spiritual powers that hold people captive (Eph. 6:11-12). Victims of those powers are loved and freed and invited into God's reign of peace (Col. 1:11-14).

Believers join Jesus' holy warfare against the powers of evil. Paul, writing to the Roman believers, makes this provocative claim: "The God of peace will shortly crush Satan under *your feet*" (16:20). John the Seer is explicit about which weapons, wielded by the saints, will ultimately bring about Satan's downfall:

> They [the believers] have conquered him by the blood of the Lamb and by the word of their testimony, for they did not cling to life even in the face of death. (Rev. 12:9-11)

Faithful believers identify with Jesus' death; like their model, they are willing to die for what is true and right. Holy warfare becomes holy martyrdom; God's weakness is greater than Satan's strength. Jesus' followers rejoice when Satan is defeated in spiritual combat. But their rejoicing is even greater that their names are written in heaven. This knowledge frees them to willingly sacrifice their own lives for the sake of the gospel of peace (Luke 10:17-20).

Jesus at Prayer

Luke highlights the theme of prayer. In his Gospel, Jesus models prayer as a time to be alone with his Father (5:16), as a preparation for major decisions (6:12), and as a small-group spiritual discipline (9:28). Jesus also prays for his disciples (22:32) and teaches them to pray (11:1), even for their abusers (6:28).

Mark has fewer references to Jesus at prayer. In fact, apart from mealtime blessings, Jesus' own praying is alluded to only three times in Mark (unless 7:34 and 15:34 are also counted as prayers). The first of the three explicit references to Jesus at prayer is in this section (1:35). After an exhausting day of ministry, Jesus rises early to pray. Communion with his Father is one of his priorities; he emerges from prayer ready to put into practice other priorities (1:38-39, notes).

The second reference to Jesus at prayer is 6:46. Jesus has completed a long exhausting day of ministry. He spends the night praying. Taking the context into account, we suspect that he is praying not only for himself. No doubt he prays also for his exhausted fellow ministers, the disciples who have served in his name (6:30) and alongside him (6:41, 43), and who are now battling with contrary winds (6:48) and with misunderstanding (6:49-52; 6:45-52, notes).

At 14:32-42, Jesus instructs his disciples to watch and pray with him in his (and their) time of need, but instead they sleep. Jesus faithfully prays, asking that the cup of suffering might be removed, yet pledging himself to face whatever God wills.

In Mark, references to Jesus' prayers are not many. They are enough, however, to show that Jesus models what he is teaching his followers. They *must* make believing prayer a priority if they want to face the challenges of ministry (9:23, 29) and see mountains moved (11:22-24). "If even Jesus found it necessary to pray, how much more should they do so" (Dowd: 120).

Leprosy and Cleansing

To understand Scriptures on the cleansing of lepers, several clarifications are needed. First, leprosy in Scripture is seldom the disease called by that name today (Hansen's disease). The word refers to virtually any skin disease, infectious or not. Most Bibles have notes to that effect at Leviticus 13-14 and/or elsewhere.

Second, the skin diseases and blemishes called leprosy in Scripture were only sometimes debilitating. In many cases the social stigmatization and restrictions resulting from the disease were worse than the disease itself. A leper was *unclean* until pronounced *clean* by the priest. Anyone who came into direct contact with a leper was unclean until appropriate cleansing ceremonies were carried out. Thus lepers could not touch or be touched; they were excluded from meaningful social and religious participation (Lev. 13:1-46; 14:1-32). Hence, though Jesus *heals* lepers, the texts regularly report that the lepers are *cleansed.* The main issue is restoration to community.

Apart from 14:3 mentioning Simon the (cured?) leper, this section contains the only reference in Mark to Jesus healing/cleansing a leper. Yet it is part of a larger pattern in Mark. Jesus is conspicuously unconcerned about ceremonial defilement. According to the standards of official religion, Jesus is frequently rendered "unclean" by direct contact with people and things that "defile." Jesus does not shy away from leprosy, a hemorrhaging woman (5:25-27), a corpse (5:41), contact with Gentiles (7:24-26), or a whole complex of defilements (Gentiles, a graveyard, a herd of pigs; 5:1-20). In his contact with unclean things and people, Jesus demonstrates that his power to cleanse is greater than the power of anything or anyone to defile.

Jesus' approach to defilement is explained in 7:15-23. For him, true defilement comes from the heart, not from external contacts (7:18-20). Jesus' approach undermines established Jewish traditions and those enforcing them (particularly the priests; Ezek. 44:23). Jesus' religious opponents rightly conclude that he is a serious threat to the status quo and to their roles in maintaining its sanctity.

THE TEXT IN THE LIFE OF THE CHURCH

The Call of the Disciples

In the notes on 1:16-20, four points related to the call of the disciples were listed. All four are crucial in the church today:

1. The call to discipleship has inseparable aspects: It is a call to follow, to be changed, and to become ministers. A literal translation of Jesus' word to Simon and Andrew clearly brings out all three parts: *Come after me, and I will make you to become fishers for people.* The same sequence is repeated later when Jesus appoints *the twelve* (3:13-15). They are called (summoned to follow), and they are commissioned to be *with him* (transformation) and to be *sent out* (mission). The Christian life inseparably unites these three aspects; a call and decision to follow Jesus must always lead to ongoing transformation and also to ministry in Jesus' name.

2. The primary ministry of the kingdom is to draw others into an experience of the reality of God's reign (*fishing for people*). Some interpreters have maintained that *fishing for people* in Mark 1:16

refers to *judgment* (cf. Amos 4:2) rather than to *disciple-making*. The context here argues otherwise. At this very moment, Jesus is calling followers and creating a kingdom people. The disciples will be trained to do precisely what Jesus is doing right now: proclaiming the kingdom, recruiting people for it, and drawing them into a community that experiences God's reign (3:13-15). *Fishing for people* is broader than a narrowly conceived evangelistic ministry and/or a preoccupation with church growth. It is as broad as the ministry of Jesus, depicted well in the section studied here (recruiting, modeling, mentoring, caring for the sick and demonized, praying, proclaiming, teaching, and so on).

3. To be a disciple is to leave everything (careers, relationships, possessions, and so on) to follow Jesus. But the things *left* are not necessarily abandoned. We leave them in our heart first (they are not our priorities; they do not control us). Then we can abandon them if God's will requires it. Mark 1:17 reports that Simon left everything; yet not a week will pass before we find him back in his own home and enjoying his mother-in-law's Sabbath dinner (1:29-31). The boats that are left behind in this text will reappear frequently (3:9; 4:1, 36; 5:18; 6:32, 45; 8:10, 13). To leave everything is to release control of things; Jesus becomes the Lord of our relationships and possessions. They no longer keep us from responding as radically to Jesus as he calls us to do (10:28-31, notes).

4. The cost of discipleship is not the same for everyone. The call may be the same, to leave everything (10:28), but it will challenge each potential disciple at different points. Different aspects of the call tempt us to make our responses conditional or half-hearted. Mark makes an interesting distinction when he reports that Simon and Andrew *left their nets* and that James and John *left their father*. All four of them left everything. Yet the text hints that Simon and Andrew found it hardest to leave behind the *nets* and all they represented (cf. John 20:3); and that it was harder for the sons of Zebedee (Mark 1:19; 3:17; 10:35; Matt. 20:20) to leave their family. The call to discipleship is a call to break all the ties that keep us from following Jesus, whatever those ties might be. D. Bonhoeffer sums up the meaning of Jesus' call to discipleship in these words:

> If we would follow Jesus, we must take certain definite steps. The first step, which follows the call, cuts the disciple off from his previous existence. . . . The call to follow implies that there is only one way of believing in Jesus Christ, and that is by leaving all and going with the incarnate Son of God. (1963:66-7)

Multifaceted Ministry

In this section, Jesus ministers in various ways (preaching, healing, casting out demons, and so on). All these are valid ministries; all serve notice that God's reign is here. If proclamation is prioritized (as it seems to be in 1:38), that is not because the other ministries are less valid, but because Jesus' proclamation explains both the need for Jesus' other ministries and their significance.

How easily the church polarizes over questions of priority. One group stresses evangelism, another relief work and development, yet another healing ministries. Ministry organizations may specialize to maximize effectiveness, and this is to be applauded. Often, however, a critical eye is cast on organizations with priorities different from our own. Then we are only a small step away from defending *our* ministries as the *important* ones and playing down the work of others as peripheral. The wholistic ministry of Jesus calls us to see all human need as God's concern, whether that need is for protection and justice, comfort and support, hope and meaning, or salvation and eternal life.

As a member of two different national boards, I remember listening to animated debates. One was a denominational board charged with the spiritual and theological oversight of a denomination. The other was a relief agency in which our denomination participated. The denominational board was doing an official investigation of the validity of the ministries and strategies of the other organization. If members thought there was too little *explicit* Christian witness evident by those digging wells and distributing food, they questioned the spirituality of the workers. If they thought there was too *much* explicit witness, they voiced suspicions the relief agency was "encroaching on our denominational mission."

Many of the comments (no doubt also some of mine!) betrayed a good deal of suspicion, turf mentality, and tendency to prioritize some ministries over others. In the last several decades, most church groups seem to have moved toward a more wholistic, cooperative stance. I hope this perception is correct.

Mark 2:1-3:6

Conflict in Galilee

PREVIEW

Mark 1 has contained no report of any direct conflict between Jesus and those who will ultimately reject him. Yet the perceptive reader has picked up hints that a conflict is brewing. How will the scribes react when the Galilean crowds prefer Jesus' teaching over theirs? How will the priests react when Jesus sends to them a man he just cured of leprosy *as a testimony to* (or *against*) *them*? Do they need to be persuaded of something? As we begin Mark 2, conflict erupts almost immediately and is sustained throughout all the material up to 3:6, where readers learn that the Pharisees and Herodians are aligned against Jesus and plotting his death.

Mark 2:1—3:6 is often called the conflict section of Mark. Actually, it is the first of two major conflict sections. This one takes place in Galilee. After Jesus arrives in enemy territory (Jerusalem), a second conflict section leads to Jesus' death (11:27—12:44).

Here in Galilee, Jesus speaks and acts in ways that directly conflict with traditional religion as defined by the scribes, the Pharisees, and other religious officials. His teaching and claims undermine their authority. In response, all the major religious leadership groups in Israel eventually reject Jesus. We need to be clear that this is *Mark's characterization* of these groups. Mark never claims that each individual in the historical situation is typical of the group as depicted here [*Israel and Israel's Leaders*].

In this section (2:1—3:6) Jesus will make significant authority claims and back them up with reasoned arguments and biblical precedents. His claims will be incompatible with those of other religious groups, but Jesus is not out to provoke the religious leaders in this section. He will not treat them as enemies until they take a stand against him, rejecting his claims and plotting to do away with him (3:7, notes).

In this section Mark is showing his readers which issues will eventually create the unbridgeable gulf between Jesus and the religious officials. Conflict will develop over Jesus' claims of authority (to forgive sins and to determine appropriate Sabbath behavior), over Jesus' association with "sinners," over religious rituals and ceremonies (e.g., fasting), and so on.

This section of Mark (like several others) features a concentric structure: a series of matching episodes surround a central core. The first and last episodes are matching pairs; so are the second and second to last. The section in the middle contains the heart and interpretive center of the unit. The device is called a chiasm, a common literary device in Mark's day (and much earlier) [Chiasm and Intercalation]. A diagram of the chiastic structuring of this conflict section appears at the end of the notes, below.

Overlapping the concentric structure is a cumulative structure, one that reveals development from beginning to end. Here it is conflict that grows, as issues accumulate that divide Jesus from his opponents. A careful reading of the original language reveals that even the words chosen to record the opponents' questions betray increasing hostility and rejection (Swartley, 1981:51-2). The section begins with internal mental reservations on the part of the scribes and ends with a conspiratorial plot.

In addition to the main theme of growing conflict, we note additional and often related themes: the authority of Jesus (esp. 2:10, 28), the new way of Jesus contrasted with the old way of Jewish piety (esp. 2:21-22), Son of Man Christology (esp. 2:20, 28), the true meaning of "life" and "death" (esp. 3:4; cf. Dewey, 1980:194-5), and the ineffectiveness of "evidence" to change the mind of those who are not open to Jesus (T. Geddert, 1989:42).

OUTLINE

A Paralyzed Man Is Healed and Forgiven, 2:1-12

2:1-4	An Implied Request for Healing
2:5	Jesus Pronounces the Man's Sins Forgiven
2:6-7	The Objection of the Scribes
2:8-9	The Challenge of Jesus
2:10-11	Jesus' Pronouncements of Authority and Power
2:12	The Responses of the Paralytic and the Crowd

The Call of Levi and His Good News Party, 2:13-17
2:13-15   The Call of Levi and His Banquet
2:16-17   The Objection of the Scribes and Jesus' Response

Feasting and Fasting: New Way and Old Way, 2:18-22
2:18   A Question About Fasting
2:19-20   The Presence and the Absence of the Bridegroom
2:21-22   Patching Clothes and Preserving Wineskins

Lord of the Sabbath, 2:23-28
2:23-24   No Threshing on the Sabbath
2:25-26   The Precedent of David
2:27   The Purpose of the Sabbath
2:28   Jesus' Authority over the Sabbath

What Is Lawful, to Save Life or to Kill? 3:1-6
3:1-4   What Should Be Done on the Sabbath?
3:5   Doing Good on the Sabbath
2:6   Doing Evil on the Sabbath

The Structure of 2:1—3:6

EXPLANATORY NOTES

The original four disciples are still following Jesus, still learning about the movement they have joined, still being prepared for the commissioning they will receive to minister in Jesus' name (3:13-15; 6:7). They have begun to learn about Jesus' authoritative teaching and popular multifaceted ministry. In this section they will learn that Jesus' authority will not go unchallenged and that the movement they have joined will soon be under severe attack.

This section does not name Simon and Andrew, and James and John. However, Jesus' *disciples* are with him in Levi's house (2:15), in a grain field (2:23), and in a synagogue (3:1-6; 3:7, notes). Mark clearly wants us to imagine that the original four disciples are with Jesus as the conflict grows and also that this disciple group is both open-ended and growing (2:14-15).

A Paralyzed Man Is Healed and Forgiven 2:1-12
2:1-4 An Implied Request for Healing

Chapter 1 closes with a report of Jesus' immense popularity (1:28, 45). The crowds prevent Jesus from ministering openly in towns, and they throng to him even in the country. Now Jesus returns to Capernaum, where his public ministry has begun (1:21). Last time he ministered in the synagogue; this time he ministers in a house. Last time the crowds marveled at his authority to teach and to drive out an unclean spirit; this time they marvel at his authority to heal and forgive sins. Last time they claimed that Jesus had greater authority than the scribes (1:22); this time they watch him demonstrate it.

A paralyzed man is brought into the presence of Jesus when four friends will not be deterred by a blocked doorway. They *unroof the roof* (TJG; Greek writers delighted in redundancy) and lower the man on his own mat into the presence of Jesus. Their intention is obvious, though no request for healing is reported.

It is possible that this incident happens in Simon's and Andrew's home (1:29; 2:1), and the four men who let the paralytic down through the roof may be the original four disciples. If they are, one difficulty is removed from the text: Simon and Andrew would have the right to tear open their own roof.

2:5 Jesus Pronounces the Man's Sins Forgiven

The persistence of the man's four friends reveals their faith in Jesus' ability and willingness to heal (cf. 1:40). Jesus responds to *their* faith by addressing the paralytic with a word of acceptance, *Son* (an endearing term, not condescending), and by pronouncing, *Your sins are forgiven.* He says this even though the participants in the story (and readers) would expect a pronouncement of healing.

Some have suggested that an earlier healing narrative has been embellished, perhaps by combining two events, thus reflecting early church debates about the relationship between sin and sickness (TBC, below). We cannot and do not need to know. Our task is to interpret the text as Mark has chosen to present it. The issue here is not the relationship between forgiveness and healing in the life of the individual. It is the relationship between these two in the authoritative ministry of Jesus.

2:6-7 The Objection of the Scribes

The narrator informs us that the scribes take exception to Jesus' pronouncement of forgiveness, and that Jesus knows what they are thinking (cf. John 2:25). Their view is that only God can forgive sins. They refer to Jesus with the derogatory *this fellow* (houtos) and accuse him of blasphemy. Jesus responds by setting up a challenge: Since they doubt that he has the authority to make this pronouncement, he will pose a question and set up a demonstration that he does. Here is where we run into some difficulties. On what point do Jesus and the scribes actually disagree? They would agree that people can forgive sins committed against *themselves*. They would agree that forgiveness in the *absolute sense* is God's prerogative. The issue then must be whether the *authority* (2:10) to pronounce God's forgiveness can be delegated to someone else. Yet the scribes would surely agree that God can and does delegate this authority. When people are forgiven, they do not hear a voice from heaven. They are assured of forgiven sins by the provisions of a covenant, its prescribed rituals, and the ministrations of the presiding priest.

Now the point of disagreement is revealed. The issue is whether Jesus can *know* that the person is being forgiven by God and can pronounce the man forgiven *apart from any of the prescribed ceremonies and sacrifices*—apart even from an explicit confession on the part of the sinner. But only God can do that! Therein lies the objection of the scribes: if Jesus claims that right, he is claiming God's prerogative for himself—and that's blasphemy!

2:8-9 The Challenge of Jesus

Jesus proposes a proof of his authority to pronounce sins forgiven. He will demonstrate that he acts on God's behalf apart from the ritual system of temple and sacrifices. His challenge involves a matter of what is easier and what is harder. If he can do the harder thing, who can doubt his ability to do what is easier? It is important to read the text carefully at this point.

The question is not about which is *easier to do*: (1) forgive sins or (2) heal a paralytic. Everyone present shares the assumption that healing is easier to do; in their view, many can heal, but only God can forgive. They do not consider it blasphemy for someone to make a healing pronouncement, because healing is not usurping a divine prerogative. To pronounce a man forgiven is another matter.

The question is about which is *easier to say:* (1) *Your sins are forgiven* or (2) *Stand up and . . . walk!* (2:9). We might be tempted to reply that both are easy to say; just say them! But how about saying them effectively? How about speaking and making them come true? A pronouncement of forgiveness produces no objective proof of its effectiveness. A pronouncement of healing does. If the man is unable to move, the pronouncement is a fraud. The issue is provability, making good on a claim. This is about speaking an authoritative word *that actually changes things!* If Jesus can now heal the man, he demonstrates that his words have effect, and their charge that he claims an authority he doesn't have will fall to the ground.

2:10-11 Jesus' Pronouncements of Authority and Power

Jesus makes two pronouncements. He first tells his audience what conclusion they are to draw from the miracle that is about to happen. It will demonstrate that the Son of Man (= Jesus himself [Son of Man]) does in fact have the authority to pronounce sins forgiven. Then he tells the paralyzed man, *Stand up, take your mat and go to your home.* The proof that Jesus does in fact have the authority to forgive is found in the effectiveness of his command to the paralyzed man.

2:12 The Responses of the Paralytic and the Crowd

When God speaks, it happens; so also with Jesus. The effectiveness of the healing word proves the effectiveness of the forgiving word.

One could still object that this is not a knockdown argument. If the ability to heal proves the authority to forgive, then either every healer is authorized to forgive, or no one but Jesus ever accomplished a healing. Both are patently false. Is something more subtle being demonstrated here? Perhaps Jesus' point is that God may well use other healers to bring about a healing. But would God use a blasphemer? If other healers started claiming the right to forgive sins, would God still heal through their pronouncements? Jesus' healing pronouncements continue to be effective. God acts through them, for Jesus is no blasphemer; Jesus is God's agent *even in the matter of forgiving sins.*

Jesus is here claiming authority directly from God. The scribes lose the debate without even speaking their objections. The crowds are amazed and glorify God, claiming never to have seen anything like this before. In the light of 1:32-34, 37, they can hardly mean they have never seen such a spectacular healing. They have never before seen someone claim the right to forgive sins and demonstrate the claim with a proof that even the scribes cannot refute. Just as in 1:22, the crowds are amazed at Jesus' authority, and again at the expense of the scribes. The areas of conflict between Jesus and the scribes are beginning to emerge; the conflict is beginning to escalate.

The Call of Levi and His Good News Party 2:13-17

2:13-15 The Call of Levi and His Banquet

The scene shifts from a house in Capernaum to the lakeshore. A crowd gathers but quickly fades into the background. Jesus has pronounced a man forgiven. Now his attention zooms in on another "sinner," a man by the name of Levi. As a tax collector, he is viewed in his society as one who has sold out to the occupying power. He is judged (or misjudged) as dishonest. His occupation puts him in regular contact with Gentiles, making him permanently "unclean." It is customary to say *tax collectors* and *sinners* in the same breath (2:15-16). Levi is high on most people's list of those to be avoided. He is high on Jesus' list of prime prospects for God's kingdom.

Jesus summons Levi to follow him. Levi leaves his *tax booth* as quickly as the first disciples have left their nets. Using the vocabulary of discipleship, Mark reports Levi's response to Jesus: he *followed him* (2:14). Levi celebrates his new life by hosting a festive meal. It is a special banquet, as shown by the fact that the guests recline (see NRSV note). It is almost certain that Levi is the host, though the Greek permits the interpretation that Jesus is.

Jesus and his disciples are there along with many *tax collectors and sinners*. This phrase (once in reverse order) appears three times in this verse and the next. If the reference to *sinners* had come only from the objecting scribes, it might refer to ordinary (even pious) Jews who are somewhat less scrupulous about legal correctness and ceremonial cleanness than the Pharisaic scribes. But Mark as narrator also refers to Levi's guests as *sinners;* this suggests that the word here refers to people known as notorious sinners, those who would agree that the designation suits them. Along with tax collectors, these people are considered religious outsiders by the scribes and Pharisees.

Levi is creating an opportunity for his friends and associates to meet Jesus. He is demonstrating that discipleship leads to mission. The table fellowship of Jesus with this group of people indicates that there is a bond of mutual acceptance and unity.

2:16-17 The Objection of the Scribes and Jesus' Response

The scribes *of* (or *and*; manuscripts vary) the Pharisees object. The reader is alerted to the issues at stake: scrupulous avoidance of contaminating contacts (Pharisaism) and meticulous concern for legal correctness, regardless of its impact on people (the domain of the scribes). Jesus does not share either of these preoccupations. He does not consider his present contacts defiling or inappropriate.

The objections of Jesus' critics are presented to Jesus' disciples; the response comes from Jesus himself. In justifying his actions, Jesus makes it clear that the objectors do not share his priorities. With a short proverb and a pronouncement, he silences them.

Those who are well have no need of a physician, but those who are sick (2:17). The tax collectors and sinners are the sick; Jesus is the physician. He has what they need: good news and the offer of a new life. Since what he offers matches their need, his association with them is justified. Jesus extends invitations to them and accepts invitations from them. It is all for the purpose of sharing the good news of the kingdom and drawing in those who will accept it.

I have come to call not the righteous but sinners (2:17). The text does not say "call sinners *to repentance*" (as in Luke 5:32), though Jesus also does that (Mark 1:15). Here Jesus calls *sinners* to celebrate new beginnings (just as Levi is doing). The focus is not on the sinners' need to change but on Jesus' offer of forgiveness. That is why this text appropriately follows the preceding one about Jesus' authority to forgive (2:10), and appropriately precedes the next one about the new way of Jesus in contrast to the old way of scribal religion (2:18-22).

Jesus' proverb and pronouncement should have undercut his critics' objections. After all, he agrees with them that these people are sinners, sick and in need of healing. Has he not by implication pronounced the scribes healthy, righteous, in no need of change? They should have responded with "Amen!" Instead, the conflict grows. They rightly suspect sarcasm in Jesus' words.

The scribes can clearly see that Jesus' way of dealing with sinners is the polar opposite of theirs. They call for repentance, they prescribe ceremonies, but they have no power to grant new life. On the other hand, Jesus offers forgiveness without ceremonies (2:5, 10); he offers fellowship with people who have neither publicly acknowledged their sinfulness nor visibly cleaned up their lives; he calls people to follow him, and in so doing their lives are transformed.

Jesus is redefining righteousness. No longer is it measured by strict moral and ceremonial criteria. It has more to do with right relationships: relationships with Jesus, with others accepting Jesus' invitation, and with God, whose forgiveness and whose reign they experience in the presence of Jesus. Everyone needs the physician (including Jesus' critics), but he can help only those who recognize and admit their need.

Feasting and Fasting: New Way and Old Way 2:18-22

Conflict is the theme that holds this entire section together, but other themes link individual units as well. Mark 2:1-12 and 2:13-17 are linked by the theme of forgiveness and new life. Jesus claims the authority to extend forgiveness (2:5, 10), then demonstrates his willingness to do so by accepting sinners (2:18-22). Both his claim and his behavior offend representatives of the religious establishment.

Mark 2:13-17 and 2:18-22 are also woven together by Mark. At Levi's feast, Jesus demonstrates the incompatibility between his own kingdom way and the old strict piety of the scribes and Pharisees. In 2:18-22 the incompatibility of *old* and *new* comes up for discussion. Jesus' opponents shift the topic from feasting to fasting. Just as quickly, Jesus shifts it back again.

2:18 A Question About Fasting

The main point of the question posed here by *some people* (NIV) is clear enough. Why do the followers of Jesus not practice one of the expected spiritual disciplines? Why do they not fast as other religious people do? Beyond that, little is clear. Who is objecting? Is it really true that Jesus' disciples do not fast (cf. Matt. 6:16-18)? Who are the Pharisees' disciples, and what are their fasting practices (cf. Luke 18:12)? Do John's disciples fast? If so, does it represent repentance (1:4), waiting for God's kingdom, or mourning John's death (1:14; 6:16, 29)? Why are John's disciples linked more closely to the Pharisees than to Jesus? Mark has chosen not to clarify these issues. His focus is on Jesus' (unexplained) parables.

2:19-20 The Presence and the Absence of the Bridegroom

Jesus' parable is a simple lesson drawn from a wedding. Weddings are joyous occasions, times for feasting, not fasting. Similarly, Jesus' disciples live in a situation (now that God's reign has arrived) where joyous feasting is more appropriate than somber fasting. It is the time to celebrate!

Fasting was appropriate in the time of waiting (as during John's ministry). It no doubt still seems appropriate to the Pharisees, for they do not recognize the arrival of the kingdom. Those who know that Jesus announces the arrival of God's reign must celebrate. Yet they will fast in the future. They feast *as long as they have the bridegroom with them*, and will fast *when the bridegroom is taken away from them*. Thus an ominous note is sounded, the first clear allusion to Jesus' fate at the hands of those who oppose him. Jesus' disciples have not rejected fasting; but they know when it is appropriate and when it is not.

Jesus' response is not about fasting as a spiritual discipline or as a legal requirement. It is about discerning the times. When feasting is appropriate, feast! When fasting is appropriate, fast! Those who have accepted Jesus' proclamation of good news can no longer practice religion as usual. Fasting will be resumed, not because a day of fasting has been prescribed on someone's religious calendar, but because the situation has changed. Meanwhile, they feast; they have the bridegroom with them.

Jesus has sounded an ominous note: the bridegroom will be removed. He will now continue to clarify how the scribal way of religious rules and ceremonies is not compatible with his own way of the kingdom. In doing so, he will hasten the day when the plot to remove the bridegroom takes effect. It is *on that day* that Jesus' followers will fast (cf. 13:32, notes on *that day; Amos* 8:9-10 in TBC for 15:16-47).

2:21-22 Patching Clothes and Preserving Wineskins

To a first-century Jew, it is obvious that old clothing is not repaired with new patches, and equally obvious that new wine is not poured into old wineskins. These are less obvious to modern readers, whose everyday experiences do not include patching clothes or making wine, at least not as these were done in the first century.

New cloth will shrink, but an old cloak will not. Thus new patches, after being sewn in place and washed, will no longer fit. The tear will be made worse as the patch (now smaller) causes the already worn clothing to tear at the place where it has been stitched in place. Likewise, a leather bottle stretches enough to withstand the pressure as grape juice turns into wine. Repeated use of the same bottle, however, stretches it beyond its limits. A burst wineskin represents a loss of both the bottle and its contents.

This much would have been understood by Jesus' hearers. But what do these parables (or metaphors) mean? Mark's first readers have struggled along with us. Is it significant that the theme of a wedding (2:19-20) is immediately followed by metaphors drawn from two of the most significant features of a Jewish wedding, appropriate festive clothing and a good supply of wine? (Muddiman: 279). Probably not. Is Jesus' real concern to preserve the old? After all, Jesus seems less concerned for the new patch than for the old garment (in contrast to Luke 5:36). Has Jesus joined the scribes in their concern to preserve the old against the threat of the new? Certainly not.

When we interpret parables, we must guard against overshrinking (claiming that parables always have only one point) and also against overstretching (claiming that some point of application must be squeezed out of every detail). Instead, parables can allude to different levels of meaning. Jesus likely wants to focus on the issue of incompatibility. Some things just don't fit together, such as new patches on old clothes, new wine in old wineskins, fasting when the bridegroom is still present, feasting when he is removed, John's ministry of preparation and Jesus' demonstration that the time of waiting is over, the scrupulous piety of the Pharisaic scribes and the celebration of those who know that Jesus has welcomed them into his kingdom.

Lord of the Sabbath 2:23-28

Jesus and those who are becoming his enemies have fundamental differences: forgiveness, association with sinners, and fasting; now Mark adds another: Sabbath observance.

2:23-24 No Threshing on the Sabbath

The disciples are journeying with Jesus through a grainfield on the Sabbath. Along the way they pick a few heads of grain, roll out the kernels in their hands, and eat them. The Pharisees object. The issue is not theft or traveling on the Sabbath. They are likely still within the limit of "a Sabbath day's journey" (Acts 1:12, about 1,000 meters/ yards; Num. 35:5), since the Pharisees are silent on that issue and seem to be traveling with them. On the Sabbath, Jesus' disciples are reaping, plucking heads of grain and presumably threshing them. Both aspects of harvesting are on the list of types of work forbidden on the Sabbath (cf. Mishnah Shab. 7:2).

The Pharisees confront Jesus about his disciples' behavior. They (correctly) assume that it is Jesus' business to instruct his disciples on appropriate Sabbath behavior. Jesus defends the disciples' right to do what they are doing. He does not, however, get caught up in picky disputes about exactly what is work and what is not. Instead, he steps back from the immediate objection and makes a series of provocative points about legalism and freedom, his own royal sovereignty, the divine purpose for the Sabbath, and his own authority to regulate appropriate Sabbath activity.

2:25-26 The Precedent of David

Have you never read . . . ? Jesus is being sarcastic; he knows that the Pharisees' problem is not too little Bible reading. The great dividing wall between him and them is how they *use* Scripture. For them, it is a catalog of laws; for Jesus, it is a pointer to God's larger purposes. They see only rules; he sees how those rules affect people and when they must be subordinated to human need.

It is not obvious how the David precedent relates to the issue at hand. The disciples who are eating grain are probably not *hungry and in need of food,* as David was (1 Sam. 21:1-6). Possibly David and his men were eating the sacred bread on the Sabbath (cf. Lev. 24:8), but Mark's text does not make reference to this. Surely Mark does not want to portray Jesus as eliminating all distinctions between sacred and profane things (bread in the illustration he uses, or days of the week in its application). He is, after all, not abolishing the Sabbath.

The main point of the David precedent is suggested by the repeated term *David and his companions* (literally, *those with him;* cf. 3:14). This was David, already anointed by the prophet and heir to the throne; it was not just any hungry passerby who requested bread from the priest. He and his men were on a sacred mission (cf. 1 Sam. 21:5). The priest discerned the times (cf. 1 Chron. 12:32) and made the legal exception for David. The beneficiaries included the men in his company, those on the sacred mission with him. So it is with Jesus, the anointed king and heir to David's throne. He, too, is on a sacred mission. If legal exceptions can be made for Jesus, then also for *those with him* (*met' autou* is used for David's men in 2:25 and for Jesus' disciples in 3:13).

Jesus claims for himself and his followers a freedom with respect to the scribal traditions about Sabbath behavior. But the OT precedent he cites goes far beyond that. David usurped priestly prerogatives. He acted against covenant regulations, not merely against human traditions. By defending David's and the priest's actions, Jesus claims a sovereignty with respect to OT laws and religious institutions. Jesus' own hermeneutic recognizes a distinction between weightier matters of the law on one hand, and on the other hand, rules that ordinarily apply but might be set aside for life-giving purposes.

2:27 The Purpose of the Sabbath

The David precedent is a provocative statement of sovereign freedom with respect to details of the law. It is an argument that Jesus' own sovereign freedom yields benefits also for his followers. But does it clarify what is and what is not lawful on the Sabbath? Not very specifically. That question is addressed more directly in Jesus' pronouncement concerning the Sabbath's purpose. God instituted it for human benefit. Regulations that subvert that original purpose are to be ignored.

Jesus is not arguing for the abolition of the Sabbath, nor is he erasing all guidelines for its observance. Yet he is preserving its function as a divine gift, given to enhance human life, not complicate it. There will be times when human need takes precedence over the usual guidelines. He himself will demonstrate that in the next episode.

2:28 Jesus' Authority over the Sabbath

So the Son of Man is lord even of the sabbath, says Jesus (referring to himself) [Son of Man]. The word so links verse 28 with verse 27. God had specific purposes for creating the Sabbath (v. 27). Therefore, God's representative on earth has the authority to regulate Sabbath behavior in line with those purposes (v. 28).

In claiming to be lord of the Sabbath, Jesus picks up a word that has appeared in 1:3. There it refers to the LORD God (within the quotation itself) and to Jesus as Lord (in Mark's context). Mark frequently uses the word Lord, making a double reference to Jesus and to God (5:19; 11:3; 12:36-37). Jesus here links his authority over Sabbath observance to his identity as Lord.

Son of Man is used here to make a claim that is parallel to 2:10. This title itself alludes to authority delegated by God. Jesus has been given authority and a kingdom (cf. Dan. 7:13-14). He is therefore authorized to interpret God's will on specific issues, even the Sabbath. That may seem like one of the lesser issues to us, but it was extremely important to a first-century Jew. In the ancient world, Sabbath keeping set the Jews apart from others.

Claiming authoritative rights with respect to forgiveness of sin (2:10) and Sabbath regulations (2:28) is tantamount to denying any authority to the whole religious system controlled by priestly ceremonies and scribal regulations. The issue of Jesus' authority continues to be a major issue of controversy throughout Mark's Gospel and erupts in full force when Jesus confronts the religious leaders in Jerusalem.

What Is Lawful, to Save Life or to Kill? 3:1-6

3:1-4 What Should Be Done on the Sabbath?

Conflict has been building between Jesus and the Pharisaic scribes (2:16). They have just locked horns over Sabbath observance. Now Jesus enters the synagogue, their stronghold. Can he do anything that will provoke them more than to initiate the healing of a man, in the synagogue, on the Sabbath, in front of his enemies? Jesus' enemies are watching closely, presumably hoping he will initiate the healing. They are looking for an occasion to accuse him, and he does not disappoint them.

Jesus knows they are trying to trap him. He is preparing a trap himself. By having the man stand up in front of everyone, Jesus turns this into a showdown. At precisely the point where we expect him to speak a word of healing to the man, he turns and asks a question of his opponents. It is a question they cannot answer: "Does the Sabbath authorize people to do good or evil, to save life or to kill?"

What can they say? Jesus' question involves a set of alternatives they do not accept. Their view is that it is right to keep the Sabbath laws, regardless of whether good or harm might result from it. They cannot respond "to do evil," for that is not the Sabbath's purpose. But if they respond "to do good," they admit that Sabbath rules can be set aside, not only in life-threatening situations (as they believed), but also in order to do good deeds. Jesus believes that (2:27); they do not. They are silent.

3:5 Doing Good on the Sabbath

The reference to Jesus' *anger* may seem surprising. Yet Mark often refers to Jesus' emotional responses, including anguish and anger. He is angry and *grieved* at their stubborn hearts. The Greek word *sullupeomai* is used only here in the NT and expresses somewhat more passion than *grieved* (cf. *deeply distressed*, NIV).

Ignoring his opponents, Jesus turns to the man who is waiting for healing. With Jesus' word, the man is instantaneously restored. To do good and to save life, that is Jesus' mission. Perhaps by healing with a word rather than a touch, Jesus avoids the charge of violating the Sabbath.

3:6 Doing Evil on the Sabbath

In a shocking statement for a first-time reader, Mark reports that the Pharisees and the Herodians initiate a death plot against Jesus. Two normally incompatible parties, one religious and one political, one scrupulously biblical, the other notoriously compromising, are drawn together in their rejection of Jesus. Later they again appear united when their plot begins to go into action (12:12-13).

The enemies of Jesus never agree that doing evil and killing are appropriate Sabbath activities. Yet without waiting for the Sabbath service to end, they walk out and plot to put him away. The irony is inescapable. The conflict has reached a climax. The death of Jesus is being planned, and we are only in chapter 3! Jesus' opponents depart to work out a death plot. Jesus departs to carry on his life-giving ministry of healing, deliverance, and building a kingdom community.

The Structure of 2:1—3:6

In the preview to this conflict section, it was suggested that 2:1—3:6 is not only structured cumulatively (rising conflict, greater clarification of the issues, and so on) but also as a chiasm. Readers not familiar with chiastic structures may consult the essay *[Chiasm and Intercalation]*. Here is a portrayal of the concentric (chiastic) structuring of this section of Mark (adapted from Harrington: 25):

> A • 2:1-9, cure by Jesus, silence of adversaries, *questioning in hearts.*
> B • 2:10-12, declaration on the *Son of Man.*
> C • 2:13-17, action of Jesus, opponents' reaction to disciples.
> D • 2:18-22, sayings of Jesus on *bridegroom* and *newness.*
> C' • 2:23-26, action of disciples, opponents' reaction to Jesus.
> B' • 2:27-28, declaration on the *Son of Man.*
> A' • 3:1-6, cure by Jesus, adversaries' silence, *hardness of heart.*

Dewey's study of this section points out many interesting and important parallels in the matching elements of Mark 2:1—3:6. Sections A and A' are about healing; B and B' are about eating; and so on. The center of the section focuses on fasting and the removal of the bridegroom (Mark's first hint of the coming passion).

Stock develops the significance of these and other parallelisms in the text unit. The primary significance is found at the center. This section is not simply about rising conflict; it is about elements that lead to the passion of Jesus. Jesus comes with good news that God is doing something *new* (new wine, new wineskins, and so on). It is precisely the newness of Jesus' message that leads to the conflict. Paradoxically, the death resulting from the conflict serves to *create* the newness that Jesus proclaims and his critics reject. When we read the whole conflict section with such awareness, these points shed new light on each incident and on the impact of the whole unit.

THE TEXT IN BIBLICAL CONTEXT
Sin and Sickness

A brief note on the relationship between sin and sickness is needed, since Jesus' act of forgiveness and his claim to have the authority to do so are tied so closely to the story of the healing of the paralytic (2:1-12). Was the man's paralysis caused by sin? Is sickness generally related to sin? Many have believed so.

The Bible supports the idea that all human sickness, suffering, and death are in some sense related to the reality of human sinfulness; we suffer in a fallen world because we are fallen people. At times in Scripture, specific incidents of sickness or calamity are directly related to specific sins: sometimes the suffering is viewed as divine judgment (e.g., 1 Cor. 11:30); sometimes people suffer the natural consequences of wrong choices (e.g., Proverbs).

The Scriptures clearly deny that *every* occasion of suffering is directly related to some *specific* sin (the book of Job; John 9:1-3; Luke 13:1-4). That, of course, does not mean a connection is never to be sought. It seems appropriate, therefore, whenever we seek and pray for physical health and well-being, at least to *consider* the possibility that guilt and sin *may* also need to be addressed (e.g., Luke 13:5, connected to 13:1-4; James 5:13-15).

The Talmud contains the following claim: "No one gets up from his sick bed until all his sins are forgiven" (Hooker, 1991:85). This view, however, is not the view of the NT. Mark 2:1-10 does not confirm such a connection, and issues of sin and forgiveness are not usually raised when Jesus performs a healing miracle.

THE TEXT IN THE LIFE OF THE CHURCH

The Christian and the Sabbath

In many denominations, minority groups give respect to the seventh day instead of Sunday. Eleven million Seventh-Day Adventists observe Saturday, not Sunday, as God's chosen Sabbath. However, most Christians throughout the past two millennia have honored the first day of the week (Sunday) as the Christian "Sabbath." When and why did the shift take place?

There is no hint in the Gospels that the church's change from Saturday (the Jewish Sabbath) to Sunday (the so-called Christian Sabbath) is based on anything Jesus practiced or taught. A few NT texts are thought to provide evidence that the shift from Saturday to Sunday happened within a few decades after the resurrection. However, a close look at those texts does not yield strong support for that view.

First Corinthians 16:2 does not clearly indicate that the church had weekly meetings on Sunday, still less that they observed that day as a Sabbath. Revelation 1:10 is more naturally read as a reference to "the Day of the Lord" than as a reference to Sunday. Acts 20:7 speaks of a special farewell gathering for Paul, who was scheduled to leave the next day, rather than a regular Sunday church service. The

NT evidence for an early shift from Sabbath to Sunday is not strong. Most likely the change came gradually during the second and third centuries, as the Christian movement found ways of distinguishing itself from the Jewish faith. An official church decision defining Sunday as the "Christian Sabbath" took place no earlier than the fourth century (Bacchiocchi; for alternative views, see Carson; Faw on Acts 20:7; Yeatts on Rev. 1:10).

Does the fact that there is not a strong justification for Sunday-keeping in the NT mean that Christians have been wrong all along? Not necessarily. The Gospels clearly reveal that Jesus did not endorse a legalistic focus on the timing of Sabbath-keeping. Jesus' primary concern was the meaning of setting aside special days for human benefit (esp. Mark 2:28), and investing those special days in ways that honor God.

Jesus' example and teaching had a profound effect on the church's later thinking about Sabbath-keeping. Jesus' disruption of the tradition did not involve shifting from one day to another; it involved a refocusing of the purpose and meaning of the Sabbath. God had originally instituted it primarily for human benefit (2:28), to give time for rest, to keep work from being an all-consuming preoccupation, to facilitate worship gatherings, to provide rest for work animals, and to commemorate both God's acts of creation (Gen. 2:2-3; Exod. 20:11) and God's acts of redemption (Deut. 5:15).

Many Christians (especially biblical scholars) are re-thinking the NT basis for Christians keeping Sunday. They note that there is no clear biblical basis for shifting from Saturday to Sunday, and also that the NT challenges the idea of its observance being regulated according to OT commands. Various NT texts imply that there is no mandatory Christian Sabbath. All days belong to God (Col. 2:16-17; and so on). If we observe special days, we do so to honor God, who rested after great acts of creation and redemption. Indeed, we are called to rest in the redemption God provides (Heb. 4:9).

Observing one special day each week as the designated day for worship and rest is a voluntary act. It symbolizes primarily the accomplished work of salvation in Jesus Christ; it facilitates the gathering of the Christian community. Sunday, the day of the resurrection, *need* not be chosen for this, but it is an appropriate choice.

As a child, I remember hearing my father preach a sermon on "Sunday-Keeping," using as his text Mark 3:1-6. His emphasis was that Sunday was not intended as a day to do nothing, but as a day to do good. Attending church, of course, fell into this category, but he suggested that acts of kindness would also fit well in a day that honors God and yet was "made for humans." Sunday afternoons in our little village usually involved a family drive after the children had played quietly so that parents could have their Sunday nap.

To our parents' chagrin, my brothers and I secretly practiced what Dad had preached by agreeing that weeding my mom's garden during their nap would be an act of kindness and therefore appropriate on Sunday. We never reflected on how our secret act of kindness would be interpreted by our neighbors already on their afternoon drive! They too had heard my father's sermon, and would never have suspected that the Geddert boys were weeding the garden voluntarily!

Sunday is deeply entrenched in our culture, and especially in our Christian culture, as the day of the week set aside to fulfill the Sabbath's true purpose. Hence, we do well to honor that day in the ways Jesus modeled and taught. Those who cannot do so because of inflexible work schedules are encouraged to choose another day, or at least to find a regular rhythm of work and rest that facilitates the Sabbath's purposes.

Where Christians are persuaded that the seventh day (Saturday) remains the God-ordained day of Sabbath rest, we admire them for their serious commitment to biblical faithfulness. Yet we encourage them to avoid the legalistic attitude to Sabbath-keeping that Jesus critiqued.

In some countries there is a growing tendency in the culture to view *Monday* as the first day of the week (as in train schedules, calendars). This shift has sometimes been welcomed by Christians, since then they can honor *Sunday* (the resurrection day) as they have always done, yet simultaneously do so on the *seventh* day of the week, as in biblical times.

Certainly Jesus' example frees Christians from a legalistic approach to the whole question. It is important to find regular opportunities for worship and fellowship (even if not always on Sunday); for physical, mental, and spiritual renewal; and for deeds of kindness. In so doing, we will honor God with our special days and also honor God more faithfully on the other days (cf. Swartley, 1983, with helpful analysis of the texts and issues).

Mark 3:7-35

From a Religious System to a Family of Disciples

PREVIEW

The previous section portrayed the rising conflict between Jesus and those who rejected his claims to authority, his contact with "unacceptable people," and his approach to such matters as religious rituals and Sabbath observance. What began as internal questioning (2:6) grew until it became a conspiracy to kill Jesus (3:6).

Jesus' response is to depart/withdraw (3:7a). He withdraws, first, from the synagogue. What has been a favorite location for ministry (1:21, 39), now becomes enemy territory (see below). Jesus now ministers to the gathering crowds at the lakeshore. In the material from chapters 3—8, we shall often find Jesus ministering to people on or near the sea. He has done this before (2:13), but now the sea becomes his favorite place of ministry until he begins the journey to Jerusalem (chaps. 8—10).

Second, Jesus withdraws from the scribes and Pharisees. This is an even more significant shift than the one from synagogues to the seashore. Jesus changes his approach to God's people and their official representatives and leaders. The scribes and Pharisees have rejected Jesus. Jesus will now officially designate new leaders for God's renewed people (*the Twelve*). Along with a shift in people comes a shift in focus. Jesus will no longer battle a religious system that centers on purity laws, ceremonies, and legal prescriptions (2:1—3:6). He will redefine God's faithful people as those who gather around himself. A religious system gives way to a spiritual family (3:31-35).

OUTLINE

Jesus Withdraws to Minister at the Lakeshore, 3:7-12

Jesus Commissions the Disciples, 3:13-19
3:13-16a   The Commissioning
3:16b-19   The Twelve

A House Divided, 3:20-30
3:20-21   Jesus' Family Is Concerned
3:22-30   Jesus' Enemies Misinterpret His Authority

Jesus Redefines Family, 3:31-35

EXPLANATORY NOTES

Jesus Withdraws to Minister at the Lakeshore 3:7-12

What was once a platform for ministry has become a place of rejection. In Mark, Jesus enters a synagogue only once more, in his hometown (6:2). He teaches there and heals a few people; it is a ministry without much success. After that time, Mark mentions synagogues only as places where scribes grasp for personal prestige (12:39) and where Jesus' followers will face rejection (13:9). From now on, Jesus' "gathering place" (meaning of *synagogue*) will be a house, a seashore, a boat—wherever people gather around him to learn God's will (3:35). That must have spoken volumes to Mark's community, perhaps struggling with their own exclusion from former synagogues and temples.

Jesus' withdrawal (3:7a) is also from his enemies. They keep coming, but only to discredit him (3:22-30), spy on him (7:1-2), and tempt him (8:12-13). No longer will Jesus patiently explain his actions to them, demonstrating his authority and interpreting Scripture. Now he will expose their misdeeds (3:29-30) and their hypocrisy (7:6-7), warn the crowds and the disciples against them (7:14-19; 8:15), and refuse to oblige them when they pretend to want more evidence (8:12). Jesus turns to those who are willing to hear, and especially to his chosen disciples.

Jesus' departure to the sea does not mean he will be alone. The crowds that gather are larger than ever. In this summary section,

Mark lists Galilee, Jesus' ministry center, and virtually all the territories around it (3:8). The only significant omissions are Samaria and the Decapolis. Mark reports no significant contact between Jesus and Samaria or Samaritans. Later Mark features ministries in the Decapolis (5:1-20; 7:31; and likely others). Though Jesus later ministers to Gentiles (certainly in 7:24-30; probably in 5:1-20; 7:31-37; 8:1-10), we assume that the crowds of 3:7-35 are mostly Jewish.

The (dis)connection between 3:6 and 3:7-8 is astonishing. A major party of spiritual leaders in Israel takes a firm stand against Jesus (3:6). Simultaneously, the people flock to Jesus from everywhere (3:7-8). The religious leaders must have little influence on the general population. No wonder they object to this teacher so strongly. His authority is eroding the little authority they still have in religious matters (on Galilean religious and social conditions, see Freyne).

Mark 3:9-10 refers to the previous healing ministry of Jesus. His effectiveness as a healer is part of the reason the crowd has gathered. They want more. Jesus recruits one of the disciples' boats to keep the thronging crowds from overwhelming him. Is Jesus trying to avoid a healing ministry here in favor of teaching (cf. 4:1-2)? Is he just organizing the healing ministry so as not to be crushed by those wanting to touch him, so he is not overwhelmed by it and everyone can have a turn? We are not told.

It seems that whenever Jesus teaches and/or heals, the demons react. We are not explicitly told that Jesus drives out demons this time, only that he silences them. They keep shouting out his identity: *You are the Son of God!* (3:11). They know who Jesus really is; but Jesus wants his identity to be discerned by faithful disciples, not publicized by demons [Messianic Secret].

Jesus Commissions the Disciples 3:13-19

3:13-16a The Commissioning

The original four disciples and others who have joined along the way (2:14-15) have been following and learning. Their original decision to leave everything and follow must have seemed like a good decision as they observed his authoritative teaching, his power over demons, his compassion, his ability to heal, his prayer life, and his passion to reach people with the good news. But does it still seem like such a good idea, now that the Jesus movement has enemies? When Jesus gives hints of coming rejection (2:20), and as opposition to Jesus grows (3:1-6), the disciples must surely be struggling with second thoughts.

Whatever doubts the disciples may have, Jesus invests a lot in them. The authorized leaders of Israel have proved unfaithful by rejecting Jesus' authority. Jesus now grants his own authority to those who have accepted his claim on them. They will be appointed as the designated leaders of renewed Israel.

Jesus does not pronounce a commission on an unsuspecting group. They are invited once more, and they respond anew (3:13). If their original yes was an uninformed, spontaneous response to a summons, their present yes is a more informed, deliberate acceptance of a call to discipleship and mission.

Mountains are regular places for spiritual renewal, meetings with God, and divine revelations. All these associations may be present in this mountaintop gathering of Jesus and those he has called out of the crowd. Exactly twelve are appointed: this suggests a specific OT text as the background for this event. Exodus 19:5-6 relates that on Mt. Sinai God established a covenant, taking twelve tribes and creating "a holy nation." Now Jesus chooses a mountain location to re-create the holy nation. These twelve men represent all Israel, the renewed Israel of the last days, a holy nation set apart to become a light to all the nations. They symbolize that nation, and they will proclaim God's good news to the rest of their nation and to the other nations (13:10).

They are given a double designation, *apostles* (3:14) and *the Twelve* (3:16a). *Apostles* are "sent ones" (*hoi apostoloi*). The title appears in Mark again only when Jesus is receiving a mission report from those he has literally sent on a mission (6:7, 30). *The Twelve* becomes a regular title for this group, distinguishing it from many others who are also called followers or disciples (6:7; 9:35; 10:32; 11:11; 14:10, 17, 20, 43). Some manuscripts lack either *whom he also named apostles* (3:14) or *so he appointed the twelve* (3:16) or both; yet the balance of probabilities is that both belong to the original text *[Textual Criticism of Mark]*.

Jesus appoints his twelve apostles to two specific responsibilities: (1) *to be with him*; and (2) *to be sent out*. They will be disciples/learners so that they can be apostles/missionaries. The Twelve will be apprenticed in Jesus' presence so that they can be his representatives in his absence. The focus will be on nearness of relationship (*with him*) and on carrying out a task (*sent out*).

Some interpreters have made the following equations:

- With him = the time before the passion.
- Sent out = the time after the resurrection.

For Mark, however, this is not accurate. Though the disciples are often literally with Jesus before his passion, they refuse to stay with him to the end (14:50); Peter even denies that he was with Jesus (14:67). Furthermore, Jesus sends them out already before his passion (6:7). The double commission involves both presence with Jesus and ministry on his behalf. The need for the first continues even after the second is inaugurated (T. Geddert, 1989:102, 165).

The second half of the double commission is itself twofold. The apostles will be sent out for two purposes: (1) to proclaim the message, and (2) to have authority to cast out demons. Jesus' priority is on proclamation (1:14-15), often referred to in Mark as teaching with authority (1:21-22). He expels demons when they react to his proclamation and his teaching (1:27-28, notes). When kingdom proclamation results in spiritual conflict, commissioned proclaimers are ill prepared if they have no resources to deal with it. The twofold sending here does not suggest that proclamation and driving out demons are equally important, but rather that proclamation will not go unchallenged. When Jesus sends out his messengers, they are equipped with authority to deal with the conflicts that kingdom ministry will generate.

3:16b-19 The Twelve

At this point the Twelve are listed. On every NT list of Jesus' twelve disciples, *Simon, James, John, and Andrew* are the first four, though the order of these four sometimes varies. In Mark, these are Jesus' closest four (1:16-20; 13:3), and the first three the closest three (5:37; 9:2; 14:33). Simon is renamed *Peter*, a name that Greek readers understand as *Rock*. From now on, the narrator will call him *Peter*. Jesus addresses Peter directly only twice, once as Satan (8:33), and once as Simon (14:37). James and John are also renamed, as *Sons of Thunder* (3:17). No reason is given, but the name appears first in Aramaic and is then translated into Greek. Luke 9:54 might indicate a historical reason for the name.

Then comes Andrew, followed by seven disciples listed in a fairly standard order, though no two lists in the NT are identical (Matt. 10:2-4; Luke 6:14-16; Acts 1:13). Apart from *James son of Alphaeus* (whose father is named, to distinguish him from *James son of Zebedee*), the only special reference is to *Simon the Cananaean*. This term *Cananaean* is basically a transliteration of the Greek word, and its translation is *Zealot* (3:18, NIV). Perhaps the name is supplied only to distinguish him from the other Simon; perhaps it identifies this Simon as a (former?) sympathizer with the militant liberationist group that later formed the Zealot party, a group that was central to the

Jewish resistance in the war against Rome (A.D. 65-70).

As always, *Judas Iscariot* is listed last (3:19). The attached remark *who betrayed him* fails to shock us, because we know the story so well. The first-time reader is astounded. It is one thing for religious opponents to plot Jesus' death. But reference to a traitor from within the ranks of Jesus' followers comes as a surprise. The reader has already learned that there is a plot against Jesus (3:6). Now the reader asks, Will it actually succeed? Though there have been allusions to Jesus' martyrdom (notes on 1:11, 14; 2:20; and so on), it is not until 8:31 that the reader hears any explicit statements from Jesus or the narrator on Jesus' anticipated death at the hands of his enemies.

A House Divided 3:20-30

The rest of the material in chapter 3 centers around two incidents: the charge of Jesus' family that he is out of his mind, and the charge of the Jerusalem scribes that he operates in Satanic power. It is arranged chiastically *[Chiasm and Intercalation]*. The pattern of this material can be diagrammed like this:

> A • Jesus and His Family (3:20-21)
> B • Jesus and Beelzebul (3:22-30)
> A' • Jesus and His Family (3:31-35)

The material within unit B can be further subdivided. The scribes bring two charges against Jesus; he answers them in reverse order. Between the charges and the answers, Jesus exposes the absurdity of the *kingdom* of Satan *divided against itself* (the section's center, 3:23-26). Putting it together, the larger section is in chiastic order as follows (cf. Harrington: 43):

> A • Jesus and His Family (3:20-21)
> B • Scribes' Charge 1: Jesus Is Possessed (3:22a)
> C • Charge 2: Jesus Casts Out Demons in Satan's Power (3:22b)
> D • Absurdity: The Divided Kingdom of Satan (3:23-26)
> C' • Response to Charge 2: Jesus Casts Out Demons Because He Is Stronger Than Satan (3:27)
> B' • Response to Charge 1: Such a Claim Is Blasphemous and Unforgivable (3:28-30)
> A' • Jesus and His Family (3:31-35)

If the author intended this pattern, then he encourages the reader to view the impending demise of Satan's kingdom in the middle section (*D*, 3:23-26) as an encouraging word, reinforced in *C'* (3:27). The kingdom Jesus represents may well face opposition from enemies or even friends/family, but it will be victorious. Verses 20-21 connect closely to verses 31-35. Yet the link between verses 20-21 and verses 22-30 should also not be overlooked. That link creates the effect of saying, This is what Jesus' family says—and if you think that is bad, you should hear what his enemies are saying! The same link also draws a connection between the divided house of Satan (3:23-36) and the other divided house (Jesus' own) that has just been depicted (3:21).

3:20-21 Jesus' Family Is Concerned

There are significant problems translating and interpreting the next two verses. Is Jesus at *home* (3:19, 21) or in *a house* (3:20, NIV)? Who is trying to *restrain him* (literally, *take him by force*)? The Greek says *those by him* or *his associates; it does not say *his family; we assume it is his family if we read verse 31 into verse 21. What are these people saying about Jesus? The word can be translated *out of his/its mind,* but elsewhere in Mark (2:12; 5:42; 6:51) it always means "amazed/astounded." And are they ascribing this state to Jesus or the crowd? The Greek is unclear.

Are Jesus' associates attempting to rescue Jesus from an overly enthusiastic crowd? Or are they criticizing aspects of his ministry that make him seem out of his mind? The decisions presupposed by the NRSV translation (*He has gone out of his mind*) are, on balance, the more likely ones. However, contrary to NRSV, we should not imagine Jesus is in his own home in Nazareth (since his family needs to travel to reach him; 3:31).

3:22-30 Jesus' Enemies Misinterpret His Authority

Scribes from Jerusalem come to Galilee to oppose Jesus, as their Galilean counterparts have already done (2:24; 3:6). Jesus' family has charged him with being out of his mind (3:21). The scribes lay two more serious charges against Jesus.

- Jesus is possessed by Beelzebul (an obscure name for Satan).
- Jesus casts out demons in Satan's power.

Jesus responds to the charges in reverse order. He begins by pointing out the absurdity of charge 2. Does Satan cast out Satan? Why would Satan do that? It is a recipe for destruction. With brief parables/analogies, Jesus illustrates this absurdity. Would a kingdom deliberately set out to destroy itself by initiating a civil war? Would a house (household) deliberately set out to tear itself apart? Satan and the whole evil kingdom would quickly self-destruct, turning on themselves, driving out their own demons.

The assumption is that Satan's kingdom is not self-destructing. It is claiming and defending its territory with as much success as ever. The amount of demonic activity Jesus has already encountered is sufficient evidence of that. Yet Jesus hints that Satan's kingdom is indeed falling apart: *his end has come.* Verse 26, by a subtle grammatical shift in Greek (*ei* = *if/since,* for a real condition), suggests that even though earthly kingdoms and houses normally remain united so that they may not fall, Satan's kingdom is *indeed* conflicted and about to fall apart. "Evil always carries the seeds of its own destruction" (D. Bonhoeffer). It will fall apart, however, not because Jesus is working in Satan's power, but because Jesus is overpowering Satan (3:27).

In verse 27 Jesus presents the truth about the scribes' second charge. Satan is indeed losing ground and being robbed of claimed property. No, there is no civil war within the demonic ranks (the implication of the scribes' charge in 3:22). Satan's kingdom is not breaking up on the inside; instead, it is being conquered from the outside. Jesus, the stronger one, has arrived. Jesus makes his point by developing the metaphor of the house. Jesus (the stronger one) has invaded Satan's (the strong man's) territory (his house). Satan is now powerless to protect stolen property and victims. Jesus is plundering the house and releasing Satan's captives (cf. Luke 13:16).

Satan's kingdom/house is indeed doomed, but not because the archfiend cannot keep the troops together. It is doomed because Jesus comes with greater power. But which power? The reader already knows (1:10) that Jesus has been endowed with the Spirit of God. God's Spirit operating in Jesus is driving out the evil spirits. Though this is not explicitly said in the text, it is the assumption behind Jesus' charge that the scribes are blaspheming against the Holy Spirit.

People can be forgiven all sorts of sins, even blasphemy. That is the claim of 3:28. But this universal guideline is then qualified in verse 29. There is one exception: people cannot be forgiven for blasphemy against the Holy Spirit. One often hears of people fearing they might have committed the "unpardonable sin." This verse, however, at least in its Markan form, has its limited application clarified in verse 30. The blasphemy against the Holy Spirit is a reference to the scribal claim that Jesus is possessed. They have declared themselves against the Holy Spirit, who is the true source of Jesus' power to cast out demons. Those who attribute the work of Jesus to Satan and satanic power cannot simultaneously receive the forgiveness that depends on recognizing Jesus as God's agent for salvation. That is what Jesus is suggesting these scribes are doing.

The charges of the scribes (3:22) have given Jesus an opportunity to do several things:

- Show how absurd the scribes' reasoning is (3:23-26).
- Make claims about his own greater strength (3:27).
- Charge them with unforgivable sin (3:28-30).

One cannot help wondering if the scribes regretted speaking at all! Jesus countered their arguments, and he has also laid heavy charges on them in doing so. He has charged them with blasphemy, the very charge they have laid on him (2:7) and for which they will condemn him to death (14:64).

Jesus Redefines Family 3:31-35

At this point Mark resumes an episode left hanging at verse 21. We learn from verse 31 that Jesus' associates, who went to restrain him when people said, *He has gone out of his mind*, are none other than Jesus' own family, his mother, his sisters, and his brothers. The Greek word for *sister(s)* is not included in verse 31 but is likely present in verse 32 (manuscripts disagree), and is certainly present in verse 35.

In 3:14 one of the key aspects of discipleship is being *with Jesus*. In this text another is added: What counts is being *around him* (*peri auton*). Those who are not *around him* are on the *outside* (*exō*). The same designations (*those . . . around, those outside*) appears in 4:10-11. Jesus' family is on the outside. They are neither *with him* nor *around him*. They misjudge him and oppose what he is doing (3:21). Their mission is to come and take him away from his present ministry (3:31).

When his family's intentions are conveyed to Jesus, he neither obliges them nor goes out to explain his alternative plans. If the reader is shocked at the opposing role of Jesus' family, the reader is no less shocked at the distancing response of Jesus. Jesus does not acknowledge them as true family. His true family does not stand outside and seek to control him. Jesus' true family gathers around him and learns from him what it means to hear and do the will of God.

What do we make of this? We could focus only on the positive teaching of the passage: Jesus is creating a spiritual family. We could imagine there are really no negative judgments on Jesus' physical family; their role is incidental to the real point. They function more or less symbolically, to help make the positive point.

Or one could go in another direction, taking the rift (mutual rejection?) between Jesus and his physical family with great seriousness. Yet that creates great dissonance with other Gospel portraits of Jesus' family, or at least of his mother Mary (Luke 1:26-56; 2:19; John 19:25-27). Some scholars assume that Jesus' family here (and elsewhere also the disciples of Jesus) are deliberately being cast in this negative light because Mark is using them to represent theological or ecclesiastical opponents in his own day.

Both of these extremes should be avoided. A negative judgment is indeed cast on Jesus' family. They are not in step with Jesus' priorities and inappropriately seek to hinder what he is doing. But he does not reject them, neither explicitly nor implicitly. He counters their request to come out with an implicit invitation to come in. They can indeed be "a true mother" and "true brothers and sisters." But that will not be the result of a blood relationship. It will not happen if they think they know better than he what he should do. It will happen if they, like the crowd gathered around him, accept that he is God's messenger. It will happen if they submit to God's will.

This entire section prepares for its final verse. The religious establishment has rejected Jesus (3:6), and Jesus has responded by shifting his focus. He will not seek to win their agreement or allegiance; instead, he will turn to those ready to accept him. That includes ministry to the crowds (3:7-12), a renewed discipleship call and commissioning of his closest followers (3:13-19), a strong critique of those who reject the divine origin of his ministry and message (3:22-30), and above all, a redefinition of what it means to be God's people (3:20-21, 31-35).

THE TEXT IN BIBLICAL CONTEXT

Jesus' True Family

By appointing *the Twelve*, symbolizing the twelve tribes (3:16), Jesus has begun to redefine faithful Israel; it includes those whom Jesus himself has gathered and who have accepted his authority and his message. By defining God's people as a spiritual family (3:34-35), Jesus takes this redefinition several steps further:

• God's family centers neither on temple nor synagogue; at present it is in a house. At other times it will be in a boat or on the shore or walking along *the way*.

• God's family is not tied to the accepted religious leadership of Israel, those *from Jerusalem* (3:22) whom Jesus has vanquished in debate.

• God's family is not based on ritual or law or tradition; it is con-
stituted by gathering around Jesus to hear God's will.

• God's family is not based on biological relationships; it is a true
spiritual family, held together by ties stronger than those from birth.

What a powerful word for early Christian communities, gathered
in homes and separated from the religious heritages of their Jewish
and/or Gentile backgrounds. Jesus invites and challenges them to
look around their own circle and see each other as brothers and sisters and mothers.

The family image becomes the dominant metaphor for the
Christian church in the NT. God is the one who creates a spiritual
family (Eph. 3:14-15) and households of faith (Eph. 2:19). Believers
are addressed as brothers and sisters (regularly in Paul's writings) and
as "my dear children" (especially in 1 John). The church is called symbolically "the elect lady and her children" (2 John 1). Jesus is our
older brother (Heb. 2:11), and we unite in calling God "Abba Father"
(Rom. 8:14-18; Gal. 3:26; 4:6-7).

The NT rarely uses "father" to refer to people within the church
family. Paul uses it occasionally when he describes his relationship to
a church or his younger co-workers (1 Cor. 4:15; 1 Tim. 1:2). Jesus
critiques the use of *father* within the fellowship of believers (Matt.
23:9). "Fatherhood" in first-century Palestine carried with it so much
hierarchical and patriarchal baggage that its use in the church family
became inappropriate. The Christian community is a family of brothers and sisters and mothers (Mark 3:35). Those who leave all, including earthly families, to follow Jesus, receive a hundredfold *brothers
and sisters, mothers and children* in God's spiritual family (10:28-
30). But there is only one *Father* (11:25; 13:32).

The Markan community, especially if it was experiencing external
threats, was challenged and comforted by what Jesus himself experienced and taught in Mark 3:31-35. Whenever *brother will betray
brother to death, and a father his child, and children will rise
against parents and have them put to death* (13:11-12), there will
be a spiritual family and a loving Father to turn to.

THE TEXT IN THE LIFE OF THE CHURCH
Binding the Strong Man

Spiritual warfare is a theme once discussed almost exclusively in
Pentecostal and charismatic circles. Today it is widely recognized in
most Christian circles and in fields as diverse as theology, mission,
spiritual growth, and therapy. What is clear from Scripture is that

Jesus came to *bind the strong man* (Mark 3:27, KJV), to limit and ultimately defeat the power of evil. What is less clear is whether evil is to be viewed primarily in terms of a personal devil, a whole army of real demons, the demonic power of structural evil, oppression and violence, psychological aberration, or some combination of these and others.

Ched Myers chose *Binding the Strong Man* as the title for his provocative political reading of Mark's Gospel. According to Myers, Mark presents Jesus as the radical liberator, binding evil and injustice through nonviolent resistance. Certainly this reading highlights one valid way of understanding evil and also emphasizes an important aspect of radical discipleship. The writings of Walter Wink have also contributed to an understanding of evil that goes beyond the personal conflict of individual people with literal demons.

On the other side, Clinton Arnold and other current writers have helped the church understand that evil can indeed take the form of real demonization. Sometimes spiritual warfare through prayer and casting out demons is needed to bring deliverance to those who are victimized.

Mark's Gospel clearly features Jesus in conflict both with the demons that afflict individuals and with the structural evil of abused power. Jesus both delivers individuals and establishes an alternative society that defeats the power of evil through nonviolent resistance and self-sacrificial cross-carrying (on issues of demonism, see also TBC for 1:16-45; TLC for 9:2—10:16; Myers; Boyd; Peck; Arnold; Wink).

Church: Institution or Family?

When Jesus creates family, he gathers believers indirectly related to each other. We are siblings, not by birth and natural relationships, but because we have been adopted by the same loving heavenly Father. All Christian relationships are *through Jesus*, God's Son and our leader and brother (Bonhoeffer, 1954:23-24). That is what Jesus' redefinition of family is all about (Mark 3:33-35; Matt. 23:9-12).

Throughout history, the Christian church has struggled to understand the relationship between natural and religious family ties. In the church, terms like *brother* and *sister* have always been used, and in the Catholic church terms like *father* and *mother* as well. Despite the language, however, churches have often become institutions whose members are strangers to each other. The language of family is retained, but the experience of it is conspicuously absent.

On the other hand, churches that have made it a priority to experience church as a close-knit caring family (as in Anabaptist churches or intentional Christian communities) face another danger. *Close* ties can lead to *closed* boundaries. Churches without a regular influx of new believers (especially new believers from diverse social and ethnic backgrounds) can easily become ingrown and culturally homogeneous; for good and for ill, church meetings often resemble family gatherings.

Anabaptist groups have often emphasized community or spiritual family more than other groups, often resulting in loving fellowships that provide encouragement and support in the challenges of life and of Christian discipleship. Sometimes, however, the emphasis on spiritual family has been to the detriment of natural families (e.g., when a ban imposed by the church forbids natural families to eat together). We want to experience church as a close spiritual family *and* simultaneously experience openness, freedom, and a celebration of diversity and growth, but this seems to be an elusive goal.

There are also challenges along another axis. Throughout history, God's family (the church) has often been excessively patriarchal. Influential leaders (usually men) have run the church. Ordinary members have little say in the life and ministry of the church; it is not surprising that they have participated minimally in the church. Conversely, when a church *distrusts* (patriarchal) leadership and is committed to consensus-building and/or democratic decision-making at all costs, it can become a stymied, squabbling church. The church is a family, but sometimes it adopts for itself less-than-ideal human family models.

Understanding Christian relationships as truly formed through Jesus Christ will go a long way toward helping the church avoid several unhealthy extremes—the extremes of anonymous institutionalism vs. enmeshed exclusivism, as well as the extremes of patriarchal leadership from the top vs. squabbling competition for influence by the many.

Mark 4:1-34

Parables: For Those with Ears to Hear

PREVIEW

In Mark 2:1—3:6, Jesus' target audience is skeptical religious leaders. When they reject him (3:6), he shifts his focus to those open to him (the crowds, 3:7) and those committed to him (the disciples, 3:13). When his "enemies" come after him, he exposes their errors (3:22-30) and turns back to his own (3:34-35).

With the shift in audience comes a shift in both method and message. Jesus is no longer polemical (claiming authority, defending it). Now he instructs his followers about the secret kingdom, using teaching techniques that require hearing ears (spiritual discernment). Mark 4 contains parables as well as discussions *about* parables, their meaning, and their purpose.

Interpreters have sometimes struggled to find a clear unity in this chapter, often arguing that there is inconsistency within it, or between Mark's presentation and what Jesus must originally have meant. They have also stumbled over some claims recorded here (4:11-12). Two important keys, however, will help us understand this chapter.

The *first key* is to recognize interlocking themes in 4:1-34:

- The nature of the kingdom of God.
- The secrecy of the kingdom of God.
- The purpose of parables.
- The need for true hearing.

If we are careful to observe which theme is being addressed and how the themes are interwoven, the chapter proves to be more unified than some commentators imagine.

The *second key* is to recognize that this section in particular (though this would really apply to *all* of Mark) communicates on two levels. Jesus is instructing those around him; Mark is instructing those reading his Gospel. When this is taken into account, this chapter emerges as an important window into Jesus' vision of the reign of God and his call for discernment on the part of those who follow him. It also emerges as a crucial chapter in the theological and literary masterpiece we call the Gospel of Mark (T. Geddert, 1989:71-76). Jesus is leading his disciples toward understanding within the narrative (the story), and Mark is guiding his readers toward understanding by the way he tells that story (the discourse).

Whatever challenges we encounter as we seek to understand the details, we must keep in mind two main lessons taught in this chapter:

• God's kingdom is destined to be ultimately victorious, no matter what obstacles may presently lie in its way.

• Jesus challenges his followers to have hearing ears and seeing eyes.

OUTLINE

The Parable of the Sower, 4:1-9
4:1-3a	Jesus Teaches and Calls People to Hear
4:3b-8	The Sower Parable
4:9	The Call to Hear the Parable's Meaning(s)

The Purpose of the Parables, 4:10-12
4:10	The "Arounders" and the Twelve
4:11a	The Secret of the Kingdom
4:11b-12	Only Parables for Those Outside

The Parable of the Sower "Explained," 4:13-20
4:13	Do You Not Understand This Parable?
4:14-20	Hearing the Word and Bearing Fruit

Hidden Revelation, 4:21-25
4:21	The Parable of the Lamp
4:22	The Purpose of Hiddenness
4:23-25	Renewed Calls to Hear

The Parable of the Growing Seed, 4:26-29

The Parable of the Mustard Seed, 4:30-32

Public Teaching; Private Explanations, 4:33-34

EXPLANATORY NOTES

The Parable of the Sower 4:1-9

4:1-3a Jesus Teaches and Calls People to Hear

Jesus is teaching again at the seashore (2:13) and again uses his disciples' boat to facilitate his ministry (3:9; 4:35-36). The huge crowd on the beach represents various groups of people: eager learners, curious but uncommitted hearers, and rejecting fault-finders. Jesus knows his movement will not be universally accepted, but he is convinced of its final victory. As Jesus ponders these things, perhaps he spies a sower in the distance, confident that the seeds he sows will produce a harvest even though not all of them will reach maturity. In the sower, Jesus sees an image of himself sowing *the word* (4:14) as he addresses the crowd before him. Thus the first parable is born.

Jesus calls his audience (and Mark his readers) to *Listen!* (4:3). This first word is more than a beckon to listen up! It is one of the two main themes of this chapter. Those with hearing ears will understand Jesus' teaching about the secretly arriving reign of God (theme 1). Those with seeing eyes will be able to discern the presence of a hidden kingdom in Jesus' ministry (theme 2). All of the parables in this chapter are about the kingdom of God, its inevitable triumph, its ultimate disclosure, its mysterious ways, and its growth from small beginnings. All the other material in this chapter is about listening: calls to listen, descriptions of the different ways people might listen, and warnings about what happens when inadequate listening takes place ("Hearing," TBC, below).

4:3b-8 The Sower Parable

This is Jesus' first full-length parable in Mark. It plays a central role in this Gospel by its focus on the kingdom and on appropriate hearing of the kingdom message. One scholar has argued that this parable and the interpretation following it function as a "plot synopsis." Throughout Mark, Jesus' kingdom message is being proclaimed and people are responding in various ways. This parable is a lens through which one can see why some are hearing and responding to Jesus while others are not (Tolbert: 175).

This parable is about a sower. It applies to Jesus, who is at that very moment sowing *the word*. But it also applies to Mark; by recording Jesus' words, he is also sowing the word. It also applies to anyone who proclaims the word of the kingdom. Within the story, an ordinary sower is doing what sowers do. The parable summarizes in realistic terms what happens when seeds are sown and (sometimes) grow. As a story about farming, the only thing unrealistic is the size of the harvest at the end. That is central to the meaning of the parable.

This parable is also about seeds and soils. The seeds meet different destinies as the soil conditions either hinder or support the growth of the plants. Interpreters are not in agreement on what kind of farming practices are presupposed. In that farm setting, do farmers plow before or after sowing?

• If plowing takes place *before* sowing, the parable seems to say: Some seed never does have a chance. But that is how it is with broadcast seeding. Inevitably, some falls in places the farmer knows are unproductive, along the (permanent) path, where rocks are present, or where plowing has not controlled the weeds.

• If plowing takes place *after* sowing, the parable seems to say: For all the farmer knows, all the seeds can contribute to the harvest. But it doesn't turn out that way. Birds come before the (temporary) path can be plowed. In the process of plowing, rocks are turned up, and not all the weeds are eliminated.

Either way, whether the farmer knows it will happen or not, some seed is lost, either immediately (to the birds), later (among the rocks), or even later (among the thorns). Either way, some seeds, because the conditions are right, contribute to the final harvest. *This harvest will exceed all expectation.* The realistic parable suddenly becomes unrealistic, at least under first-century Palestinian conditions.

The surprise ending provokes each hearer to choose a response:

• That's a crazy story; nobody gets that kind of harvest.
• Well, it shows that Jesus doesn't know much about farming.
• I wonder what Jesus is getting at? To what does the seed refer? What kind of harvest can be that abundant?

It is this third reaction that Jesus is after. If his goal were to make things self-evidently plain, he would not use parables. His goal is to draw the hearers into active, discerning listening and growing understanding. If they do not grasp it right away, the important thing is to stick with Jesus and above all to be open to whatever will be revealed.

4:9 The Call to Hear the Parable's Meaning(s)

Just as Jesus' listeners puzzle over an appropriate response, he adds a closing line to his parable: *Let anyone with ears to hear listen!* A parable about God's *kingdom* (4:11) is preceded and followed by a call to listen.

If the focus is on the abundant harvest, the parable is clearly about the kingdom of God, and about Jesus' proclamation of it. Then the message would be this:

> There may be many obstacles along the way; there may be times when you are tempted to doubt the final victory of God's kingdom. But don't lose courage. A great and glorious harvest, greater than anything you can imagine, will finally be gathered in.

If the focus is on the different kind of soils and the different destinies of the individual seeds, then it is a parable about how to hear the word of the kingdom. That is suggested in the calls to hear and is developed in the interpretation recorded in 4:14-20.

Parables are always somewhat open-ended. We hear a powerful message and wonder if there is more. The main message of the sower parable seems to be that a glorious final kingdom harvest is promised, even if there are setbacks along the way. Yet is it also an encouraging word for those sowing the word and struggling to keep courage when they see so much of it bearing no fruit? Is Jesus' reference to an impossibly large harvest a way of saying, "Only God can possibly bring about that kind of result!" and therefore also a reminder that God's kingdom is a gift, not something we achieve? Are the large numbers a hint that great numbers of people will finally accept the kingdom message? Can they even be an allusion to the future Gentile mission and its promised success?

The Purpose of the Parables 4:10-12

4:10 The "Arounders" and the Twelve

Suddenly Jesus is alone with the "arounders" and the Twelve. Where did the crowds go? When exactly do they come back into the picture (cf. 4:33)? Mark does not clarify this; his concern is with the *themes* developed (parables, listening, kingdom, secrecy). The unity of this chapter is to be found in the development of these themes, not the choreography of the events.

Those . . . around him and *the twelve* identify certain *kinds* of people, without giving clues on how many and which people are in Jesus' audience at any given time. We should probably assume that much of the chapter (at least the material in 4:21-32) is addressed to the original large mixed group of people, though the chapter never makes that explicit. Verses 10-12, 34, and maybe 13-20 represent private teaching, regardless of when and where it happened.

Jesus is with the *arounders and the twelve*. These refer to those who are responding with openness to Jesus' teaching. They ask Jesus *about the parables*. What exactly they ask is unstated, but in the following verses Jesus talks about the *theme* of the parables (4:11), their *purpose* (v. 12), and what facilitates *understanding* of them (vv. 13-20).

4:11a The Secret of the Kingdom

To you has been given the secret of the kingdom of God. After Jesus enters Galilee announcing the arrival of God's reign, he never explicitly refers to that reign again until here. Is the arrival of God's reign the topic of Jesus' Galilean preaching or not (1:14-15)? Something mysterious is going on. That is the whole point.

Jesus is proclaiming a kingdom. But he is not doing so by going around and telling people, "Here is the kingdom!" Instead, he goes around recruiting disciples, teaching with authority, driving out demons, healing the sick, cleansing the lepers, pronouncing forgiveness, accepting the sinners, challenging the status quo, vanquishing the enemy, renewing the people of God, and creating a spiritual family.

Is Jesus announcing the arrival of God's kingdom? Not overtly. Not for those who do not have ears to hear what he is really saying. Not for those who do not have eyes to see what he is really doing. But if those around Jesus allow their ears to truly hear and their eyes to truly see, they will discern in Jesus' words and deeds the arrival of God's kingdom. It is not a kingdom established by the political systems of this world. It also is not one that arrives with apocalyptic fanfare, nor one that centers on the temple or the law or the religious leaders. It is a kingdom that comes imperceptibly, from small beginnings, but with a great destiny [Kingdom of God in Mark; Messianic Secret].

What is the secret of the kingdom? Countless answers have been suggested by commentators. Here is a sample of options:

- Jesus himself is the kingdom.
- The kingdom will arrive at any moment.
- Jesus is the Messiah, the Son of God.
- Jesus will be crucified.
- Jesus' crucifixion is really an enthronement.
- Jesus will come in glory as the Son of Man.

However, if Jesus' way of proclaiming the *presence* of the kingdom is not by explicit announcement, but by making it *present* for those with hearing ears and seeing eyes, then surely the secret is the secrecy itself. First-century Jews had diverse expectations of what the kingdom would be like. Some expected great military conquests, some expected signs in the heavens, some expected visible religious reforms. All were certain that *when* the kingdom arrived, people would *know* that the kingdom had arrived. That is where Jesus differs from all of them. Contrary to all expectation, the kingdom comes secretly; its presence is discerned only by those who recognize God at work in the ministry and message of Jesus. The secret is that the kingdom comes secretly.

This is what those around Jesus are privileged to understand. Perhaps Jesus explains this to them overtly. More likely Jesus asks them to discern its truth, as Mark asks his readers to do. Readers discern the kingdom's secrecy as they grasp the real meaning and significance of Jesus' words and deeds. That includes hearing the parables of this chapter.

If this is what Jesus (and Mark) mean, then we understand why Mark says Jesus has come to Galilee proclaiming the arrival of *the kingdom of God* (1:14-15) and then seems to drop the subject. He narrates the rest of the Galilean ministry (to 8:27) without a single reference to Jesus announcing the kingdom's arrival. In Jesus' entire Galilean ministry, the word *kingdom* appears only in 4:11, spoken in private to Jesus' followers; and then in 4:26 and 4:30, in parables that outsiders did not understand (4:33-34). Jesus is proclaiming a secret kingdom, and he does so secretly. But why?

4:11b-12 Only Parables for Those Outside

This chapter refers to three kinds of people:

• Arounders and *the twelve* (4:10), people committed to Jesus.
• Outsiders (4:11b), people who have rejected Jesus and his message.
• The *crowd* (4:1), a mixed group of the undecided (see below).

Verses 11b and 12 are about those who have taken their stand against Jesus. Jesus has given up trying to persuade them (see "Preview," above). For them, *everything comes in parables*. If they had hearing ears, they could understand the spoken parables. If they had seeing eyes, they could understand the acted parables (Jesus' deeds). They have neither; as a result, the whole meaning of Jesus' life eludes them, and they are unaware of the hidden presence of the kingdom. This situation will not change as long as they reject Jesus, for spiritual insight is given only to Jesus' followers (4:11a). Jesus does not make anyone into an outsider. But he does speak and act in such a way that outsiders will not understand. Parables make unbelief possible for people who do not want to understand. It permits people to remain in darkness if that is what they choose. It allows people to choose a stance against Jesus and the Spirit at work in Jesus; that stance prevents their forgiveness (3:29-31).

In 4:12 Jesus adapts Isaiah 6:9-10, clarifying that those who have already rejected him are excluded from insight and forgiveness. They are consigned to the ignorance and guilt they have chosen for themselves. Mark 4:12b carries irony: *After all, you wouldn't want people to repent* (TJG; on this, see TBC, below).

We can paraphrase Jesus' words in 4:11b-12 in this way:

> Some people have hardened their hearts and rejected me and my kingdom message. They are therefore unable to penetrate the mystery of God's kingdom or discern its arrival in my words and my works. As a result they also cannot respond to its call for repentance. For them, *everything comes in parables*. They cannot see past the surface of things to their meaning. There is no point in calling for repentance when people cannot see and hear; and there is no way for people to see and hear if their hearts are hard.

Jesus aims to keep people in the dark if they persist in staying outside. Those who are willing to learn God's will from him (those who have become *arounders;* 3:34; 4:10) will be granted true insight. There also are many people who are neither among the committed (the arounders) nor among the rejecters (the outsiders); these are the ones who have not yet made any decision, certainly not a final decision. They hear the parables and understand some. They watch Jesus and understand some. Their hearts may not be ready to say an unequivocal yes to Jesus, but their hearts are also not defined as hard beyond hope. Arounders are given special revelations, whereas outsiders get only parables. All the rest are privileged to hear Jesus teach and are called to listen carefully and respond appropriately.

The Parable of the Sower "Explained" 4:13-20

4:13 Do You Not Understand This Parable?

Mark probably intends us to understand verses 13-20 as a continuation of Jesus' private session with those committed to him (4:10).

They know about the kingdom's secrecy (v. 11) and are now given private instruction on how to understand parables (v. 13).

Many interpreters accuse Mark of seriously misrepresenting Jesus in 4:14-20. Jesus presents the parable of the sower to teach about the kingdom. By the time Mark is finished with it, it is not about the sower and not about the kingdom. It is not even a parable; it is an allegory about seeds and soils, and it teaches about true hearing (so the argument goes). However, such a negative judgment on Mark is not necessary.

Contrary to what is often claimed, parable and allegory are not mutually exclusive categories; parables often have allegorical features, and this one certainly does. Thus it is also able to make more than one point. It teaches about the kingdom and also about the ways people hear. These are inseparable themes for both Mark and Jesus. People hear the kingdom message with varying degrees of receptivity. As a result, some seed is lost, but still there is an unexpectedly large harvest.

Moreover, Mark's text never claims that 4:14-20 is the interpretation of the sower parable. The question that verses 14-20 answer is this: *How will you understand all the parables?* (4:13b) *[Questioning Jesus]*. The details of the sower parable are recounted, but they are used to teach about parable interpretation. They reveal the kind of hearing that makes it possible to understand *all the parables* (including the sower parable!). We can say this another way: The sower parable is about the kingdom. But the kingdom comes secretly (4:11a); it comes *in parables* (v. 11b). Thus the sower parable is a parable about speaking in parables. And the "interpretation" (4:14-20) is about how to interpret parables.

Mark's teaching here is much more profound than is recognized by some interpreters. Verse 13 does *not* say, "Do you want to know how all the parables should be interpreted? As allegories—just watch how easily it's done!" *Nor* does it say, "If you can't even understand this one, the easiest of all, how will you hope to understand any of the others? They are much more challenging than this one." Instead, verse 13 says, "If the message of the kingdom falls on fruitful soil (if you have *ears to hear*), you will learn to understand its meaning and perceive its presence, even though it comes secretly." The sower parable is about the kind of kingdom Jesus proclaims and the kind of hearing needed to understand.

Everything falls in place nicely if only we assume that 4:14-20 directly answers the question that immediately precedes it:

Question: How will you understand any parable? (4:13b)
Answer: By correct hearing. (4:14-20)

I have tried to make sense of a very difficult part of Mark's Gospel (4:10-13). Many commentators have said it is the most difficult in all of Mark. Some things may still seem unclear or unsettling. If they do, we should view that as a challenge to keep seeking the discernment this passage teaches about. Jesus deliberately did not make things as clear as possible, and Mark models himself after Jesus. We, too, are often challenged to hear and understand, but then not told everything we would like to know (see esp. "Hearing Ears and Seeing Eyes," 7:31—8:26, notes).

4:14-20 Hearing the Word and Bearing Fruit

Jesus provides this interpretation (or further reflections) on the sower parable to help his hearers understand what it means to truly hear parables of the kingdom (4:13, notes). Though somewhat allegorical, the details should not be pressed too far; sometimes the various hearers are the seeds, sometimes the growing plants, and sometimes the soils (Harder: 107). The main message is clear:

> Some people hear the Word, but because their hearts are not fully receptive to the Word, they do not bear fruit in the end. Only those who truly accept the Word ultimately bear fruit.

This is a personalization of a parable about the fate of the kingdom. We discern in 4:3-8 that a great kingdom harvest will one day be gathered in. Then we learn from 4:14-20 that there can also be a great harvest in our own lives if we learn to listen and respond correctly. Verses 3-8 encourage us that the great harvest is not in jeopardy even if some seed is lost along the way. Then verses 14-20 challenge us to make sure that we are not among those lost along the way. We discern in verses 3-8 that the great harvest is a future hope and that our role is to discern the secret advancing of the kingdom in the germination of seed and the growth of plants. We realize from verses 14-20 that we also play a role in the process of germination and growth. Otherwise, we will not be among those who are gathered in at the great harvest.

The specific threats and dangers along the way are spelled out clearly in the text. Hard-hearted people do not let the seed penetrate and germinate in their lives. Enthusiastic responses count for nothing, if there is no depth and persistence. Positive response to *the word* means rejecting competing words. If temptations of various kinds are given room to grow, they will displace an original wholehearted commitment to God's kingdom. Only receptive hearts, deep commitments, and single-minded allegiance can truly result in a harvest that corresponds to the bumper crop Jesus describes.

The last word of this text, *a hundredfold,* foreshadows what Jesus will say in 10:29-30. Those with a wholehearted commitment to Jesus and the gospel are promised *a hundredfold* return on their investment, even in this life, and eternal life in the next.

In summary, Mark 4 has thus far taught: The kingdom will flourish no matter who rejects it (vv. 3b-8). See to it that you respond correctly, and you will be part of the ultimately victorious kingdom (vv. 14-20). Your access to greater insight depends on your response to Jesus and his kingdom message (vv. 10-13). Therefore *Listen!* (vv. 3a, 9).

How much of this is verbatim recording of what Jesus actually said on the Galilean lakeshore? How much of it is molded and shaped by Mark and the needs of the church to which he wrote? There is no way we can know. But there is nothing in these 20 verses that Jesus could not have said; and all of it is what Mark wants to say. It should be received that way by the reader.

Hidden Revelation 4:21-25

4:21 The Parable of the Lamp

After a private session with committed followers, Jesus is again teaching the crowds (cf. 4:10, notes). Verse 21 functions like a parable, though it consists of only two questions (Greek/NIV) and is unlike the other parables of this chapter (which are about seeds and growth). Like the other parables, it is about God's kingdom and about the secrecy surrounding its coming (4:11, notes).

Translated literally this parable says,

> A lamp does not come in order that it might be placed under a bushel basket or under a bed, does it? [It comes] in order that it might be placed on a lampstand, doesn't it?

The first question implies a "no" answer, and the second a "yes." Lamps always exist to be seen and to shed light on other things. But is this a specific lamp? The opening words in Greek say *the lamp comes* and not that it is *brought* (as in NRSV). If no specific lamp is in view, then the meaning of this parable can be summarized as follows:

Lamps are for seeing and shedding light. That makes them just like parables, for they too are given to be understood, and so that other things can be understood by them.

This interpretation would highlight the positive function of parables (to enlighten those with spiritual perception), rather than the negative function highlighted elsewhere in this chapter (to keep those without spiritual perception in the dark).

However, it may be that a specific *lamp* is intended. The fact that *the lamp comes* suggests two options:

1. Jesus may be referring to *himself*. He is the lamp who, though not presently understood and recognized, will eventually be openly proclaimed and recognized. Any present hiddenness (nonrecognition) is temporary. Someday the identity of Jesus will be openly proclaimed, and eventually it will be universally recognized (cf. 13:26; 14:61-62; John 1:9; 7:3-4).

2. Jesus may be referring to the *kingdom*. It is presently coming secretly (4:11), but people eventually will see that it *has come with power* (9:1). There is a hiddenness at present, but it did not come to remain hidden. The kingdom will eventually be openly proclaimed and universally recognized.

The ambiguity of verse 21 permits us to accept multiple meanings for the lamp that comes. Neither the identity of Jesus nor the presence of the kingdom are destined to remain hidden forever. There is some secrecy at present, but it will eventually give way to full disclosure and ultimate recognition. Yet even now Jesus' followers are granted the privilege of penetrating the secrets. Parables are explained to them (4:34). The secret of the kingdom is given (v. 11). Before the chapter is over, Jesus will be giving them glimpses of his secret identity (v. 41).

4:22 The Purpose of Hiddenness

Jesus is no longer talking about the lamp, for lamps are not first hidden and then eventually put onto a lampstand. He is talking about things that the lamp illustrates—parables, Jesus, the kingdom. Jesus' coming and the kingdom's coming are both designed to have two phases: first, the time of secrecy and hiddenness; then, the time of disclosure and open revelation.

Verse 21 states that the ultimate goal is not hiddenness but revelation. Verse 22 indicates that the present hiddenness also has a purpose. Jesus *intends* to create a separation between those who truly see and hear and those who do not. The parables help to create that separation. So also does the secrecy surrounding Jesus' identity and the kingdom's coming. By preventing outsiders (4:11, notes) from perceiving what is really happening, Jesus gives arounders and *the twelve* (4:10, notes) time to penetrate the mysteries. Present hiddenness enables revelation to some and concealment from others.

Present hiddenness also permits Jesus to control the pace at which his identity and the presence of the kingdom are disclosed. Jesus' identity as Messiah would be revealed much *less clearly* if it had been openly proclaimed from the start, leaving everyone to their own preconceived notions as to what *Messiah* means. So also with God's reign. If Jesus had made it his goal to persuade everyone that God's kingdom had arrived, would anyone still be listening when he begins teaching that in God's kingdom servants are great, children are models, crosses become thrones, and defeats become stepping-stones to victory? Would not that sort of teaching be lost in the cries for military conquest or apocalyptic signs or religious reform?

4:23-25 Renewed Calls to Hear

Verse 23 is almost identical to verse 9 (4:9, notes). Verse 24a is a brilliant mixed metaphor, reminding the hearers that hearing ears and seeing eyes go together. Literally, verse 24a reads, *See what you hear.* The two verbs are the same as those used for seeing (or looking) and hearing (or listening) in verse 12. The material surrounding the sower parable focuses on hearing, and the immediately preceding parable (the lamp) focuses on seeing. Seeing eyes and hearing ears belong together as code terms for the spiritual discernment needed to truly understand and recognize what the secret kingdom, the hidden messiahship, and a chapter full of parables are all about.

Verses 24b and 25 belong together, with verse 25 explaining verse 24b. This is not a recipe for getting richer, nor is it merely about the truism that often the rich get richer and the poor get poorer. This is about spiritual perception. Interpreted in *this* realm, Jesus' statements are indeed a recipe for gaining more. He promises that having leads to receiving still more. Some truly listen and truly see, gather around Jesus with the Twelve, and listen without allowing the tempter or persecution or competing interests to block the growth. They are the ones who will indeed bear a rich harvest, a harvest that includes more and more understanding, more and more faithfulness, and a greater portion of the rewards promised to those who give up all for the sake of the gospel (8:35—9:1; 10:29-31). On the other hand, those who are deaf and blind miss out on the harvest.

The Parable of the Growing Seed 4:26-29

The next short parable explicitly claims to be an illustration of the nature of the kingdom of God. What is not explained is what aspect of the farmer's (in)activity and/or aspect of the seed's/plant's progress is to be compared with the kingdom of God. Is the focus on the patience of the farmer during the time of growth? Is it that the plant (kingdom) grows independent of human effort? Is it that the seed grows irresistibly once it is sown? Is it that the plant must go through different stages before the harvest can come? Is it about the imminence of the final judgment (*sickle*; cf. Joel 3:13)? Is the parable a call for patience? trust? discernment? preparation?

This parable seems to focus on the farmer's inactivity and lack of understanding. If so, then presumably the farmer is not being compared to Jesus but rather to the disciple who, though given more and more understanding (4:25), is never given full insight. During the present stage of the kingdom's presence and growth, there will not be many assurances of the kingdom's ultimate success [*Kingdom of God in Mark*]. Setbacks may occur (or so it will seem). But the seed has been planted. The promise has been given. The disciples need to trust and be patient.

The Parable of the Mustard Seed 4:30-32

The final parable of this chapter concerns the contrast between the smallest of seeds (the mustard seed, proverbially regarded as the smallest of all seeds) and the much larger plant that grows from it. The kingdom may have a small beginning; it may be overlooked by all but the most discerning; but its growth will eventually result in something that cannot be overlooked. *That which is hidden now will eventually be revealed* (restating 4:21-22).

The reference to birds nesting or finding shelter under its shade emphasizes the large size of the full-grown garden *shrub*. In Mark, Jesus does not call it a "tree," and the Greek text does not necessarily mean that birds build nests in its branches (as in NRSV). These features of Matthew's and Luke's versions carry additional meanings not necessarily taught in Mark (TBC, below).

This parable stands alongside all the other material in this chapter in its central message: present smallness and hiddenness notwithstanding, the kingdom will someday be revealed to be *the greatest*. At present there is need for much discernment and trust. Some day all things will be made clear [*Kingdom of God in Mark*].

Public Teaching; Private Explanations 4:33-34

With Jesus' teaching complete, the narrator makes four final comments on parable teaching. First, Jesus spoke many more parables than those recorded here. We have often been informed that Jesus taught in synagogues, open places, and at the seashore. Seldom are we given glimpses of what he taught. Now we learn that he typically spoke in parables.

Second, Jesus taught *as they were able to hear it*. This likely means that some of the hearers benefited more and some less from Jesus' teaching method. It all depended on their ability to see and hear; that in turn depended on their commitment to Jesus and his teaching (4:10-12, 24-25, notes).

Third, Jesus taught *only* by means of parables. Since Mark records much teaching that seems nonparabolic, this must mean that in *everything* Jesus taught, there were deeper meanings than the most obvious ones.

Finally, Jesus disclosed some of the deeper meanings to his followers. No doubt Jesus provided some parable interpretations. Perhaps he also pointed out how they are to discern the secret arrival of the kingdom in Jesus' life and ministry (4:11).

Since the first verse of Mark's Gospel, the reader has known things hidden from the human characters in the story. Now we are confronted with the reverse. The disciples have been given private teaching, and we are not told what they learned. Mark is preparing us for what lies ahead. Later Jesus will chide his disciples for not understanding things that readers are also not told (e.g., the secret meaning of the feedings). Mark challenges *readers* to use the same seeing eyes and hearing ears that Jesus challenges his *disciples* to use (cf. esp. 8:14-21).

What does this chapter teach about God's kingdom? Jesus has announced the arrival of God's reign in his own ministry and proclamation right from the beginning (1:14-15). Now we learn that he is proclaiming a *secretly arriving* kingdom, giving glimpses of its presence in his deeds (for those with eyes to see), and speaking of its nature and destiny in riddles and parables (for those with ears to hear; 4:11b-12, notes). The kind of kingdom Jesus proclaims does not manifest itself with obvious proofs of its presence and power. For that reason, those committed to God's kingdom need assurances that the kingdom for which they are investing their lives will one day be fully manifest and will be victorious over competing kingdoms.

This chapter gives those assurances. Despite rejection, a great harvest is guaranteed (the sower parable). Present hiddenness will surely give way to future visibility (the parable of the lamp). Though we may not understand the process, we need not doubt the final results (the parable of the growing seed). Small beginnings do not preclude large endings (the parable of the mustard seed). The composite picture says, God's reign is destined to grow and be victorious, however insignificant or incomprehensible it might now seem. Mark's Gospel teaches that even seeming defeats can contribute to the final victory (cf. 1:14, notes).

THE TEXT IN BIBLICAL CONTEXT
Hearing

"Hear, O Israel: the LORD our God, the LORD is one" (Deut. 6:4-5, NIV) So begins the oft-repeated Hebrew *Shema* (named after the Hebrew word for "hear, take heed, obey"). The *Shema* represents the most important teaching of the Torah (Mark 12:28-29). By opening his parable discourse with the word *Hear!* (4:3, TJG), Jesus sets his teaching of the kingdom alongside the greatest teachings of the OT.

The Greek word *akouō* covers the same range of meaning as the underlying Hebrew. In this chapter, *akouō* (*hear/listen*) appears no less than thirteen times. An interesting exercise is to take all the words of Jesus in this chapter and divide them into two parts: one part for the parables, the other for all the rest. The parables take verses 3-8 (starting with the second word of verse 3), verse 21, and verses 26-32. The rest are the following:

4:3 • *"Listen!"*
4:9 • "Let anyone with *ears* to *hear, listen!"*
4:11-12 • Jesus' words about the secrecy of the kingdom and about seeing with perception and *hearing* with understanding.
4:13-20 • The (so-called) interpretation of the sower parable, with four references to ways in which people *hear* the word.
4:22-24 • Jesus' words about secrecy and revelation, including "Let anyone with *ears* to *hear listen!"* and "Pay attention to what you *hear!"*

After we have thus divided Jesus' words into two parts, we can easily see that all the parables are about the nature of the kingdom and all the rest is about hearing. These two themes are inseparable in this chapter. Jesus' concern that his followers hear the message of the kingdom can well be called the new *Christian Shema.*

Human Choice and Divine Predestination

In 4:10 Jesus refers to *those who were around him along with the twelve* (Jesus' followers, his family; cf. 3:13-19, 32, 34-35). In 4:11

he refers to *those outside* (those who reject Jesus' authority [2:7], plot his death [3:6], call him possessed, crediting his works to Satan [3:22], and so on); such people put themselves outside and make themselves unforgivable (3:29). Mark 4:11b-12 is not about Jesus arbitrarily facilitating or preventing true hearing and seeing, but about Jesus' way of dealing with people who have taken their stand for or against him.

Various Scriptures wrestle with the issue of human choice vs. divine predestination (e.g., Rom. 9). Will people ultimately be saved because of God's choice or their own? While it is possible to read individual texts as though they place the entire decision in God's hands, most often the context indicates that human choice is also a deciding factor (e.g., Rom. 9:32). Other texts clearly say or imply that anyone can choose to accept the gospel. God wills for all to be saved; those who accept the salvation God offers will in fact be saved (2 Pet. 3:9). At any rate, despite some scholars' protests to the contrary, Mark 4 does *not* teach that Jesus makes anyone into an outsider; outsiders are where they have chosen to be (see below, next).

"So That They May Not . . . Be Forgiven"

Jesus explains his treatment of outsiders in Mark 4:11-12 by means of Isaiah 6:9-10. The prophet Isaiah's preaching was designed to accomplish three things:

- Make the heart of this people calloused (hard).
- Make their ears dull.
- Close their eyes.

What is the goal? "Otherwise they might turn . . . and be healed" (Isa. 6:10b, NIV).

Mark's quotation from Isaiah ends, "So that they may not turn again and be forgiven" (4:12). We might well word it like this: "After all, you wouldn't want people to repent and be forgiven, would you?" Clearly there is irony intended here (and probably in Isaiah as well). Jesus is not really aiming to *prevent* forgiveness. Instead, forgiveness is declared unavailable to those who reject God's messenger. Human choice is not excluded, a point that becomes obvious when we note that Mark has significantly *omitted* a line in Isaiah: "Make the people's hearts hard" (Isa. 6:10a, TJG). Mark has told us that Jesus' enemies have already hardened their own hearts (Mark 3:5). Jesus' enemies have made *themselves* outsiders.

The apostle Paul, reflecting on the mystery that not all Israelites recognized Jesus as Messiah, writes, "A hardening has come upon part of Israel" (Rom. 11:25). They have stumbled (Rom. 9:32), but their rejection is used by God to bring salvation to the Gentiles. The salvation of the Gentiles will in turn be used by God to bring Israelites who presently reject their Messiah back into the true people of God (Rom. 11:11-12, 25-26). Forgiveness is conditioned upon returning to God, who keeps drawing and calling and inviting.

The Mustard Seed Parable and the Gentile Mission

The mustard seed parable may allude to the future Gentile mission. This is particularly true for Matthew's and Luke's versions of the parable, where the mustard seed becomes a large "tree" in whose branches the birds make nests (cf. Matt. 13:31-32; Luke 13:18-19). In the background here are several OT texts that speak of great earthly kingdoms (trees) allowing birds (peoples) to build nests (find political protection) in their large branches (cf. Ezek. 17:22-24; 31:3-10; Dan. 4:10-27). A reference to birds finding shelter in the mustard plant/tree may well allude to the nations (Gentiles) finding a future home in God's reign.

In contrast to the OT texts, Jesus' parable (especially in its Markan form) speaks of a mysterious hidden kingdom, not political alliances, military might, and earthly securities. Indeed, Mark seems to *resist* the idea of a "grandiose tree." R. W. Funk in an article with the provocative title "The Looking-Glass Tree Is for the Birds" argues that Mark's version preserves something essential about Jesus' kingdom vision. Unlike earthly kingdoms, God's kingdom does *not* exalt greatness and strength. Instead, "it will erupt out of the power of weakness and refuse to perpetuate itself by the weakness of power" (7). This is an attractive suggestion; while it remains uncertain whether this lesson is taught in Mark 4, it is certainly taught elsewhere in Mark (10:15, 43-44).

To make the same point, Paul uses a different metaphor for the Gentile mission. He speaks of grafting "wild branches" into the olive tree (the People of God; Rom. 11:11-24). As God's kingdom is established, Gentiles will find in it (in God's eschatological plant/tree) a home alongside believing Jews. Paul's use of "mystery" to describe this (Rom. 11:25) corresponds to Mark's emphasis in his parable chapter. This parallel further suggests that those who presently have hardened hearts (Mark 4:11-12) are not beyond hope of final redemption (Rom. 11:25-26).

THE TEXT IN THE LIFE OF THE CHURCH

A Kingdom That Cannot Fail

Throughout church history, Christians have struggled to understand NT teaching about the kingdom of God. When does it come? What is its relationship to the church? Is it a visible kingdom, and if so, when does it appear?

If Jesus had shared the views of his contemporaries, Mark 4 would not have been possible. In a kingdom focused on "marching armies, heroic deeds, and valorous exploits" (Stock, 1982:94), there is no need for careful discernment. The kingdom Jesus proclaims is nothing like that. It is best illustrated with vulnerable seeds and delayed harvests. Those who share his vision are challenged to listen carefully, watch closely, and wait patiently. Jesus will go on to teach his disciples that by giving up personal treasures, by placing great value on children, by pursuing servanthood, and by carrying a cross, they will be pursuing the kingdom of God.

With varying emphases, Mark's view of the kingdom is shared by all the writers of the NT. It is sad that the church throughout its history has not always shared this biblical perspective. Sometimes God's kingdom has been mistakenly identified with the (very visible) institutional church, complete with grandiose temples, elaborate rituals, political influence, and sometimes even armies. Other times it has been identified with national entities, as though Jesus, who denied he was setting up a kingdom "from this world" (John 18:36), would have nations to do so on his behalf!

A more subtle error occurs when God's reign is (slightly) detached from *political* structures and then identified with a particular culture or ideology, a particular political direction, a popular movement, or an anticipated millennium in which the returned Jesus and national Israel share the rule. Some Christians have distanced themselves from such worldly ideas of God's kingdom, only to fall into an error on the other side. They have limited God's reign to an inner spiritual or mystical experience, or more frequently to a future hope in heaven (cf. Snyder).

Deceived leaders and teachers have often claimed to know exactly when God would set up the final kingdom; they have summoned their followers to abandon normal patterns of life in order to make special pilgrimages, or else idly to await the great and imminent event. Paul opposes just such an error in 2 Thessalonians 2:1-2 (cf. 3:6). In the sixteenth century, Balthasar Hubmaier addressed such a movement:

I very strongly opposed Hans Hut and his followers when they hood-
winked the simple people by claiming a definite time for the last day,
namely, next Pentecost. They convinced them to sell their property and
leave wife and child, house and field behind, and are now without means
of support. Thus the poor people were convinced to follow him by a
seductive error which arose out of ignorance of Scripture. (via Klaassen,
1981:324)

In the last few decades, not a few false teachers have deceived
masses of followers with erroneous views of God's kingdom or predictions of Jesus' return. Political developments, sometimes even the
movements of comets, are wrongly interpreted as signs of the kingdom. Hopes are raised, only to be dashed when expected events do
not materialize. Sometimes tragedies like mass suicides are the end
result of these misguided speculations.

We live in a day when one-sided and often erroneous visions of
God's kingdom abound. Some Christian cultures identify the kingdom
and its coming with spiritual warfare, some with church growth, some
with mystical experiences, some with political activism, and some
with either the life within or the life beyond. Seldom have followers
of Jesus more desperately needed to learn from the vision of Jesus in
Mark and thus also from Mark's vision of a mysterious hidden kingdom, one that can be seen and heard, if we are looking and listening
for the right things!

There is evidence of the presence of this kingdom everywhere,
says Mark, if only we know how to interpret the evidence [Kingdom
of God in Mark]. Calls for repentance are going forth (Mark 1:15).
Lives are being changed (1:17). A community of brothers, sisters, and
mothers gathers around Jesus to learn God's will (3:35). People are
restored to health and sanity (1:32-34; 5:1-20). Social outcasts are
invited to dine with Jesus (2:15-17). Cups of cold water are given in
Jesus' name (9:41). Children are valued and welcomed into Jesus' circle (10:13-16). Disciples are learning that salvation is found in self-
denial and self-sacrifice (8:34-35).

Such evidences indicate that God's kingdom is far more than an
inner or mystical spirituality. These are visible signs of a kingdom that
is truly being established. Yet this kingdom is mysterious and con-
founds expectations, for who would have thought that the reign of
God would be established like that?!

Mark 4:35—5:43

Victories over Storms and Satan, Sickness and Death

PREVIEW

Jesus has just challenged his audience (and Mark his readers) to have hearing ears that can truly understand the *parables* (4:1-34) and the message of the kingdom that they convey. Mark's Gospel now shifts to *miracles* and challenges the readers to have seeing eyes that can truly understand what they mean *[Miracles in Mark]*.

There is no great disjunction between words and deeds in Mark's Gospel. Both demonstrate Jesus' authority, and both convey hidden meanings. Both have the potential to reveal the identity of Jesus, the nature of his mission, the presence of the kingdom, and the implications for discipleship. *Everything comes in parables* (4:10-12). In this "miracle section" of Mark, the reader is challenged to learn along with Jesus' disciples about Jesus' power, his priorities, and most of all, his true identity.

This section includes four miracles, each narrated in detail: stilling a storm (4:35-41), salvation from demon possession (5:1-20), salvation from illness and uncleanness (5:24b-34), and resurrection from death (5:35-43). The careful structuring of this section is revealed by observing how each one shares significant features with the one immediately preceding and/or following it.

The first two are linked by the themes of the sea (home of the demonic?) and demons (who perish in the sea). The first asks of Jesus, *Who then is this?* (4:41); the second provides an answer, *Son of the Most High God* (5:7). Both teach about discipleship: it entails courageous faith when the storms of life threaten and Jesus seems absent (4:35-41); it entails faithful witness, when Jesus sends us out in his name (5:18-21).

The second and third miracles focus on individuals whose conditions are unimaginably pitiable. A man is driven to insanity by a legion of demons and a woman to despair by health problems, exploiters, and an ostracizing social religious system. Both victims experience complete healing, including social restoration and full salvation.

The third and fourth miracles are linked structurally. They are woven together, urging the reader to explore the significance of their common features *[Chiasm and Intercalation]*. Both are concerned with faith and what happens when it is exercised.

We can also draw comparisons between the first and last miracles reported here, since Mark frequently frames a larger section with matching narratives (cf. 7:31-37 and 8:22-26 as the framework for the section "Hearing Ears and Seeing Eyes"). In the first miracle, Jesus demonstrates mastery over wind and sea; in the last, over death itself. The experience of these great acts of God astounds those who experience them and provokes reflection on who Jesus really is.

That Jesus can indeed accomplish works of power is by now accepted by disciples, curious onlookers, and even Jesus' enemies (not present in this section). Jesus' companions and Mark's readers are being challenged to look beyond sheer *power* to the *meaning* of all this. What sort of Jesus works like this? What sort of kingdom is being proclaimed as these stories are narrated?

OUTLINE

Jesus Triumphs over Wind and Sea, 4:35-41
4:35-36	Setting the Scene
4:37-39	Calming the Sea
4:40-41	Calming the Disciples

Jesus Saves a Gerasene Demoniac, 5:1-20
5:1-5	Setting the Scene
5:6-10	The Demoniac and the Legion of Demons
5:11-13	The Demons and the Swine
5:14-17	The Swineherds and Their Countryfolk
5:18-20	The Healed Man and Jesus

Jairus Calls for Jesus, 5:21-24a

Jesus Saves an Unclean Woman, 5:24b-34
    5:24b-26   An Unclean Woman in the Crowd
    5:27-29   The Physical Healing of the Woman
    5:30-32   Jesus and the Crowd
    5:33-34   The Full Healing and Salvation of the Woman

Jesus Triumphs over Death, 5:35-43
    5:35-36   The Need for Renewed Faith
    5:37-40   Witnesses of the Resurrection
    5:41-42a   Jesus Raises the Girl
    5:42b-43   Responses and Restrictions

The Purpose of This Miracle Section

EXPLANATORY NOTES

Jesus Triumphs over Wind and Sea 4:35-41

The disciples have just heard Jesus teach about a secretly advancing kingdom that is guaranteed to reach its goal, whatever setbacks may be experienced along the way. One may hope that when the next threat to their security arises, they will remember and maintain courage, perhaps asking Jesus, "Is this what you were talking about?" Instead, they panic, charge Jesus with not caring, and react with astonishment when he rescues them. If we view the last episode of chapter 4 as the test at the end of the day's teaching, the disciples do not demonstrate they have mastered the material.

Mark has already alluded to the disciples' misunderstanding (or nonunderstanding; 1:36-37; 4:13). This section will bring it out into the open. Soon the inadequate responses of the disciples will become a major theme of the narrative (6:52; 8:14-21, 32-33; and so on).

4:35-36 Setting the Scene

Verse 35 connects this episode to the day of parable teaching; this is the test at the end of the lecture. The statement that they take Jesus *just as he was* is puzzling but probably means only that Jesus was already in the boat (4:1) and they simply leave. *Other boats* are mentioned (v. 36), perhaps hinting that Jesus' acts of deliverance on behalf of his followers can result in blessings also for others around them. On the other hand, the reference to other boats may represent reminiscences of an eyewitness, likely the source of other details (the

time, the vivid description of the boat as *already being swamped*
[v. 37], the position of Jesus in the boat, and so on).

4:37-39 Calming the Sea

A great windstorm arose, as it often does on the Sea of Galilee.
Even experienced fishermen consider it life-threatening, but not
Jesus; he sleeps. Sleep can be the wrong response in a crisis (cf.
14:37-42) or a sign of trust. "I will both lie down and sleep in peace;
for you alone, O LORD, make me lie down in safety" (Ps. 4:8).

The reader is expected to see Jesus' sleep as a sign of trust; the
disciples interpret it as lack of concern. Waking him, they ask, *Do you
not care that we are perishing?* Did they want him to help bail out
water? to get up and "pray to his God" (cf. Jon. 1:6)? to get up and
calm the sea? They don't seem to anticipate this last option (cf. Mark
4:41). It is possible to translate their words as a direct reproach (not
a question at all): *You do not care that we are perishing!*

This is only the second time in Mark that the disciples speak to
Jesus. In 1:37 they criticize Jesus for wrong priorities. Now they
chide him for not caring. The next time they speak to him, they criticize him for asking a foolish question (5:31). Mark's portrait of the
misunderstanding disciples may be subtle, but it is persistent.

Jesus demonstrates his concern and his power by mastering the
wind and the sea. The wind he rebukes (*epitimaō*), and the sea he
muzzles (*phimoō*). The great windstorm (*lailaps megalē*) is replaced
by a great calm (*galēnē megalē*). That is the easy part. Jesus has
more trouble calming his disciples.

4:40-41 Calming the Disciples

As often in Mark, Jesus sets fear and faith as opposites: *Why are
you afraid? Have you still no faith?* (4:40; 5:36). The questions use
present-tense verbs. The questions can mean one of these options:

• After all the mighty works you have seen me do, why do you
respond with fear when danger threatens?

• In the light of all the assurances you heard today about the final
triumph of God's kingdom, why do you fear that a storm at sea will
bring it down?

• Why are you *still* panicking; the great storm has already given
way to a great calm?

Word repetition to the point of redundancy is used effectively in
Greek. Our English distaste for it often obscures the meaning of the

original. In Greek, this text speaks of a *great calm* replacing a *great storm*. The disciples' reaction is reported thus: They feared a *great fear*. To translate it with the positive-sounding *they were filled with great awe* (as NRSV does) gives the disciples the (probably unwarranted) benefit of the doubt.

Yet they do ask the right question. *Who is this?* This story is not about raw power. It is about the identity of Jesus. He is the *Christ* and *the Son of God;* this is something readers know (1:1), but the disciples do not. Yet this miracle points beyond titles to other features about the nature and identity of Jesus. The psalmist said,

> Some went down to the sea in ships; . . .
> they saw the deeds of the LORD. . . .
> For he commanded and raised the stormy wind,
>   which lifted up the waves of the sea.
> They mounted up to heaven, they went down to the depths;
>   their courage melted away in their calamity; . . .
> Then they cried to the LORD in their trouble; . . .
> he made the storm be still,
>   and the waves of the sea were hushed. (Ps. 107:23-29; cf. 89:9)

Who is this one who does what only God can do? Mark never clearly affirms divinity for Jesus but frequently suggests it. Only God can forgive (and therefore Jesus can! 2:5-7); God determines the purpose of the Sabbath (therefore Jesus can regulate its usage; 2:27-28); only God is good (but so is Jesus! 10:17-18); only God can calm the waves of the sea (who then is Jesus who can do that?). The next time Jesus rescues his disciples at sea, he will identify himself as *I AM* (6:50, TJG; cf. Exod. 3:14). He does this more than once (14:62), but always in contexts where the Greek can also mean something else as well. Mark is dropping some bold hints (but they are only hints) that Jesus may be God and not just *Son of God* (1:1, 11).

First-century Jews identified the sea not only with danger and threat to human life, but with primeval chaos and the demonic. In light of this, it is surely no coincidence that Mark uses precisely the same verbs in 4:39 as he does in 1:25:

• With reference to the storm: He rebuked (*epitamaō*) the wind and said to the sea, "Be muzzled" (*phimoō*).

• With reference to the demon in the Capernaum synagogue: He rebuked it (*epitamaō*) saying, "Be muzzled" (*phimoō*).

"Who is this man, that in him even the primeval forces of demonic chaos find their master?" (Achtemeier, 1962:176) *[Three Lessons from a Boat]* (on the sea and the demonic, see TBC, below).

Jesus Saves a Gerasene Demoniac 5:1-20

5:1-5 Setting the Scene

The storm is over. The question is still in the air, "Who is this?" The boat comes ashore on the east side of the Sea of Galilee, in the area of the Decapolis, a federation of ten cities east of Galilee and Samaria. The scene is near the lake, a cemetery, a hillside where swine were feeding, and the town. Scholars ancient and modern have puzzled over which town: Gerasa? Gergesa? Gadara? (NRSV notes; NRSV's *Gerasa* is 33 miles SW of the lake; Gadara is 6 miles SW of a steep shore; Gergesa is on the eastern shore).

It is not certain whether the demonized man is Jew or Gentile, though clearly Gentiles constitute the vast majority in the Decapolis, where Greek culture is dominant. The presence of a herd of swine indicates the Gentile character of the region.

The demonized man is described in detail. His pathetic condition is emphasized by—

• his *habitat. The tombs* are proverbially the haunt of demons and were for Jews permanently unclean (5:3).
• his *diagnosis.* He has an *unclean spirit* (v. 2); we later learn he has thousands of them (v. 9).
• his *uncontrollability. The shackles and chains* testify to the danger he poses (v. 4).
• his *massive strength.* When he tears the chains, he is not escaping his tormenters; instead, his tormenters are proving stronger than his restrainers (v. 4).
• his *howling.* It conjures up images of a demented animal howling in the night (v. 5).
• his *self-mutilation.* The use of *stones* to bruise and cut perhaps indicates attempted suicide (v. 5).
• his *nakedness.* We learn of this later through the amazement of those who see him *clothed* (v. 15).

5:6-10 The Demoniac and the Legion of Demons

Much in this text is unclear. When is the demon/*unclean spirit* acting and speaking, and when is the man? What do the actions and words mean? Do the demons make the man run to Jesus (5:2, 6)? Is that foray to dissuade Jesus from acting against the demons? Is the bowing a recognition of Jesus' greater power, or a begging for mercy, or both? Do the demons shout out Jesus' identity to gain power over him? Are they trying to distance themselves from Jesus by asking, *What have you to do with me?* (cf. 1:24). What are we to make of the *demons* invoking *God's* protection against the overpowering presence of Jesus (5:7)?

Is the unclean spirit's self-identification as *Legion* (5:9) an attempt to avoid giving out real names and losing an advantage? Or since a legion is a big force of 3,000 to 6,000 soldiers, is it an attempt by the demons to overstate their own power? Does *he, it,* or *they* (the Greek can be translated all three ways!) beg Jesus to let the demons stay in the area (v. 10)? Why is Jesus' earlier command to the demons not effective (v. 8)? Why does he not silence them as he usually does?

In all the pathos and confusion of the situation, it also is hard not to laugh. Invoking God against Jesus? All this terror at the presence of Jesus? It seems a little overdone, no doubt because we understand too little of the demons' fear of Jesus, their desire to keep their prey, their abhorrence at disembodiment, and their beliefs about name-calling and name-hiding.

5:11-13 The Demons and the Swine

The story takes a surprising turn. Jesus agrees to the demons' request to remain in the area, allowing them to inhabit a herd of swine. Yet as soon as they enter the pigs, the herd rushes headlong down the slope and is drowned in the sea. We remember from the previous incident that the sea is associated with chaos and the demonic (4:40-41, notes; TBC, below). The demons have been sent where they belong.

When Mark's Gospel was publicly read in the Christian gathering, at this point there would surely be some snickers or Alleluias, if not boisterous laughter:

> Unclean spirits, unclean animals, all destroyed in one headlong rush! Serves them right. Jesus sure got the best of those demons. And they thought they were getting what they wanted! If they died with the pigs, they're finished. If not, they're disembodied after all. Now they'll have to leave the region anyway!

Those who were suffering under Roman military occupation or persecution might have been tempted to add, "If only it were that easy with a real legion!"

We who know the story well probably suppress such reactions, but the story still troubles us. Does Jesus foresee the destruction of the swine? Granted that swine are unclean animals for Jews, does that mean Gentiles should be denied the right to own them? Would the death of the herd not represent a colossal waste, perhaps even severe economic hardship to the owners and their families? The narrative shifts its focus onto these people.

5:14-17 The Swineherds and Their Countryfolk

Those tending the herd of swine run off (in terror?) and report what has happened. Their report generates a stampede in the opposite direction. People cannot believe what they have heard and come to check it out. They see the evidence for themselves and are given further explanation from the swineherds who have returned.

Mark has reported the destruction of the demons and the pigs. But only now, from the perspective of the gathered crowds, does he report the healing of the demonized man. Indeed, their disbelief is reflected even in the grammar of the report. They see the *demonized* (present tense) *man*, but what is this? He is sitting, he has clothed himself, and he is in his right mind. The narrator identifies the man again, switching the present tense to a past tense construction: the one who *previously* had the legion of demons.

The local people respond in fear (v. 15). Is it terror in reaction to a display of strange power? Is it an appropriate fear (a reverent awe) in the presence of a power so great? Likely not: they beg Jesus to leave their region. Do they really prefer to cope with demons than with a power great enough to expel them? Or do they just value their pigs more than the life that was saved when the pigs were lost? The narrative leaves these questions open. The man sits there calmly. The crowd is in a panic. He has experienced the Lord's *mercy* (v. 19); they are calculating their losses and risks.

5:18-20 The Healed Man and Jesus

Jesus leaves; he does not stay where he is not welcome. The healed man wants to be *with him* (met' autou, the expression used in 3:14 to define discipleship). Instead, Jesus sends him away to proclaim (kērussō; cf. 3:14) the good news of his healing.

Usually Jesus counsels silence after a mighty miracle. Here the healed man is commissioned to spread the word. The people already know the details of the story (the manner of the healing, the consequences). What they need to hear is that this is the Lord's mercy. Jesus commissions the man to tell what the *Lord* has done (v. 19); he obeys by proclaiming what *Jesus* has done (v. 20). As readers ponder the shift from *Lord* to *Jesus*, they are drawn back to the question posed in the previous incident, *Who is this?* (4:41).

The man's mission field is his own home. His audience is his friends (NRSV) and family (NIV). Swartley sees a strong emphasis on the Gentile mission in Mark's Gospel: "The healed Gerasene demoniac must 'go home,' but only because his home is already where the mission is, among the Gentiles" (1981:197). His mission work is not without effect, as shown in the final words of the narrative: *Everyone was amazed* (v. 20).

Why was such a story remembered and passed on? Surely not just for its entertainment value. Perhaps it was preserved because it so vividly portrays the destructive power of the enemy and the even greater healing power of Jesus. A man is naked, howling, uncontrollable, self-mutilating, unclean, and demonized. Then Jesus comes along, and soon the man is sitting, *clothed and in his right mind* (v. 15). He was bound, shackled, and ostracized by his society; now he is at home, proclaiming the Lord's mercy.

We may still be wondering whether the pigs needed to be lost for this to happen. But if we mourn the economic loss more than we rejoice in the man's full salvation, we side with the Gerasenes; Mark's goal is to draw us to side with Jesus, and to speak also to our family and friends of the Lord's great mercy.

Jairus Calls for Jesus 5:21-24a

Jairus and his immediate need are introduced here, but before the end of the story is told, Mark narrates the full healing Jesus brings to a needy woman (5:24b-34). By then, Jairus' need (and his daughter's need) will have become greater and consequently Jesus' ultimate response even more astonishing.

The large welcoming crowd back in Galilee, on the western side of the lake, stands in stark contrast to the rejecting crowd Jesus has just left behind, to the east. The present crowd follows Jesus as he leaves with Jairus and will be a significant factor in the intervening narrative.

Jairus is a synagogue leader (5:22). Jesus' relationship to the synagogue was once close (1:39) but has became increasingly distant (cf. 3:1-6; 3:7, notes). Most religious officials have proved unreceptive to Jesus. Here is one who is willing to humble himself before Jesus, even in the presence of the crowd. He bows down and pleads with Jesus. We recall that in the previous incident, the demons did the same (5:6, 10). Both times there is recognition of Jesus' great power. There it is a response of terror, an attempt to ward off Jesus' power (5:7-12). Here it is an act of faith, a request to experience Jesus' power.

Jairus asks Jesus to come and place his hands upon his dear little daughter (the endearment term is used). The purpose is (literally) *that she may be saved (sōzō) and live* (TJG). His request is for more than he himself realizes (5:34, notes). Jesus follows him and so does the crowd, including a woman who should not have been there.

Jesus Saves an Unclean Woman 5:24b-34

5:24b-26 An Unclean Woman in the Crowd

In the crowd is a very needy woman. The narrator tells us that she has had continuous (presumably vaginal) bleeding for twelve years. The loss of blood makes her highly anemic. But her problems are much greater than that. She has suffered many indignities at the hands of doctors who know no effective remedy (for a list of some bizarre attempted cures, see Lane: 192, n. 46; cf. G. Geddert: 109-113, whose study of this text supplies many of the following ideas).

Mark is rather blunt about the incompetence of the doctors and the futility of their methods (cf. Luke 8:43; written by a doctor?). His goal is not to discount the medical profession of the day, but to magnify the greater healing resources of Jesus. Treatments by doctors have been counterproductive, have not led to healing, have made things worse, and have used up all her financial resources.

The text only alludes to her most serious problem: she is unclean (cf. Lev. 15:25-27). She is untouchable, forbidden normal human contact (especially sexual contact), and excluded from religious services and ceremonies. If she has ever been married, she is almost certainly now divorced.

5:27-29 The Physical Healing of the Woman

This woman, desperate for health and restoration to normal life, has heard about Jesus. If she has heard reports such as we find in 3:10, she may well have believed that her only chance for healing is to push through the crowd and touch Jesus. Thus, fearful of the crowd and yet secretly pressing through to Jesus, she sneaks up from behind; she surreptitiously touches his cloak and immediately knows that she is healed. Presumably some physical sensation indicates that her bleeding has stopped. Literally translated, the healing is reported this way:

And immediately the flow of her blood dried up, and she knew with respect to her body (or in her body) that she was healed from the illness.

Everything in this verse points to *physical* healing. Her presenting problem is taken care of, but all her other problems (those that may have contributed to the flow of blood and those that resulted from it) are left out of the picture. Her loneliness, her social rejection, the inner damage resulting from twelve years of shame and humiliation—these have not yet been addressed. These will be dealt with later.

5:30-32 Jesus and the Crowd

The narrative perspective changes. The narrator has told of the woman's experience: her prior suffering, her knowledge of Jesus, her inner thoughts, her secret and daring foray into the crowd, and her equally daring touch of Jesus. Tradition and purity laws barred women, especially "unclean" women, from doing that. We have read about her experience of physical healing. Now the focus shifts to Jesus' experience.

Jesus is aware that healing power has flowed *out of* him (just as the woman knows that it flowed *into* her). Perhaps he has felt something; perhaps it was an inner knowledge similar to what Mark has reported on other occasions (2:8; 3:5; 12:15; and so on). If the latter, then Jesus' next question is probably to be taken not as lack of knowledge on his part, but as an attempt to draw out the woman.

Who touched my clothes? Jesus asks (v. 30), in a crowd where everyone is crowding against him. In verse 32, Jesus follows up the question with a searching glance, presumably waiting for the woman to come forward. But Mark's narrator first reports the disciples' inappropriate interruption. This is now the third time in Mark's Gospel that the disciples have spoken a word directly to Jesus. All three times they chide him (1:37; 4:38, notes). Mark does not want the reader to identify too closely with the disciples. Discipleship is not learned by following their examples; it is learned from Jesus. Ignoring the disciples' interruption, Jesus casts his searching glance around himself until the woman who has touched him steps forward.

5:33-34 The Full Healing and Salvation of the Woman

She comes trembling with fear. Is it awe and wonder at the divine power she has experienced? Is it fear lest Jesus not approve of what she has done, a woman in a public place, touching him, drawing on his power from God? Or is it the terror of possible exposure? What if the whole crowd learns that she, an unclean woman, has jostled many of them on her way to Jesus and has made him unclean by a deliberate touch?

Likely this last possibility explains both her terror and the reason Jesus has brought her to the attention of the crowd. What she has done *needs to be exposed* in the crowd, not because it was wrong, but because it was right. The crowd has not become unclean by her touch; instead, she has become clean by touching Jesus. The crowd needs to know that.

It would be a huge challenge for her to persuade anyone afterward that she managed to sneak into the crowd, experience healing in the presence of Jesus, and sneak back out without being noticed. It would be the ultimate indignity to continue to be shunned and excluded as unclean, even after being healed and cleansed. This woman's humiliation has been public knowledge; her healing must be public knowledge as well. Her public confession in the crowd and a pronouncement of full healing by Jesus facilitates a healing far beyond the physical problem. It has a social and spiritual dimension as well.

Thus, Mark reports her healing again, but with a difference. Verse 29 reports a physical healing; verse 34 reports restoration and salvation. Each word and phrase contributes to its impact:

Daughter! The word could sound paternalistic in a patriarchal society. But coming from Jesus in this context, it is a term of endearment, acceptance, relationship. Imagine the impact on one who has been shunned, excluded, and cut off from relationships.

Your faith has made you well. The crowd and the disciples (not to mention Jairus, who has been waiting for Jesus to have time for his request) see here a model of courageous faith. Perhaps the woman needs to be clear that it was her *faith* that made the difference, not the physical contact with the garment, certainly not any magical properties in it. Faith was the conduit through which Jesus' power could flow to her need.

Her faith resulted in her full salvation. The word for *made you well* is not the word used for physical healing in verse 29. It is *sōzō* (*to save*), a word much fuller and richer than any one English equivalent can capture. It can speak of healing, rescuing, preserving, forgiving, delivering, making whole. *Your faith has made you well* speaks to her past; *Go in peace* speaks to her future. Literally, the text says, *Go **into** peace*. Peace in the NT often carries with it the full meaning of the underlying Hebrew *shalom*. Jesus dismisses the woman into a new life, a life of well-being, right relationships, and peace with God. *Go into peace* signals the beginning of a journey out of hopelessness into wholeness.

Why would the early church have remembered and retold this story? Why would Mark have recorded it? I suggest several reasons:

1. *It provides a model of faith and courage.* The woman takes great risks; she throws her whole destiny on Jesus; she trusts him to

rescue her from her past and renew her future.

2. *It depicts the breadth of the salvation and wholeness Jesus provides.* The vocabulary of healing, saving, acceptance, and peace is rich enough to deal with the wide range of problems she has brought along with her into Jesus' presence.

3. *It portrays Jesus as one who freely crosses the restrictive boundaries of religious scruples and ceremonial restrictions.* The previous narrative featured unclean spirits (Legion), an unclean place (the graveyard), unclean animals (pigs) in an unclean land (Decapolis). Jesus was not at all reluctant to minister there. Nor will he hesitate to touch an unclean corpse when he arrives at Jairus' house. Here Jesus affirms the faith of an "unclean" woman who expresses her faith by touching him.

4. *It preserves a picture of a woman who, like Jesus, has not let ceremonial restrictions prevent her from breaking through boundaries.* Along with other NT writers, Mark highlights those women who break through barriers caused by oppressive purity regulations and unfair restrictions based on gender. The Markan community found in this text encouragement for the gender equality they were (or should have been) practicing.

5. Finally, *it strengthens faith in Jesus' healing power,* something rather important for Jairus within the narrative and for readers who have been wondering since 5:24 what will happen to his daughter.

Jesus Triumphs Over Death 5:35-43

5:35-36 The Need for Renewed Faith

While a woman's twelve years of suffering is brought to an end through healing, a twelve-year-old girl's suffering ends in death. At home the family assumes this is the end. They hire mourners and send word to Jairus. Messengers deliver the news of the girl's death and call off the request for Jesus' healing touch; it's too late.

Jesus, however, does not accept the finality of the girl's death. Is Jesus *overhearing* (NRSV) or *ignoring* (NRSV note) the message? The word used can mean both, and Mark might well have intended both. Jesus hears the words but refuses to accept them. He calls on Jairus to renew the faith he has already expressed: *Do not fear,* **keep on** *believing* (v. 36, literally).

5:37-40 Witnesses of the Resurrection

Peter, James, and John (cf. 9:2; 14:33) are permitted to accompany Jesus. The crowd and most of the disciples are left behind; Jesus now has to deal with the mourners. He dismisses them, claiming the child is not truly dead, only asleep (5:40). Their (professional) mourning quickly shifts to (unprofessional) laughing. Who does Jesus think he is? Would the family have hired them if the child had not died? What does Jesus know about the girl's condition? He has not even entered the child's room!

Jesus' comment has occasioned considerable discussion among commentators. If the child's family has pronounced her dead and Jesus pronounces her only asleep, whom are we as readers to trust? Mark's narrator does not explicitly confirm that the girl is dead (cf. Matt. 9:18; Luke 8:53), yet his text strongly suggests that this is a resurrection, not merely a healing. For example, Jesus does not contradict the initial report of the girl's death, but instead calls for renewed (even greater?) faith; Jesus limits the number of observers; he restricts news of the event; Mark reports extreme amazement after Jesus raises the girl; and so on.

The mourners are correct: she is dead. Jesus is also correct: she is but asleep. He will wake her with words this girl might have heard her mother speak almost every morning. Leaving the mourners out of a job, Jesus now enters the room with the girl's immediate family and his three closest disciples (cf. 9:2; 14:33).

5:41-42a Jesus Raises the Girl

The Aramaic words Jesus uses as he raises the girl are *Talitha cum*. If Mark had only transliterated the words, his Greek-speaking readers would have imagined some foreign magical formula was being invoked. Mark's translation of the words cancels this impression. The girl is being awakened from her sleep: *Little girl, get up!* The narrator reports an immediate and complete restoration to life. Lest the reader be surprised that she can walk, the narrator clarifies that she is not an infant; she is already twelve.

5:42b-43 Responses and Restrictions

The command to feed the girl expresses care for someone who would by now be hungry. Her eating might well also function as proof that she really is there in flesh and blood, fully alive (cf. Luke 24:41-43).

The command to silence allows the facts to speak for themselves. Those with eyes to see and ears to hear find further evidence that God's reign is advancing. Those *outside* (4:11-12) are allowed to go on disbelieving; they can conclude, if they insist, that she was truly only asleep. The command to silence may also give Jesus a chance to move on before being mobbed with people more curious than ready to follow him. Mark does not report whether the command to keep quiet about the miracle is obeyed. It is hard to imagine that the event could be kept secret very long.

Why did Mark weave together the story of the healed woman and the story of Jairus' daughter? Is that simply the way it happened and/or the way the tradition was preserved (cf. Matt. 9:18-26; Luke 8:41-56)? Perhaps; but even if it were so, Mark could easily have told only one story or told both but in different contexts.

Presenting them together is, at least, good storytelling. As a dramatic device, it gives time for the situation at Jairus' house to deteriorate. For the reader, it raises suspense as a girl at the point of death is ignored for a time. It increases our estimation of both the woman's faith and Jesus' compassion: they did not converse during a rest period, she sought him out while he was on an important mission, and he interrupted it to minister to her. It portrays Jesus' commitment to ministry on the run, as he meets pressing needs without losing sight of the larger picture. It increases our sympathy for Jairus, who anxiously awaits Jesus' attention to *his* need.

Putting the two stories together also draws attention to similarities between the two narratives. Some similarities are incidental: both are about females, feature the number twelve, and contain foolish comments by the bystanders. Other similarities are important: both highlight faith and the salvation/life that can flow from it. This last theme remains in focus as Jesus leaves for his hometown and we find out what happens when faith is absent (6:1-6a).

The Purpose of This Miracle Section

Mark's Gospel does not usually highlight the apologetic value of miracles: they are not designed primarily to persuade people to believe. Instead, they are reported to demonstrate how fully Jesus can meet human need. They are designed to provoke reactions that lead to reflection, insight, and convictions about the arrival of God's reign. They also reveal the true nature and identity of Jesus. As we summarize this miracle section, we pose questions reflecting these priorities:

• *What needs do these miracles meet?* The need for safety at sea (4:35-41), deliverance from demons, subsequent restoration to sanity and society, discipleship and mission (5:1-20), healing from an ailment and subsequent acceptance, reintegration into society, personal wholeness and salvation (5:24b-34), and restoration of physical life (5:21-

24a, 35-43). Jesus' miracles touch on every aspect of existence.

• *What reactions do the miracles provoke?* Fear in the case of the disciples who experience the storm-stilling; fear and rejection in the case of the residents of Gerasa who receive back a demonized man and lose 2,000 pigs; devoted following and obedience on the part of the restored man; no reaction on the part of the crowd that experiences the healing of the woman; fear on the part of the healed woman until Jesus restores her status in society and pronounces her both restored and saved; exceedingly great astonishment on the part of those who experience the raising of Jairus' daughter.

• *How do these events serve as signs of the reign of God?* The storm-stilling builds on the theme of the parables, that the kingdom will prove invincible, no matter what setbacks occur; the healing of the demoniac and of the woman point to the ultimate *shalom* and salvation that divine intervention makes possible; the resurrection of Jairus' daughter is a sign that God's reign will finally conquer even death itself.

• *What do these events say about Jesus?* The first and last episodes in this section reveal his mastery, first over wind and sea, then over death. The middle episodes reveal him as compassionate and powerful, willing and able to restore complete wholeness, even if he must cross boundaries of uncleanness to do so.

Literally translated, the first episode of this section is about a *great storm* that gives way to a *great calm* and leads to the disciples' reaction: *They feared with a great fear* (4:41). Using the same redundant style and the same adjective, Mark reports the reaction to the final miracle: *They were amazed with a great amazement* (5:42). This entire section puts a question mark over both responses. Jesus does not do great works of power to produce fear or amazement. He does so to point to his identity and to the nature of God's reign for those with eyes to see and ears to hear *[Miracles in Mark]*.

THE TEXT IN BIBLICAL CONTEXT
The Sea and the Demonic
Both the OT and the NT reveal that in the ancient world the sea was considered a place of terror, the unknown, insecurity and disaster, evil beasts and demonic powers.

OT writers often picture God slaying the monster of the deep waters to create a place of security. For example, the psalmist speaks of God's salvation in the following terms (Ps. 74:13-14a):

You divided the sea by your might;
   you broke the heads of the dragons in the waters.
You crushed the heads of Leviathan.

Similarly, Isaiah combines creation and redemption motifs in this appeal for God to act once more in restoring the covenant people (51:9-10):

Awake, awake, put on strength, O arm of the LORD!
Awake, as in days of old, the generations of long ago!
Was it not you who cut Rahab in pieces, who pierced the dragon?
Was it not you who dried up the sea, the waters of the great deep;
Who made the depths of the sea a way for the redeemed to cross over?

Both of these texts borrow the language of Near Eastern mythology, where there was no security unless the monsters of the deep were slain first. Storms at sea were especially associated with terror and evil. Psalm 107 (quoted in notes to 4:35-41) speaks of sailors' "courage melting away in their calamity" (v. 26). In John's vision of the new heaven, he saw "no more sea" (Rev. 21:1). This was a comforting scenario for a man exiled on an island and for one who had seen visions of an evil beast rising out of the sea (13:1). Some day the raging sea and all the chaos and evil it stands for, will "be no more," or will be replaced by a "sea of glass, like crystal" (4:6). When Jesus calms a storm on the Sea of Galilee, he is foreshadowing God's victory over all God's enemies.

During the second and third centuries, the persecuted church in Rome drew on the catacomb walls a boat on a storm-tossed sea. They were symbolizing the beleaguered church, reminding themselves that the raging tempest would not last forever.

Resurrections

Mark's Gospel features three resurrections:

1. The raising of Jairus' daughter (5:35-43)
2. The resurrection of Jesus (16:1-8)
3. The general resurrection from death (12:18-27)

The raising of Jairus' daughter foreshadows Jesus' own resurrection, though it is clear to Mark and his readers that Jesus' resurrection is of a different order. Jairus' daughter is merely resuscitated to continued mortal living (and is expected to die again). The resurrection of Jairus' daughter also foreshadows the general resurrection, though again the two events are of a different order. This foreshadowing function is indicated by Jesus' comment that *the child is not dead but asleep* (5:39). She had actually died, but Jesus' own view is that when God's resurrection power is at work, death is no more terminal than is natural sleep.

Consistent with this viewpoint and with the language, the early church regularly referred to the death of believers as "falling asleep," rather than as "dying" (Acts 7:60; 1 Thess. 4:13-15; 1 Cor. 11:30; 15:6, 18, 20, 51). On the only occasion when a believer is explicitly said to have "died" (Acts 9:37), she is raised back to life (9:40). Dorcas was, after all, only "asleep."

Paul never refers to occasions where Jesus resurrected/resuscitated people who had died. For him, the resurrection of Jesus becomes the central event in salvation history. It is the crowning evidence that Jesus is the Son of God (Rom. 1:4); it demonstrates and makes effective the salvation accomplished through the cross (Rom. 6:8-11); and it is the guarantee of the final resurrection yet to come (1 Cor. 15:20-23). Indeed, for Paul, Christ's resurrection does not only foreshadow and guarantee the future resurrection; it is also the first part of it. He calls it the first fruits (*aparchē*) of those who have "fallen asleep" (1 Cor. 15:20). If part of the harvest has already been gathered, God someday will bring in the full harvest. As someone said, "One of us has already made it!"

Paul's "resurrection chapter" (1 Cor. 15) draws out a whole set of implications and applications of the fact that Jesus was raised. This chapter is not (as some have thought) aimed primarily at proving that Jesus was raised, even though it opens by recounting a series of resurrection appearances (15:5-7; for Paul, these count as irrefutable evidence that Jesus really was raised). The chapter is primarily about what we can experience and know, *because* we know that Jesus was raised. These include the following:

• We have a solid basis for faith and proclamation (15:14-17).
• We have assurance of forgiven sin and victory over sin (vv. 18, 56-57).
• We have certainty that we will also be raised and will inherit God's kingdom (vv. 18-22, 26, 50).
• We have the necessary motivation for sacrificial living (vv. 19, 30-32).
• We have assurance that our service for God is not in vain (v. 58).

Miracles

Mark's Gospel reports many miracles (about 16), yet scholars are divided as to whether Mark is encouraging his readers to value and to expect miraculous interventions, or warning them against an excessive fascination with them (see esp. Dowd: 163-5). The position taken in this commentary is that he does some of both (see esp. 6:45-52, notes; essays) [Three Lessons from a Boat; Miracles in Mark].

Both concerns are well represented in Scripture. Sometimes God's people are chided for overlooking, not expecting, or even forgetting divine interventions (e.g., Ps. 78:11-16; 106:13); sometimes for overdependence on them (Matt. 12:38-39; 1 Cor. 1:22). A close look at miracles in Scripture reveals that they are not at all evenly distributed.

The Hebrew prophets and the apostle Paul are virtually silent on the topic, apart from prophecies of future judgment and salvation. Apart from Daniel and Jonah, miracle reports are virtually absent from Job through Malachi and from Romans through 3 John! Yet in the parts of Scripture where miracle reports are given, they often play a significant role in revealing the character and purposes of God, and in particular God's faithfulness and acts of deliverance and healing.

In Mark miracles (or signs and wonders) do not effectively counteract unbelief. Faith and insight come, not because the evidence is so compelling, but because there is an openness to the presence of God and a submission to God's ways. To demand signs, to ask for unmistakable proofs, to impose conditions on our response to God—these are not expressions of faith. Piling miracle upon miracle can have no life-changing effect on those who do not want to believe. Nor can miracles lead to understanding for those who eat the bread and count the baskets but have no eyes to see the meaning (8:14-21). Insight comes for those whose eyes are opened to see the handiwork of God. That is Mark's view.

Mark's view is not emphasized as strongly by all biblical writers, though it does find echoes in many places. The Bible contains other emphases as well. Luke, for example, seems to take a much more optimistic stance on the effectiveness of miracles to persuade the unconvinced (e.g., Acts 4:16; 5:12-14; 8:6; 14:3). Mark is very cautious on this point.

There are times to quote Mark and there are times to quote Luke. Christians who have lost confidence that God is at work in the world, who are somewhat embarrassed by the *miracle talk* in the Bible—such believers should spend more time reading Luke and watching for God's mighty works. Christians who crave signs and wonders, who are sure that proofs will overcome unbelief, and whose own faith shrivels without a continual supply of evidence—such believers should take a careful look at the message of Mark's Gospel. Ultimately,

Mark's and Luke's viewpoints both belong to a biblical perspective. Ignoring half the picture distorts that biblical perspective.

Some commentators do not use the word "miracles," instead preferring "portentous actions," "marvels," or "acts of power." In this commentary, I sometimes use the term "miracle," since it is so commonly used, but it is a slippery word. While most Christians believe in the reality of miracles, most would also have a difficult time defining a miracle or clarifying its function within Christian theology, apologetics, and experience. Four main biblical terms reveal different facets of the events we call miracles:

Dunamis, "power" or "work of power," focuses on the source of the energy producing events that we would not expect from nature/creation left on its own. Since the Bible recognizes other powers besides God, its use of this word for miracles puts emphasis on the divine *origin* of the events themselves.

Ergon, "work," focuses on the divine *goal* in God's exercise of miraculous power. Those who work miracles on God's behalf are not merely displaying power; they are fulfilling God's purposes in the world and in individual lives.

Sēmeion, "sign," focuses on the *meaning* of a supernatural event. Miracles do not merely display power or bring about desired changes; they are signs that point beyond themselves to God's nature, to the authority of God's representatives, to the meaning of God's work in the world, and to the nature of God's reign and salvation.

Teras, "wonder," focuses on the astonishment caused in humans when they observe or are the beneficiaries of a divine intervention. In Scripture, miracles are intended to evoke more than wonder; they are to lead to insight, belief, gratitude, humility, and so on.

These biblical terms testify to the depth and the breadth of the biblical concept of miracle, in turn challenging believers to be open to the broad range of ways in which God acts in our experience, whether God's acts are called miracles or not (see below).

THE TEXT IN THE LIFE OF THE CHURCH

Miracles and the Christian Church

Biblical terms for the miraculous cover a wide range of events that are viewed as acts of divine intervention ("Miracles," above). The biblical concept in its depth and breadth has not always been preserved as theologians have tried to define miracles and analyze their relationship to "nature" or their contribution to Christian apologetics (rational defenses of the faith).

Augustine was convinced that God never contradicts the normal course of nature. Events *appear* miraculous, because we do not know exactly how nature works. For Calvin, miracles were sacramental signs; for Luther they were God's masks and garments (they indirectly revealed God); for C. S. Lewis, they were "interferences with nature by supernatural power" (1996:12).

Colin Brown has shown that throughout church history miracles have shifted from a *foundation* for faith, to a *crutch*, and finally to a *cross* that Christians must bear. For the early apostles, miracles were foundational; the apostles appealed often to God's miraculous interventions. However, their motivation for doing so was not merely apologetic—as though they could prove a doctrine by appeal to the miraculous. In fact, where people readily accept the reality of "miraculous" events and where they believe that many people can produce them (as in the first century), "miracles" as raw acts of power would not be of much apologetic value, anyway.

In the first century, the power behind miracles could be attributed to any one of a number of sources (divine, demonic, magical). The events themselves certainly would not be taken as evidence of divinity. P. J. Achtemeier points out, "Whatever miracles as such would prove about Jesus, they would also prove about a number of his contemporaries" (1962:169). When early Christian preachers recounted Jesus' miracles, these were used to illustrate the nature and the purposes of God, and to show that God's purposes were being fulfilled. In that sense, miracles were part of the foundation of faith.

Over time, miracles became less foundational and more of a crutch for faith. They lost their focus on the object of belief and became (mere) supporting evidences for the doctrines of the faith. Speaking of Jesus, Calvin (echoing Gregory of Nyssa) said, "How plainly and clearly is his deity shown in miracles" (Brown: 5-6). The *meaning* of miracles was being lost as they were treated only as part of a *proof*. Sometimes the use of miracle as "supporting evidence" deteriorated even further; miracles were treated as allegories, with details illustrating specific doctrines and thus demonstrating their truth.

Much later, in the rationalistic modern age, Christians struggled to maintain belief in miracles in the face of cogent arguments by their critics. Empiricists, rationalists, and deists all considered belief in the miraculous to be impossible, unintelligible, incredible, or incompatible with belief in a truly transcendent God. Where belief in miracles is unpopular (or considered naive), theologians have sometimes been tempted to sacrifice belief in miracles to make Christianity palatable to naturalists in a modern scientific world. From aids to faith, miracles had become barriers to faith! No longer was faith bolstered by miraculous events; instead, Christians needed to take a leap of faith to continue believing in miracles. Belief in miracles had become a cross for Christians to bear.

Many Christians maintain a belief in miracles today for one reason only: The Bible is to be trusted (even) when it reports that miracles happened. That is fine, but one can hardly believe in miracles because of biblical inspiration, and in biblical inspiration because of miracles. One of these two must come first, as Colin Brown points out:

> What we cannot do is to appeal to the miracle stories as compelling, objective evidence for the divine inspiration of Scripture, and at the same time to appeal to the inspiration of Scripture as the ground of our claim for the historicity of the miracle stories. (103)

Some theological traditions minimize the significance of miracles (even in Scripture), perhaps finding inspirational value in some of the miracle reports, perhaps "demythologizing" them to find an underlying "truth" beyond the factual claims, but otherwise not knowing what to do with them. Some traditions argue on (shaky!) theological grounds that miracles were indeed real in biblical times, but that they are no longer occurring. They were designed to facilitate the founding of the Christian faith and should not be expected today.

A better approach is to understand "miracles" as broadly as Scripture does. We should not pit miraculous events against "nature," as though God does not fulfill divine purposes through "natural" processes. Nor should we claim the ability to analyze a miracle in a test tube. Unusual events, especially if they point to the nature of God's reign, should be viewed as divine *works*, as evidences of God's *power*, as *signs* of God's presence in the world, and as occasions for *wonder* that leads us on to worship, to faith, and to obedience.

Two readable attempts to understand and defend the reality of biblical miracles are *That You May Believe* (Brown) and *Miracles and the Modern Mind* (Geisler). I also recommend *Miracles,* a classic Christian treatment of the topic by C. S. Lewis.

I have four personal reasons for accepting that God did and still does miraculously intervene in the "normal course of nature":

• *Theological grounds.* I believe that the whole fabric of Christian faith, especially the incarnation and resurrection of Jesus, depend on acceptance of such interventions.
• *Historical grounds.* I believe that the historical evidence for at

least some miraculous interventions in the past is sufficient to persuade all but those who rule out the possibility of miracles in principle.

- *Personal grounds.* I believe that I have (occasionally) experienced such events and/or witnessed them around me.
- *Rational grounds.* I believe that "nature" is not a closed system. It normally operates according to predictable "laws," where effects are determined by prior causes; yet this natural sequence can be influenced by acts of the will (and therefore also by God). If this were not so, then we would have to exclude not only *divine* intervention but also *human* intervention (acts of free will). Our only "defense against miracles" (as C. S. Lewis calls it) is to suppose without argument that there are no free wills (and therefore no God) that can act upon the natural order.

Today many Christians overemphasize miracles in their ministry to sick and hurting people, in their expectations of charismatic phenomena during worship, or in their concept of evangelism. That is no reason why the rest of us should underemphasize them. According to Scripture, miracles play a significant role in Christian faith. They can do the same today if we aim to grasp their significance along biblical lines (T. Geddert, 1986; Kydd).

Mark 6:1-29

The Rejected Prophets

PREVIEW

The previous section (4:35—5:43) stressed miracles. It revealed Jesus' power to rescue at sea, cast out demons, heal the sick, and raise the dead. The section features a mixture of negative responses to Jesus (the Gerasenes, the disciples, the mourners) and positive responses to Jesus (the demonized man, Jairus, the woman).

The present section (6:1-29) features *lack* of faith more than faith, rejection more than acceptance. If the Gerasenes, who do not know Jesus and have just lost 2,000 pigs, do not welcome Jesus, that is one thing. Here Jesus is rejected by his own native village. He calls himself the rejected *prophet*. As he sends the Twelve out on mission, he instructs them on how they should react when *they* are rejected. Then comes a detailed account of the macabre death of another prophet, Jesus' forerunner, John the Baptist. This section seems not to be about Jesus, yet it functions as a foreshadowing of the terrible unjust death that Jesus himself will face.

Yet not everything is dark. If there is a foreshadowing of Jesus' death here, there is also a foreshadowing of his resurrection. If two prophets face rejection, there are twelve apostles carrying out an effective ministry. Here again is evidence of a carefully structured text. The mission trip forms a centerpiece, surrounded by the reports of the rejected prophets [Chiasm and Intercalation].

Interpreters regularly comment on the "ominous cloud" that hangs over the disciples' mission. What can they expect if those who preceded them are rejected thus? One frequently hears comments about "suffering in the midst of ministry" and "suffering that results from ministry." Yet seldom does one hear the reverse emphasized. There is also ministry in the midst of suffering and ministry that results from suffering. Mark's Gospel juxtaposes ministry and suffering in many contexts (1:14; 13:9-11). Mark calls on those who are given *the secret of the kingdom* (4:11) to recognize that even in passion and death, there is the hope of resurrection and the assurance of final victory. The mission of the kingdom cannot be stopped by Nazareth's lack of faith or Herod's foolish oath.

OUTLINE

The Rejection of Jesus at Nazareth, 6:1-6a
6:1-3	Nazareth's Reaction to Jesus
6:4-6a	Jesus' Reaction to Nazareth

Expanded Mission of Jesus and the Twelve, 6:6b-13
6:6b	Jesus' Ministry in the Surrounding Region
6:7-11	Jesus Sends Out the Twelve
6:12-13	The Disciples' Mission

The Passion of John the Baptist, 6:14-29
6:14-16	Herod's Reaction to Jesus and John
6:17-20	Herod's and Herodias' Reactions to John
6:21-23	A Party, a Dance, and a Foolish Oath
6:24-29	The Beheading and Burial of John

EXPLANATORY NOTES

The Rejection of Jesus at Nazareth 6:1-6a

6:1-3 Nazareth's Reaction to Jesus

Jesus enters the synagogue in Nazareth (cf. 1:9). It is his first and final entry into one since he was rejected in a synagogue by the religious leaders (3:1-6). This time his fellow townspeople do the rejecting.

Their response to Jesus sounds positive enough at first. *Many* (the word can mean *all*) are *astounded*, just as the synagogue crowd in Capernaum was (1:27). There, however, astonishment was accompanied by an affirmation of Jesus, and people came out in large numbers to experience Jesus' healing power (1:27, 32). Here amazement gives way to disdain. People speculate about the source of Jesus' wisdom and power, but in the end they reject the prophet because they know him, or think they do. We are not told that they attribute his supernatural powers to demonic connections (cf. 3:22), but we are left wondering what other alternatives they have considered. They know he is (only) a *carpenter*. Who does he think he is? They know his family. In fact, he is known in Nazareth as *Mary's son* (NIV; an unusual link to the mother's name instead of the father's). Mark's first readers might have heard echoes here of Jesus' virgin birth (if they knew the traditions Matthew and Luke incorporate). But Mark is surely not attributing such an intention to those rejecting Jesus in Nazareth. Far more likely, they are obliquely reflecting rumors that his birth was illegitimate.

Earlier Jesus' own family reflected misunderstanding and lack of support for his ministry (3:21, 31-35). Now his village is scandalized (*skandalizō*) by him. This word, when used in the passive voice (as here), does not imply that Jesus causes their stumbling (as some commentators suggest). As a passive, it means they themselves are rejecting, deserting, or having doubts about him. Those rejecting Jesus are responsible for their wrong response.

6:4-6a Jesus' Reaction to Nazareth

Mark records three reactions by Jesus. The first is a proverbial saying: *Prophets are not without honor, except in their hometown.* Jesus likely expands it to fit the situation. Its use does not imply that *prophet* is considered an adequate identification of Jesus. The addition on being without honor *among their own kin, and in their own house* likely reflects the rejection by people closest to Jesus, including his family (3:21). Readers see in the text intimations of a broader rejection of Jesus by many of his contemporaries and especially by the religious authorities.

Jesus' second reaction is a minimal healing ministry. The text says he could do *no deed of power*, then states the exception (6:5). A few were done. Lack of faith is the reason why so few were healed. There are two possible ways of understanding this:

1. People doubt that Jesus can heal. Therefore, few come to Jesus, and he has little opportunity to heal.
2. People do not exercise faith in Jesus (though they may still believe he is an effective healer; cf. 6:2). Therefore, Jesus considers a healing ministry inappropriate.

There are two additional but *unlikely* ways of understanding this:

3. The *power* in Jesus (5:30) is somehow diminished through the lack of external faith responses.
4. People come for healing and try to exercise faith, but Jesus,

knowing that the faith is not large enough, refuses to heal. (This last explanation is common as a rationalization for unfulfilled healing requests today, but it is not a biblical concept.)

Jesus' third reaction is amazement. The people are astounded at what he can do (6:2); he is amazed at their inappropriate responses (6:6a). Jesus has likely entered the synagogue in Nazareth hoping that *at least here* the synagogue might still be a fruitful mission field. But that is not to be. Throughout his Gospel, Mark speaks freely of Jesus' emotional responses such as anger, exasperation, anguish, distress, and feelings of abandonment. Here his reaction is surprised disappointment.

Expanded Mission of Jesus and the Twelve 6:6b-13

6:6b Jesus' Ministry in the Surrounding Region

Perhaps verse 6b can be included with the previous episode, counting as a fourth response by Jesus to the lack of faith in Nazareth. He is rejected there, but his ministry is not hindered. He moves out to the smaller villages around Nazareth. Connecting verse 6b to this episode, however, also fits Mark's larger pattern. The sequel to rejection is expanded ministry. We have often seen this in Mark:

• When demonic opposition arises, it is quickly subdued, and Jesus' fame spreads (1:23-28).

• When religious leaders begin to question Jesus, his fame attracts great crowds (2:6-7, 12-13).

• When the Pharisees and Herodians initiate a death plot, Jesus is quickly surrounded by crowds from virtually every region in Palestine (3:6-8).

• When family and foe alike oppose him (3:21-22), Jesus is surrounded first by faithful followers (3:34-35), and then by the largest crowds to date (4:1).

So it is here also: Jesus is rejected in his hometown, and immediately the narrative shifts to the enlarging ministry of Jesus (among the villages; 6:6b) and its multiplication through those he sends out (v. 7).

6:7-11 Jesus Sends Out the Twelve

The mission of the disciples is sandwiched between two stories of rejected prophets. The pattern may hint that mission is bound to lead to rejection. But more clearly it shows that rejection gives way to expanded ministry.

Mark suggests this also by taking the disciples' mission and making it a framework around the story of John's passion. Before John's passion is narrated, we read of the disciples' commissioning, their instructions, and even the results of the ministry. The story is actually over. But after the passion of John is narrated, a sequel is recorded. *The apostles gathered around Jesus, and told him all that they had done and taught* (6:30). By framing John's passion with the disciples' mission, Mark again hints that there is a silver lining around the dark clouds (notes for 1:14 and 6:30).

The disciples are sent out in pairs, perhaps for protection and mutual support, more likely because a valid testimony requires two agreeing witnesses (cf. Deut. 19:15; Matt. 18:16, 20). Jesus has endowed them with authority to drive out demons, but later we learn that they carried out other ministries as well (6:12-13).

The instructions for the journey are given (6:8-10): some normal provisions for a journey are permitted (shoes, staff), some are not (food, a bag [possibly for begging], money, extra clothing). Both Luke and Matthew record more stringent restrictions: no staff or sandals (Luke 9:3; 10:4; Matt. 10:10). In contrast, Mark's text permits (or even requires) both. The staff (which may echo Moses' use of a staff) helps with walking and warding off stray dogs or other animals. The shoes are not absolutely necessary but are more comfortable than walking barefoot, which was also done.

The provisions allowed are clearly minimal, for the missionaries are not to be encumbered with unnecessary luggage; they are to trust God (acting through those who hear them) to meet their needs. Staying in only one home is probably to prevent embarrassment for the host/hostess, if they are inclined to accept another invitation. Alternatively, it might be to discourage them from seeking more luxurious accommodations. The concern is to travel and live simply but not so as to endure hardship (TLC, below).

In 6:11 Jesus instructs them on how to respond to rejection. It is not surprising that they too will face rejection, as hinted by the rejection of the other prophets (Jesus and John). Yet there is no indication that they will suffer persecution (cf. Matt. 10:17-23 in context of 10:5-16). When people do not accept their ministry and message, they are to shake the dust off their feet as they leave the village, a symbol of judgment and exclusion from the people of God (TBC, below).

6:12-13 The Disciples' Mission

The disciples have been recruited (1:16-20) and commissioned

(3:13, 16). Both times it is made clear that they are being called to a mission. Being with Jesus is preparatory to being sent out by Jesus (1:17; 3:14). Here again they are called (6:7a), organized (v. 7b), authorized (v. 7c), and instructed (vv. 8-11).

Their mission is briefly reported. They preach repentance, cast out demons (cf. 3:14b-15), and heal the sick. Their *works* are similar to Jesus' except that they use oil when healing (Jesus is never reported to do that). Yet their *words* are more like John's: they preach repentance and do not announce the kingdom's arrival (cf. 1:4, 14-15, notes). A ministry that resembles John's but foreshadows Jesus' functions well to prepare the way for Jesus to come afterward to these towns (Luke 10:1). The resemblance of the disciples' ministry to both Jesus' and John's is picked up in the next episode (6:14b), where people speculate about the connection between Jesus and John.

The Passion of John the Baptist 6:14-29

This is the only extended narrative in Mark's Gospel not directly about Jesus. In Greek, Jesus' name does not appear between 6:4 and 6:30, though two pronouns in verse 14 almost certainly refer to him. At a deeper level, Mark alludes to Jesus throughout this text; John's passion clearly foreshadows Jesus' death and resurrection. Even the one who has beheaded John believes (or fears) that he has risen from the dead (Senior: 19).

6:14-16 Herod's Reaction to Jesus and John

Mark 1:14 reported how John was *handed over* (TJG). It was the final act by which he prepared the way for Jesus' ministry to begin. Now we discover what that handing over meant: arrest, imprisonment (many translations inappropriately insert these at 1:14), and martyrdom.

Jesus' expanded ministry (6:6b) and that of his representatives (vv. 7-13) have not gone unnoticed by the political authorities. King Herod (technically, only a tetrarch) hears speculation about Jesus' identity. *These powers* at work in Jesus must mean he is some great prophet come back to life (cf. 8:28). Is he Elijah? Some other ancient prophet? Herod agrees with a different opinion; Jesus is John the Baptist, recently executed, now come back to life. Perhaps Herod merely opines, "That's John the Baptist all over again!" More likely, however, his speculation is about a literal resurrection of John: perhaps John has brought great powers with him when returning from the other side of death. The reader, of course, knows that the source of Jesus' power is his status as the Christ, the Son of God (1:1), and the presence of the Holy Spirit in him (1:10).

In stating his own opinion about Jesus, Herod speaks of *John, whom I beheaded.* Thus the door is open for the narrator to take over and report, with all the gory details, how it is that John the Baptist was beheaded in spite of Herod's intention to protect him (6:20). It happened at the hands of an executioner, but behind him stood Herod, Herodias, the daughter who danced, and a crowd of courtiers, officers, and leaders in Galilee (v. 21).

6:17-20 Herod's and Herodias' Reactions to John

This section has been described as a complicated, entangled narrative with backtracking and explanatory comments (cf. Fowler, 1991:93). Yet it is not half as complicated and tangled as the family tree of the Herods. I will let other commentators try to figure out who was married to whom at any given time, which relationships are technically incestuous, and so on. Mark's text makes sense with only a few explanations (though it does not agree exactly with Josephus' report of this event).

In this text, *King* Herod refers to Herod Antipas, tetrarch of Galilee and Perea, who has married Herodias during the lifetime of Herodias' former husband, Antipas' brother, Philip. John the Baptist confronts Herod with the sinfulness of his action, and Herodias takes exception to John's intrusion into their affairs. Herod (perhaps at his wife's insistence) throws John in prison. Herodias wants more; she requests John's death, but Herod refuses. Herod is afraid to harm someone he considers *righteous and holy* (6:20a). The report of Herod's reaction to John (v. 20b) is confusing: some manuscripts say *he was greatly perplexed;* others say *he did many things* (whatever that means). The verse closes by reporting that Herod gladly listened to John. One commentator suggests that "Herod loved to be upset by John" (Hamerton-Kelly: 97).

6:21-23 A Party, a Dance, and a Foolish Oath

We now learn how it happened that Herod made a foolish promise to his daughter (or stepdaughter). Manuscripts are divided on whether the dancing girl is *his daughter, Herodias* or *the daughter of Herodias.* Manuscript support for the first option is better, but the context (esp. 6:24) lends more support for the second. NRSV goes with the first option, in which case there are two different persons named Herodias, Herod's wife and his daughter. Following the second option allows us to attribute the name Salome to the girl, following information from the Jewish historian, Josephus. The story seems more plausible if the girl is Herodias' daughter and therefore Herod's stepdaughter [Textual Criticism of Mark].

Herod is celebrating his birthday, likely at his palace in Tiberias, on the Sea of Galilee. He is surrounded by leading political officials, people in front of whom he can scarcely afford to lose face. His (step)daughter is summoned (or offers) to dance, and her performance elicits from Herod a foolish offer. The expression up to half my kingdom (6:23, NIV), though hyperbolic, obligates Herod to fulfill anything but the most outrageous request.

At this point interpreters often let their imaginations run wild and historians become skeptical. Legends of a highly erotic dance that brings a crowd of half-drunken men to frenzied excitement are just that—legends. Historians insist that a prostitute could be hired for such a dance, but it would be unthinkable for a princess to perform it. The text says nothing about the nature of the dance or the condition of the guests who enjoyed it. Though we cannot be sure what in the Herodian family would be considered unthinkable, elaborate reconstructions of triangulated and incestuous lusts (cf. Hamerton-Kelly: 97-9) go far beyond the evidence.

6:24-29 The Beheading and Burial of John

Perhaps Herod's wife merely seizes the opportunity provided by Herod's promise. It is possible, however, that her schemings precede the dance itself; Herod's promise might be precisely what she herself, via the dance, schemed to elicit. If so, the girl has accomplished the first part of the plan and then asks her mother what she should request from Herod. The girl is either in full agreement with or completely controlled by her mother. The text emphasizes the haste with which the girl reenters the banquet hall and makes the request.

To take advantage of such a situation by requesting an execution is unthinkable enough. The macabre stipulation that the head is to be brought to her on a platter (during a banquet!) should bring illness to everyone present—and to every reader since. If familiarity with the story has blunted the sickening edge of this detail, it is restored in Alec McCowan's addition: "With an order of French fries?" (98).

Herod quickly realizes the foolishness of his promise and attempts some damage control. It is a sad commentary on the quality of his guests, that Herod loses face less by carrying out the horrible promise than he would have by breaking the oath (6:26).

The storyteller leaves nothing to the reader's imagination, narrating in full detail Herod's order to decapitate John, the soldier's fulfillment of the request, and even the grisly report that the head is served up on a platter and carried first to the girl and then to the mother. Only at the crucifixion of Jesus, should Mark's reader be even more horrified.

Mark's text provokes the following reflections: If John's handing over led to this (1:14), to what might the handing over of Jesus lead (3:19)? Is this the end for John? What of the rumors that he has been resurrected (6:14; 8:28)? And what about Jesus? Even before Jesus explicitly predicts his own martyrdom and resurrection, there is foreshadowing of both in the text.

Reference to John's disciples burying him (6:29) enlarges the connection. Will Jesus' own disciples be as faithful? Will they be there to provide a proper burial if his betrayal also leads to this? The answer, as the reader eventually learns, is that his disciples will abandon him (14:50), leaving a stranger to bury Jesus (15:46).

Why would this story have been remembered in the early church? Why would Mark have included it? I can suggest three answers:

1. John the Baptist played a crucial role in the founding of the Christian faith. An account of his death, though gruesome, is something early believers would care to preserve and retell.

2. John's passion foreshadowed Jesus' own death (cf. 9:12-13).

3. John's death is the first in a series of deaths, each preparing *the way* for the ministries of others. John prepared the way by going this way. Jesus goes the way and thereby also prepares the way for others. These others, the reader remembers, are out there on their first mission trip, even as John's death is being narrated. The next verse in Mark (6:30) deals with the end of their mission trip and the return of the Twelve to report to Jesus, who sent them. John, Jesus, the Twelve, and all who follow are bound together by their commitment to walk in *the way* and by their faithful service to prepare *the way* for those yet to come.

THE TEXT IN BIBLICAL CONTEXT

Shaking Off Dust

R. Guelich suggests that shaking off dust from the feet, the symbolic act that Jesus' disciples were to carry out when leaving a rejecting village (6:11), has a threefold meaning (322-3):

• It announces the inevitability of judgment (since further contact and opportunity for repentance is symbolically cut off).

• It declares that the missionaries have done their job and are washing their hands of further responsibility (Ezek. 3:21; 33:1-9).

• It labels that village as pagan.

Of these three, the third is the most provocative. Jews would shake off "pagan" dust before entering the "holy land" (Str.-B, 1:115). Likewise, Jesus' emissaries demonstrate that villages rejecting them and the one who sent them have lost their inheritance in the people of God.

A similar message is conveyed via John's symbolic act of baptizing Jews (1:5), an act normally reserved for *converts* to Judaism. John is thereby symbolically reinstating Jews into the people of God, implying that without his baptism, they are outsiders to Israel. The present text about shaking off "pagan dust," however, takes this a step further. People are invited to reinstate their membership in the people of God; those who reject God's messengers are symbolically excluded.

Other NT references to shaking off dust include all three of the meanings suggested above, though sometimes one of them is more prominent than the others (Matt. 10:14; Luke 9:5; 10:11; Acts 13:51; 18:6). Acts 18:6 in particular seems to highlight all three aspects. As he leaves the Corinthian synagogue, Paul shakes the dust off his clothing and says, "Your blood be on your own heads [meaning 1]. I am clear of my responsibility [meaning 2]. From now on I will go to the Gentiles [meaning 3]" (NIV). With his final line, Paul reverses the usual Jewish practice of cleansing their feet before moving from Gentile to Jewish territory. Paul is moving from Jewish territory (the synagogue) to Gentile territory (the house of Titius Justus) and shaking off the dust before doing so. Believing Jews join him as he moves toward a more fruitful mission field.

OT Parallels to the Martyrdom of John

Many commentators point out parallels between the story of Herod, Herodias, and John on the one hand; and Ahab, Jezebel, and Elijah on the other. In a nutshell, both John and Elijah were persecuted by wicked women and weak kings. It is possible that the parallels between Ahab and Herod contributed to the fivefold identification of Herod as a *king* in this section (though tetrarch is more accurate).

Both Ahab and Herod sinned similarly: Ahab by marrying Jezebel, and Herod by marrying Herodias (1 Kings 16:31; Mark 6:18). Both are pictured as too weak to stand up to the influence of their wives (1 Kings 21:5-16; John 6:24-27). Both feared the respective prophets Elijah and John, and yet were confronted by them (1 Kings 21:20-29; Mark 6:18-20). The prophets, for their part, courageously preached against the sins instigated by the political rulers (1 Kings 20:41-43; 21:20; Mark 6:18), and both faced the uncompromising rejection of the queens (1 Kings 19:2; Mark 6:19). The great difference is that Jezebel failed to bring about Elijah's death, whereas Herodias succeeded in bringing about John's.

The parallels between John and Elijah are especially significant, since Mark's Gospel counts John the Baptist as the returned Elijah (cf. Mal. 4:4-5; Mark 1:6; 9:11-12). This identification counters speculation that *Jesus* is the returned Elijah (cf. 6:15; 8:28). The correspondences between Elijah and John might help solve a puzzle in Mark. Scholars have wondered which OT text Mark thought was fulfilled by the passion of the returned *Elijah* (cf. Mark 9:13). He may well have meant that John experienced situations already foreshadowed in the OT record of Elijah.

There are also interesting parallels between the banquet Esther prepared for king Xerxes and Herod's birthday banquet (cf. Esther 5:1-8; 6:14—7:10; Mark 6:14-29). The reference to the king's pleasure in seeing Esther stands as a parallel to the pleasure Herod had in the dancing girl. In each case, the banquets become occasions for the women (Esther and Herodias) to make their requests of the king. The specific promise by the king to give anything up to half of his kingdom is a verbal parallel (cf. Esther 5:3; 7:2; Mark 6:23). In both cases, the end result is the death of the queen's enemy. Here again, there is a significant difference: justice is meted out in response to Esther's request, but a great injustice comes from Herodias' request.

THE TEXT IN THE LIFE OF THE CHURCH

Mission Strategies

The commissioning of Jesus' disciples for their mission (6:7-11) provokes an important question: What living standard should characterize cross-cultural missionaries today? I know missionaries who are frustrated with what they perceive as a great inequity. They are asked to sacrifice greatly while mission board members live at a higher standard.

Even more disturbing, what about inequities between missionaries and native Christians in the cultures where they serve? Missiologists disagree on when and to what extent the lifestyle of a missionary should match the lifestyle of the people who are to be reached (cf. Bonk). Sometimes missionaries live on a much higher standard than the surrounding culture. This can lead to several dangers: People may become converts in the hope of cashing in on material benefits. The resources of the missionary translate into power and therefore control. As a result, it becomes difficult for converts to develop self-governing and self-supporting congregations. Finally, converts and congregations are easily distracted from their own mission by a pursuit of the missionary's lifestyle.

Still, it is often unrealistic for missionaries to fully adopt their host culture, especially if that means doing without necessary tools for ministry (such as computers for Bible translation, airplanes for mobility, household help to free up more time for ministry, and so on).

Each of the Gospels outlines the minimal provisions Jesus permitted his disciples on their mission (6:8-10, notes). Some commentators suggest that the diverse restrictions (Matthew and Luke are more restrictive than Mark) are traces of early church disputes about how much deprivation should be expected from Christian missionaries. Paul seems to give evidence of such disputes in 1 Corinthians 9:3-7 and elsewhere. The issue has not gone away with the passage of time! In all the NT texts, it seems clear that Jesus expects those who receive the Gospel to take care of those who have come to proclaim it to them (Matt. 10:10; Mark 6:10; Luke 9:4; 10:7; 1 Cor. 9:3-14). Where that is not being done (or is not possible) it seems obvious that a sending agency needs to provide adequately for the real needs of those they send out.

Paul was willing to "endure anything" (1 Cor. 8:12) to further the work of the Gospel. Yet he fought to establish the principle that adequate (or even *doubly* adequate; cf. 1 Tim. 5:17!) compensation be paid to ministers of the Gospel (1 Cor. 9:3-12). Meanwhile, Peter exhorts workers to avoid greed and to keep their eyes fixed on the final glorious reward (1 Pet. 5:1-4). Given these diverse concerns, it seems clear that there will be no simple guidance for mission agencies.

As Hare points out, the main issue is clear: "Jesus' representatives must not allow the profit motive to obscure the Gospel" (71). Beyond that, it seems clear that the NT expects of missionaries no more and no less than of all Jesus' disciples: selfless service in the assurance that God supplies all our needs and that no sacrifice will ultimately go unrewarded.

Mark 6:30-56

The Misunderstood Miracle-Worker

PREVIEW

The material beginning at 6:30 is one of the most intriguing sections of Mark's Gospel. Everything moves quickly, too quickly it seems, for Jesus' disciples. They participate in the action, but as Mark clearly informs his readers (6:52), they do not understand what it all means.

In only twenty-seven verses, Mark leads his readers through a series of rapid changes of scene: on land, across the lake, up onto the shore, down on the grass, up into the hills, back on the lake, back on shore, into villages, towns, countryside, and marketplaces.

The scenes are filled with action. The section begins with so much commotion that Jesus and his disciples cannot even find time to eat (6:31). Their attempt to find a quiet place for rest and food does not succeed. The crowds will not leave them alone (vv. 32-33). Quickly changing plans, Jesus spends the day teaching the people (v. 34). Then suddenly we are listening in on an emergency business meeting to solve the newest problem: crowds of hungry people and almost no food (vv. 35-38). The solution turns out to be an awe-inspiring miracle when a small lunch is turned into a feast (vv. 38-42).

The miracle on land is followed by a miracle on the lake. Jesus' disciples are battling a storm-tossed sea. Before morning dawns, Jesus is seen walking over the tossing waves toward his struggling disciples (6:45-52). The minute they disembark, people are running everywhere, carrying the sick on mats, listening for rumors as to where Jesus might be, and then coming for healing (vv. 53-56).

Mark's text has been compared to a slide presentation flashing glimpses of fast-paced action past the reader. This section of the text lends itself to such a description, at least on the surface. But beneath the surface something else is happening. Though the narrative moves rapidly, it also offers details that make the reader pause and reflect, such as the time references. Jesus makes his hungry, exhausted disciples wait all day while he teaches the crowd. He leaves them fighting the waves all night while he prays. Why?

Even more puzzling is the fact that the feeding event has a *secret meaning* (6:52). Because the disciples are blind to this secret meaning, they misunderstand what is going on when Jesus walks on the sea and identifies himself to his disciples (vv. 47-51).

The hero of the story is the miracle-working Jesus. The supporting roles (though they are not always supportive!) are played by the uncomprehending disciples. They are present when it happens; they participate, they see and hear, but they do not understand.

In 4:41 the disciples are asking, "Who then is this, that even the wind and the sea obey him?" As the miracles continue, so do the questions: Who is this? He heals the paralyzed and the lepers, casts out demons, multiplies loaves and fish, walks on water, teaches and feeds and heals and saves. Who is this?

Mark's Gospel has rightly been described as *action-packed*. But it also calls for deep reflection. Just as Jesus' actions have *hidden meanings*, so does Mark's text. The reader is left asking, What are the disciples supposed to understand? Why does Jesus not tell them? Why does Mark not tell his readers? Readers of Mark's Gospel face the same challenge that Jesus' first disciples faced—the challenge to have *hearing ears* and *seeing eyes* (cf. 4:12; 8:18).

OUTLINE

Jesus Multiplies the Loaves and Fish, 6:30-44
6:30	A Dark Cloud and a Silver Lining
6:31-34	Changed Plans
6:35-38	How Can the Crowds Be Fed?
6:39-40	Groups on the Green Grass
6:41-44	The Feeding Itself

The Secret Meaning

Jesus Walks on the Water, 6:45-52
6:45-45	Evening Plans

6:47-48   A Night of Rowing and a Surprise
            Passing By
            It Is I/I AM
            The Meaning the Disciples Missed
6:49-52   The Miracle and the Misunderstanding

Jesus Heals Many Sick People, 6:53-56
6:53-55   The Persistent Crowds
6:56   Healing Miracles

EXPLANATORY NOTES

Jesus Multiplies the Loaves and Fish   6:30-44

There is a *secret meaning* to this feeding miracle (cf. 6:52). We have to read the narrative with care. Good detectives know that every detail is potentially important when there is a mystery to be solved.

6:30   A Dark Cloud and a Silver Lining

The disciples (here called *apostles* because they have been *sent out*) return from their short-term mission trip and report to Jesus on their success. John the Baptist's martyrdom is reported between the sending out of the missionaries (6:7-12) and their return to report (6:30). That is effective storytelling; it gives the feeling of time lapse. But more than that, it is effective teaching, highlighting the double-sidedness of the Gospel. There is a *glory* side (glowing reports of missionary success), and there is a *cross* side (courageous and costly self-sacrifice). Mark ties the two tightly together.

Looked at one way, the text seems to hang a dark cloud over the proclamation of the Gospel. Mark seems to be saying, "The mission of the church is not all success and glory; it also involves a cross; see what has happened to John!" Looked at the other way, Mark hints that even this dark cloud has a silver lining: "Does John's martyrdom seem like a tragedy, a defeat? Look closer: there are now twelve new missionaries carrying the work forward."

By linking together John's martyrdom and the disciples' mission, the story foreshadows Jesus' own ministry. Dark clouds will cover his ministry, too. Yet beyond the darkness of the cross will be the bright sunshine of Easter morning. Mark's narrative also foreshadows the missionary outreach of the disciples and the Christian church, a ministry characterized by a cross, with the guarantee of victory beyond. Yes, it will cost much (10:28; 13:9-13), but it will also bring great reward (10:29-31; 13:13, 27).

6:31-34 Changed Plans

The crowds prevent the returning missionaries from getting food (6:31) and rest (vv. 33-34). They cross the lake by boat to find a solitary (literally, *desert*) place. But their plans to rest and eat are short-circuited by the crowds who have run along the shore. Jesus, whom Mark here characterizes as a compassionate shepherd, promptly turns his attention to the shepherdless sheep. This is a clear indictment on the religious leaders whom God commissioned to make sure the people were not shepherdless (cf. Num. 27:17). The reference may also allude to Jesus' coming role as the end-time Shepherd of God's people (cf. Ezek. 34:23; Jer. 23:3ff.).

6:35-38 How Can the Crowds Be Fed?

The day of teaching is over. Everyone is hungry, especially the disciples (v. 31, notes). But how can five thousand men (plus women and children?) be fed in this desert place? The word *desert(ed)* seems to be emphasized, appearing in verses 31, 32, and 35. That may be a clue pointing to the secret meaning (see below).

The disciples and Jesus discuss three possibilities:

1. Send the people to buy food for themselves (v. 36).
2. Go and buy food for them (v. 37).
3. Make do with what is available (v. 38).

Jesus immediately rules out option 1. A good shepherd does not disperse a hungry flock. He provides for their needs. That includes leading the people in "paths of righteousness" (= Jesus' teaching; cf. Ps. 23:3, KJV). But it also includes preparing "a table" for them (cf. Ps. 23:5). The Good Shepherd motif in our text parallels Psalm 23 and yields further clues as to the secret meaning.

Option 2 (going away to buy food for the crowd) might be possible. Mark does not say whether or not the disciples have the suggested 200 denarii, whether they have seriously considered spending it, or how long the errand would take.

Jesus chooses option 3. Five small loaves and two fish in Jesus' hands are more than enough.

6:39-40 Groups on the Green Grass

Mark next vividly describes the orderly seating of the crowds *on the green grass*. Is he just creating a vivid narrative? Is he preserving historical reminiscences, passive proofs that the account is factually reliable? Or is he dropping hints as to the *secret meaning* of the feeding? Interpreters have suggested that there are subtle clues here:

1. *Green grass* is possible in this desert place only in early spring, thus around Passover time. That may mean that the feeding foreshadows the Lord's Supper and Jesus' death as the Passover lamb.
2. *Green grass* echoes Psalm 23:2; "He makes me lie down in green pastures." Mark is still portraying Jesus as the Good Shepherd.
3. *Green grass* is not characteristic of a desert. The greening of the desert is evidence that God is fulfilling end-time promises (cf. Isa. 49:9-10; 51:3). That in turn makes the meal a foretaste of the end-time feast that God prepares. NRSV says the people sit, but the Greek says they recline, the posture of a feast, not a normal meal.

What about the groups of *hundreds* and *fifties?* Does it just mean some groups are larger, and some smaller? The Greek text literally says *according to a hundred and according to fifty.* Does that mean 50 groups of 100, or 100 groups of 50, or even (as NEB translates it) *a hundred rows of fifty each?* In each case, it comes out to 5,000. Or is the issue more than mathematics?

Many commentators have seen in these numbers, *hundreds* and *fifties,* a reference to the organizing of the Israelites during their desert wandering (cf. Exod. 18:13-27). Some of Jesus' contemporaries live in religious communities in the desert that actually have modeled themselves after the Exodus 18 pattern. They seat themselves "according to a hundred and according to fifty" for special meals designed to symbolize the final end-time feast in God's kingdom (Pesch, 1976:352). Perhaps the secret meaning is that Jesus is even now gathering together the end-time people of God.

6:41-44 The Feeding Itself

Neither the miracle nor the reactions it provokes are described. The text says only that all are satisfied, and that there are twelve baskets of leftovers.

The disciples play an active role. They are consulted at the planning stage (6:35-38), and they work hard as the plans are implemented (vv. 39-43). Are the disciples here ministers-in-training, learning about their future role as Christian ministers? Jesus is the one who provides; but his followers are to be active in bringing the provisions to those in need.

The narrative leaves an interesting question unanswered: When do the disciples eat? They are the hungriest of all, and the crowds have prevented them from eating (cf. 6:31). The narrative implies that while the others eat, the disciples are busy with the arrangements

(v. 39), the distribution (v. 41), and even the cleanup (v. 43).

Presumably the disciples do eventually eat (v. 42, *all ate and were filled*). Collecting exactly twelve baskets of leftovers can hardly seem anything but providential to twelve starving and exhausted men. Yet the narrative portrays Jesus' compassion for the crowds much more clearly than his compassion for his own followers.

The Secret Meaning

In all this, there is apparently a secret meaning that the disciples do not understand (6:52). What is it? Following are some of the most frequently defended alternatives:

1. Jesus is the "one like Moses" (Deut. 18:15), organizing (cf. Exod. 18) and teaching his people in the desert, feeding them with manna (cf. Ps. 78:19, 29), and preparing to lead them to the Promised Land (Kee: 111-2).

2. Jesus is the promised Messiah, preparing in the desert the anticipated end-time banquet (Mauser: 137). What the disciples then fail to understand is that the *secret kingdom* (4:11) is already here and advancing toward its final fulfillment.

3. Jesus is the compassionate shepherd, modeling himself after the good shepherd in the Psalm 23. Thus Jesus reveals the very presence of God. More support for this view is in 6:50, notes (cf. 4:41, notes).

4. Jesus is foreshadowing the soon-to-be-instituted Lord's Supper (Quesnell) and therefore symbolizing the giving of his life for others. The language of taking, blessing, breaking, and giving in 6:41 and in 14:22 is almost identical. If that is the secret meaning, then the disciples have failed to understand the mystery that this miracle-worker will soon be offering up his own life. Perhaps the disciples (like the crowds in John 6:14-15) are excited about the wonderful power of Jesus, but are far from ready to follow him on the road to the cross.

5. Jesus' action foreshadows the later mission of the church to Jews and Gentiles. This interpretation proposes that the two feeding miracles (6:35-44 and 8:1-10) prefigure mission to Jews and Gentiles, respectively. The locations, the numbers, and various other details symbolize Jews and Gentiles. Other interpreters see a hint of the Gentile mission in the leftover crumbs (cf. 7:28). This suggestion will be addressed in 8:14-21, notes.

It is not necessary to defend one of these suggestions and deny all the others. Texts are often multilayered and can hint at various meanings. All the above themes can be found in Mark, even if interpreters are unsure whether all are found in this text.

While Markan interpreters often choose one of the above five options, I want to propose a sixth. Perhaps the secret meaning can be formulated like this: *Although Jesus has the power to do mighty deeds, he does not always exercise it in order to lighten the load for his followers.* This may seem a surprising suggestion. But as we see in the following narrative (6:45-52) and again later (cf. 8:1-21), there is much to support this view. We turn now to the miracle on the lake.

Jesus Walks on the Water 6:45-52

6:45-46 Evening Plans

The crowds have been taught and fed. Jesus determines where everyone is to go next. The disciples are sent out onto the lake in the boat, perhaps no longer hungry, but by now certainly very tired (6:31, 41-44, notes). The crowds are sent back home. The Good Shepherd has provided nourishment for their souls and for their bodies. Jesus himself heads up into the hills to pray.

6:47-48 A Night of Rowing and a Surprise

The disciples' boat leaves before darkness sets in, and almost immediately a storm picks up. Jesus sees the disciples *straining at the oars against an adverse wind* (6:48). The last time they battled a storm, Jesus was with them in the boat and wondrously calmed the storm (4:39). What will happen this time?

Mark reports the chronology of the events, clearly suggesting that a whole night passes *after* Jesus knows his disciples are struggling but *before* he comes out to them (clearer in the Greek and most English translations than in NRSV). In the evening (6:00-9:00 p.m.; cf. also 13:35), Jesus sees his disciples struggling on the lake. *Early in the morning* (literally, *about the fourth watch*, 3:00-6:00 a.m.), Jesus comes walking on the water. Jesus does not look up from prayer, discover his disciples are in need, and immediately come to their aid. Instead, he deliberately waits an entire night before making a move to help them. The disciples spend the night fighting the wind and waves; Jesus spends it praying.

To understand why Jesus has waited so long, it is necessary to understand why he finally comes. He does *not* come to join his struggling disciples in the boat and calm the storm (even though in the end he does that). His purpose is to walk past them (6:48).

Some commentators have suggested that Jesus only makes it look as though he would walk past them; he wants to give his disciples an opportunity to invite him into the boat. But that is not what the text says. Mark says Jesus *intended* to pass them by, or more literally, *to pass by* (Berg: 111).

6:49-52 The Miracle and the Misunderstanding

Why then does Jesus change his plan, enter the boat, and calm the storm? Evidently because his disciples fail to understand what he wants to do. They do not even recognize that it is Jesus. Just as Jesus has changed his plan at 6:31-34 to accommodate the needy crowds, so now he changes his plan to accommodate his uncomprehending and frightened disciples. He wants to walk past, but the disciples fail to recognize him. They are terrified, misidentifying him as a ghost. He speaks to calm them. He identifies himself with the words *It is I*. Then he enters their boat and calms the storm.

His original intention, however, is to *pass by*. Can that possibly be true? What can it mean? If it is puzzling to us, it is even more puzzling to the disciples. *They were utterly astounded, for they did not understand about the loaves* (6:51b-52a). Are they amazed that Jesus can do such mighty deeds, like multiplying loaves, walking on water, and calming a storm? Is Jesus trying to raise their hopes for his miraculous intervention? I do not think so.

The opposite is nearer the truth. The disciples are not amazed that Jesus can do mighty deeds; instead, they are amazed that he would wait so long before coming, and then would intend to walk right past (8:14-21, notes). The disciples may well understand the miraculous feeding as a guarantee of Jesus' immediate intervention every time life becomes difficult. If so, it is not surprising that they also misunderstand what has happened on the lake. Mark's narration includes clues to the meaning the disciples missed.

Passing By

Passing by (*parerchomai*) is an important OT motif. It is a technical term for an epiphany, for God "passing by." When God "passes by," it is *not* a sign of unconcern or noninvolvement; it is a sign of caring *presence* (Guelich: 350). Exodus 33:15-23 provides a close parallel to what the disciples face on the stormy sea. There Moses struggles to maintain courage in a difficult situation, praying, "If your Presence will not go [with us], do not carry us up from here" (33:15). God comes to encourage Moses, not by changing Moses' difficult circumstances, but by *passing by*, by revealing divine goodness and glory. The epiphany assures Moses that God will be with him on the hard road ahead. Jesus knows that his disciples need *this assurance* more than they need another storm-stilling miracle.

It Is I/I AM

Mark reports that Jesus identifies himself to his disciples with *egō eimi*. In the Greek translation of the OT (LXX), that is how God's name, Yahweh (I AM), is translated. It is also Greek for the ordinary self-identification, *It is I.* Here is where translating becomes a difficult task. The usual translation, *It is I*, is correct; it tells us what Jesus says and indicates what the disciples hear and understand. But it is also an incomplete translation. It does not indicate the deeper meaning that Jesus hopes they will understand: *I AM.* Some translations use a footnote to solve the problem.

But why should these words be translated as *I AM* in this passage? Again we turn to Exodus 33. After God said, "I will make all my goodness pass [by] before you" (Exod. 33:19a), God offered Moses something else. "And [I] will proclaim before you the name, 'The LORD'" (33:19b). The name *LORD/Yahweh* is *I AM* (in Greek, *egō eimi*). It is a name that promises, "I am with you; I will accompany you into an unknown future and reveal myself to you along the way" (cf. Janzen).

The Meaning the Disciples Missed

Jesus intended to *pass by*, to assure his disciples that God, in the person of Jesus, is present with the disciples in the storm. The disciples do not understand (6:52). They have eyes, but do not see (8:18). They think it is a ghost and are terrified.

To calm their fears, Jesus speaks the words, *egō eimi*. The disciples hear, "It is I!" Those are comforting words to Jesus' disciples, assuring them this is no ghost; it is Jesus, their friend. But if they had ears to hear (8:18), they would also hear *egō eimi* as meaning "I AM." If they would understand, they would hear Jesus pronouncing the divine name in their presence. They would experience what Moses experienced, the assurance of God's presence even in difficult times. They would know that in the presence of Jesus, they are in the presence of God, a God who will go with them on the difficult journey ahead, even when miracles are denied.

Mark's narrative portrays a wonder-working Jesus. It also portrays disciples who have yet to learn that God's presence is with them even if they must battle the waves all night. They can be thankful that Jesus does not give up on them. Later they experience another amazing feeding (8:1-10), and then, again on the sea, Jesus will try to lead them to understanding (8:14-21) *[Three Lessons from a Boat]*.

The great feeding and sea-walking episodes present Jesus as the new Moses, the Good Shepherd, the promised Messiah, the presence of God. Earlier *the disciples* have been asking *each other*, "Who is this?" (4:41). Later *Jesus* will ask *them*, "Who do you say that I am?" (8:29). Meanwhile, the disciples are struggling to understand.

Jesus Heals Many Sick People 6:53-56

6:53-55 The Persistent Crowds

Why Jesus and his disciples disembark in Gennesaret, after planning to go to Bethsaida (6:45), is not explained. Perhaps the storm has changed their course. The persistent crowds in Gennesaret may well be the same people who prevented the disciples from eating and resting the day before (vv. 31-34).

Mark portrays a flexible Jesus, responding spontaneously to the needs at hand. In 6:34 he delays his plans for rest as he ministers compassionately to the *sheep without a shepherd*. In verse 49, to accommodate his uncomprehending disciples, he changes his plan to *pass by*. Now, as the small group comes ashore, Jesus allows the pressing needs of the crowd to set the agenda. Earlier in the Gospel (1:35-39), Jesus has tried to escape the crowds clamoring for healings. He needs time for public preaching and for private prayer. Here in Gennesaret, he turns his full attention to the sick and hurting. Yesterday was a day of teaching (6:34); last night was a night of prayer (v. 47); today is a day of good news for the sick.

6:56 Healing Miracles

Numerous and remarkable healings occur. The sick need only to touch Jesus' cloak, and they become well. Mark thus continues to portray Jesus as the compassionate one who does great deeds on behalf of the needy. For those with eyes to see, he is revealing his identity and showing that God's reign is breaking in. The disciples, however, the very ones who have been given the secret of God's kingdom (cf. 4:11), do not understand. If they believe that in times of trouble divine intervention is always just a prayer away, they still need to have their eyes opened. Otherwise, they will not be ready for what lies ahead *[Miracles in Mark]*.

Those who truly follow Jesus know a theology of glory—five thousand fed with a few loaves, Jesus walking on the water, Jesus healing the multitudes. They also know a theology of the cross—a hard and tiring mission, the promise of rest that gets thwarted, a struggle on the stormy sea.

They know that neither theology is correct unless it is connected to the other. That is the part that the disciples are having difficulty grasping. That seems to be the primary message of this fascinating but challenging section of Mark's Gospel.

THE TEXT IN BIBLICAL CONTEXT
Meals

Among the many Markan (and biblical) themes reflected in this passage is the theme of meals. Scripture often portrays meals as sacred events where covenants are sealed, victories celebrated, and relationships deepened. Meals are special times of celebrating peoplehood and God's presence (cf. Gen. 18:1-15; Exod. 24:11; Ps. 23:5; Luke 24:13-35; and so on).

Scripture carries thousands of references to food and mealtimes. Someone has noted that *every* chapter of Luke's Gospel refers to eating or drinking (if we count mentions of feasting and fasting)! If we narrow our focus to the journey section (9:51—19:44), we see these significant references to food and feasting in Luke:

- Sharing food as an act of participation in mission (10:7).
- Daily food as God's gracious provision (11:3, 8; 12:22-24, 29).
- Banquets as rewards for faithful service (12:37) and opportunities for faithful service (12:42).
- A feast to celebrate gathering the lost into God's kingdom (13:29).
- Jesus' instructions about taking a humble seat at a banquet (14:8).
- Jesus' instructions on whom to invite to banquets (14:12-14).
- Jesus' warning against lame excuses for not entering God's eschatological banquet (14:15-24); or (depending on how this text is interpreted) the story of a rich man qualifying for divine blessing by practicing the kind of meal hospitality (inviting the outcasts) that Jesus requires (J. Green, 1997:560-3).
- Jesus' parable about a celebration banquet for the returning prodigal (15:23-24).
- The rich man's banquet table that excluded poor Lazarus (16:19-21).
- The duty to serve at the table before presuming to share in the table's benefits (17:7-8).
- The danger of eating and drinking, oblivious to impending disaster (17:27-28).

- The folly of fasting as a spiritual discipline, while maintaining self-righteous pride in the heart (18:11-12).
- Jesus' redemptive reception of Zacchaeus' hospitality (19:5-9).

Clearly, mealtimes are strategic opportunities for evangelism, provision for missionaries, celebration of success in mission, places of testing and rewarding faithfulness, opportunities to practice trust, humility, generosity, and spiritual wakefulness.

Meals are extremely important events in Mark as well. Jesus eats with *sinners* to reveal the nature of his saving mission (2:15-17); the focus here is on the grace of God, freely extended to all who will receive Jesus. Jesus uses a *wedding banquet* to explain why his disciples should feast and not fast while the Bridegroom (Jesus) is with them (2:18-21); here followers of Jesus are encouraged to rejoice in anticipation of the wedding supper of the Lamb.

Jesus feeds *crowds in the desert* (Mark 6:30-44 and 8:1-10), thus symbolizing a range of themes (see notes, above). Jesus uses *crumbs* falling from a rich person's table to symbolize God's grace available even to Gentiles (7:26-28); he means that the time is not far away when rich and poor, righteous and sinner, Jew and Gentile will have equal opportunity to share meal fellowship with Jesus and each other.

Finally a *Passover meal* serves as the occasion for Jesus to symbolize the giving of his life for his followers (Mark 14:12-25); this self-giving, celebrated by the church at its communion fellowship, is what makes all of the above possible. Mark's account encourages readers to see all these elements reflected in the more-than-enough festive meal that Jesus shared with the five thousand on the shores of the Sea of Galilee.

Compassion and the Sovereignty of God

God's compassion is expressed in Scripture by means of a variety of Hebrew and Greek nouns and verbs. The OT teaches that God's constant loving care and sometimes dramatic interventions are available to God's people because God's compassions never fail (Lam. 3:22; Ps. 103:13). In the NT Jesus expresses divine compassion and calls his followers to do the same: "You must be compassionate, just as your Father is compassionate" (Luke 6:36, NLT).

This section of Mark directly refers to the compassion of Jesus only in 6:34, but it is demonstrated throughout the text. Jesus shows compassion by being willing to forego a planned retreat so that he might minister to the crowds (vv. 31, 34); he also shows it in his widespread healing ministry (vv. 56-57). Though Jesus expresses so much compassion to the crowds, he does not make life easy for his disciples. Because of his care for the crowds, the disciples (the hungriest of all) have to wait longest before eating. Because Jesus gives priority to the crowds, the disciples never get their much-needed rest. They even spend the whole night rowing.

What does Jesus want them to learn? Here Exodus 33 helps us once more (Mark 6:49-52, notes). God promises Moses to "pass by" and to pronounce the divine name (*I AM*) in his presence (Exod. 33:19); the key verse adds, "I will have mercy on whom I will have mercy, and I will have compassion on whom I will have compassion" (NIV). That is also part of what *I AM* means: God acts with sovereign freedom, and we will not always understand God's ways.

In the OT God rescued Israel marvelously, miraculously, and often—but not always. The same God who prepares for some a "table in the presence of [their] enemies" lets others walk "through the valley of the shadow of death" (Ps. 23:4-5).

In the NT Jesus rescues and helps many people, but sometimes he allows them to go through difficult times. This chapter of Mark's Gospel highlights the difficulties of the disciples (not to mention the martyrdom of John). The first half of Mark's Gospel narrates numerous miracles, the second half hardly any. Many experience deliverance, healing, safety, and even new life in the presence of Jesus; some experience that following Jesus is a hard and costly choice. Jesus does not promise that he will always smooth the path for those who follow him.

The disciples are hungry; the crowds are fed. The crowds recline on the green grass; the disciples struggle against the waves. "I will have compassion on whom I will have compassion" (Rom. 9:15). It is part of the mystery of God's sovereignty that some are rescued and some not, some healed and some not, some fed and some not.

THE TEXT IN THE LIFE OF THE CHURCH
Preaching the Stories of Jesus

Even before the Gospels were written, the apostles and others were preaching the stories of Jesus. Miracle stories, like The Feeding of the Five Thousand (6:30-44) and Jesus Walking on the Water (6:45-52), were rich sources of insight concerning Jesus' person and mission. Early Christian expositions of these events have left traces in the texts where OT allusions and christological reflection are often evident.

Some scholars spend much effort trying to figure out what *really happened* on the shores of Galilee. They are sometimes motivated by skepticism of the Gospel record, sometimes by a desire to harmonize the various accounts. The focus of the Gospel records, however, is less on proving and more on presenting Jesus and proclaiming the arrival of God's reign.

Throughout the history of the church, miracle reports have played many roles. They have served as glimpses of God and God's reign, they have been used to "prove" the truth of the Gospel, or (conversely) they have been explained away to let modern minds believe the Gospel without having to accept "the miraculous." Christians would do well to de-emphasize the aspects of proving and explaining away. A biblical worldview involves having eyes to see God at work, however "miraculous" or "nonmiraculous" God's handiwork seems. God is at work when astonishing things happen that nature/creation left to itself would not have produced as well as when God walks with us through tough times.

Biblical interpretation should focus on how "miracle" reports function to reveal God's presence and God's reign; it should not major on hazardous reconstructions of the historical events that lie behind the biblical accounts (TLC for 4:35—5:43) *[Miracles in Mark]*.

Expecting Miracles Today

Many Christians struggle to understand why "miracles" do not always happen when we pray for them. Is it lack of faith? Perhaps at times it is (as in Mark 6:4-6), but more often the explanation is not that easy. Often we are faced with the mystery of a God whose ways we do not fully understand, a God whose self-designation is "I AM" (Exod. 3:14), meaning "I am here; I am faithful; I am your companion and guide on the journey." This God says, "I will have compassion on whom I will have compassion" (Rom. 9:15; Exod. 33:19).

Throughout the ages, believers have struggled along with Job, trying to understand a God whose ways do not seem fair. God's answer was then and is now: "I am God; I know what I am doing." Jesus in Gethsemane also struggled to know and accept the incomprehensible ways of God. For Jesus, "Not my will but yours" was the bottom line. Christians too easily use the presence or absence of miracles to draw conclusions about God's power and love, God's presence or absence. When God marvelously smooths our path, we conclude that God is loving and caring. When life is hard, we wonder if God knows or cares, or is even there.

This unit of Mark's Gospel urges readers to be open to other options. The presence of God is revealed also when God's ministers faithfully care for shepherdless sheep, even though they themselves are tired and hungry. God's presence is revealed when a great wonder occurs and minimal provisions are astonishingly multiplied. But God's presence is also revealed when things take a more normal course, as God's people recognize a need, make plans, look after arrangements, distribute food, and clean up messes, all so that others can experience the miracle of enough to eat. God's presence can be known in the midst of life's storms, even when God's people must trust that Jesus is praying for us or passing by, though we may wish he would enter our boat and calm our storm.

This section of Mark calls readers to acknowledge a God whose love and power are accepted in faith, whether or not a miracle takes place, whether or not things turn out as we had hoped and prayed [Three Lessons from a Boat].

Scholars sometimes refer to a *Theology of Glory* and a *Theology of the Cross*. The first emphasizes God's gracious provision, and our experiences of victory, joy, abundant life, and miracles. The second emphasizes God's call to walk the narrow road of self-sacrifice, discipleship, and the cross. To choose one and reject the other is to distort the Gospel. It is not a biblical understanding of glory if it is divorced from the cross—the cross of Jesus and also the cross his followers are called to bear. It is not a biblical understanding of the cross if it ends in death and not in the glory of the resurrection and God's final victory.

Pastors and teachers are often asked to give easy assurances that God will indeed intervene in answer to prayer, especially when we pray for healing. Some Scriptures seem to offer assurances of God's intervention in response to believing prayer; yet much of Scripture provides a more nuanced perspective or even explicitly denies that God is obligated to respond to our requests.

Glib assurances such as "All things work together for good" (Rom. 8:28) are often even less helpful than attempting to discern what God will do in a specific situation. That is especially so, since the probably correct translation of Romans 8:28 is as follows: "And we know that God is working for good in all situations together with those who love God, with those who are called according to God's purpose" (TJG). Taken this way, believers are not promised that "everything always works out" for us. Instead, they are challenged to be God's co-workers, bringing about good purposes in a world where things do not always turn out as we hope.

Mark 7:1-30

Breaking Down Barriers

PREVIEW

In chapter 6, Mark's portrait of Jesus, the miracle-worker, reaches a high point. He has just fed five thousand, walked on water, and healed many sick people. He is a famous teacher, a compassionate helper, a wonder-worker. The mood is upbeat. What a shock, then, to begin reading Mark 7. Jesus' enemies, the Pharisees and scribes, have arrived. The Pharisees were last seen in 3:6, responding to a miracle of Jesus by plotting his death. The scribes from Jerusalem were last seen in 3:22, accusing Jesus of working miracles in Satan's power.

This time the issue is ceremonial cleansing. It is as though the Pharisees and scribes point to Jesus and his disciples and say, "Wash your hands, you sinners!" (cf. James 4:8a). Jesus looks them straight in the eye and retorts, "Purify your hearts, you double-minded!" (cf. James 4:8b).

Niceties are set aside, the mood is tense, and the words are harsh. One suspects that Jesus' opponents are being caricatured. Nevertheless, the point Jesus (and Mark) are making is crucially important: human tradition can become the enemy of God's word. When that happens, the guilty must be confronted, and the causes of the problem must be exposed.

The real issue for the Pharisees and scribes turns out to be broader than merely washing ceremonies; it includes all the scribal traditions that regulate eating habits and ceremonial purity. The real issues for Jesus, however, are hypocrisy, the law of God, and internal purity. Jesus redefines *defilement* as a matter of the heart. In this section

Jesus works at breaking down great barriers—barriers of ceremony and legalism that kept the *pious* walled off from the ordinary Jew, and barriers of ritual and tradition that prevented Gentiles from joining the people of God.

This text must have be very important for Mark. He has lived through some of the struggles of the early church, as barriers between Jews and Gentiles were tumbling down. He wants his readers to know that Jesus is the one who authorized those great changes. Mark even slips his own interpretive comment into the text: *Thus he declared all foods clean* (7:19b), making sure his readers do not miss the point.

Attached to this long controversy over rituals and defilement is a short narrative about a Syrophoenician woman. The narrative has been called "difficult, surprising," even "offensive." It is also beautiful! It reports an exorcism, but more important, it reveals that the wall separating Gentiles from God's grace is breaking down.

In this section Jesus meets his match. But it does not happen when a powerful coalition of Pharisees and scribes try to trap him. It happens when a witty Greek woman simply will not take no for an answer. If Jesus works from the Jewish side, chopping at the foundations of the great dividing wall, this faith-filled Gentile stands on the other side, waiting for a crack to open up. When it does, she simply pushes her way through, and Jesus ministers to her.

One can hardly doubt that D. McKenna also has a point here:

> My guess is that the woman also ministered to Jesus. After laboring with hard-hearted Pharisees and dull-minded disciples, the interlude with an open spirit and a lively mind must have been as good as a night's rest. (158)

OUTLINE
Controversy with the Pharisees and Scribes, 7:1-13

Teaching for the Crowd and Disciples, 7:14-23
   7:14-15   Public Teaching
   7:17-23   Private Explanation
                Nothing from Outside Defiles, 7:17-19a
                Cleansing All Foods, 7:19b
                Defilement Comes from the Inside, 7:20-23

The Persistent Faith of a Gentile, 7:24-30
   7:24   Breathing Room
   7:25-26   A Gentile with a Need
   7:27   Jesus' Shocking Refusal
   7:28   The Woman's Witty Reply
   7:29-30   Grace Flows to a Gentile

EXPLANATORY NOTES

Mark's text often flows from one unit into another, making it difficult to divide it into sections. Changes in target audience (as in 7:17) or location (as in 7:24) are not reliable indicators that a new section begins. Developing themes is much more important to Mark than organizing events on lines of chronology or geography. Thus 7:1 marks the beginning of a new section, even though neither a temporal nor a geographical shift takes place. What shifts here is the theme.

Issues of ritual purity, scribal traditions, and the breaking down of Jew-Gentile barriers do not appear in the preceding section; here they are central. After 7:23 come major shifts in geography and type of literature, but the theme continues to develop. Separating the incident of the Syrophoenician woman from the controversy over clean and unclean would obscure one of the main points in Mark's text. He is concerned here to show the opening of the door of salvation to the Gentiles. Thus the unit beginning at 7:1 continues at least until 7:30.

Many commentators carry the present unit through to the end of the chapter, since the material in 7:31-37 is also viewed as a Gentile healing, and since the doxology in 7:37 must refer to more than one miracle. However, as we see in the next major section, there are good reasons to link 7:31-37 with the material following it.

Still, we should not forget that all structural boundaries are in one sense artificial. They are created to make commentary writing (and reading) more manageable. Not only individual texts but also larger units should be interpreted with both the immediate and the broader context of the Gospel in mind.

Controversy with the Pharisees and Scribes 7:1-13

7:1-5 The Opponents' Attack

The Setting for the Controversy 7:1-2

Mark 7 opens ominously. The Pharisees and scribes are gathering around Jesus. These are his declared enemies (cf. 3:6, 22); their gathering is not accidental.

Since they *come from Jerusalem,* this will not be a friendly theological discussion about eating habits. It will be a critical interrogation sponsored by what will develop into the official opposition centered in Israel's political and religious capital. Jesus' enemies have previously accused him of blasphemy (2:7), of keeping bad company (2:16), of breaking the Sabbath (2:24; 3:2), and of working in Satan's power (3:22). What will they find wrong this time?

They noticed that some of his disciples were eating without washing their hands (abridged). The reader hardly knows whether to laugh or cry. Is that all they can find?

The way Mark's narrative is structured, one gets the impression the disciples have just returned with Jesus from the marketplaces (6:56). There they have been in contact with ritually unclean people. Now they are eating *bread* (7:2, KJV; NRSV omits *bread/food*). Are they still eating leftovers from the great miracle (6:43)? But Jesus' enemies are not impressed with the healings or the feeding miracle. They have no eyes for such evidences of God's gracious provision. They see only unwashed hands.

What if those hands have been defiled in the marketplace? What if the grain for the bread has not been tithed? What if the farmer has sown the grain in violation of Sabbath laws? The Gentiles among Mark's original readers are left shaking their heads. Mark pauses to give them some background information—but *not* to justify the charges; Mark just wants his readers to understand what the enemies are saying.

Parenthesis: What All the Jews Do 7:3-4

Mark says that *all the Jews* observe elaborate cleansing rituals, especially when coming from the market. The issue is not hygiene; it is ceremonial purity, and behind that, religious tradition. Various ceremonial washings have been prescribed in the OT for priests on duty (cf. Exod. 30:19). Hygiene has not been the issue there, either. Nor did God intend to promote empty rituals, meaningless but obligatory ceremonies. Instead, the washings are designed to symbolize that God is a pure God and demands purity of the people so that they can serve

God through clean hands and an upright heart.

The OT prescribed cleansing rituals, particularly for priests and their households before they ate consecrated food (cf. Num. 18:11-13). The Pharisees, however, wanting to appear especially pious, have adopted them for themselves and expanded them to cover all manner of cleansing rituals for hands, food, and eating utensils (Mark 7:4). They have tried to impose their traditions on their fellow Jews, questioning the piety of those who ignore these traditions.

By referring to *the tradition of the elders*, Mark introduces the real issue at stake. The Pharisees have substituted their own traditions for the will of God.

The Pharisees are naturally of a different opinion than Jesus. To them, the traditions of the elders are designed to support and safeguard the written law. The traditions interpret the law, clarify debatable points, and provide specific applications to everyday situations. The traditions are for them a guardrail around the law, ensuring that no one will inadvertently step over the line (Mishnah Aboth 1:1).

According to the Pharisees, these supplements to the written law are more than mere traditions (in the sense of *customs*). They are *faithfully transmitted obligations*. Some Pharisees even claim that they were part of God's revealed law, given orally at Mt. Sinai along with the written law, and then faithfully passed down through the centuries. It is the mission of the scribes and Pharisees to interpret and enforce them.

In reality, the additional weight of these added traditions make the law an almost unbearable burden. People who try to live by them almost inevitably are caught up in *doing* things or *avoiding* things, forgetting what really matters—the heart. For the benefit of Gentile readers, Mark lists parenthetically some of the traditions followed by *all the Jews* (7:3). It is hyperbole to claim that *all the Jews* practice these things; after all, the disciples and the common people do not.

The Question of Jesus' Opponents 7:5

Mark's parenthesis has already shifted the focus from the issue of washing to the real issue—the scribal traditions. Mark's readers are now ready for the question posed by the enemies of Jesus, *Why do your disciples not live according to the tradition of the elders?* (7:5). The reader expects Jesus' answer, but it does not come—at least not directly, at least not yet. Instead of explaining the disciples' "disobedience," he tells the Pharisees and scribes what is wrong with *their* "obedience."

7:6-13 Jesus' Counterattack

The Quotation from Isaiah 7:6-8

Jesus' response is harsh and to the point, and it comes with the authority of a biblical quotation (Isa. 29:13). Jesus calls the Pharisees *hypocrites;* their words make them sound spiritual, but their hearts prove they are not. They are insincere, and that makes their worship useless. Jesus gives his own summarizing assessment: *You abandon the commandment of God and hold to human tradition* (Mark 7:8).

The Corban Example 7:9-13

Jesus here uses an example to show how traditions can cause people to abandon the commandment of God. Note how Jesus introduces the example: *You have a fine way of rejecting the commandment of God in order to keep your tradition!* (7:9).

You have a fine way is an attempt to translate a Greek adverb "beautifully" (*kalōs*). It is the same word Jesus has used when he said, *Isaiah prophesied* **rightly** (*kalōs;* 7:6). With his wordplay, Jesus says (ironically), "Isaiah did a beautiful job of describing you, and you do a beautiful job of living up to the description."

The Greek words indicate that Jesus' accusations are getting progressively stronger (Guelich: 370). In verse 8 Jesus has accused them of *abandoning* or *neglecting* God's law; in verse 9 he accuses them of *rejecting* or *nullifying* it; in verse 13 he accuses them of *making void/annulling* it. The descriptions of the tradition are also becoming more negative. First it is the tradition of the *elders* (of *esteemed* people, 7:5), then *human* tradition (of *ordinary* people, v. 8), and now *your* tradition (of *hypocritical* people, v. 9).

In support of Jesus' charge that his accusers are rejecting God's law, Jesus cites one example, but claims that many others could be cited (7:13). The example chosen is perhaps hypothetical and likely extreme, but it makes the point well. It involves the swearing of a *Corban* oath, dedicating a property gift to God (or to the temple), and thus making it unavailable for secular/profane use by anyone but the donor (cf. Lev. 27; Num. 30). Jesus is not criticizing the giving of *an offering to God* (Mark 7:11); it is the abuse of the Corban oath that is unacceptable.

Declaring something *Corban* does not necessarily mean actually giving it to God. One verbally sets it aside (like a trust fund) yet may retain use of it. It simply becomes unavailable to other people *as if* it has been given to God. A son may go so far as to inform his parents with a vow that anything they might have expected to receive from him (support in their old age) is now *Corban* for them, not available for their benefit. The son could then keep for himself what he actually owed his parents, who could not touch it. And the religious establishment stands on the side of the son who has made the oath! (cf. Mishnah Ned. 8:7—9:1; M. Sheni 4:10).

Jesus considers this a breach of the commandment to honor parents (7:10) and therefore in principle deserving of death. The Pharisees, according to Mark 7, would defend such a Corban oath (v. 12), thus setting their tradition above God's law (v. 13).

Jesus' counterattack has been forceful. Taken on its own, it appears unfair: the Pharisees and scribes have merely posed a question (7:5). Do they really deserve all that? But in the context of Mark's whole Gospel, the picture looks different. Jesus' opponents have done nothing but find fault. At first Jesus responds to the criticisms and attacks with positive teaching (2:17), careful explanations (2:19-22), and biblical examples (2:25-28). Only after his enemies start plotting his death (3:6) do Jesus' responses take on this tone. As long as their rejection and hypocrisy continue, Jesus will continue to expose them.

Teaching for the Crowd and Disciples 7:14-23
7:14-15 Public Teaching

The summoning of the crowd indicates that Jesus has finished dealing with his opponents. He has criticized their misuse of traditions but has not answered the question they posed in 7:5. What follows is general teaching for those willing to learn from Jesus. They will hear why Jesus' disciples do not observe the traditional washing ceremonies. *Listen . . . and understand* hints that the meaning or application of the coming statement might not be obvious. This is true, as we see from the disciples' need for additional clarification (vv. 17-23).

Jesus cares very much about issues of defilement. However, for Jesus, defilement is not something that enters a person through unclean hands or unclean food. It is something that is born in the heart and works its way outward. The implication is that only *people* can be unclean, not things; and people are not made unclean by things, but by the thoughts and actions devised in their own hearts.

There are two parts to Jesus' statement; both parts are further clarified in the private instruction Jesus gives his disciples. Verses 18-19a state that nothing coming from outside defiles. Verses 20-23 declare that defilement comes from inside a person. Between these two parts, Mark inserts a short phrase literally translated *cleansing all foods* (19b). This editorial insertion points to the far-reaching implications of what Jesus is about to tell his disciples.

7:17-23 Private Explanation

Nothing from Outside Defiles 7:17-19a

There is no verse 16. The most reliable manuscripts do not contain the words *Let anyone with ears to hear listen* (included in many older translations) *[Textual Criticism of Mark]*. The idea captured by these words is nevertheless present. The mention of the *house* suggests a place of private instruction and revelation (7:17; Lane: 255). The reference to *parable* (v. 17) suggests there is a hidden meaning. The penetrating question to the disciples, "Do you also fail to understand?" is surely an implicit challenge to those who have *ears to hear*.

Jesus' explanation is simple: So-called *defiled food* cannot defile a person; it simply passes into the mouth, through the stomach, and out into the sewer. The person (the *heart*, here) is left untouched. Jesus is not creating an artificial sacred/profane distinction here, as though the spiritual life is important and the physical life is not. If anything, he wants to break down such a distinction. Jesus' opponents are the ones thinking special ceremonies are necessary to make profane things sacred again. Jesus' words affirm the basic goodness of God's creation (cf. 1 Tim. 4:4).

It is doubtful that Jesus' first audience would imagine that he is encouraging them to eat swine, camel, or other meats forbidden by OT law (Nineham: 192). Yet Jesus' radical claim that *there is nothing outside a person that by going in can defile* (7:15a) seems to extend beyond the question of defiled hands and defiled (but still kosher) foods. That extension is slipped into the text by Mark's editorial comment (19b).

Cleansing All Foods 7:19b

It is possible (though unlikely) that the three words in Mark's editorial comment should be translated, "Foods are cleansed when they pass through the body." More likely the NRSV correctly interprets what Mark intends to say: "All foods may now be considered clean."

What Mark is claiming is that when the church later learned that OT food laws are no longer binding, their newfound freedom was consistent with what Jesus had taught. Mark is not claiming that the disciples understand Jesus' statement in this text as an abrogation of all food laws, nor that Jesus expects them to do so. That food laws were no longer binding was something the church learned much later and only through great struggle. First came Peter's vision at Joppa (Acts 10:9-20), the conversion of *God-fearers* and *Gentiles* (Acts 10:44-48; 11:20-21), and several conferences (Acts 11:1-18; 15:1-35). Only then was the church able to accept Mark's editorial comment: *Thus he declared all foods clean.*

The words of this declaration may well reflect the words Peter heard God say to him, "Do not call unclean what God has made clean" (Acts 10:15). In Acts the issue is inseparably tied to the spread of the Gospel to Gentiles. As we shall see, that also is the bottom line in Mark 7. Mark's editorial comment shifts the focus from *how* one may eat to *what* one may eat. This shift, Mark believed, is warranted by what Jesus said.

Defilement Comes from the Inside 7:20-23

Jesus continues to clarify his statement on defilement (7:15). The first part, that externals cannot defile, has been clarified in verses 17-19. Now Jesus moves to the second part of the claim in verse 15, that defilement comes from inside. The focus shifts from food to the heart. *Heart* represents the source of thought, deliberation, and decision that leads to action. Jesus has already criticized the condition of his opponents' hearts (v. 6). Now he explains to his disciples what *heart* and *defilement* have to do with each other.

The word *intentions* (7:21) should be understood as *devisings* or *schemings*. Jesus' point is that a person is not defiled through food entering the stomach, but through reasonings, schemings, and finally actions flowing out of a defiled heart. As W. Lane points out, "Jesus does not alleviate the demand for purity but sharpens it" (258). Washing hands is relatively easy compared to overcoming greed, pride, and other evil desires.

The list of things that defile is carefully constructed in the original text. The first six nouns are given in the plural, suggesting a reference to repeated acts. The last six nouns are given in the singular, pointing rather to various vices that eventually result in evil actions.

The Pharisees are concerned about defilement, so they watch what goes into the body. Jesus is concerned about defilement, so he watches what comes out of the heart. They were concerned with hands and food. He tells his disciples:

• Defilement is a matter of the heart, not the hands.

• Observing the ancient purification ceremonies will not keep the heart pure.

• What or how one eats is not crucial; what counts are one's thoughts and actions.

Let us be glad that Mark 7:1-23 with its stern warnings and its long list of vices is not the whole Gospel. Otherwise the Christian faith would seem to be nothing but a long list of prohibitions and a constant joyless struggle with moral issues. The next episode in Mark's Gospel will help balance the picture.

The Persistent Faith of a Gentile 7:24-30

7:24 Breathing Room

After a long text that begins with harsh criticism (7:1-13) and ends with heavy moral obligations (7:14-23), it is a wonderful breath of fresh air to read of the daring, persistent faith of a Syrophoenician woman.

Jesus travels northwest toward the coastal city of Tyre, a region far more Gentile than Jewish. We are not told whether his disciples are with him. If they are, this trip might be designed to provide breathing room, the rest and privacy that neither the wilderness (6:30-33) nor Gennesaret (6:54-56; 7:1) permitted. Nothing in the text indicates that Jesus is setting out on a missionary trip to Gentiles. The text says he wants to remain hidden (7:24).

7:25-26 A Gentile with a Need

In the previous chapter, Mark portrays Jesus as one who responds to need, even if that requires setting aside prior plans. It happens again here when Jesus permits a needy woman to invade his privacy, and then once more when he grants her request after first refusing.

Jesus' reputation for healing and casting out unclean spirits has preceded him to Tyre. No sooner has he found privacy in a house when an unlikely candidate for his healing ministry is at the door. As R. Martin points out, she is a born loser on three counts: She is a *woman*: social mores discouraged such contact between men and women. She is *Greek*: the focus here is on her religious status (Gentile). She is of *Syrophoenician* origin: this identifies her by race, linking her with the OT Canaanites and associating her with the "bastardized religion" of Tyre and Sidon since queen Jezebel's time (1981:40).

This woman comes to request that Jesus drive a demon from her daughter. Jesus has just redefined defilement. Mark has just hinted that the wall between Jew and Gentiles is coming down. But does that mean that Jesus will begin a ministry to Gentiles? Declaring foods clean is one thing. This is something else.

7:27 Jesus' Shocking Refusal

Jesus says, *Let the children be fed first, for it is not fair to take the children's food [lit.: bread] and throw it to the dogs.* Jesus' answer seems to be "Sorry; it just would not be right." It is a flat refusal, playing on one of the most derogatory terms Jews used when referring to Gentiles—*dogs!* Is this Jesus talking? The reader of Mark's Gospel cannot hear Jesus' tone of voice: how serious is he? Nor can we watch his eyes: are they twinkling? Is Jesus perhaps only jesting and testing her faith? We do not know. What we can do, however, is listen carefully to how Jesus words his response.

He says, *Let the children be fed **first**,* thus implying that there will be a serving for others later. That in turn is a broad hint that a refusal now has nothing to do with ritual uncleanness, racism, or even paganism. If Jesus refuses, it will be because the right *time* has not yet come. Jesus is doing what must be done *first.*

Then, too, the Greek word that NRSV translates as *dogs* is a diminutive; Jesus actually said *puppies* (*kunaria*), not dogs (*kunes*). The diminutive can even be a term of endearment: *dear little puppies.* Most commentators are reluctant to soften Jesus' words that much. Yet we must at least recognize that Jesus refers to household pets, not to wild dogs. Furthermore, Jesus does not actually *call* her a dog/puppy. The term is used only as part of an analogy.

Readers should also notice Jesus' reference to bread for the children. Jesus has just miraculously fed a crowd, and Mark has hinted that there is a secret meaning to the feeding miracle (6:52). In the present context, *the children* can only refer to Jews (7:27). Does this provide a clue as to the significance of the first feeding miracle, suggesting that it symbolizes God's provision for Israel? If so, could the leftover pieces mean that there is more than enough for the Jews? Soon Mark will narrate a second feeding miracle. Will it perhaps symbolize God's provision for the Gentiles? (8:14-21, notes). Mark provides significant textual hints that Jesus is alluding to more than is on the surface.

Jesus' refusal sounds much different when all that is taken into account. But it is still a refusal, until the woman changes Jesus' mind.

7:28 The Woman's Witty Reply

Luther comments that this woman has grasped Jesus' reply with unshakable faith and dared to see beyond Jesus' "No!" to God's secret "Yes!" (Gnilka, 1978:295). There must be something in Jesus' answer that still gives her hope. We also cannot hear the tone of the woman's voice or watch the twinkle in *her* eye. She clearly chooses her words with utmost care.

Her first word to Jesus is *nai* (not translated in NRSV), meaning *Yes.* "Yes, Lord! Yes, I know that we Gentiles have no place at the table (not yet, at any rate). Yes, I know that the Messiah's mission is to the Jews. Yes, Jesus, what you say is right. I accept that."

Her second word to Jesus is *Kurie* (translated *Sir* in NRSV). Even if she meant to say no more than *Sir*, that would still be remarkable in the light of Jesus' words to her. But *Kurie* can also be translated *Lord.* This is the only time in Mark's Gospel that anyone addresses Jesus as *Kurie,* and the word surely has a confessional ring to it. The only person in Mark who confesses that Jesus is *God's Son* is also a Gentile (15:39).

The woman's third word to Jesus is an important little word, *kai,* translated in NRSV as *even.* It usually means *and*, sometimes *but.* Here it is probably somewhere between these two. *And yet* captures the meaning well. The woman is saying, "That is all fine and good. I accept all that about Jewish priority. *And yet*, remember that I was not asking for a seat at the table. I would gladly accept a small crumb that falls while the children are enjoying their feast; that will surely be enough." This woman does not cringe at being called a *puppy.* She seizes the label and uses it to make her request irresistible. All the Pharisees and scribes could not make Jesus change his mind. The playful, persistent faith of a pagan woman has succeeded.

7:29-30 Grace Flows to a Gentile

Jesus announces that the woman's request is being granted. When she arrives at home, she will find that the demon has left her daughter. Yet as important as the healing of her daughter is to this woman, it is not the main issue for Mark. This is a story of persistent faith, not a deliverance story. The dialogue takes center stage, and Mark highlights the woman herself, her great exercise of faith, and the fact that Jesus crosses the barrier to a Gentile. Or is the woman the one who has broken through?

God's grace is not reserved for those who are scrupulous about religious ceremonies (7:1-13). Nor is it reserved for those who avoid all the vices flowing from a defiled and defiling heart (vv. 14-23). It is for those who are open to receive it and who know they are undeserving. This needy Gentile woman moved the heart of Jesus by her

open heart, her empty hands, and her daring confidence that whatever Jesus would give would be enough.

THE TEXT IN BIBLICAL CONTEXT
First the Jews, Then the Gentiles

Whether or not the feeding miracles point symbolically toward the
future Gentile mission (see above; 8:14-21, notes), this unit surely
does (7:1-30). Mark's comment in 7:19b (*cleansing all foods*) and
especially the example of the Gentile woman make this point unmistakable.

That the Jews are to be fed *first* (7:27) finds echoes in Paul's missionary agenda, "first for the Jew; then for the Gentile" (Rom. 1:16).
It also finds correspondence in the practice of the earliest missionaries (Acts 13:46; 18:6; 28:28; cf. Matt. 10:5-6). The Jews have historical priority. Even the Syrophoenician woman acknowledges this,
and that is what makes her faith so great. As Guelich points out (387),
the loophole she finds is not implied by Jesus' reference to *first* (for
then she would have to wait). She does not deny that the children eat
first, nor does she claim they have already eaten and the *dogs* should
have their chance. In faith she perceives that even the crumbs that
accidentally fall during the children's meal would be enough.

An important question remains: When does the *first* give way to
the *second*? When is the time for the Gospel to go out to the
Gentiles? Even in OT times, there was a celebration of non-Israelites
accepting and/or benefiting from Israel's faith (Rahab, Josh. 2 and 6;
Ruth; the widow of Zarephath, 1 Kings 17:9-24; Naaman, 2 Kings
5). In Jesus' ministry not only the Syrophoenician woman but other
Greeks and some Samaritans also came into contact with Jesus. Yet
these are viewed as exceptions.

Theologically, the transition from *first* to *second* is anchored in
the post-resurrection commissioning of the apostles to "make disciples of all nations" (Matt. 28:19). Historically, the transition took
place in sometimes painful stages during the first two decades after
Pentecost. Peter's vision of unclean animals (Acts 10:11-15, 28-29),
the subsequent conversion of Cornelius (Acts 10:44-48; 15:7-9), and
the Jerusalem council (esp. Acts 15:11), were major turning points.

According to the Gospels, however, this later transition is justified
by what Jesus himself said and did. Already during Jesus' ministry, *first*
is beginning to give way to *second*. Mark, at any rate, grounds the
later Gentile mission theologically (7:1-23) and symbolically (7:24-30)
in the material of this section, even though his Gospel locates the full-

scale mission to the Gentiles in the post-resurrection period (13:10).

Mark might intend his readers to find more than *grounds* or *justification* for the Gentile mission in this text. He might have expected them to find increased *motivation* as well. His point would then be that if Jesus was willing to respond to this Gentile's faith even *before* his death tore down the great dividing wall (cf. 15:38), how much more should the Christian church expand its mission work among Gentiles in the time after his death (Harrington: 105).

Law and Grace, Rituals and Purity

It is often said that the OT emphasizes law and the NT grace. Texts like Mark 7 are then viewed as Jesus' critique of law and celebration of grace. But that is not quite what Mark 7 (or the rest of the NT) actually says. Certainly some aspects of OT law are rendered void (especially for Gentiles) in the NT, but law itself does not end with the OT, nor does grace begin with the NT.

The OT law prescribes and prohibits a wide range of activities—moral issues, social issues, religious issues—and these are often not clearly separated from each other. While strict obedience was required, the emphasis, even in the OT, is not simply on legalistic compliance, but on hearing and obeying God's voice and on maintaining covenant with God and God's people.

Religious ceremonies of all kinds were regulated by the law. Within the OT the prophets insist most strongly on the priority of heart condition over religious practices (e.g., Hos. 6:6; Mic. 6:8; Jer. 31:33; cf. Ps. 51:16-17), while priestly traditions (much of the Pentateuch) hold these in balance.

Mark 7 exposes the emptiness of mere ritual observance, just as the OT prophets had often done (Isa. 1:10-20; Amos 5:21-27; cf. Hurtado: 99). While Mark 7 highlights the centrality of a pure heart and faith in God's grace (cf. 7:15, 24-30), these themes are not exclusive to the NT; they are major themes in the OT as well. Indeed, there is nothing in Mark 7 which could not have been said by the OT prophets. In fact, Jesus critiques the Pharisees precisely by citing Isaiah!

With the NT we see a strong shift away from ceremonial and ritualistic aspects of religion to a focus on relational issues, inner attitudes, and external freedom. Mark in particular highlights Jesus' disregard for boundary conditions and purity codes. Mark 7:1-23 helps readers understand why Jesus does not hesitate to touch a leper (1:41) and a corpse (5:41), why it is alright for a ceremonially unclean woman to touch him (5:27-31), why he can eat with *sinners* (2:15) and extend God's grace across gender, racial, and religious boundaries (7:24-30). His heart is pure; external contacts cannot defile him.

Jesus came, not to abolish the OT law of God, but to fulfill it (Matt. 5:17). As a consequence of fulfilling God's law, certain aspects of OT religious practice lose their significance and become irrelevant, especially for Gentiles (cf. Acts 15:10-11). God's moral law, by contrast, has continuing relevance for all Christians; walking in the Spirit enables Christians to fulfill its requirements (Rom. 8:4).

The church gradually learned that the distinctive marks of Jewishness (circumcision, food laws, the observance of the Sabbath, and Jewish festivals) were neither conditions of salvation nor moral/spiritual requirements for believers. Gentile Christians are free to ignore such things; Jewish Christians must learn that these are not essential parts of what it means to be Christian. Virtually the whole purity system is defined as essentially neutral by the Jerusalem Council (Acts 15). The turning point at that gathering came when Peter insisted, "We believe it is through the grace of our Lord Jesus that we [Jews] are saved, just as they [Gentiles] are" (Acts 15:11; cf. Col. 2:16-17).

Paul counsels freedom with respect to foods that have been offered to pagan gods, though one's own attitudes and the likely effects on others puts some restraints on the exercise of that freedom (1 Cor. 8:7-13). We even read, "Everything created by God is good, and nothing is to be rejected, provided it is received with thanksgiving" (1 Tim. 4:3b-4).

With respect to the ritual aspects of Jewish religion, the OT demanded both pure hearts and ceremonies designed to symbolize them. As portrayed in Mark 7, the Pharisees were content to observe the ceremonies; Jesus was content with pure hearts.

THE TEXT IN THE LIFE OF THE CHURCH
Religious Traditions and Ceremonies

This section raises a whole series of interrelated issues that have figured prominently in ethnic and religious conflicts throughout history. Traditional cultures and religions have often developed elaborate guidelines defining proper and improper behavior. Purity codes, cleansing ceremonies, and religious rituals are often inseparable components of what defines a social group. They perform the positive function of creating group solidarity. But they do it at the cost of emphasizing the boundary and not the heart of a group's identity.

Rigid insider/outsider categories can easily develop, and these then isolate the group from outsiders and marginalize those who are insiders but not scrupulous about living by the accepted norms.

OT religious law and NT Christian traditions share aspects of this social function of ritual (both positive and negative). The OT prophets and especially Jesus played down the importance of ceremonies and rituals. Their concern was for the heart of true religion. That does not mean that defilement was no longer an important issue; it was, but it was defined as a matter of the heart (cf. Ps. 51:16,17; Jer. 7:21-23; Hos. 6:6; Mic. 6:8; cf. TBC, above, and for 11:27—12:44).

Mark 7:1-23 teaches that defilement is not related to *how* we eat or to *what* we eat. Mark 7:24-30 teaches us that it is also not related to gender, race, or creed. If it took the Christian church several decades to recognize this, it has taken several millennia to learn to practice it. Precisely for fear of defilement, many Christians experience contact across gender, racial, or creedal lines to be threatening rather than wholesome. Some are not even open to people whose eating (or drinking) habits are different than their own.

The history of the Christian church is replete with examples of believers avoiding contact with "the world" for fear of defilement. That is what Jesus' opponents in this text are doing. Mark surely wants us to take our cues from Jesus, not from those he opposes. Jesus' word is unmistakably clear: defilement comes not from the outside; it comes from the heart.

The believers church tradition has struggled with many aspects of this theme. For some groups, rigid boundaries separating insiders from outsiders were occasioned by external persecution or by restrictions on proselytizing. Just as often contributing to the problem, however, is a lack of clarity about what is cultural and what is biblical, or a legalistic concern to preserve cultural peculiarities. At times authoritarian leaders who established and enforced the rules of the community only compounded the problem.

Today many of these same groups have gone to another extreme. Wanting to break down barriers to evangelism and to the incorporation of newcomers, cultural and theological distinctives alike are downplayed or denied. The danger is that the church becomes unclear about its own identity and boundaries, becoming so "seeker-driven/sensitive" (to use current phrases), that newcomers can virtually join the church without realizing they have done so.

Many churches value rituals and traditions, both as enhancements to worship and as aids to establishing and defining group identity. In some churches elaborate rituals are incorporated into worship experiences. In others, special church events (retreats, drama productions, ministry venues) become focal points of group identity. Such rituals contribute positively both by helping to define a group and build solidarity, and through the intrinsic value of the worship and ministry that result from the events.

Church traditions often relate to how Christians dress, what songs they sing, what amusements they avoid, what organizations they support, and so on. Often such traditions develop accidentally in the life of the church. Sometimes they were deliberately initiated to safeguard the clearly revealed will of God (clear to us, at any rate). Danger sets in when they become more important than the core of the Gospel.

Mark 7:1-23 is about traditions that get out of hand. D. McKenna claims the church is in danger of doing exactly what Jesus says the Pharisees and scribes have done:

> Christian history is tragically replete with examples of a spiritual Truth being represented by a meaningful symbol, elevated to a required ritual, substituted for the original truth, and finally perverted to justify an evil act. (154)

Not all traditions are bad, nor are all innovations good. But the church continually runs the risk of letting traditions crowd out precisely those things they were designed to safeguard. When our traditions become rigid, when they blind us to aspects of the truth we are overlooking, when we confuse our traditions with the will of God— then Mark 7:1-23 has much to say to us.

Mark 7:31—8:26

Hearing Ears and Seeing Eyes

PREVIEW

The next section seems at first glance to be just a collection of diverse and odd incidents. First Jesus performs an unusual healing, one that involves sticking fingers in a man's ears, applying saliva, and uttering strange sounds. Then he does a repeat performance of the great feeding miracle (cf. 6:30-44), only the details all seem to have changed a little (clues as to the secret meaning?). Next he rebuffs a group of Pharisees who request a sign, and then promptly confuses and embarrasses his disciples, who cannot understand what this all means. Finally, he restores a blind man's sight, but it takes two tries before he gets it right (or so it seems on the surface, at any rate).

Five mystifying episodes are strung one after the other. It would take a genius to make a coherent teaching unit out of such odd and diverse materials. Mark rises to the occasion! One of his favorite writing techniques is to place individual narrative units next to each other in such a way that an interpretive context is produced. He then drops hints that there is more going on than meets the eye, and leaves it to readers to work out the intended meaning.

That is what happens in this section. Mark has not placed five odd incidents randomly one after the other. He has carefully selected five incidents that develop an important theological theme, one we can entitle *Hearing Ears and Seeing Eyes* (cf. 4:12). The reader gradually senses that these units have much depth below the surface. The reader is drawn into the story, hearing with Jesus' disciples his penetrating question, *Do you have eyes, and fail to see? Do you have ears, and fail to hear?* (8:18).

This section is about miracles and their meaning, a topic of perennial interest to Christians. In every age Christians have pondered the mystery of a God who can act miraculously, but often chooses not to do so. Today some Christians praise God with the crowds in the Decapolis: *He even makes the deaf hear and the mute speak!* (7:37). Others hear Jesus' words to the Pharisees: *No sign will be given to this generation* (8:12). Why this difference in emphasis? Why do some feast abundantly and have food to spare (8:8), while others hold one loaf in their hands and fear they shall go hungry (8:14, 16)?

The perplexity and incomprehension of the disciples are prominently featured in this section; yet Mark hints that their confusion will not be permanent. Signs of hope surround the challenge to understand. Jesus can heal deaf ears (7:31-37), and he can open blind eyes (8:22-26). Just like the physically deaf and blind, so also Jesus' disciples and Mark's readers can be granted hearing ears and seeing eyes.

OUTLINE

EXPLANATORY NOTES
The Healing of a Deaf and Dumb Man 7:31-37
7:31 The Roundabout Journey

To travel from Tyre to the Sea of Galilee and the Decapolis (Ten Towns) via Sidon is quite roundabout indeed. Many commentators have blamed Mark for not knowing his geography very well. However, Jesus' purpose for this trip was privacy (cf. 7:24), and he has already interrupted his plans once to minister to a Gentile (7:25-30). A long roundabout journey through Gentile territory can facilitate privacy or further Gentile ministry or both. This journey ends on the east side of the Sea of Galilee, in the Gentile region of the Decapolis.

7:32 A Deaf Man Is Brought to Jesus

Mark clearly intends readers to understand that the deaf man and his friends are Gentiles. The geographical location (Decapolis) and the thematic development (see previous section) both indicate this.

The man is *kōphos* (deaf) and *mogilalos* (with *an impediment in his speech*, NRSV). The Greek word *mogilalos* is rare, found only twice in the entire Greek Bible, here and in Isaiah 35:6. Isaiah 35 addresses Israel's end-time hopes, and Mark uses this section to show that in Jesus they are being fulfilled (7:37, notes; TBC, below).

The deaf man's friends want Jesus to *lay his hand on him*. They want more than a blessing; they ask for healing. Jesus fulfills the request for healing, but in a more elaborate manner than they expect.

7:33-34 The Odd Methods of Curing the Man

Instead of healing by a simple touch or an authoritative word, Jesus' usual methods, he does some seemingly odd things:

1. He removes the man from the crowd. This point is strongly emphasized in the text, as NRSV clearly shows: He takes him aside, in private, away from the crowd.

2. He thrusts/sticks his fingers into the man's ears. The Greek word suggests a more aggressive approach than gentle touching.

3. He applies saliva to the man's tongue. The Greek text does not make clear whether he spits directly onto the man's tongue or onto his own hand, then applying the saliva to the man's tongue. Either way, the act is dramatic and unusual.

4. He looks to heaven and sighs. *Groans heavily* would also be an appropriate translation. Some have suggested that the reference is to a deep and exhausting prayer (Moule: 58); others say that Jesus is

in combat with the powers of Satan (Cranfield, 1966:252). The language of releasing/loosing in 7:35 does suggest demonization (cf. Matt. 16:19; Luke 13:16).

5. He speaks Aramaic, *Ephphatha*. Mark translates it for his readers: *Be opened!* It seems strange that Jesus uses Aramaic words in a Gentile setting.

Such methods were common among magicians in the first century, but they are odd for Jesus. Is he simply trying to make contact with the man? Is he trying to awaken his faith? Is he showing the man symbolically what he intends to do for him?

Amid all the questions, two things should not be overlooked. First, Jesus' upward look clearly points to the divine source of his healing power. He does not heal by getting the magical techniques and incantations right, but by God's power. Second, even though some unusual actions accompany the command, the healing occurs in response to Jesus' authoritative *word*: Be opened! (Guelich: 395).

Why is this healing miracle so different from the majority of Jesus' other healings? Perhaps because it forms a pair with the healing of the blind man at the end of this section. Both suggest that opening deaf ears and blind eyes can be a long and difficult process, especially so when the ears and eyes belong to Jesus' disciples! (see "Reflections on Mark's Teaching Pattern," below).

7:35-37 The Miracle and the Crowd's Response

The man's ears are opened and his tongue loosed. There seems to be special emphasis on the next phrase: *He spoke plainly* (lit., straight/correctly). Not only the deaf man's tongue is loosed; the crowds burst out in praise for what Jesus has done. Despite Jesus' instructions to keep quiet about the miracle, they spread the word zealously and with joy. It is the same thing that has happened in 1:44-45, where the spreading of the good news (contrary to Jesus' instructions) also put an abrupt end to Jesus' privacy.

Mark does not seem to criticize the crowds for acclaiming Jesus. Instead, he quotes their astounded jubilant response. He does so in a way that subtly points to the significance he sees in this miracle of Jesus. God's original work of creation merited the acclamation, "It was very good!" (Gen. 1:31). Here the crowd's similar words, *He has done all things well*, hint that God has again been at work restoring his creation.

The crowd's final words, *He even makes the deaf to hear and the mute to speak*, allude to the same chapter in Isaiah where that rare word *mogilalos* is found. Mark is saying, "God's end-time promises to Israel are even now being fulfilled." The remarkable thing, however, is that it is Gentiles who here acclaim the mighty works of Jesus (TBC, below).

The Second Feeding Miracle 8:1-10
The Two Feedings: Similarities

Mark 8:1-10 reports an incident much like the more well-known *Feeding of the Five Thousand* (6:30-44, notes). The two accounts are so similar that some commentators have wondered whether they are not variant accounts of the same event. Both take place in a desert setting (6:35; 8:4). Both portray the disciples baffled about how to feed the crowds (6:37; 8:4). In each case Jesus asks, *How many loaves do you have?* (6:38; 8:5). The miracle itself proceeds along similar lines: the crowd reclines; Jesus blesses and breaks bread and fish; the disciples distribute the food; all eat and are satisfied; the leftovers are carefully collected (6:39-43; 8:6-8). Even the conclusions sound similar as Mark reports the dismissal of the crowds and a boat journey across the lake (6:45; 8:9-10).

The Two Feedings: Differences

Yet for all the similarities, there are many (and potentially quite significant) differences. Most obvious are numerical differences:

	First Feeding	**Second Feeding**
Loaves	5	7
Fish	2	a few
People fed	5,000 (men?)	4,000
Baskets full of leftovers	12	7

The location is also different: the first was in Jewish territory; this one is in Gentile territory. Another significant difference is the presence of numerous allusions to the OT in the first one, and their virtual absence from the second. In the first, Jesus is portrayed as the Good Shepherd, the New Moses, and the long-awaited Messiah. Even seemingly incidental details such as the green grass and the seating in numbered groups apparently indicate a hidden symbolic meaning: *Jesus has come to fulfill the hopes of OT Israel* (6:39-44, notes).

None of these OT allusions seem to be present in the second feeding account. Instead, we see an expression often used in Scripture to refer to Gentiles. The people have come *from a great distance* (8:3; lit., *from afar, apo makrothen*). As so often in Scripture, Gentiles have come *from afar* to seek and find favor with the God of Israel (cf. Josh. 9:6; Acts 2:39, 22:21; Eph. 2:12-13, 17). The distance they travel helps explain the need for food, but the word also alludes to the significance of the miracle: It is especially for the Gentiles.

The Two Feedings: Mark's Meaning

Mark wants us to recognize the second great feeding as a Gentile feeding, symbolically showing that God's grace through Jesus is also for the Gentiles.

This part of Mark's Gospel has been moving inexorably in this direction. It starts with the abolition of the food laws that have created a barrier between Jews and Gentiles (7:19b). Then a Gentile woman breaks through the barrier and receives God's grace (7:28-29). Jesus' ministry in Gentile territory continues with the deaf man in the Decapolis and the doxology of the Gentile crowd (7:32-37). Now in Gentile territory, a crowd of four thousand is fed, not with mere crumbs this time (7:28), but with a satisfying meal.

In the first century, this would be understood as an authorization of the expanding Gentile mission of the church. Even if this crowd is a mixture of Jews and Gentiles (as likely), Mark still makes the point that God's grace is now available also to Gentiles. But he would then be making the additional point that God's plan is for Jews and Gentiles to sit together in meal fellowship. That too would encourage and challenge Mark's original readers—and should do the same today.

As early as Augustine of Hippo, interpreters of Mark's Gospel have seen the two feedings in Mark as for Jews and Gentiles, respectively. The first shows how God fulfills Israel's hopes; the second shows how God also intends to give grace to the Gentiles.

Once that conclusion is accepted, the interpreter faces a new challenge: how many more clues are there in the text? Are the numbers symbolic of Jewishness (5/12) and Gentileness (4/7)? Why are two different Greek words used for *basket* when referring to the leftovers? We return to these questions when Jesus himself asks the disciples whether they understand the meaning of the numbers and the baskets (8:14-21).

The Pharisees Ask for a Sign 8:11-13

8:11 The Request

Jesus and his disciples arrive in Dalmanutha (back in Jewish territory, cf. 8:10) and are confronted by a group of Pharisees. We have seen how Jesus treated them in 7:1-13 when they wanted to talk about the tradition of the elders. Now we see what happens when the

Pharisees come to Jesus, seeking a sign from heaven.

The vocabulary Mark uses to relate this incident is significant. The Pharisees come *to argue with* him (8:11), not to make a polite request. They come *seeking* (RSV; *asking for,* NRSV) a sign. The word for *seek* is regularly used in Mark with reference to those who want to distract Jesus from his purpose or worse still, to oppose him directly (as in 11:18; 12:12; 14:1, 11, 55). They come *to test him,* the same word used to report Jesus' temptations by Satan (1:13). They come seeking a sign *from heaven,* either a great sign displayed in the heavens or something else that is undeniably from God. They are blind to what they have already seen, or have rejected it. With a setup like that, it is easy to imagine a suitable response.

8:12-13 The Refusal

Jesus' refusal consists of an exasperated question, *Why does this generation seek a sign?* (RSV), and an emphatic declaration that *no sign will be given to this generation.* The wording is significant. *This generation* does not refer in a neutral way to Jesus' contemporaries. In the OT the phrase refers to the evil generation judged in the great flood (Gen. 7:1ff.) and to the *crooked* and *perverse* generation of Moses' day (Deut. 32:5, 20), who saw God's mighty works and yet came *testing* and *trying* God (cf. Ps. 95:8-11). It is as if Jesus were saying, "You Pharisees are just as blind and corrupt, and just as ripe for God's judgment as those people were!" Jesus refuses categorically to produce a sign and turns on his heel; *getting into the boat again,* he leaves his enemies standing on the beach (8:13).

Why does Jesus refuse to give a sign? First, the Pharisees' come insincerely, to trap Jesus rather than to learn from him. Jesus gladly interrupts his plans to minister to and teach needy people. But he is impatient with those who come seeking evidence against him.

Second, Jesus (in Mark) never produces signs in the sense of indisputable evidence. Miracles (Mark calls them *mighty works,* never *signs*) are not overt *proofs* that God is acting in Jesus (H. Anderson: 199). They call observers to *discern* that God is at work. Jesus calls for faith and for insight (15:32, notes) *[Messianic Secret].* Miracles can guarantee neither of these *[Miracles in Mark].*

The Dialogue in the Boat 8:14-21

One of most baffling texts in Mark's Gospel is this dialogue between Jesus and his disciples as they again cross the Sea of Galilee. The disciples talk about their lack of food; Jesus talks about their incompre-

hension, their failure to understand the meaning of the feeding miracles. Jesus' part in the conversation consists of a warning against the
Pharisees' and Herod's *yeast* and then nine questions, mostly rhetorical. It is mystifying to the disciples and to readers.

Some interpreters simply throw up their hands in despair and say,
"Mark has bungled." They refer to Mark's "non-logical" (Turner: 150)
or "clumsy" construction (Meagher: 59). Many claim that verse 15
(the warning against the yeast) causes all the problems and does not
fit in the text. The disciples certainly do not understand Jesus' warning, but that is no warrant for removing the verse. On the contrary,
verse 15 is central to the meaning of the text. Mark wants his readers to understand precisely what the disciples have failed to grasp.

8:14 The Situation

The text begins by setting the scene. Jesus and his disciples are
once more crossing the lake in the boat. The crisis this time is not
another storm, but a lack of provisions. NRSV says, *The disciples
had forgotten to bring any bread: and they had only one loaf with
them in the boat.* It is an odd sentence, odder still in Greek. Mark
seems to deny that there is any bread, then corrects himself by mentioning the one loaf.

Only one loaf, hardly worth mentioning, indeed! But then why
mention it at all? (Guelich: 421). Commentators choose one of four
main positions:

1. The reference to the *one loaf* is not intended to be taken literally. There are no *physical* loaves with them; but they do have Jesus,
the one sufficient loaf, the *bread of life,* who alone is all they need.
A variation of this view recognizes that they do indeed have exactly
one physical loaf, but they ought to have seen in it a *symbol* of Jesus,
the "one loaf with them in the boat."

2. The mention of the one loaf is intended to evoke images of the
eucharist/Lord's Supper. Jews and Gentiles have just been fed by
Jesus (but separately). The time will come, however, when Jew and
Gentile will commune together at a common table, sharing *one loaf*
and becoming *one body* (cf. 1 Cor. 10:16-17).

3. Mark's point is that the stage is set for another feeding miracle—there is need, there are limited resources, and there is Jesus who
can multiply bread. The *one loaf* is clearly sufficient. How can the disciples *still* be worried about not having enough to eat? Do they not
yet believe that the presence of Jesus guarantees the meeting of their
every need?

4. The fourth option is the opposite of the third. The disciples do not doubt that Jesus can multiply their one loaf; they even think they can presume on him to do so. Will their one loaf lead them to *seek signs* (8:11-13), the very thing for which Jesus just criticized the Pharisees? Do the disciples really think that is the lesson to be learned from the feeding miracles? Will Jesus provide a picnic on the lake whenever they are hungry?

The first two options seem unlikely. There are numerous references to bread in this section, and some of them clearly have a symbolic function (esp. 7:27-28). But they do not seem to point to Jesus himself or to the Lord's Supper. It is true that Jesus will later take a loaf of bread and say, *This is my body* (14:22). But it is hard to see how the reader of Mark's Gospel can make that connection already in chapter 8. It is even harder to think that Jesus expected his disciples to do so.

In the two feeding miracles, Jesus feeds both Jews and Gentiles, but Jesus is not presented in the text as either the *bread of life* or the *communion loaf*. Some have argued otherwise, pointing to the language used in the two feeding miracles. Each time, Jesus takes the bread, gives thanks, and breaks it. It is just as in the Lord's Supper. That is true, but it is also just like *every* other Jewish meal.

Deciding between the third and fourth options is more difficult. Will Jesus chide his disciples for *not* expecting a miracle? Or will he chide them for *presuming* on him to perform one? We need to read farther into the text before deciding.

8:15 The Warning About the Yeast

As the disciples ponder their situation (13 men in the boat and only one small loaf), Jesus interjects a warning: *Watch out—beware of the yeast of the Pharisees and the yeast of Herod.*

This is the verse that many interpreters claim does not fit. It has nothing to do with the situation in 8:14, the disciples do not understand the statement or make reference to it, and the matter of *yeast* never comes up again in the discussion (so the argument goes). But Mark surely intends for the reader to make a connection between Jesus' warning and the circumstances into which it was given. To see that we must ask what Jesus means by the Pharisees' and Herod's yeast.

Scholars have suggested that the yeast may stand for religiosity, legalism, nationalism, a failure to recognize and believe in Jesus, or wrong attitudes to Gentiles, and so on. Mark's context, however, points in another direction. The *yeast* has to do with demanding signs and understanding miracles.

As Guelich points out (423), Mark explicitly informs his readers of *Herod's* response to Jesus' miracles. Herod can speculate about their source and nature, but he is led neither to faith nor to understanding by them (6:14-29, esp. 6:14-16; cf. Luke 23:8). Mark tells us about this immediately before narrating the first feeding miracle. Then right after narrating the second, Mark writes of the *Pharisees'* request for a sign. They too have observed Jesus' miracles but have failed to understand the source, nature, and purpose of them.

One may diagram this section as a chiasm:

A • Herod's Wrong Attitude to Miracles/Signs (6:14-29)
 B • The Narration of the First Feeding Miracle (6:30-44)
  C • Accounts of Various Other Miracles (6:45—7:37)
 B' • The Narration of the Second Feeding Miracle (8:1-10)
A' • The Pharisees' Wrong Attitude to Miracles/Signs (8:14-21)

Mark 8:14-21 thus contains Jesus' warning against the Pharisees' and Herod's *yeast* (8:15, referring to A and A'); and Jesus' call to understand the feeding miracles (vv. 16-21, referring to B and B').

In this context, *yeast* is misunderstanding Jesus' miracles and falsely assuming he will produce *miracles on demand*, that is, signs (6:14-16; 8:11; cf. Luke 23:8). Hence, 8:15 is a call to learn from and avoid the errors of the Pharisees and Herod. The disciples have observed and participated in the two feeding miracles. What have they learned? Have they understood? Will they respond in faith to the Jesus who has performed them? Or will they stoop to the level of the Pharisees and Herod by demanding signs?

This helps us see why Jesus gives the warning precisely at the point where the disciples are discussing their *one loaf*. Thus we see how the third and fourth interpretations (above) *both* apply. The miracle-worker is with them; why are they fretting about meager provisions (option 3). On the other hand, likely with greater emphasis, a strong warning is in order (option 4). The disciples dare not stoop to the level of the sign-seeking Pharisees. Do they really think they can count on Jesus to provide a miraculous picnic on the lake every time they have forgotten to make proper arrangements? *[Three Lessons from a Boat].*

8:16-21 The Disciples Fail to Understand

The disciples have not yet come to understand the miracle-worker and his ways. They fail even to understand his warning in 8:15.

They go on discussing their lack of provisions. It is a symptom of a larger problem: ears that cannot hear, eyes that cannot see.

The first function of Jesus' nine questions in verses 17-21 is to demonstrate the disciples' need for insight. They were present, they saw, heard, and participated. They recall all the details: 12 baskets of leftovers after the 5,000 were fed; seven baskets after the 4,000 were fed. Their memories are flawless. Why then do they not understand? They are deaf and blind to the real significance. Borrowing words from Jeremiah 5:21 (cf. also Isa. 6:9-10; Mark 4:12), Jesus asks two penetrating questions: *Do you have eyes, and fail to see? Do you have ears, and fail to hear?* (Mark 8:18).

The disciples clearly do not *see* and *hear*. Yet in and around this text are two small signs of hope, hints that the disciples (and readers) can indeed come to understand. The first is in Jesus' final question: *Do you not **yet** understand?* That little word *yet* may register some impatience, but it also suggests that the disciples *will* someday come to understand. The second sign of hope is found in the opening and closing miracles of this section. Jesus heals deaf ears and blind eyes. It may take more than one touch (as it does in both), but in the end ears are indeed able to hear and eyes to see. That is what the disciples also need. Jesus will not give up on them until they understand.

The second function of Jesus' quiz might be to point to symbolic numbers in the feeding accounts. The number of baskets of leftovers after the respective feedings is carefully rehearsed. Is this information included only to show how good the disciples' memories are? Many interpreters think there is more to this. The numbers are clues to the secret meaning, and the vocabulary in Jesus' questions confirms it. Mark 8:14-21 not only identifies the disciples' problem, it also helps solve it.

In the *Jewish feeding,* the numbers 5 and 12 figure prominently. There were 5 loaves (and 5,000 people). There were 12 baskets of leftovers. Both these numbers have strong Jewish associations (5 might recall the 5 books of Moses, 12 symbolizes the 12 tribes of Israel, and so on).

In the *Gentile feeding,* the numbers 7 and 4 figure prominently. There were 7 loaves, also 7 baskets of leftovers, and 4,000 people were fed. Here the speculation runs wilder. The number 4 is sometimes identified with the "4 corners of the earth" or with the "4 winds," from which God gathers his end-time people (cf. Mark 13:27); it represents universality, and hence the Gentiles. The number 7 has been connected with the 7 deacons in Acts 6:1-6, the mission of the 70 in Luke 10:1ff., the 7 commands in God's covenant with

Noah (Gen. 9:1-17), or more often with the idea of completeness or perfection as suggested in the 7 days of creation, 7 churches in Revelation, 70 nations into which Jews divided the Gentile world, and so on. All of these would then point in the direction of the Gentiles.

The outcome of this way of reading the text is that when the symbolic numbers are decoded, the secret meaning of the feeding miracles emerges: the first for Jews, the second for the Gentiles.

In 8:19-20 Jesus uses two different words for *basket*, carefully preserving the vocabulary differentiated in 6:43 and 8:8. In the Jewish feeding, *kophinos* appears for *basket;* in the Gentile feeding, *spuris* is used for a larger *basket*. According to some interpreters *kophinos* has stronger Jewish associations, and *spuris* Gentile associations. If the disciples had listened carefully to the vocabulary and correctly decoded the symbolic numbers, they would have come to understand the meaning of the feedings. So goes the argument.

Some readers of Mark find this both too subtle and too strange; yet there is much to be said for it. There is sufficient evidence, apart from the baskets and the symbolic numbers, showing that the two feedings are associated respectively with Jews and Gentiles (8:1-10). Why then should not the carefully rehearsed numbers and the carefully preserved vocabulary also point in the same direction?

In addition, what about the material recorded *between* the two feedings episodes. There we are specifically shown that God's grace provides more than enough bread for the Jews, and there is sufficient for Gentiles (esp. 7:27-28). The Jews are to be fed first, but that implies there is also a time for the Gentiles to be fed! Interestingly, the word translated *fed* in 7:27 actually means *to be satisfied* and is found elsewhere in Mark only in the two feeding miracle reports (6:42; 8:4, 8).

A variation has been suggested by M. Hooker (1983:50): Since the Syrophoenician woman is satisfied with crumbs, the crumbs left after two feedings may symbolize the Gentile mission. When Moses fed Israel with manna, leftovers spoiled and could not be eaten. Now the New Moses is here; he also feeds the Jews, but now his followers are to collect the crumbs. They symbolically represent the bread of life that will be carried even to the Gentiles.

Are the two feedings both for Jews and the leftovers for Gentiles (Hooker)? Or is the first feeding for Jews and the second for Gentiles (many commentators)? The second option is more likely, in my opinion, even if decoding the symbolic numbers seems strange.

For those who are persuaded that the numbers symbolize Jews and Gentiles respectively, two cautions are in order. First, the main point of 8:14-21 is still a warning against sign-seeking and a call for discernment. There will not always be symbolic numbers to decode; instead, hearing ears and seeing eyes make it possible to understand what God is doing. Second, the feedings (esp. the first) have a range of hidden meanings (6:41-44, notes). If we focus on the symbolic numbers and ignore the rest, we miss the better part of the meal.

The Healing of a Blind Man 8:22-26

The healing miracle in or near Bethsaida (8:22-26) is similar to the one in the region of the Decapolis (7:31-37). Both men are brought to Jesus by others. Both times Jesus uses unusual methods of cure (with saliva). Both times two touches are needed. The two miracles are clearly a matching pair. There are also significant differences worth pondering; they may well help us see how Mark has intended these miracles to be understood.

The most obvious difference is that 7:31-37 reports the healing of a deaf man, and 8:22-26 the healing of a blind man. At one level, that appears irrelevant. Jesus' power and compassion are equally available to the deaf, the blind, the lame, the demonized, the hungry, the storm-threatened. Each receives God's grace as it is needed. But there is another level, the symbolic. The disciples also need *hearing ears* and *seeing eyes* (8:18). Without them, they cannot hope to avoid the yeast of the Pharisees and Herod or understand the meaning of the feedings (8:14-21).

Mark presents the two miracles as actual (literal) occurrences in the ministry of Jesus. But it is not a coincidence that these two episodes provide the framework for this section. Mark has used the healing of deaf ears and blind eyes to direct the reader's attention to the main issue addressed here. These miracles combine to show what can (and must) happen to the disciples.

The second difference between the two miracle accounts is the way they end. The first leads to a doxology, almost a confession of faith (7:37). At first glance, the second appears to lead nowhere, ending abruptly with the command not to enter the village (8:26). But the next unit shows that this is not really the end. In the following episode we find penetrating questions about Jesus' identity: *Who do **people** say that I am?* (v. 27). *Who do **you** say that I am?* (v. 29). The Gentiles have responded to Jesus' miracles with amazing insight (7:37). How will the disciples respond?

Perhaps the most remarkable difference between the two miracles is that in the second one, Jesus first causes the man to *see* (8:24), and then with the second touch to understand what he sees (v. 25). At the literal level, that seems surprising. Are Jesus' powers fading? (McCowan: 125). Does the man (or his friends) have insufficient faith? Is the disease unusually difficult to cure? (H. Anderson: 204). At the literal level, we are left without clues. The two stages are simply narrated, making this healing unique among all Jesus' recorded miracles. But it is precisely this uniqueness that has made it so useful to Mark at this point in the narrative. He wants readers to consider a deeper, symbolic level.

The two-stage healing is a perfect reflection of the disciples' situation. Just as the blind man has gained sight gradually, so will the disciples. After the first touch, the man sees without understanding. After the second, he sees *everything clearly*, with understanding. At this juncture in Mark's Gospel, the disciples are standing between the two touches. They have seen the feeding miracles, yet they do not see *clearly*. In the next unit, they will see that Jesus is the Christ, but again they will see without understanding. Still, there is hope that they will *yet* understand (8:21). Jesus is not finished with them *[The Discipleship Journey]*.

Mark's Teaching Pattern in 7:31—8:26

We have divided Mark 7:31—8:26 into five subsections (just as NRSV does). The divisions are based on scene changes and correspond roughly to changes in subject matter. However, it can be appropriate to separate 8:14-21 (the dialogue in the boat) into two parts: the warning against the yeast, and the discussion about the meaning of the feeding accounts. The resulting divisions can then be set out as a chiasm *[Chiasm and Intercalation]*:

> A • Jesus Heals Deaf Ears (7:31-37)
>   B • The Second Feeding Miracle (8:1-10)
>   C • Jesus Refuses to Give a Sign (8:11-13)
>   C' • Jesus Warns Against Sign-Seeking (8:14-15)
>   B' • The Meaning of the Feeding Miracles (8:16-21)
> A' • Jesus Heals Blind Eyes (8:22-26)

By means of this construction, Mark draws attention to the main issue, the correct apprehension of Jesus' miracles. The middle two parts (C and C') expose a wrong attitude, against which the disciples are warned. These are surrounded by an example of a miracle to be understood: B narrates the feeding, and B' addresses the issue of its meaning. The outer framework contains two literal miracles that have been used symbolically to show what the disciples need in order to come to understand.

THE TEXT IN BIBLICAL CONTEXT
Seeing Eyes and Hearing Ears

This section of Mark helps focus the real meaning of Jesus' mighty deeds. Jesus' deeds reveal to those with seeing eyes that God's reign is being established, that God's secret kingdom is advancing in Jesus' ministry. This section also tells us what Jesus' mighty deeds are *not*. They are not objective proofs that will persuade sign-seeking people like the Pharisees. They are not guarantees that Jesus will alleviate every felt need of his followers. But if Jesus will not multiply loaves every time the disciples are hungry, he does promise to open their deaf ears and their blind eyes if they are willing to let him.

The Scriptures are full of texts that speak of the need for eyes that truly see and ears that truly hear. Several are cited below, but there are many others (e.g., Deut. 29:4; 2 Kings 19:16; Isa. 6:10; 30:30; Jer. 23:18; Ezek. 40:4; Luke 10:24; Acts 28:27; Rom. 11:8).

> Incline your ear, O LORD, and hear; open your eyes, O LORD, and see. (Isa. 37:17; cf. Dan. 9:18)
> The hearing ear and the seeing eye—The LORD has made them both. (Prov. 20:12)
> Listen, you that are deaf; and you that are blind, look up and see! (Isa. 42:18; cf. Jer. 5:21; Ezek. 12:2)
> On that day the deaf shall hear the words of a scroll, and out of their gloom and darkness the eyes of the blind shall see. (Isa. 29:18; cf. 32:3; Matt. 11:4-6)

When God's people are in danger, they call on God to have open ears and eyes, so that God might deliver them. More often still, God is the one who calls on humans to use the ears and eyes with which God created them, to discern truly how God is at work among them. The promise is given that someday both the physically and the spiritually deaf will hear again, both the physically and the spiritually blind will see again.

Where blindness and deafness persist, it is because hearts are hard (cf. Isa. 6:9-10; Matt. 13:13-17; Mark 4:12; 8:17-18; Acts 28:27; Rom. 11:8). Jesus has come to heal the deaf and the blind. He does so on the physical level, yet not just to alleviate human suffering and not just to demonstrate that OT prophecies are being fulfilled. He heals also to symbolize what is possible in the realm of the spiritual. Jesus promises his disciples spiritual discernment, if they will continue to follow and learn, and not let their hearts grow hard.

The Fulfillment of Israel's Hopes

The Gospel writers were convinced that Jesus came to fulfill God's ancient promises to Israel. Thus it should not surprise us if their Gospels show parallels to those OT texts that articulate Israel's hopes. Consider, for example, Isaiah 35, a chapter promising the renewal of joy as God comes to redeem Israel. Here are five of its key promises/hopes (NIV):

> The desert and the parched land . . . will see the glory of the LORD. (Isa. 35:1-2)
> Those with fearful hearts will be told, "Be strong, do not fear; your God will come . . . to save you." (35:4)
> Then will the eyes of the blind be opened and the ears of the deaf unstopped . . . and the mute tongue shout for joy. (35:5-6)
> A highway will be there . . . for those who walk in that Way. (35:8)
> They will enter Zion with singing. (35:10)

Jewish interpreters expected this chapter to find its fulfillment in the days of the Messiah. Mark was convinced that this is precisely what happened with the coming of Jesus. The correspondence between these *promises* and the *fulfillments* Mark narrates is surely not coincidental. Note how the following five points from Mark correspond to the five from Isaiah 35:

1. God has been revealing his glory, most notably in the two great feeding miracles that are explicitly said to have taken place *in the desert* (Mark 6:35; 8:4). Both Jews and Gentiles are recipients.

2. "Take heart! Do not be afraid!" says Jesus to his terrified disciples on the lake (6:50), revealing himself as God who *passes by* (6:48) and calling himself "I AM" (6:50).

3. The references to opening blind eyes and unstopping deaf ears unmistakably link this section of Mark to Isaiah 35; so does the rare word for a speech impediment (*mogilalos,* 7:32, notes). The crowds allude to this chapter when they acclaim, "He even makes the deaf hear and the mute speak" (7:35).

4. Jesus and his disciples are about to begin a journey to Jerusalem, a literal journey, but also a symbolic one (10:32). Nine times Mark refers to this discipleship journey as *the Way (hē hodos).* That corresponds remarkably with the promise of Isaiah 35:8.

5. At the end of *the Way,* "they will enter Zion with singing" (Isa. 35:10). Jubilant crowds join in the acclamations, "Hosanna! Blessed is the one who comes in the name of the Lord!" (Mark 11:9).

The parallels are close and the chronological order identical. The similarities between Isaiah 35 and this section of Mark are significant, yet so are the differences between them. In Isaiah 35 there is no countercurrent; everything moves inexorably toward the glorious finale: "Everlasting joy will crown their heads. Gladness and joy will overtake them, and sorrow and sighing will flee away" (35:10, NIV).

In Mark, there is a strong countercurrent. Jesus does indeed reveal his glory in the desert, but the disciples fail to understand (6:52; 8:17-21). He seeks to calm their hearts and reveal himself as God come to them, but they neither recognize him nor understand what he is trying to do (6:49). While Jesus is healing deaf ears and blind eyes, he is also challenging his disciples with penetrating questions: *Do you have eyes, and fail to see? Do you have ears, and fail to hear?* (8:18). On the way to Jerusalem, the disciples will be physically following their Master. But at every turn, they reveal that they are not on the same wavelength (8:32; 9:34; 10:37). Even the singing as they enter Jerusalem will be based on a misunderstanding. Like the exuberant Jerusalem crowds, they celebrate their king, but do not understand his mission.

Jerusalem/Zion will not be a place of gladness and joy, where sorrow and sighing flee away. Not yet, at any rate. Not for the misunderstood Messiah and his misunderstanding disciples. How desperately the disciples will need the *hearing ears* and the *seeing eyes* that this section of the Gospel promises them! How else will they ever be ready for the journey ahead?

THE TEXT IN THE LIFE OF THE CHURCH
Expressing Christ's Compassion in Word and Deed

The word *compassion* is used at an important juncture in both feeding reports. In 6:34 we read of Jesus' compassion for the *shepherdless* crowd; he expresses it by teaching them. In 8:2 we read of Jesus' compassion for the *hungry* crowd; he expresses it by feeding them. The implication is clear: Jesus' compassion leads him to meet whatever needs are present, and when there is need for both teaching and feeding, he does both.

A third time Mark refers to Jesus' exercise of compassion. In 1:41 we read of Jesus' compassion for an ostracized, unclean leper; he expresses it by reaching out, touching, and cleansing the man. Jesus always ministers according to the need of the hour (6:53-56, notes). There is no attempt in Mark to separate Jesus' spiritual ministry and his physical ministry, still less to prioritize them as more important or less so.

D. McKenna refers to the "darkest days of American Christianity" when "liberals" and "conservatives" divided up and prioritized "social" and "spiritual" ministries. In this section, Mark is surely calling his readers to see the need for faithful ministry in *word* and in *deed*, whether that be teaching or admonishing, feeding or healing. When the tasks seem too great, then we are called to remember the miracles in this section. We can learn from the feeding miracles:

> God only asks that we give Him what we have so He can show us how He works miracles with our meager resources. The situation has not changed. What we have to give can never match the size of the need. Only God can fill in the gap. (McKenna: 165-6)

L. Williamson proposes that we learn about compassionate ministries by reflecting on the two-stage healing of the blind man. The goal of the second touch is to see all things clearly: ourselves, other persons, human need, and the presence of God. The second touch may not come easily for comfortable disciples in a complacent church and an affluent society. "It is as though Christ spits in our eyes." Sometimes that is necessary before we can see clearly (149).

When we see clearly, how can we not feel passionately and act compassionately? The Greek verb for "expressing compassion" is *splanchnizomai;* the related noun for "compassion" is *splanchna.* From these words comes the English word *spleen,* and from this, in turn, the KJV references to being *moved with compassion* (Mark 6:34) or even "putting on *bowels* of mercies" (Col. 3:12; cf. 1 John 3:17).

Christians who see clearly have a gut-wrenching ache for the needy and take concrete steps to meet their needs in the name of Christ. My own church tradition has sought to do this through the work of Mennonite Central Committee and other denominational, interdenominational, or local efforts (cf. Hoover). We can challenge each other to follow Jesus' example in holding together ministries of word and of deed.

Part 2

Journey to Jerusalem, the Cross, and Beyond

Mark 8:27—16:8

OVERVIEW

In many ways, the first half of Mark is like the preparation for a journey. John prepares Jesus' way; Jesus prepares disciples to join him on the way. With Peter's confession that Jesus is the Messiah, the journey of the second half of Mark's Gospel can begin.

Jesus announces that this journey will lead to his suffering and death, and beyond that to resurrection. The disciples are not sure they are ready for such a journey, but they (at least physically) follow as Jesus goes from near Caesarea Philippi to Jerusalem (see map).

Along the way, Jesus teaches about God's kingdom, clarifying its nature, its demands, and its rewards. The literal journey becomes a symbol of discipleship, of following Jesus. The disciples sometimes imagine that the journey will lead them to glory, but Jesus keeps clarifying, "Not without first going the way of the cross!"

After narrating the journey to Jerusalem, Mark's Gospel features Jesus' ministry in Jerusalem (especially in the temple). Conflict with the political and religious establishment in Jerusalem grows until Israel's ruling council secures a death sentence and hands Jesus over to the Romans for crucifixion. The journey leads to the cross, but it does not end there. Mark continues with another journey projected, to Galilee. Jesus has emerged from death and is ready to lead his disciples again. Their journey has taken a detour; they have abandoned the Way to the cross. But they can return and follow. Will they?

Mark's Gospel does not explicitly tell us what the original disciples do after the resurrection. He is more interested in challenging his *readers* to face the questions that affect *them:* "What will *we* do, now that Jesus has been raised? Will we find in Jesus' death and resurrection forgiveness and a new beginning? Will we follow Jesus as faithful disciples? Will we announce the good news to others?"

Jesus' journey led into glory only by way of the cross. Mark invites us to follow Jesus on that journey. (For outline of Part 2, see contents.)

Mark 8:27—9:1

A Promise of Glory by Way of the Cross

PREVIEW

No section of Mark's Gospel draws together the main themes of the whole Gospel as clearly as does 8:27—9:1. In my judgment, the five most important themes in Mark are the following:

1. *Christology.* In Mark 8:27-30, Jesus directly challenges the disciples to take a stand on Jesus' true identity. Peter's confession (on behalf of the other disciples) that Jesus is the Christ represents a major step forward, as they continue seeking answers to their own key question, *Who then is this?* (4:41).

2. *The Passion.* In Mark 8:31, Jesus unambiguously predicts his coming death, something only alluded to or foreshadowed earlier in the Gospel (1:11; 2:20; 3:6, 19; 6:27). The messianic confession of Peter provides the opportunity for Jesus to begin explaining that he will be a Messiah who will die and rise again.

3. *Discipleship.* Mark 8:34 represents the clearest statement to this point in the Gospel on what it means to follow Jesus. It means self-denial and cross-carrying; it means accompanying Jesus, even a Jesus who has just predicted his own martyrdom. The meaning of 8:34 is developed in the following verses.

4. *Discernment.* Jesus' teaching on discipleship is bracketed by evidence that Peter does *not* yet see clearly (8:31-32) and by Jesus' promise that some will not die until they *see* that the kingdom of God

197

has come with power. The theme of spiritual perceptions (seeing eyes and hearing ears) will be developed in new ways in the second half of Mark's Gospel.

5. *The Secretly Coming Kingdom.* The promise that some will see the kingdom having come (9:1) raises questions: who? when? how? where? Jesus has been speaking of the kingdom's arrival and of its secrecy. Now he begins to teach about its characteristics and its connection with the King who is crowned on a cross.

This section marks the most significant turning point in Mark's Gospel. The messianic confession is a culmination of all that has gone before. Jesus' compassionate ministries, his parable teaching, his supernatural works, his attempts to lead the disciples to greater insight—these all culminate in what is at least a partial breakthrough: Jesus' followers recognize that he is the Christ. Jesus' first prediction that he will be killed and then rise again is a preview of all that is yet to come. When the disciples reveal their unwillingness to accept the idea of a suffering Messiah, Jesus introduces the main theme of the next two chapters, the nature of discipleship.

Even geographical shifts mark this as a turning point. Thus far Jesus has traveled in and around Galilee. Now begins a clearly signaled journey from the far north (Caesarea Philippi) to the far south (Jerusalem). It is the way *to* the cross that becomes symbolic for the way *of* the cross [*The Discipleship Journey*].

Exactly where should the turning point be located? Some make the major break after 8:30. Doing so clearly shows that the first half of the Gospel has led the disciples to discover Jesus' identity and that the second half consists of the cross-journey (literally and figuratively). Yet a break after 8:30 separates the messianic confession (8:27-30) from Jesus' discipleship teaching (8:31ff.), creating a break where Mark creates a connection: *He **then** began to teach them* (8:31). Thus many interpreters (wisely) include the messianic confession with the second half of the Gospel. But then why not bring 8:22-26 along with it into the second half? The story of the blind man healed in two stages is inseparably linked to the messianic confession and is unmistakably part of a framing device surrounding and interpreting the whole journey to Jerusalem section of the Gospel (see below).

The path of wisdom and humility is to admit that we are not clever enough to write commentaries doing justice to Mark's careful structuring of the material. We draw our dividing lines (as between 8:26 and 8:27) and then immediately look back and wonder if the line should be there. Mark clearly goes in a new direction in 8:22-26, but he does so by means of what some have called a "hinge transition" (Stock, 1985), a text that "looks both ways." Mark 8:22-26 clearly closes off and belongs to the material that precedes it, yet just as clearly it introduces and belongs to the material that follows.

Two structural diagrams show this hinge clearly. The first appears in the preceding section as a chiasm (see "Mark's Teaching Patterns," after 8:26, notes). It sets forth the structure Mark has provided for 7:31—8:26.

In the final episode (8:22-26), Jesus heals a man in two stages. After the first stage, the man sees *vaguely*, without proper understanding. After the second, he sees *clearly,* with understanding. In their puzzlement over the meaning of the feedings, the disciples are just like the man before the second touch. The section as a whole (7:31—8:26) provides Jesus' promise that the disciples will yet be given hearing ears and seeing eyes.

The following diagram also uses 8:22-26 and represents in broad strokes the next section in Mark's Gospel. This diagram is refined and elaborated in later sections (esp. "Preview" for 9:2—10:16).

A • The Healing of a Blind Man (8:22-26)
  B • Confession of Jesus as the Christ (8:27-30)
    C • Discipleship Teaching "on the Way" (8:31—10:45)
  B' • Confession of Jesus as the Christ (10:46-48)
A' • The Healing of a Blind Man (10:49-52)

The two-stage healing of the blind man (8:22-26) is used to comment on the disciples' struggle to understand Jesus' identity (not just the feeding miracles). The disciples need a second touch from Jesus. Their messianic confession is seeing without really perceiving. Their understanding of discipleship is severely deficient. But the final episode of this journey-to-Jerusalem section symbolizes discipleship based on true sight that leads to following Jesus *on the Way* (10:52).

The miracle in 8:22-26 is a hinge transition. We have examined it in relation to the theme of discernment in the preceding section. We will examine its relationship to the theme of discipleship in the material to follow.

OUTLINE

Peter's Confession of Christ, 8:27-30
    8:27a   The Beginning of the Journey (the Way)
    8:27b-30   Who Do People Say That I Am?

Jesus' First Passion-Resurrection Prediction, 8:31

The Mutual Rebuke by Peter and Jesus, 8:32-33

Jesus Teaches About the Nature of Discipleship, 8:34—9:1
8:34   The Definition of Discipleship
8:35-38   Metaphors and Paradoxes of Discipleship
9:1   A Promised Vision of the Kingdom

EXPLANATORY NOTES
Peter's Confession of Christ 8:27-30
8:27a The Beginning of the Journey (the Way)

Caesarea Philippi was a city dedicated to Roman rule, named after Herod Philip and the Roman emperor (Caesar). It boasted a temple honoring the emperor as lord and liberator. In the villages around this imperial city, the man who has been proclaiming *another* kingdom asks his disciples if they recognize who he truly is. Their answer and the following teaching mark a new beginning. The disciples begin to journey with Jesus on the road to the cross.

Mark's code word for the journey is *the Way (hē hodos)*. The journey starts north of Galilee, leads through Galilee (9:30, 33) and parts of Judea and Transjordan (10:1), and then on through Jericho (10:46) and toward Jerusalem. References to *the Way* (9:33-34; 10:17, 32, 46, 52; 11:8) remind readers that this is a journey, but also that this is not only a journey from Caesarea Philippi to Jerusalem; it also shows the way from human perspectives to divine perspectives, from popularity to the cross. This is a journey of discipleship, of learning and following, of keeping the goal in mind and sticking to Jesus, who goes on ahead (10:32).

8:27b-30 Who Do People Say That I Am?

John came to *prepare the way (hodos,* 1:2-3). The way John prepared and has gone, the way Jesus now goes is the *way of the cross.* For Mark, the cross cannot be separated from the identity of Jesus, nor Jesus' identity from the way of the cross. Thus, at the beginning of the journey, Jesus asks, *Who do people say that I am?* It is clearly a request for a recital of popular opinion. But we learn in 8:33 that discipleship is all about moving beyond *human perspectives* and grasping the *divine perspective.* Jesus' first question is about human perspectives. Those without hearing ears and seeing eyes have opinions about Jesus' identity. Jesus asks the disciples what these are.

Three opinions are shared: John the Baptist, Elijah, one of the prophets (cf. 6:14-15). All three opinions give Jesus high acclaim and allude to divine authorization. Those who hold these views clearly recognize Jesus' status as a messenger from God. Yet all three fall short of the truth. The persons named are those whose ministries *prepared for* the coming one. Yet readers know that in Jesus, the Coming One has *arrived*, the promised kingdom has drawn near.

What then is the view of the disciples? Jesus' second question stresses *you*: **You,** *however, who do you say that I am?* (TJG). This captures the emphasis of the Greek. Will their viewpoint represent a true perspective, Jesus' perspective, the divine perspective?

You are the Messiah, answers Peter on behalf of the disciples. Although the term "the Messiah" does not appear often in Jewish literature, and as a title not at all in the OT, its reference is clear enough. Jesus is being identified as the expected Coming One, the heir to David's throne, the one who establishes God's kingdom. When the NRSV translates the Greek word *Christos* as *Messiah* (rather than *Christ*), it captures the focus on Jewish expectation; but NRSV thus sadly obscures the literary connection to Mark 1:1, where it gives *Christ* for the same Greek word. What the readers have known from the beginning, the disciples now also confess.

Jesus does not congratulate Peter on his great insight (cf. Matt. 16:17). He does not even affirm that the confession is correct. What are we to make of this? Commentators are divided. Some claim that Mark sees no need to record an affirming word (after all, readers know from 1:1 that Peter's confession is correct). Others insist that Peter, though "technically correct," shows in everything that follows how wrong he really is.

What about the stern order to silence (8:30)? Some interpreters argue that, since Peter does not truly understand who Jesus is, he is not permitted to spread his inadequate understanding. Others claim that secrecy is required so that people can discern Jesus' identity for themselves, or perhaps so that Jesus will not be mobbed by enthusiastic but uncomprehending supporters [Messianic Secret].

Not to be overlooked (or underestimated) is the fact that Mark does not help us much with our conjectures. He lets the text stand without explanation. A literary critic would call that indirection. Mark has deliberately left the reader to puzzle over the options. He does it so that we will be forced to read on, asking whether *Peter* truly understands what it means to confess the messiahship of Jesus, and whether *we* understand. We know (1:1) as Peter knows (8:29) that Jesus is the Messiah. But do we know any better than Peter does what that means for Jesus, and what it means for us?

As the narrative moves on (8:31-32), we will learn that "Peter's confession is accurate only in its vocabulary" (Camery-Hoggatt: 157). As readers, we are challenged to move past Peter's lack of insight to the full sight that Jesus offers. That brings us back to 8:22-26, the narrative of the man who needed two touches by Jesus before he could clearly see. There is a symbolic connection between that text and this one. Yet we must discern the exact *nature* of this connection. Some have argued that those recognizing Jesus as John, Elijah, or a great prophet are those who "half-see." They know Jesus is someone great but have not seen clearly. Peter sees everything clearly, and confesses the messiahship of Jesus. But the narrative to follow forces us to see the symbolic connection differently.

Those who have not yet grasped that Jesus is the Christ are actually still in the dark. They are blind, not able to see from a divine perspective (8:28, 33). Peter is like the man whose eyes have been touched once, who sees people *like trees* (8:24). Some light has dawned, but it will take another touch before he will see *everything clearly*. He needs truly seeing eyes before he will be ready, like healed Bartimaeus (10:46-52), to follow Jesus *on the way (hodos)*. The discipleship journey begins *on the way* (8:27) and also ends *on the way* (10:52). The journey is the way of the cross. It requires having eyes that correctly perceive the character of the One who leads along this way, and it requires a willingness to follow him.

The reader remembers that the opening verse of Mark's Gospel gives Jesus *two* crucial titles: Christ, and Son of God. At 8:29 Jesus is first confessed as Christ. Much later he will be confessed as *God's Son* by a Roman centurion (15:39). The placement of these two confessions can hardly be accidental. The first marks the beginning of a journey; it becomes the occasion for Jesus to call his disciples to follow him on the cross-journey. The second marks the end of that journey; it is the immediate sequel to the announcement that Jesus takes his last breath and dies on the cross. A true confession of Jesus as Christ and Son of God requires a recognition of and an acceptance of the way of the cross. That is what disciples (and readers) are expected to learn as they journey with Jesus from popularity in the north to rejection in the south *[The Discipleship Journey]*.

Jesus' First Passion-Resurrection Prediction 8:31

Most Markan interpreters speak repeatedly of Jesus' "passion predictions." There are none in Mark; there are only passion-resurrection predictions. By separating the predestined passion from the predicted resurrection, we hang a dark cloud over Mark's Gospel, one that Mark never intended. His Gospel is entitled *good news,* and we must let him define his own focus. Never is death the final word. Just as Jesus' death leads directly to his resurrection, so also the failure of the disciples leads to their final restoration (16:7-8). Mark's Gospel is good news indeed!

We cannot be sure whether the disciples know of the earlier death plot against Jesus (3:6) nor whether they were present when Jesus referred to the coming removal of the bridegroom (2:20). We know they did *not* have access to the opening confession (1:1) nor to the divine voice at Jesus' baptism, with its telling OT allusions (1:11). We can be sure that Judas has not been introduced to *them* as *the one who betrayed Jesus* (3:19). No wonder they are caught off guard by Jesus' clear prediction of his own death.

Then he began to teach them (8:31) hints that the messianic confession opens the doorway to the new teaching (and fewer miracles) that fill the next few chapters. Referring to himself again as Son of Man (for the first time since 2:28) *[Son of Man],* Jesus predicts that he will be rejected by the various groups making up the Jewish Sanhedrin (elders, chief priests, scribes). He will suffer and die at their hands, but will rise again after three days.

Son of Man was used as a title to affirm Jesus' authority. He claimed authority to forgive sins (2:10) and to regulate Sabbath observance (2:28). His claims have set him against the priestly religious establishment, the custodians of the ceremonies and sacrifices needed for forgiveness. They also have set him against the scribal/Pharisaic establishment, those claiming authority on biblical and legal interpretation. Their rejection of his authority leads directly to the passion he now predicts.

The first word of the passion-resurrection prediction is *it is necessary* (8:31, TJG; Greek: *dei*). This refers to the will of God and the prophecy of Scripture. Jesus predicts that his coming death will fulfill Scripture and his commission from God (1:11, notes). In that sense, his death *must* come and will be followed by a resurrection.

Mark uses the phrase *three days later* (cf. 9:31; 10:34) in signaling the timing of the resurrection. In Jewish reckoning, this is equivalent to Matthew's and Luke's "on the third day" (parts of days counted as whole days; cf. 14:58; 15:29).

The Mutual Rebuke by Peter and Jesus 8:32-33

This is the only time in Mark that Jesus is said to have spoken *plainly* (8:32, NIV; *parrēsia*). Peter rebukes Jesus, not because he *misun-*

derstands Jesus but because he *understands* him. The predicted passion is totally at odds with Peter's concept of *Messiah*. Peter presumes to pull Jesus to the side and tell him that he has it all wrong. Indeed, he begins to *rebuke* (*epitimaō*) Jesus. This is the same strong word used to report Jesus' *stern order* to keep silent about his messianic identity (8:30).

Moreover, the same word appears in the next verse as well. Jesus, in front of all the disciples, *rebukes* Peter with the shocking words, *Get behind me, Satan!* As soon as the word *Satan* is uttered, the reader remembers that Jesus has been rebuking Satan all along: when a demon shouts out that Jesus is the *Holy One of God* (1:25), and when unclean spirits shout, *You are the Son of God* (3:12). Prior to this text, every occurrence of *epitimaō* represents a rebuke of Satan (4:39, notes). Like Peter's confession, the demons' confessions of Jesus are accurate only in their vocabulary. A confession of Jesus uttered by one who opposes Jesus elicits Jesus' rebuke.

So Jesus rebukes Peter for his rebuke and calls him back into line. *Get behind me* is an ambiguous command. It can mean, "As long as you play the role of Satan—the false confessor, the tempter—get out of my sight!" But it can also be understood as Jesus inviting Peter to return to a proper discipleship stance: "Peter, I address you presently as Satan, for you speak Satan's words. But if you *get behind me* (*opisō mou*), you will return to your position as a disciple. *Opisō mou* is precisely what Jesus used when first calling Simon Peter to follow him (1:17). In the next verse, Jesus uses *opisō mou* to define more clearly than anywhere else what discipleship really involves (8:34).

Why has Jesus charged Peter with playing Satan's role? It is because Peter's thoughts are human thoughts, not divine thoughts; human ways, not God's ways (cf. Isa. 55:8-9). Jesus is declaring that when the human way opposes God's way, it is demonic; the divine way corresponds to the teaching and lifestyle of Jesus.

On this journey, Jesus clearly predicts his death/resurrection three times (8:31; 9:30-31; 10:32-34). Each time the disciples respond with clear evidence of their misunderstanding and/or nonacceptance of this way of the cross. Each time they do, Jesus provides clear teaching concerning what the way of the cross means for discipleship (8:34—9:1; 9:35-37; 10:38-45; cf. structural diagram in "Preview" of next section). The other seven distinct episodes in this journey section (9:2-29; 9:38—10:31) seem to be held together by Jesus' concern to clarify what are "divine thoughts" on these diverse topics, and how they differ from "human thoughts" (Kingsbury, 1989:116).

Peter has clearly heard Jesus' prediction that he must suffer and die. He does not understand that the messiahship of Jesus must include this. Nor does he understand that the secretly coming kingdom (4:11) also requires it. No doubt Peter's messianic confession is linked to a kingdom perspective different from the one Jesus is teaching. A great and powerful Messiah brings about a glorious military victory. But what kind of kingdom can come by means of a suffering Messiah? Peter cannot imagine. The reader is challenged to learn about that from Jesus.

Jesus Teaches About the Nature of Discipleship 8:34—9:1

8:34 The Definition of Discipleship

Jesus summons the crowds to join his disciples. What follows is an invitation to discipleship. Those already called and already with Jesus learn more clearly what discipleship involves. They must continually reaffirm their willingness to stay with Jesus. Others are tacitly invited to begin the journey with Jesus.

Those who confess Jesus as Messiah must accept that he will die and rise again. But what must they accept about themselves? *If any want to become my followers, let them deny themselves and take up their cross and follow me.* This translation from the NRSV obscures the fact that two different expressions are used for following. In the first line, the phrase *become my followers* uses the expression *opisō mou*. A follower/disciple is thus defined as one who has taken up a position behind Jesus. The second reference to following uses the verb *akoloutheō*, a word that implies movement along with (but still behind) Jesus. Thus discipleship (following after Jesus) is defined with three qualifiers, each of which deserves a few comments:

• *Self-denial* does not focus on denying *things* to ourselves or living as an ascetic. The self is denied as the controlling center. Jesus and his cause are taken up as one's chief loyalties. There are two options: one lives for self, or one lives for the one who is confessed as the Christ. To do the former is to remain tied to *human things;* to do the latter is to give allegiance to *divine things* (8:33). Indeed, the word for *deny* (*aparneomai*) is used only here and with reference to Peter's denial of Jesus (14:30-31, 72). In Mark, one either denies self or one denies Christ. That is what the paradoxes in verses 35-38 are designed to clarify.

• *Cross-carrying* is loaded with a wealth of associations, especially for later Christian readers who know the outcome of the story and understand a NT theology of the cross. From this perspective, cross-carrying may well allude to such diverse elements as a willingness to suffer (even martyrdom), crucifixion of the flesh (Gal. 5:24), the acceptance of and proclamation of the gospel, a commitment to non-retaliation, peacemaking and reconciliation, freedom from the law, and so on. But in the context of Mark's narrative (and of the historical Jesus' teaching around Caesarea Philippi), cross-carrying has a more restricted meaning: willingness to submit to God's will (and Jesus' teaching), no matter what the cost (on cross-carrying, see TBC, below; TLC for 14:27—15:15) *[The Meaning of Cross-Carrying].*

• *Accompanying Jesus* as he journeys toward Jerusalem involves active identification with Jesus, and acceptance of what he teaches. The disciple who has denied self (ceased to live for oneself) and taken up the cross (submitted to God's will) is free to follow (keep in step with Jesus as he models and teaches God's way). All these elements together define what it means to come after Jesus (8:34).

8:35-38 Metaphors and Paradoxes of Discipleship

After each passion-resurrection prediction, Jesus makes a universal statement that helps clarify what is entailed in the *divine things* that define discipleship (cf. 9:35; 10:43-44).

He says, *Those who want to save their life will lose it, and those who lose their life for my sake, and for the sake of the gospel, will save it* (8:35). Humans cannot save themselves; they can only lose themselves (deny themselves, 8:34) and thus find salvation in the one whom they follow. *For my sake* is not in all the manuscripts, but it is likely original. If Mark's Gospel was written to a persecuted Christian community (as I think likely), 8:35 would take on special meaning. When hauled into court and offered the opportunity to recant, Christians would have to choose between declaring allegiance to Jesus (losing life in the persecution and saving it ultimately) or recanting (saving life in the immediate situation and losing it ultimately). This makes Peter's wrong choice in 14:66-72 all the more serious.

Verse 36 is a rhetorical question provoking disciples to evaluate priorities. The things of this *world* (riches? recognition? acceptance?) are surely not to be compared with ultimate salvation, are they? The hearer and reader are left pondering.

Verse 37 puts the highest priority on ultimate salvation and asks if it can be achieved any other way than by losing one's life for Jesus and the gospel. Jesus implies that there is no other way; that in turn means that self-sacrifice, cross-carrying, and accompanying Jesus (cf. 8:34) will bring rewards that overshadow any costs.

Verse 38 recognizes that it may well be costly to side with Jesus. The scoffing and disbelief of *this adulterous and sinful generation* can easily intimidate would-be followers. Yet anticipation of final glory and fear of its loss can be a powerful motivator to stay with Jesus, although not strong enough (it turns out) to keep Peter from shamefully denying Jesus (14:66-72, notes).

After predicting his resurrection (8:31), Jesus now speaks for the first time of his role *beyond* the resurrection. He will come in glory, *with the holy angels*, the first hint that the kingdom presently coming secretly will someday be manifest publicly. The reference to *glory* in this text is Mark's first of three. The second is in the misguided request of James and John to gain glory by bargaining and making glib promises (10:37-39). The third is in the great promise to which verse 38 of this text alludes: *They will see the Son of Man coming in clouds with great power and glory* (13:26).

Jesus is not reluctant to speak of glory, but it is located on the other side of his death and resurrection. The way of the cross is the way of glory. Some have argued that Mark's Gospel seeks to replace a "theology of glory" with a "theology of the cross." It is more accurate to say that Mark knows these two must be tied inseparably together.

In summarizing the immediately preceding discipleship sayings, Morna Hooker aptly notes,

> In Mark's context, the sayings point to the fact that the crucial divide is not between those who acknowledge Jesus as the Messiah and those who do not, but between those disciples who are prepared to follow him on the way of suffering and those who are not. (1991:208)

When Peter confesses that Jesus is the Christ, he reveals that he is not completely blind; he sees, however unclearly. Only those who are prepared to learn from Jesus what such a messianic confession truly means (both for Jesus and for themselves) can experience the second touch, enabling them to see all things *clearly* (8:25, notes).

9:1 A Promised Vision of the Kingdom

Jesus' teaching about discipleship closes with a promise, one that Mark uses to make a connection between the preceding definition of discipleship (8:34-38) and the following account of the transfiguration

(9:2-8). In this context, the meaning of the promise depends on its connection with both discipleship and transfiguration.

Truly I say to you is a solemn word of affirmation. *Taste death* is a reference to dying. But beyond that, not much is clear. Who are those standing here? (1) Jesus' disciples? (2) The crowd? (3) *Mark's* contemporaries? (4) Invisible but nevertheless present OT heroes? The first two options are the most natural readings. The third confuses the time frames of Mark and Jesus. The fourth would not be considered if not for the possibility that Jesus is speaking of Elijah and Moses, who appear in the (following) transfiguration account.

Most interpreters assume that Jesus is promising a great future event, one to happen so soon that not all those standing around him will have died. If Jesus intends that, we still wonder, To what great event is Jesus referring? Is it the transfiguration? Peter, James, and John would then be the ones *standing here* who see the great event that powerfully brings in God's kingdom. But why then the reference to some not dying before the event takes place? The statement would be technically correct, but quite odd. Hardly anyone and perhaps no one who heard Jesus that day will die in the next six days (9:2).

Hence, interpreters usually pick some other event to match the *kingdom of God* coming *with power* (9:1):

• The crucifixion, which paradoxically brings in the power of the kingdom through the weakness of self-sacrifice.

• The resurrection, which surely represents a great event in the kingdom's ever more powerful coming.

• Pentecost, about which Mark is silent except perhaps for 1:8.

• The destruction of the temple, as an act of judgment and therefore part of the establishment of God's reign (13:1-4, 30).

Finally, many suggest that the return of the Son of Man referred to in 8:38 is intended here (and also in 13:30), and that this event is predicted to occur within one generation. The kingdom is present secretly until then, but in power thereafter. This view, however, flies in the face of Jesus' own declaration of ignorance about the timing of *the end* (13:7, 32). It also would mean that both Jesus and Mark prophesied falsely.

The best solution is probably to read the text differently. It is not a prediction of a great future event that brings the kingdom in power. It is rather a prediction that in the future some will have the eyes to see that it has *already* come in power *[Kingdom of God in Mark]*. Happily, the NRSV has adopted this view in its translation: *until they see that the kingdom of God has come with power*. What is promised is not an event in the progressive coming of the *kingdom*, but a future enlightenment of the *disciples*.

With the advent of Jesus, the kingdom has already come in power. But it has come in such a way that one needs special discernment to recognize its presence, let alone its power. What is promised here is that some of those around Jesus will someday understand that the kingdom has (already) come with power.

Thus Jesus promises that whatever difficulties his followers may have seeing all things clearly now (8:26), their eyes will yet be opened. Those who truly deny themselves, take up their crosses, and accompany Jesus (some of those *standing here*) will be granted a vision of what Jesus, his ministry, and his death and resurrection truly accomplish—a powerful inbreaking of God's kingdom.

As a first glimpse of all this, a small number of those standing with Jesus are privileged to be present six days later on the mountain of transfiguration. There they see a foretaste of the final vision of God's kingdom (9:2-8). But it is only a foretaste of what is yet to come. The resurrection is the event par excellence through which blindness gives way to sight for those who meet Jesus in Galilee (16:7).

Thus this discipleship section ends with a promise of eventual seeing. It is an important promise, for faulty seeing will continue to plague the disciples all along this discipleship journey. But if they will stay on the road with Jesus, they will be given sight. That is the promise that makes discipleship part of the good news. Discipleship is itself the way of salvation (8:35). It is the way in which we participate in God's reign (on cross-carrying, see below). It is the pathway to glory and to ever greater glimpses of a kingdom that has come in power.

THE TEXT IN BIBLICAL CONTEXT
Cross-Carrying

Taking up the cross and identifying with Jesus in his death hold a wide range of associations in the rest of the NT. Some are drawn simply from the meaning of the metaphor and the model of Jesus. These include a willingness to suffer unjustly (1 Pet. 2:19-21), to pay the ultimate price of faithfulness (Heb. 2:17-18), and to trust in God's vindication (1 Pet. 2:23). They also include a renunciation of self-defense and retaliation (Matt. 26:52-53; cf. 5:38-48), a forgiving attitude toward the enemy (Luke 23:34), and a relinquishing of oneself into the hands of God (Luke 23:46).

Paul testifies in Galatians 2:19-20 that he has himself suffered crucifixion as a follower of Jesus. Paul's former life came to an end when Paul identified with Christ's death. The life he lives on the other side of the cross is the resurrection life of Jesus, who now lives in him.

Paul also appeals to Jesus' cross in his exhortation for Christians to live in humble unity (Phil. 2:1-11). The mind of Christ Jesus (his self-giving humility) has resulted in an emptying, which in stages brought Jesus all the way down from the highest heaven to the most degrading of deaths—the crucifixion of a slave. God in return has exalted Christ above all things earthly and heavenly. Christians willing to humble themselves as Jesus did can also trust God to take care of them; furthermore, they will be able to live in unity with each other.

Numerous other NT themes are also associated with the cross, cross-carrying, and the disciples' willingness to identify with the crucified one, such as the following:

- A "daily" recommitment to be a follower of Jesus (Luke 9:23).
- Depending on God's revelation, even when neither visible signs nor human logic confirm it (1 Cor. 1:21-24; 2:1-5).
- A Spirit-empowered renunciation of sinful passions and desires (Gal. 5:22-26; cf. Rom. 8:13; Col. 3:5).
- A commitment to Christian fellowship across racial and ethnic lines (Eph. 2:13-16).
- Reconciliation with God (Col. 1:19-20), made possible because God forgives sin and has disarmed the enemy (Col. 2:13-15).
- Perseverance in the struggle against sin, and in the face of hostility to the gospel (Heb. 12:1-4).

Some interpreters have suggested that taking up the cross can also mean accepting for oneself the atoning sacrifice won for us by Christ. Still others suggest that to carry the cross involves the spreading of the message of the cross (evangelistic preaching; cf. M. P. Green).

The historical Jesus would not have expected his first disciples to link all the ideas listed above with his first reference to cross-carrying. Nor would Mark have expected his readers to bring that whole range of ideas with them in seeking to understand Mark 8:34. Yet since the cross of Jesus is so central to Christian faith, it seems appropriate to associate it symbolically with many aspects of salvation, personal discipleship, interpersonal relationships, and Christian mission.

One aspect of cross-carrying is more basic than all of the above and underlies them all. Ultimately, Jesus went the way of the cross, not simply because his enemies orchestrated his death, but *because God willed it.* The divine necessity of the cross (8:31, notes) is combined with Jesus' own commitment, *Not what I want, but what you want* (14:36). This suggests that ultimately carrying the cross means saying yes to God, yes to whatever it might be that the discipleship road demands of each one of us. For another way of looking at the meaning of cross-carrying that ultimately leads to the same conclusion, see the essay on this *[The Meaning of Cross-Carrying].*

Understanding the root meaning of cross-bearing as saying *yes* to God's way presents cross-carrying in a much less morbid light than traditional interpretations sometimes do. The cross is not a symbol of horror and should not be thought to define discipleship in negative terms. Discipleship is, at its heart, saying yes to God; thus it is participation in the reign of God, with all the related blessings and challenges, costs and rewards. The cross is a way of *living*, not just a way of *dying* (T. Geddert, 1989:152).

This understanding of cross-carrying is surely closer to what Mark must have in mind than the trivialized version one often hears in popular culture, religious or not. When life's small inconveniences are labeled "the cross I have to bear," then we have substituted something else for Jesus' call to radical discipleship.

Cost and Reward: Two Sides of Discipleship

Related to the above discussion of cross-carrying is an underlying question: Is discipleship primarily about *cost*? Wherever God's people presume on God's grace, accepting salvation as a gift but not seriously following Jesus as a consequence, we need to hear prophetic words like those of Dietrich Bonhoeffer. He called the church to rediscover *The Cost of Discipleship* (cf. writings of Søren Kierkegaard). Discipleship is not merely reaping the benefits of grace; discipleship is responding to the responsibilities and challenges that Jesus links to following him.

Yet to think of discipleship *only* in terms of cost is to drive a wedge between the costs and the benefits of following Jesus. The NT does not do that. In fact, the costs and the benefits of being committed to Jesus are all subsumed under being his disciple. The end of the road of discipleship is not crucifixion; it is resurrection. That is made clear in every passion-resurrection prediction in Mark. Moreover, as I have written elsewhere,

> Mark 8:34-38 is not finally about losing one's life, forfeiting the world, and unashamedly joining the Son of Man's rejection. It is finally about saving one's life, gaining one's soul, and seeing the kingdom. (T. Geddert, 1989:153)

So it is everywhere in Mark. The dialogue with the rich man in 10:17-21 is not about the necessity of self-sacrifice, but about the means of gaining eternal life. The way of the cross is not a popular way. It is not a broad road that all delight to travel; it is a narrow road that many reject (Matt. 7:13-14). Indeed, the disciples gradually learn that they have joined a movement harassed by enemies, rejected by the majority, and opposed by the powerful. Yet Mark does not emphasize how difficult the life of following Jesus will be, but how rewarding it is. Despite persecution, self-sacrifices will be generously rewarded, and eternal life granted as well (10:28-31). Discipleship, for Mark, is the secret means of gaining glory (cf. Mark 13:26-27; John 6:67-68; 1 Pet. 5:4).

THE TEXT IN THE LIFE OF THE CHURCH
Discipleship

Christology is the central theme of all the Gospels. In Mark, a correct Christology always implies an apprehension and an acceptance of the way of the cross. That is why Jesus immediately supplements Peter's messianic confession with his word about his own impending passion and resurrection, and with his word about discipleship, defined as self-denial, cross-carrying, and following Jesus on the road of obedience, even to death.

An early Anabaptist, Hans Denck, maintained that "no one may truly know Christ except one who follows him in life" (via Klaassen, 1981:87). Mark's Gospel makes the same claim in the ironic wording of Peter's denials: *I do not know this man you are talking about* (14:71). In his failure to truly follow Jesus, he has lost clarity concerning the identity of the one he once publicly confessed (8:29).

Many church traditions seek their primary definitions of the Christian life first and foremost in the writings of Paul. Thus terms like "sanctification," "walking by the Spirit," and "exhibiting spiritual fruit" become key descriptions of Christian living. These terms are virtually absent from the Gospels, where the key terms are those of discipleship and following. By beginning with the Gospels, we have the advantage of keeping central the underlying basis for all Christian living: commitment to Jesus and obedience to him.

Many church traditions also rightly see the cross of Christ as the means of forgiveness and of reconciliation with God, again leaning heavily on the teaching of Paul. It is better to begin with Christ's cross in the Gospels, and in particular with his word about cross-bearing. The Gospels help Christians maintain a balance between the grace side of Christianity (what God has freely done for us) and our response (what we do in gratitude and obedience). None of the more radical discipleship themes are absent from Paul, but they are less centrally focused, especially the way Paul is usually interpreted.

One Anabaptist writer has suggested,

> If in Catholicism the cross was made contemporary in the mass, and if in Protestantism it happened through the faithful dispensing of Word and sacrament, the cross became contemporary in Anabaptist thought in its function in the lives of the disciples. (Klaassen, 1981:85)

Sadly, even when long-forgotten truths are recovered (as I believe they were by the sixteenth-century Anabaptist movement, and others since), there are never guarantees that rediscovered truth will not be abused. Many of the church traditions looking back to the sixteenth-century Anabaptists for their theological inspiration have experienced periods of time where discipleship was hard to distinguish from a judgmental legalism that knew all too little about grace. Mark's Gospel is one that profoundly links the radical call to live a committed costly discipleship with the good news of forgiveness and grace. Jesus *knew* his disciples would fail before they did so. He promised them renewal and forgiveness beyond their failure, based on *his* faithfulness alone (esp. notes on 14:28 and 16:7-8). That is grace.

Mark 9:2—10:16

Divine Thoughts—
Human Thoughts

PREVIEW

After Peter's messianic confession (8:27-30), Jesus has begun preparing the disciples for what is to come. For him, there will be suffering, death, and resurrection (8:31). For them, Jesus gives a renewed challenge to take their discipleship calling seriously (8:34—9:1). Peter, though technically correct in calling Jesus the Christ (8:29), does not yet see *all things clearly* (8:26, 32). But Jesus promises that faithful disciples will indeed someday have their eyes opened to see the present advent of God's powerful reign (9:1).

All this happens at the start of a literal journey from Caesarea Philippi to Jerusalem, and a symbolic one from popularity to the cross. Jesus calls the disciples to progress from *literal* walking behind him to the true following that involves self-denial, cross-carrying, and ultimate loyalty to him (8:34).

Jesus begins the journey southward, leading his disciples through Galilee and into Judea and Perea. Along the way they ascend and descend a mountain, enter and exit several homes, interact with crowds and religious opponents, miracle-workers and children. But the focus is on the slow-to-understand disciples. They argue with the crowds and each other, fail in an attempt to drive out a demon, and exhibit fear and misunderstanding in various contexts. Jesus patiently teaches them *along the way [The Discipleship Journey].*

I have chosen to include in this section all the material up to

10:16, as varied as it may be. At that point the focus is again (as in the previous section) on the cost and reward of discipleship, as Jesus and his disciples approach the gates of Jerusalem. At the center of this section is Jesus' second passion-resurrection prediction, followed (like the first one) with blatant misunderstanding by the disciples and clear discipleship instruction by Jesus. Surrounding this central block are various episodes, sometimes clearly linked to what precedes and follows, sometimes not.

A schematic diagram of the larger context appears in the "Preview" for 8:27—9:1. The diagram emphasizes that this discipleship section is inseparably connected to the issues of true seeing (healing blind eyes) and Christology (Who is Jesus?).

We now turn our attention to Mark's structuring of the large central block, called "Discipleship Teaching." In the following diagram, I have marked with numbers the recurring pattern of (1) prediction, (2) misunderstanding, and (3) teaching. The remaining episodes have been simply listed and marked with an asterisk (*).

Discipleship Teaching "on the Way" (8:31—10:45)

FIRST UNIT
1. Jesus' First Passion-Resurrection Prediction (8:31)
2. The Mutual Rebuke by Peter and Jesus (8:32-33)
3. Jesus Teaches About the Nature of Discipleship (8:34—9:1)

* The Transfiguration (9:2-8)
* The Coming of Elijah (9:9-13)
* Casting Out an Unclean Spirit (9:14-29)

SECOND UNIT
1. Jesus' Second Passion-Resurrection Prediction (9:30-31)
2. The Disciples Misunderstand and Argue About Greatness (9:32-34)
3. Jesus Teaches About True Greatness (9:35-37)

* An Unknown Man Drives Out Demons (9:38-40)
* Sayings About Water, Fire, and Salt (9:41-50)
* Marriage and Divorce (10:1-12)
* Jesus Blesses Children (10:13-16)
* The Rich Man (10:17-22)
* Rich People and the Kingdom (10:23-27)
* Gaining True Riches (10:28-31)

THIRD UNIT
1. Jesus' Third Passion-Resurrection Prediction (10:32-34)
2. The Misguided Request of James and John (10:35-40)
3. Jesus Teaches About Authority and Service (10:41-45)

Here is an important question: What do the episodes marked with an asterisk have in common? What thread holds them together? What are we encouraged to watch for as we aim to understand them? Various answers have been proposed:

1. Mark includes the marked episodes as "community rules," to give explicit guidance to his church community on issues they face. Reply: Mark's Gospel is anything but "rule-oriented." Moreover, one finds such guidelines in Matthew more easily than in Mark.

2. The marked episodes correspond to the experiences of Israel on their own journey from Egypt to the Promised Land. Mark is then interpreting Jesus' journey along similar lines. Reply: There are some clear parallels between Israel's experience at Sinai and the story of the transfiguration. Beyond that, one can find some parallels, but the section is hardly held together or explained by them.

3. The marked episodes are a sample of experiences and issues teaching the disciples how to think *the things of God* (8:33, TJG). In these texts, I have often noted how Jesus' teaching helps clarify the nature of true discipleship, the values of the reign of God, and the desired characteristics of Jesus' spiritual family (for Mark, this is the Christian community). Reply: The third option, I suggest, is the thread holding these episodes together. If this is correct, then we do well to focus our attention on what, for Mark, is the core issue: What is God's perspective on the issues addressed here?

That means we will be leaving other questions to the side. Commentaries often devote many pages to various issues: What historical event lies behind 9:2-8? Were several episodes combined to create 9:14-29? When and how were the sayings in 9:41-50 brought together? I refer readers to those other commentaries if they want to explore such matters. Robert Gundry gives a comprehensive discussion of multiple options. Morna Hooker offers briefer discussion and good judgment in recommending the most probable option.

In this section, I focus on the *human thoughts* betrayed by the disciples of Jesus and others around him, and on the *divine thoughts* that Jesus' teaching represents (8:33; cf. Isa. 55:8-9). This is all about the training of the disciples, a concern that has been central to Mark from the beginning. It is also about the life of a Christian and a Christian community dedicated to the values of the secret kingdom. We notice some of the themes of this section: ultimate allegiance to Jesus and his words, ministry that trusts in God rather than techniques, humility, servanthood, openness to outsiders, acts of kindness, concern for the weak and vulnerable, purity, fellowship, integrity, equality, and faith.

OUTLINE

The Transfiguration, 9:2-8

The Coming of Elijah, 9:9-13
9:9-13   Secrecy and the Resurrection
9:11-13   The Suffering of Elijah and the Son of Man

Casting Out an Unclean Spirit, 9:14-29
9:14-16   The Crowd, the Scribes, and the Disciples
9:17-18   A Distraught Father and Unsuccessful Disciples
9:19   Jesus' Frustration
9:20-24   Jesus and the Boy's Father
9:25-27   Jesus Drives Out the Unclean Spirit
9:28-29   Jesus and the Disciples

Jesus' Second Passion-Resurrection Prediction, 9:30-31

The Disciples Misunderstand and Argue About Greatness, 9:32-34

Jesus Teaches About True Greatness, 9:35-37

An Unknown Man Drives Out Demons, 9:38-40

Sayings About Water, Fire, and Salt, 9:41-50
9:41   Giving a Cup of Water
9:42   Protecting Little Ones
9:43-48   Avoiding Scandal
9:49-50   The Salt of Testing, Preservation, and Fellowship

Marriage and Divorce, 10:1-12
10:1-2   The Pharisees Test Jesus
10:3-5   Moses' Concession
10:6-9   God's Original Intention
10:10-12   Divorce, Remarriage, and Adultery

Jesus Blesses Children, 10:13-16

EXPLANATORY NOTES
The Transfiguration 9:2-8

On an undesignated mountain, Jesus is transfigured, his clothes shine, Elijah and Moses come to talk with him, and God's voice affirms him as the divine Son. What a drama! There are special lighting effects, special sound effects, and appearances out of the past. Yet the narrator is constantly shifting the focus back onto the stunned disciples. Jesus is transfigured *before them* (9:2). Elijah and Moses appear *to them* (9:4). The voice of God addresses *them* (9:7). Throughout the whole experience, Jesus does and says nothing.

Peter fumbles around for an appropriate response, finally coming up with a foolish proposal, in Mark's opinion: *Let us make three dwellings* (9:5-6). The original makes Peter look even more foolish than the NRSV, which fails to translate several words. In Greek, Peter *answers* (v. 5), even though no one asks him any questions. He speaks *because* he doesn't know what to say (v. 6). The whole experience is for their benefit, but they struggle to understand its meaning. So also do the commentators. Some things are clear:

1. The voice of God affirms the divine sonship of Jesus. The disciples have already confessed Jesus as *the Christ*. Now the voice of God addresses him as *my Son*. The disciples have now caught up with the readers. What we learned in Mark 1:1, the disciples have now confessed (8:29) or heard God confirm (9:7). Jesus is Christ and Son of God. The reader and the disciples must now continue on the journey to learn what it *means* to confess Jesus in such terms.

2. A correct Christology without obedient response is of no value. *Listen to him!* says the divine voice (9:7). Jesus has begun to explain the more challenging aspects of discipleship. Disciples (then and now) need not bother fine-tuning their Christology if they are not willing to follow Jesus in life.

3. There is glory on the other side of the passion. Exactly what the gleaming robes represent is not clear. Is it a preview of Jesus' resurrection glory? Is it a glimpse of the *great power and glory* that will characterize the final coming of the Son of Man (13:26)? Is it (less likely) a temporary removal of the veil that hides the ever-present glory of the divine-human Jesus? Whatever it is, it should remind the disciples that even though Jesus has begun to speak of suffering and death, these do not represent the final destination of the journey they are on.

Some things are far less clear. For example, what are Elijah and Moses doing there?

1. Do they represent the prophets and the law respectively? This is a popular but improbable view. The names are in the "wrong" order (the usual reference is to the law and the prophets); Elijah does not typically represent "prophets"; Moses is considered a prophet as much as a lawgiver; and even if they represent prophecy and law, what is Mark's point?

2. Do they represent two OT leaders who "did not taste death"? First-century Jews circulated legends that Moses did not in fact die, despite Deuteronomy 34:5. This view provides for a possible fulfillment of the promise in 9:1. But there are better interpretations of that verse (9:1, notes).

3. Do they represent two great OT leaders who foreshadow Jesus? Elijah and Moses both suffered for their faithfulness. Both were strengthened in a special meeting with God on a mountain. Both (at least according to Jewish legend) experienced transfigurations instead of deaths. Are they there in solidarity with Jesus? Are they there to remind the disciples that God's way has often been the way of rejection, but that God vindicates in the end?

4. Do they represent two great OT leaders who play preparatory roles for the coming (now present) Messiah? Moses is the precursor and Elijah the preparer (Mal. 4:5-6). Elijah's preparatory role is much more strongly emphasized in Mark, explaining the order in which they are listed (cf. 9:11-13). According to Malachi, final preparations for God's intervention include careful attention to the commands God gave Moses on the mountain (4:4), and a spiritual renewal initiated by the returned Elijah (4:5-6).

This fourth option is the one I prefer, though the third one also contains attractive features. The danger on any view is to link Elijah and Moses too closely to Jesus. The whole point, probably, is that they are to be carefully distinguished from Jesus. Elijah and Moses are preparers only; Jesus is the fulfillment. Elijah and Moses had mountaintop experiences with God; only Jesus is affirmed there as God's beloved Son. Elijah and Moses may have survived death, but Jesus will experience it to the full and emerge in resurrection glory on the other side. Elijah and Moses may make an appearance, but Jesus is the central figure, the one who is transfigured and whose clothes shine with an unearthly glory.

This understanding helps us identify what was wrong with Peter's proposal to build three dwellings/tents. Peter errs by trying to prolong an experience of glory, not realizing it can only be glimpsed now. Its full experience is withheld until Jesus has completed the journey to

Jerusalem and the passion that awaits him there. Peter errs also by insinuating that Jesus, Moses, and Elijah are all on par, equally great. They are not: Jesus far supersedes the greatest prophets of the old covenant. Indeed, all they accomplished is but a preparation for what Jesus now fulfills.

That brings us to the last important issue. There are a whole series of parallels between the transfiguration account here and Moses' experience at Mt. Sinai. There is the six-day waiting period for the divine revelation, a cloud that covers them, God's voice in the cloud, and dazzling glory (cf. Exod. 24:15-18; 34:30). Even Moses' encounter with *his* faithless people after he descends (Exod. 32:7-8) finds its parallel in Jesus' frustration over the *faithless generation* he must deal with when the mountaintop experience is over (Mark 9:19).

If Mark has deliberately preserved and highlighted these connections, his point is not only that Jesus supersedes Elijah and Moses; Jesus also establishes a greater covenant than the one these two great leaders inaugurated and preserved. Moses came down the mountain with two tablets of stone, preserving the words God had spoken. Jesus comes down the mountain as the living voice of God. *Listen to him!* God's voice says (9:7). That makes this unusual event an appropriate inclusion in Mark's discipleship journey.

This text is not only about future glory. It is also about present discipleship. Jesus is even now the beloved Son of God, the authoritative voice of God. Jesus is moving toward Jerusalem, where he will establish God's new covenant in which God's laws are not written on tables of stone but on the heart (cf. Jer. 31:33; 2 Cor. 3:3). The voice dies away, the cloud melts away, and the two great OT heroes disappear; but Jesus is still there (9:8). He is the one on whom the disciples must keep their focus.

The Coming of Elijah 9:9-13

9:9-10 Secrecy and the Resurrection

As Jesus and his disciples descend from the mountain of transfiguration, he orders secrecy about their experience until after the resurrection *[Messianic Secret]*. Jesus' resurrection will create new opportunities for seeing Jesus (16:7) and for experiencing the victory side of the cross (10:35-40). Those with eyes to see will know that God's secret kingdom has arrived (9:1). Then it will be appropriate to discuss openly experiences like the transfiguration.

This does not mean, however, that for Mark all secrecy ends with Jesus' resurrection. It does not, for Mark and his readers still live in the era of the secret kingdom, visible only to those with seeing eyes (4:11-12). The veil of secrecy will be finally removed when the Son of Man returns with great power and glory (13:26) *[Son of Man]*.

Somehow Jesus' disciples misunderstand his reference to the Son of Man's resurrection. Do they still not accept that he must die and rise again (8:31)?

9:11-13 The Suffering of Elijah and the Son of Man

The following questions show that the disciples are still puzzled about these things. So also are interpreters! Various parts of the next three verses can be punctuated either as statements or questions, and so translations often vary. The main lines of the discussion are reasonably clear.

The disciples have nagging doubts that their messianic confession was premature (8:29). They wonder how the Messiah can already be here if Elijah has not yet come, as the scribes say he must (8:11). Jesus agrees that Elijah's coming precedes the coming of the Messiah. He claims, however, that both have already arrived. Jesus does not explicitly say that Elijah has come in the person of John the Baptist, but his allusion is clear. *They did to him whatever they pleased* (9:13); they handed him over (1:14) and later executed him (6:27).

Behind the disciples' questioning, one suspects, is puzzlement over the necessity of Jesus' suffering. When Elijah comes, he will prepare people's hearts for the coming of the Messiah. After Elijah's work is complete, they expect no rejection and suffering for the Messiah.

Jesus turns this reasoning on its head. Elijah has indeed come. He has indeed prepared the way for the Messiah; but the way is the way of the cross. Yes, John led a renewal movement, leading many to repentance and baptism. But his final act of messianic preparation was to be *handed over* (arrested, 1:14). It is faithfulness, not mass acceptance, that prepares for the coming of God's reign. Jesus took John's own passion as the signal that all preparations were complete. *After John was handed over, Jesus came into Galilee proclaiming* (1:14, lit. trans.).

Jesus' contemporaries expect neither a suffering forerunner nor a suffering Messiah. Jesus affirms that the suffering of both is predicted in Scripture. Christians have found various OT texts, especially Isaiah 53, that count as prophecies of a suffering Messiah. They have found fewer texts that speak of a suffering forerunner. But the close

parallels between John the Baptist and historical Elijah (esp. their suffering at the hands of wicked women and weak kings) may well count
as prophecies of a suffering forerunner (TBC for 6:1-29).

The *human thoughts* of the disciples in this text all revolve
around their attempt to deny the necessity of suffering. Accepting
divine thoughts means accepting the way of the cross—recognizing
that God's way is often through persecution and death—and believing that there is a resurrection beyond.

Casting Out an Unclean Spirit 9:14-29

9:14-16 The Crowd, the Scribes, and the Disciples

The transfiguration experience is over. Jesus has clarified some
things about *Elijah* (= John, the forerunner). He has reaffirmed that
his own coming suffering is part of a divine plan, and so was John's
suffering. The privacy of the preceding two episodes is over.
Overwhelmed crowds, faultfinding scribes, defensive defeated disciples, a half-trusting and half-despairing father, a tormented boy, and
in reaction to all this, a frustrated Jesus—these all play their roles in
the following incident.

An awestruck crowd enthusiastically greets Jesus, though the
cause of their reaction is left unspecified. Some have speculated that
Jesus is still "shining" from the transfiguration experience, but this
finds no support in the text (cf. Exod. 34:29-35).

The scribes are present, too. They have been among Jesus' greatest critics (e.g., 3:22) and thus also the object of Jesus' strongest
counterattacks (e.g., 7:5-8, 13). In Jesus' absence they have been
arguing with his disciples (not with the crowd, the Greek makes clear),
the nine disciples not with Jesus on the mountain.

9:17-18 A Distraught Father and Unsuccessful Disciples

Jesus asks what the argument is about. In response, a man in the
crowd speaks up. He describes the pitiable condition of his son. He
has a spirit causing dumbness, convulsions, paralysis, and so on. The
description sounds like what is today called epilepsy ("Demonization"
in TLC, below). The father's final line explains the reason for the
argument: The disciples of Jesus are unable to drive out the evil spirit.

The father claims to have brought the boy to *Jesus: I brought* you
my son (9:17). Clearly he (and presumably the scribes) believe that
the disciples' authority is to be equated with Jesus' own. By the same
token, their failure reflects directly on Jesus. The scribes have interpreted the disciples' failure as a discrediting of *Jesus'* authority.

9:19 *Jesus' Frustration*

Is Jesus exasperated with the scribes for drawing his disciples into an argument over his own authority? Is he exasperated with the *amazed* but uncomprehending *crowd*? (9:15, KJV). Is he exasperated, seeing the destructive power of evil in the helpless boy and the distraught father? Is he exasperated with his disciples who have too little faith to minister in his absence? Maybe all of these play a role. Imagine Jesus spending a quiet time conversing with Elijah and Moses on the mount of revelation, hearing God's voice affirm him as the beloved Son, and then coming down to this!

In answer to *them*, Jesus expresses his exasperation, calling *them* a *faithless/unbelieving generation* (the Greek word means both). It sounds a lot like one of God's outbursts in the OT (cf. Num. 14:11-12). But who does Mark refer to as *them*? The text is unclear, since the previous speaker was the man (singular).

9:20-24 *Jesus and the Boy's Father*

In Jesus' presence, *the unclean spirit* (9:25) reacts, causing the very symptoms the father has just described. Yet Jesus does not immediately drive out the demon. With the boy still rolling on the ground and foaming at the mouth, Jesus converses with the father.

The condition is both long-standing and dangerous, explains the father, obviously seeking to persuade Jesus to act. The father prefixes his desperate plea for help with the conditional clause *If you can!* (9:22, NIV). Perhaps he has become less certain after the disciples have failed. Seizing on the man's words, Jesus introduces the central theme of this long text: believing.

Jesus' statement in verse 23 should be read something like this: *About this "If you can . . ."—all things are possible for/by the one who believes* (TJG). This is an ambiguous statement. Is Jesus affirming that everything can be done *for* or *by* the person(s) with faith? Is this about the faith of the man making the request, or about the faith of the disciples, who were asked to fulfill it?

Mark is not a careless writer. We should give him credit for challenging both the father and the disciples with the same statement. The father's request can be granted, providing his faith is adequate. The disciples were unsuccessful and thus demonstrated that their faith has not been adequate. To his credit, the man hears the challenge to his faith. The disciples apparently do not get it. Later they are still at a loss as to why they were unable to drive out the evil spirit.

Meanwhile, the boy is still rolling and foaming and a crowd is gathering. The father utters what has been called "perhaps the most human confession in all the Bible" (Hamerton-Kelly: 105). *I believe: help my unbelief.* Faith is measured in degrees of genuineness, not in degrees of certainty. This man's faith is adequate.

9:25-27 *Jesus Drives Out the Unclean Spirit*

Now Jesus acts quickly. A stern rebuke, a violent reaction by the spirit, and the spirit is gone. Where the reader expects an announcement of the boy's full healing, we are told that he looks *like a corpse.* The bystanders think he is dead. Jesus takes the boy's hand and raises him up. The narrator reports this (9:27), using vocabulary that exactly parallels his report of Jesus raising Jairus' daughter (5:41-42). Both texts reflect uncertainty about whether the child is truly dead. Both "resurrections" foreshadow the greater resurrection Jesus has already predicted for himself (8:31), and thus should assure the disciples that whatever trials and evils *the way* contains, there is ultimate victory at the end of the road. Instead, the disciples are still puzzling over their inability to perform the healing.

9:28-29 *Jesus and the Disciples*

The disciples cannot explain their inability to expel the spirit; Jesus again focuses on the issue of faith. He says that only prayer makes it possible. One wonders what incantations and formulas they may have tried. Jesus says that it does not depend on technique but on prayer and the faith that makes prayer effective.

The paradox of this text is that some later Christian scribes modified it in precisely the *wrong* direction: *This kind can come out only through prayer **and fasting**,* as in many inferior Greek manuscripts and English translations. But this reintroduces technique as the crucial factor, missing the whole point of the text.

Why have the disciples successfully driven out demons during their mission trip (6:7, 13), but fail here? Perhaps their faith was more genuine on the mission trip authorized by Jesus than here in front of an awestruck crowd, where they are trying to prove to critical scribes that they really do have enough authority (cf. 9:37, notes).

In this text "thinking human thoughts" leads to a preoccupation with competition, techniques, and the need for success. "Thinking divine thoughts" means trusting in the unlimited power of God, and humbly asking for increased faith.

Jesus' Second Passion-Resurrection Prediction 9:30-31

Jesus travels *through* Galilee, but this is not part of the Galilean ministry, which ended at 8:27. He is passing through on a journey. His focus is on instruction for the disciples, not on ministry to the needy. Indeed, to focus on instruction, Jesus aims to keep their presence in Galilee a secret. In contrast to *every* other attempt, this one succeeds. From here until Jesus reaches Judea and Perea, only one person comes into contact with Jesus and his disciples. That is a child whom Jesus takes into his arms (9:36).

The second passion-resurrection prediction is uttered in private. It is the shortest and the one most clearly focused on God's invisible guiding hand. *The Son of Man is being handed over* (TJG). The construction is called a divine passive. Before Judas can hand Jesus over into enemy hands, God hands Jesus over into human hands. Those human hands will kill him; they will not hold him. *He will rise again.*

Three times on this journey, at the beginning (8:31), here in the middle, and once more at the end (10:32-34), Jesus predicts the coming passion and the resurrection to follow. Each time the disciples respond with misunderstanding. Each time Jesus seizes on their failure to provide clear discipleship teaching.

The Disciples Misunderstand and Argue About Greatness 9:32-34

Verse 32 records the disciples' response to Jesus' prediction, but it also explains their behavior in verses 33-34. They have misunderstood Jesus' words and act accordingly. They have not understood *the things of God* (8:33, TJG) and do not practice them.

Jesus has just caught the disciples arguing with the scribes (9:14); now they have been at each other. Of all topics, they are arguing about who among them is *the greatest!* Perhaps Peter, James, and John claim the prestigious positions. After all, only they were invited to see the resurrection at Jairus' house (5:37); only they were invited to join Jesus on the mountain (9:2).

Maybe the others, those who had just botched their attempt at healing the child (9:18), are trying to find the real culprit, denying personal responsibility, trying to regain status in the eyes of the three "special ones." One can almost imagine them tripping over each other (and Jesus) as they vie to be on Jesus' left or right (cf. 10:37). Feigning ignorance, Jesus asks: *What were you arguing about* **on the way***?* They are silent.

Jesus Teaches About True Greatness 9:35-37

Sitting down (= preparing to teach; cf. Luke 4:20), Jesus explains the inverted hierarchy of God's way. The way to the front of the line is to volunteer to go to the back. Greatness is measured by service. The paradoxes are not designed just to confound. Nor is Jesus giving strategies by means of which one can become greatest after all. Instead, he is redefining greatness. He is not showing individuals how to move forward but providing a strategy for moving the whole community forward. Any personal gain in influence, ability, or opportunity increases one's responsibility to invest it on behalf of those who lack influence, ability, and opportunity.

Then comes the object lesson. With the disciples in their proper positions around Jesus (cf. 3:34-35), he draws one, the greatest one, into the center of the circle. Is it Peter? John? Any other would-be great one? No, Jesus draws to himself a child. What constitutes true greatness? Being last, like the child; serving even the child; being like the child; welcoming the child. If the disciples can invert their standards of greatness, they will also welcome Jesus and become like him; in turn, they will welcome God and become like God (9:37).

Perhaps the disciples' inability to cast out an unclean spirit in the preceding incident (9:28) is made more understandable here. Did they really care about the tormented boy? Did they welcome the child? Or were they trying to look great, trying to impress the scribes and the crowds? According to Jesus' words here, they were not welcoming God into the situation at all (v. 37).

One may hope that this time they have learned their lesson. But the evidence of 10:13 convicts them, and so does the attitude expressed in the next episode *on the way.*

An Unknown Man Drives Out Demons 9:38-40

For this episode, my edition of NRSV adds the title "Another Exorcist." The word *exorcist* does not appear in the Greek text of Mark, and I have reservations about using it, especially with reference to Jesus and his disciples (TBC, below).

If "the three special ones" have claimed to be greater than the other disciples (9:32-34, notes), Mark's narrator puts them back in their place. Peter, James, and John are regularly singled out as those who say and do the most inappropriate things. Peter rebukes Jesus after the first passion-resurrection prediction; James and John act atrociously after the third one. On the mountain, Peter says all the wrong things. Here it is John who is wrong!

Jesus pronounces people "outsiders" only after they have taken a stand against him. The rest are invited to become "arounders" (3:31-35; 4:10-11). The disciples are less generous. Whoever this man is, John is sure he should be prevented from acting in Jesus' name; after all, he doesn't belong to their group. The disciples try to prevent the man from *casting out demons* (of all things). Perhaps their own recent failure to do the same (9:18, 28) has increased their motivation to discredit someone who is succeeding.

Jesus has taken the position that Satan is not divided against himself (3:23). In what other power, then, can the man be working, if not in God's power? Why then should he be stopped? Jesus declares that the man is *for us*. He should be permitted to do further deeds of power in Jesus name. After all, he is not *against us* and not likely to run off and join Jesus' enemies (9:40).

This short episode is not designed to answer diverse questions about driving out demons, or about who is inside and who is outside the circle of those allied with and authorized by Jesus. It is about attitudes. The disciples are exclusionary; Jesus is inclusionary. They want to protect their prerogatives; he wants to see God's reign established. They are thinking "human thoughts"; Jesus is calling them to think "divine thoughts" (8:33). Cicero the Roman orator once characterized an inclusivist: "While we considered all who were not with us as our enemies, you considered all who were not against you as your friends" (Hooker, 1991:230).

Sayings About Water, Fire, and Salt 9:41-50

What follows is a series of linked sayings. Verses 44 and 46 do not appear in the best Greek texts. An early Christian scribe inserted the contents of verse 48 at two earlier points in the text, creating verses 44 and 46, which the NRSV rightly omits. The sayings that belong to Mark's text seem to cover a wide range of topics and to be linked by nothing but a few catchwords (like *water, fire,* and *salt*). Yet on closer inspection, they do relate well to each other and the larger context.

9:41 Giving a Cup of Water

Jesus has just spoken a word of inclusion concerning a man who drives out demons in Jesus' name. He now promises a reward to all who minister for his sake: *because you bear the name of Christ.* Neither the size of the ministry nor the recipients are the crucial factors. That ministry is done in *the name of Christ* is what guarantees eternal significance for it. Again, it would be hazardous to distill prin-

ciples about the nature of heavenly rewards and who qualifies for
them on the basis of such a saying. Jesus is teaching about attitudes:
generosity, acceptance, humility, and faithful service.

9:42 Protecting Little Ones

Just as little children are highly valued (9:37), so also those who
are little in the faith, those who are vulnerable. People who *put a
stumbling block before* (Greek: *skandalizō*) them, will suffer a fate
worse than being drowned. Neither this statement nor the next four
should be used to construct a "biblical theology of judgment and hell."
Like the preceding saying and the preceding episodes, this is about
attitudes: the vulnerable are to be protected and cared for. They are,
after all, the most important ones in the community of faith (9:34-
37).

Both this saying and the preceding are about water. They are also
about reward and/or punishment. They are about the greatness of little ministries that help little people. Most important, they are both
concrete applications of Jesus' teaching on true discipleship. Next
come three sayings about fire.

9:43-48 Avoiding Scandal

Jesus has just said that a terrible fate awaits those who cause others to sin. Using the same word, *skandalizō,* he now calls on disciples to deal seriously with those things in their *own* lives that will lead
them into sin. Two destinies are possible, *life* or *hell* (*geenna*),
reminding us of Moses' words, "I have set before you life and death,
blessing and curses. Choose life!" (Deut. 30:19). Here Jesus presents
hell/Gehenna (a place that is permanently worm-infested and burning; 9:48) as a circumstance so horrible that one would obviously
choose life/the kingdom, even if one has to become maimed, crip-
pled, and blind to enter it.

Literal mutilation is not intended here, nor would such mutilation
actually bring anyone closer to life. The point is that there are activities we engage in (with the hand), places we go (by foot), and things
we see (with the eye) that can become sources of temptation. Using
graphic hyperbole, Jesus says, *Cut it off, . . . cut it off, . . . tear it
out.* He means it seriously, or he would not have supplied the equally hyperbolic alternative, being thrown into hell.

The word *hell* requires several comments:

1. The word is actually *Gehenna*, derived from the Hebrew name
"Valley of Hinnom." This valley, just outside Jerusalem, had become

a garbage dump, which explains the imagery—worm-infested and continually burning. Such metaphorical language gives no solid footing for a doctrine of hell.

2. Nothing in this text suggests permanent suffering. Never dying and never being quenched refer to the worms and the fire, not to suffering souls.

3. This reference to hell/Gehenna, the only one in Mark, is used as a motivator to serious discipleship, not as a threat to unbelievers.

This text says that discipleship is costly; there are things to be given up, but it is the way to life. It pays to take the demands of discipleship seriously! *Those who lose their life for my sake . . . will save it!* (8:35). Without completely changing topics, Jesus now utters three sayings about salt.

9:49-50 The Salt of Testing, Preservation, and Fellowship

The next three sayings are all somewhat ambiguous. This first one (9:49) likely is a general statement that hardships will come; "causes of stumbling" will abound; the way of discipleship is not without pitfalls. Just as salt penetrates the places where it is sprinkled, so also trials will come, even to the most faithful disciple. These times of testing are likened to fire, which can burn but can also purify (cf. 1 Cor. 3:12-15).

The second saying (9:50a) refers to salt's usefulness as a preservative and flavor-enhancer. The salt stones used in the first century could lose their salt content, however, and would thus become useless. This saying is a call to be genuine, the real thing, the kind of disciple that preserves and enhances the community.

Jesus ends this rather long and diverse teaching session the way he has begun, with a reference to the disciples' arguments over greatness. *Be at peace* is the final exhortation. It is linked to the final salt saying (9:50b). The best translation is probably *Have salt among [not in] yourselves.* Leviticus 2:13 may be in the background. There salt is prescribed for all sacrifices. The disciples have been taught that they too must become willing sacrifices, taking up their crosses (8:34) and giving up their selfish desires for greatness (9:34-35). People who make such sacrifices can *be at peace with one another*.

With his salt sayings, Jesus may also be alluding to table fellowship (cf. Ezra 4:14). Who knows? Maybe Mark wants us to imagine that their host had just called them to the evening meal. Jesus in effect says, "You were fighting on the way [9:36]. Can we share a meal of reconciliation?"

Marriage and Divorce   10:1-12

Why we have chosen to call this text "Marriage and Divorce" rather
than "Divorce and Remarriage" will become clear in the comments
that follow, here and in TLC below.

10:1-2 The Pharisees Test Jesus

The geographical markers remind us that this is a journey. The
travelers have begun at Caesarea Philippi (8:27) and are now nearing
Jerusalem. Perhaps the geographical markers hint at something else
as well. The Pharisees are coming to test Jesus with a question about
divorce. They are in the region where John the Baptist was thrown
in prison for taking a stand on the divorce of Herodias and her remarriage to Herod. That cost John his life!

Are the Pharisees trying to trap Jesus by getting him also to speak
a word that condemns the marriage of Herod and Herodias? Perhaps.
From other sources, we know that the rabbis in the first century were
somewhat divided on the divorce question, some following
Shammai's more rigorous view, and some following Hillel's more per-
missive view. Again, we are not explicitly told that the Pharisees' *test*
revolves around this dispute. We are only told that the Pharisees ask
Jesus about the legality of divorce. They obviously mean, "Does
Scripture condone it?"

10:3-5 Moses' Concession

As often, Jesus responds to a question with a question
[Questioning Jesus]. The Pharisees respond to his question by quoting a text (Deut. 24:1-4) that does not in fact speak to the rightness
or wrongness of divorce. It speaks to the prescribed procedure one
must follow *if* divorcing, a procedure designed to curb divorce and to
protect the wife in case a husband chooses to go ahead with the
divorce. In the OT, divorce was completely in the hands of the husband.

Jesus points out the inappropriateness of their textual choice.
Deuteronomy 24:1-4 represents a concession, not God's real intention. He explains that hard-heartedness necessitated this provision,
clearly implying that the present Pharisees share such hard-heartedness (*because of* **your** *hardness of heart,* Mark 10:5). Jesus then
directs them to the appropriate place for guidance.

10:6-9 God's Original Intention

God's creation intention was that one man and one woman be

married for life. They are to be legally bound to each other; they are to be fully united in a union that is closer even than ties to their natural families, a realignment of allegiances far more radical in their day than in ours. Married people should find their guidance in God's original plan (Gen. 1:27; 2:24).

Jesus' reference to Genesis 1:27 and 2:24 is worth pondering. It shifts the focus from a *divorce* question to a *marriage* question. Those who strive to conform to God's *marriage* ideal will hardly need (nor would they likely benefit from) technical discussions by those who debate the biblical divorce texts.

Jesus has not cleverly sidestepped the Pharisees' question about divorce. Nor has he told them to what extent he agrees or disagrees with the options they are disputing among themselves. What he has done is refocus the question. God's original plan does not include divorce regulations. It consists rather of marriage guidelines. These ought to be the focus (TLC, below).

10:10-12 Divorce, Remarriage, and Adultery

Here Jesus seems to reintroduce rules about divorce right after arguing that texts containing such rules are not to be the focus. Yet there is another way of interpreting these verses. Everything depends on what question Jesus is answering. Here are two possibilities:

1. When is divorce and/or remarriage wrong?
2. Is it still adultery if I first divorce my present wife and then marry the person I want to sleep with?

If Jesus is answering the first question, his answer here is "Always." But this approach creates tension not only with the message of the rest of Scripture, but also with the focus of Mark 10:1-9, where Jesus is not preoccupied with rules about divorce.

If Jesus is answering the second question, his answer here is, "Yes." Jesus is then insisting that God calls for marital faithfulness; he does not permit legal games to justify sin. This approach is better both because it preserves the focus of the preceding section, and because it leaves unanswered the question whether in different circumstances divorce and/or remarriage can ever be right.

Mark 10:10-12 denies that adultery can be legalized and therefore justified by means of divorce and remarriage. God calls people to align themselves with God's ideal, faithfulness in marriage (10:6-9), even if that means severing an illegitimate relationship. This way of reading the text does not produce clear guidelines about when divorce and/or remarriage is right or wrong. But that is precisely why it is probably the *right* way to read the text; Jesus has just steered the focus away from such guidelines and focused on God's intention in creation (TBC, below).

Does that mean Jesus declares Deuteronomy 24:1-4 invalid or unbiblical? Not at all. It was originally designed to control abuses of divorce and protect the victims of divorce. Properly applied, it can still have that function. It was never designed to guide people in decisions about their marriages. The impact of Mark 10:10-12 is the same as the impact of 10:1-9. It is a call to shift one's focus away from divorce texts (like Deut. 24:1-4) toward marriage texts (like Gen. 2:24).

This section treats women and men as equally responsible for the maintenance and quality of their marriages. In Jewish contexts in Jesus' day, only men could divorce (this was less true for Gentile contexts in Mark's day). By the husband's choice alone, a marriage either continued or ended. Moreover, adultery could be committed only against a man. If a man had sexual relations with another man's wife, that was not viewed as a sin against one's own wife. Instead, it was a sin jointly committed by the man and the woman against the woman's husband (cf. Prov. 6:34; R. deVaux: 37). This text puts all that into new focus.

To commit adultery is to sin, first and foremost, against one's own spouse. That is true both for men and for women. Moreover, women are as responsible as men to avoid the adultery that divorce-and-remarriage rules are thought to legalize. This text is a radical statement on the equal dignity and value of women. It appropriately makes women as responsible as men to work toward permanence and integrity in marriage. In a day when all the control was (at least officially) in male hands, that was a radical word!

This section, like many of the preceding texts on this discipleship journey, is about protecting and valuing those who were, in that culture, less powerful, less influential, and more vulnerable. In this case it is women (cf. 9:36-37, 42), and especially women married to philandering and/or abusive husbands.

Like all texts on this journey, this one is about "thinking divine thoughts" rather than "thinking human thoughts" (8:33). Thinking human thoughts leads to justifying lust and sexual sin, seeking easy ways out of challenging situations, and playing games with texts. Thinking divine thoughts means looking for God's true intentions, resisting temptations to sin, and living lives of purity and integrity.

Jesus Blesses Children 10:13-16

The final text in this block (though in Mark the discipleship journey continues) may have been connected with the preceding one because marriage and children are properly related. But it also fits well into the larger unit. On several occasions, Jesus has already spoken of *children* and of *little ones*. He is instructing his disciples about kingdom values. In the kingdom, value is not placed on greatness (defined in human terms). It is placed on service, humility, welcoming the weak, and protecting the vulnerable (cf. 9:34-37, 42; 10:11-12; and so on).

Just as the disciples have tried to stop an unknown man from driving out demons in Jesus' name (9:38), so they try to stop those wanting their children blessed (10:13). Indeed, the disciples *rebuke (epitimaō)* them. The same strong word is used as in 8:30, 32-33. The disciples are still concerned about keeping people away from Jesus; they are still more exclusivist than inclusivist. That they try to keep *children* (of all people) from Jesus shows how little they understand of Jesus' object lesson in 9:36-37.

Jesus is indignant with them, as he has been rather often on this journey. "Get out of the way; let the children come," he instructs his disciples (TJG). When the children come, Jesus embraces them and blesses them.

We should not imagine Jesus placing a sacramental blessing on the heads of infants (though people might be bringing some infants as well). The word for *children* here is the one used for the twelve-year-old girl in 5:39. This is an act of loving acceptance, an object lesson on inverted values. This text does not allude to initiation into Jesus' spiritual family (as maintained by some who link this text to discussions about infant baptism).

The challenge in this text is to understand verses 14b and 15. God's reign belongs to *such as these* (10:14b). What characteristics of children are in focus here? Clearly not their age, for Mark believes adults too can enter the kingdom! Is the focus then on their humility? their openness to Jesus? their ability to embrace Jesus without reservation? their lack of status and rights?

What does it mean to receive the kingdom *as a child* (v. 15)?

- Receiving as one receives a child (with open arms)?
- Or receiving as children receive it (without reservations)?
- Or receiving it by becoming childlike (without status and rights)?
- Or receiving it when *it* comes like a child (eager for our acceptance)?

Perhaps we ought to be content with not knowing for sure! It is an acted parable, and in Mark, parables are there not so much to make a clear point as to provoke careful reflection. What does it mean to grasp God's reign? What does it mean to be grasped by it? How is that like and unlike children? How is that like and unlike the way we receive children?

My personal reflections on this include some of the following thoughts: children are neither innocent nor sinless (don't I know!). But they are forgiving and humble (usually), and exhibit a remarkable faith. In Jesus' day, they were not highly valued and had few or no rights. As I reflect on what that says about God's reign, I think of terms like "inclusiveness," "without pretensions or hesitations," "claiming no personal rights," "exhibiting faith," "admitting dependence," and "relying on grace." Children have much to teach us.

THE TEXT IN BIBLICAL CONTEXT

The Disciples' Journey and OT Backgrounds

Mark and the church to which he writes clearly share the conviction that the experiences of Jesus' followers are understood only against the backdrop of God's Word, which for them is the OT. In the OT God called Israel into a covenant relationship, based on knowledge of God and a mutual commitment of faithfulness and loyalty. Now Jesus has been doing the same thing with his disciples. He has called them (1:16-20), they have come to know him (8:27-30), and now he has been spelling out for them the responsibilities and the blessings of their covenant relationship (8:31—9:1).

It should not surprise us, then, that there are significant parallels between Israel's experiences with God in the OT, and the disciples' experiences with Jesus. This section, perhaps more than most sections in Mark, highlights some of these parallels [The Discipleship Journey].

The Journey. The first significant parallel between Israel's experience and that of the disciples is the journey each of them makes. Israel was summoned by God to abandon Egypt, the land of captivity, to cross the sea, to join God in covenant relationship at the mountain (Sinai), and then to begin a journey toward the Promised Land. All along the way they were learning to know, to trust, and to obey God.

Just so, Jesus' first disciples were summoned to abandon their former lives and all those things that held their hearts captive (1:16-20), to go by way of the sea (3:7-9), and on toward a mountain (3:13), where they too were drawn into a special relationship with their leader (3:13-19). As they travel with him, they learn to know him (8:27-30), and they learn what it means to trust him, obey him (8:31—9:1), and follow him obediently on the way to their own inheritance (cf. 8:35; 9:1). W. Swartley (1981: 212) writes,

> Mark's Gospel draws upon the place-sequences of the Old Testament story of salvation for a structural pattern, a conceptual framework for organizing the teachings and deeds of Jesus' life and ministry.

Thus two journeys are made: Israel goes to the Promised Land, and Jesus goes with his disciples to the glory on the other side of the cross (8:31; 9:1). As the disciples begin their journey with Jesus, OT background texts and experiences often enlighten them and us as to the significance of what they are experiencing. In several incidents in this section, this is clearly evident.

The Transfiguration (9:2-9). Here the presence of Elijah and Moses, the allusions to Malachi 4, the construction of tents, and the images of God's covenant with Israel at Sinai (6 days waiting, the cloud, the mountain, the voice, the glory, even the faithless crowds in the valley below)—these all link OT precedents with this NT re-enactment/fulfillment (for details on such parallels, see notes, above).

The Coming of Elijah (9:9-13). Jesus explains both his own role and that of his forerunner, John, in terms of OT prophecies concerning Elijah and the Messiah/Son of Man. For Jesus, the OT does not predict a "successful" forerunner and a "glorious" Messiah, the view of many of Jesus' contemporaries. Instead, Elijah (cf. Mal. 4:5) has come as a suffering forerunner, preparing the way for a suffering Messiah/Son of Man (cf. Isa. 53). Jesus affirms that John's sufferings and his own are *written about* (9:12) in OT Scripture (see notes, above).

Casting Out an Unclean Spirit (9:14-29). OT allusions are less obvious in this unit, but Jesus' outburst at the faithless generation he must deal with (9:19) is a close parallel to God's outburst at faithless Israel (cf. Num. 14:11-12). Moreover, the faithless disciples and crowds Jesus encounters when he descends from the mount of transfiguration are a close parallel to the faithless Israelites Moses had to deal with when he came down from his parallel experience on Sinai. "Both Moses and Jesus descend from the mountain to face the unbelief of the people (Exod. 32:9; 34:9; Mark 9:19)" (Swartley, 1994:104).

Sayings About Water, Fire, and Salt (9:41-50). Mark draws various parallels between OT texts and Jesus' sayings about water and about salt. Jesus' references to hell (*Gehenna*), to the necessity of choosing life, to salting with fire, and so on, take on new meaning when the relevant background texts are considered (see notes, above).

Marriage and Divorce (10:1-12). This text is about marriage and divorce and also about how to use the OT as a guide for Christian living. The Pharisees ask the wrong question (what are justifiable grounds for divorce?) and go to the wrong text to find an answer (Deut. 24:1-4). Jesus says the OT should be used to learn about God's *purposes* (not God's *permission*, or minimal requirements); thus he points to the right text for the topic at hand (Gen. 1:27; 2:24).

Readers may wish to explore further the OT precedents, allusions, and paradigms reflected in the Synoptic Gospels and in Mark (especially in this journey section). I recommend the writings of W. Swartley, especially *Israel's Scripture Traditions* and his unpublished dissertation "A Study in Markan Structure: The Influence of Israel's Holy History upon the Structure of the Gospel of Mark."

THE TEXT IN THE LIFE OF THE CHURCH
The Child and the Circle

We often symbolize greatness, power, importance, and influence with reference to "being on top." The unimportant, the weak, the downtrodden, are "at the bottom." People clamor their way up the ladder of greatness, often on the backs of their competition.

Jesus chose another image, the image of "arounders." Jesus is in the middle, and true inclusion in Jesus' circle involves positioning oneself "around Jesus" (3:31-35; 4:10). Those around Jesus do not need to jockey for positions in the inner ring. There is room for everyone in the circle of arounders. Those who refuse the invitation are "outsiders" (4:11).

One day Jesus' disciples have been arguing about who is the greatest. In Capernaum Jesus teaches them an object lesson on greatness (9:33-37). In the city, in the house, in the circle, in the arms of Jesus, that is where the child is seated. At the center of power is a no-power, no-greatness, no-influence child—in Jesus' embrace. Jesus is vividly symbolizing true greatness (Hamerton-Kelly: 107).

We might say Jesus has turned the pyramid of greatness upside down (cf. Kraybill). *Jesus* would say the disciples have been turning the true circle of greatness inside out. This section and much of the material to follow it focuses on setting aside "human thoughts" in favor of "divine thoughts" (8:33); that involves discernment and correct assessment (of true greatness, in this case), according to the norms of the kingdom. The disciples have been arguing *on the way* (9:33). They have been having a hard time following Jesus on this discipleship way. In a variety of ways on this journey, Jesus has been defining a community that does not show partiality to the strong or the influential. If Jesus' disciples are being prepared for leadership in this community, they have a great deal to learn.

I cherish the memory of three enriching years in the Mennonite church in Ingolstadt, Germany. In this church, my family and I were drawn into some of their many circles. In North America, we call them groups or teams (home fellowship groups, Bible study groups, leadership teams, and so on). In Ingolstadt they are called circles (*Kreise*). There was a *Leitungskreis* (leadership circle). There were several *Bibelkreise* (Bible study circles). There were many *Hauskreise* (home fellowship circles). I love the imagery; it is the imagery of Jesus. The primary focus is not on structure or administration or leader. It is on the one around whom we are gathered. As we support each other, study the Word, and provide leadership for the church, we recognize the presence of Jesus in the center of the circle.

Demonization, the Bible, and Psychotherapy

It is not easy to know exactly what it means to "be biblical" in our understanding and handling of demonization. Certainly it is not simply a matter of reading Bible stories about demons and looking for similar things today, or of reproducing today the techniques employed back then. In aiming to "be biblical," I suggest that we seriously consider at least the following guidelines:

1. *Choose "demonization" language carefully.* Popular terms for so-called "demon possession" abound. Yet if we mean that a demon possesses a person, there is no such expression or claim anywhere in the Bible. People can have demons or be plagued by them, but demons never *own* anyone. The most neutral biblical term for "demonization" is *daimonizomai* (demonized). It is used in various kinds of situations where something demonic is going on. Beyond the neutral term, Scripture uses various metaphors to help visualize the reality of demonization and of God's victory over demonic powers (e.g., demons can "bind" or "inhabit" people; by God's power they can be "cast out" or "driven away"; often the texts simply say they "leave"). The Bible does not make the distinctions we sometimes make (e.g., between "possession" and "oppression," and so on).

Apart from Acts 19:13 (where "exorcists" are discredited), no word relating to exorcism is found in Scripture. The verb from which the English word derives (*exorkizō*) actually means something quite different ("to put under oath," as in Matt. 26:63). Terms like "exorcism" are loaded, popularized by the entertainment industry, and misunderstood by many Christians. We also need to be cautious about terms like "spiritual warfare" and "deliverance ministry." They easily become code words for someone's theory about them, or they conjure up standardized procedures for dealing with demons.

Standardization should be avoided, both in language used and in techniques adopted to diagnose or treat cases of "demonization." To standardize is to assume there is a "normal pattern." But demons are decidedly paranormal, and our language should never suggest otherwise. Anyone who claims to have a neat system that explains exactly how demonism works is automatically unbiblical.

2. *Avoid simplistic views of the relationship between sickness and demonism.* Sometimes "demonism" is linked to physical illnesses (cf. Mark 9:17-18). Sometimes demonism and illness are clearly distinguished (cf. Luke 9:1-2). No doubt "the destroyer" is at work whenever sickness and/or demonism destroy people, but wherever the destroyer is working, there God is also working, seeking to bring about divine purposes.

Sometimes God's purposes result in healing, sometimes in comforting, sometimes in lifting our eyes beyond present evils to the coming victory of God. It is unbiblical to claim demonism is regularly present whenever sickness and/or sin destroy human lives. We need sensitivity and discernment. There is hardly anything more "demonic" than so-called exorcists trying to persuade all suffering people that they are not only sick and hurting but "demon possessed" as well.

3. *Don't explain every problem with reference to demons.* Demonic influences are sometimes cited in Scripture to explain human evil and destructive events in nature. Often, however, the Bible refers to God's judgment, or to wrong human choices, or simply to disasters that "come upon the land." People who want to find direct demonic involvement whenever something bad happens, may well be underestimating *human* potential for good or evil; or they may be forgetting that *God* is ultimately sovereign over all that occurs. People who live with the constant fear of demonization may need help in dealing with their fears, not with demons.

4. *Expect modern medical and psychological findings to correctly explain some "demonization" in the Bible.* Some "demonized" people whose cure is reported in the Gospels probably suffered epilepsy; others likely suffered schizophrenia. In response to such

claims, many people cry, "Unbiblical!" "Demythologizing!" "Explaining away!" But consider a comparable example. In earlier times many different skin diseases were called "leprosy." Few were what we today call "Hansen's disease" (1:40-45, notes). By learning how to differentiate between various kinds of skin diseases, we learn how to develop effective treatments. So it is with demonization. We should be just as willing to fine-tune our diagnoses of the various aberrations that in earlier times were all called by the generalized term "demonization." That leads to the next point.

5. *While the need for a deliverance ministry should not be ruled out, careful psychological diagnosis should accompany every situation where "demonization" is suspected.* In the case of a broken bone, we readily seek the help of an orthopedic surgeon, even while we pray to God for healing. In cases of "demonization," we should seek the help of competent psychotherapists alongside prayers for deliverance. That is especially true if we pray in Jesus' name, command demons to leave, and there is no obvious improvement. True, we have no record that Jesus ever used extended psychotherapy, but then he never set a bone or used a cast either! His healing word or touch fixed bones, and his word of command drove away demons. One finds here no warrant for the double standards we sometimes adopt, running for medical help when a bone is broken, and relying on prayer alone when "demons" are destroying a mind or spirit.

6. *Be open to the possibility that the demonic can truly be present, however difficult it might be to understand and deal with it.* I wish I did not have to believe that. I want the world to be predictable and normal and wholesome. I don't want to have to reckon with demons. Yet the world is even more unpredictable and abnormal if the enemy is seeking to "kill and steal and destroy," and if we do not take into consideration all the ways Satan might do damage. I believe one of these ways is through "demonization"—something not easy to diagnose, understand, or deal with.

Personally, if I were confronted with a situation where I had reason to believe some form of demonization was at work, I would never deal with it alone. Nor would I call in a "practiced exorcist" or a "deliverance ministry team" *unless* these included people that I would also consider competent biblical theologians (T. Geddert, 1996). For a detailed treatment of this topic that is balanced, biblically based, and tested in ministry settings, I especially recommend the writings of Clinton Arnold.

Divorce and Remarriage

Individuals, couples, churches, and scholars alike have struggled to find "the biblical position" on questions of divorce and remarriage. There are several tough questions: Is it divorce or is it remarriage that the texts seek to prevent? How should we understand the so-called "exception clause"? ("except for unchastity," Matt. 19:9; cf. 5:32). Why do some NT texts seem to allow for an exception while others do not (e.g., Mark 10:11-12; Luke 16:18)? Are there other possible "exceptions" not addressed by the Gospel texts (cf. 1 Cor. 7:15)?

Traditions maintaining that no divorce is ever allowed (or even possible) sometimes use "annulment" virtually as a legal manipulation to preserve a principle in theory, but not in practice. Other traditions struggle to know under what conditions a divorce or remarriage might be right or at least permitted. Often individuals and couples are left without guidance in their own real struggles with these questions.

Biblical interpreters often confidently defend their own views on the subject and claim to have found "the biblical position." The strategy is usually to line up all the "divorce texts," interpreting them in the light of each other, and searching for the correct harmonization. What is found is often poles apart from what someone else finds! The uncomfortable feeling I have is that this whole approach is far closer to the approach of the Pharisees, which Jesus critiques, than it is to Jesus' own way.

Meanwhile, people in deteriorating marriages and in the churches that stand alongside them are frustrated. Does the Bible have a clear word or does it not? Any struggling couple can easily find a biblical scholar, a book, a therapist, a pastor, and/or a Christian congregation to support any position they themselves have reached (or want to reach) on the question of divorce and remarriage. In the end those in struggling marriages would probably benefit more by focusing on "marriage texts" than on "divorce texts," which is exactly what Jesus modeled in Mark 10:5-9.

I have suggested in the notes that Mark 10:1-12 is a marriage text more than a divorce text. The Pharisees want to know when divorce is allowed. Jesus refocuses on God's intention to preserve marriages. But does Jesus then produce a divorce text of his own by absolutely prohibiting divorce and remarriage (cf. 10:11-12)? Is he creating a new divorce regulation? I am not persuaded that this is what he does, not if we interpret this part of the text in the light of the rest.

The content of Mark 10:11-12 is fairly clear: Men and women both commit adultery against their first spouse if they divorce and then marry someone else. What is less clear is what situation Jesus has in mind. I suspect he is addressing the situation that may well have motivated the Pharisees' own debates: A man finds another woman more attractive to him than his own wife. Knowing that adultery is sin, he divorces his wife and marries the other woman in order to pursue his attraction. Jesus responds that the divorce-remarriage procedure is no less adulterous than if the legal proceedings had not taken place. The man has still destroyed God's ideal for the existing marriage.

If this is what Jesus means, then his absolute prohibition of divorce and remarriage here would not stand in contradiction to the texts with a so-called exception clause (e.g., Matt. 5:32; 19:9). The Matthean texts grant no divorce permission to people living in adultery or to those seeking to justify it by the legal route. They speak, instead, of the options available to a person being victimized by such unfaithfulness. That situation is not addressed in the Markan text.

People often find themselves in situations not directly addressed by any of the so-called divorce texts in Scripture. Their marriages seem to have become untenable as a result of serious abuse, neglect, or repeated unfaithfulness by their spouse. Such people need to hear a clear word from Jesus, a word that directs them away from divorce texts and toward texts in which God speaks to their situation. Where marriages are in trouble, but both partners are willing to keep seeking God's ideal, there is no better text to be found than the one Jesus has highlighted, God's creation ideal. Where this is not the case, we do well to look for a guiding word from God in texts that speak of forgiveness, of new beginnings after failure, or of the church as a supportive community.

Mark 10:17-52

The Cost and the Reward of Discipleship

PREVIEW

In this commentary, the journey to Jerusalem (8:27—10:52) is perhaps rather arbitrarily divided into three blocks of material, each block centering on one of the passion-resurrection predictions. The purpose of the division is to facilitate commentary writing and reading. Yet various themes from the preceding section continue in this section, themes such as entering the kingdom (cf. 10:15; 10:23) and learning a new value system (cf. 10:13,14; 10:23-26, 42-45). Above all, the *journey itself* links the present section with the preceding one (and the one before that). Jesus continues teaching his disciples about the necessity of his passion and resurrection, and about the nature of true discipleship.

The journey to Jerusalem has begun near Caesarea Philippi (8:27). It is preceded by an episode in which Jesus heals blind eyes (8:22-26); it closes with another episode in which Jesus heals blind eyes (10:46-52). In fact, Jesus has been opening eyes all along the way, and so has Mark. Disciples of Jesus, then and now, have been learning that it is not enough to confess Jesus as the Messiah (8:29-30). What is needed is to deny oneself, take up the cross, and follow Jesus (8:34). Those who do that will see all things clearly (8:25). Those who see clearly, faithfully follow Jesus *on the way* (10:52).

In truth, however, neither seeing nor following are ever perfect. We are always on a journey, learning more and more what it means to set our minds *on divine things* and not *on human things* (8:33). On this journey, the disciples of Jesus have not fared well. Each time Jesus has predicted his death and resurrection, they have blatantly betrayed their misunderstanding, their blindness to the things of God.

The present section (10:17-52) brings Jesus and his disciples within sight of their destination, the city of Jerusalem (cf. 11:1). Thereafter, everything will center in and around Jerusalem and the temple, as the narrative moves inexorably toward the passion and resurrection of Jesus.

A structural diagram of the whole journey (8:27—10:52) is provided in the "Preview" of the preceding section (9:2—10:16). Clearly depicted there is the framework of the entire journey: three passion-resurrection predictions, each time followed by discipleship misunderstanding and then discipleship instruction. The rest of the material concerns the issue of divine and human perspectives (8:33). The disciples are being taught how to think the things of God. In this section three connected episodes involving *wealth* precede Jesus' passion-resurrection prediction. Following these, as usual, are incidents involving discipleship misunderstanding and additional teaching. The story of what happens to a poor blind beggar brings to a close the section and the journey *[The Discipleship Journey]*.

The individual episodes in 10:17-52 are about misguided priorities (10:17-22), about grace and what blocks it (10:23-27), and about the true costs and rewards of following Jesus (10:28-31). They are about glory and the cross (10:35-40), and about lordship and servanthood (10:42-45). Finally, they are about seeing eyes and obedient steps (10:46-52).

OUTLINE

The Rich Man, 10:17-22

Rich People and the Kingdom, 10:23-27

Gaining True Riches, 10:28-31

Jesus' Third Passion-Resurrection Prediction, 10:32-34

The Misguided Request of James and John, 10:35-40

Jesus Teaches About Authority and Service, 10:41-45

EXPLANATORY NOTES

The Rich Man   10:17-22

This episode has traditionally been labeled "the rich young ruler," though Mark's readers would not know that the man is either young or a ruler (cf. Matt. 19:20; Luke 18:18). Even that he is rich is disclosed, for dramatic effect, in the last line of the episode. Mark tells the story of *a man* invited to give up everything to follow Jesus. The reader's mind goes to Simon and Andrew (1:16-18), James and John (1:19-20), and Levi (2:13-14). *Everyone else* in the Gospel to whom Jesus says, "Follow me!" has left everything to do so. Will this man?

The man shows the seriousness of his quest for eternal life by running up to Jesus and kneeling before him (10:17). Calling Jesus *Good Teacher* honors Jesus and recognizes his authority. Jesus accepts the man's claim to have lived in obedience and expresses his love for this man (10:21a) by identifying the one thing this man still lacks, a willingness to give up everything to follow Jesus (cf. 8:36). By asking him to sell his possessions and give to the poor, Jesus helps the man discover what is still lacking: he is still living for himself. Change is still possible for him. Instead, the man clings to what he owns and leaves in sadness. Then Mark adds words that put a whole new slant on this incident, *for he had many possessions* (v. 22b).

This incident is not merely about honoring Jesus, obeying the law, or seeking eternal life. It is not even ultimately about concern for the poor. It is about the seductive power of wealth to hold people captive. It is about a man who seems to have done everything right, but to have done it all in service of the wrong master, himself. This text thus leads directly into the following two textual units. The next one further develops the theme of earthly riches and God's kingdom. The one after that speaks of true riches and heavenly rewards.

There are several additional aspects to this text, however, that provoke questions and require comment. The first relates to the title this man gives to Jesus, *Good Teacher*. Jesus does not comment on the designation *Teacher* but deflects the man's adjective with the question *Why do you call me good? No one is good but God alone.* It is a wonderfully ambiguous response to the man, implying any or all of the following:

1. I, Jesus, am not good. How could I be if only God is?

2. Why are you concerning yourself with *my* goodness? Your concern should be with *yours* and *God's*. Yours is insufficient to lead to eternal life; your salvation depends on God's.

3. If you call me good, you must be prepared also to call me God.

The *first* interpretation would, of course, not correspond to Mark's own view of Jesus, but that does not mean Jesus would not test the man's views by making him wonder if that is what he's saying. The *second* interpretation would cohere well with what follows, for verses 19-22 function as evidence that however "good" the man is, he is not good enough. Verses 23-27 function to show that it is not possible to be good enough to inherit eternal life; inheriting eternal life (or entering the kingdom of God) depends not on our goodness, but on God's. The *third* interpretation coheres with hints elsewhere in Mark that the real divinity of Jesus is being affirmed (cf., e.g., 2:7; 4:41; 6:50; 14:62).

This text also provokes questions about the role of obedience to the law. If *God alone* is good, then this man is not. Yet he has obeyed the law. Jesus seems to agree that he has been an exemplary law-abiding person. But is there not at least one law that he has broken? Jesus' list of commandments closely follows the last six in the Decalogue (though not quite in the original order) except that "do not defraud" is substituted for "do not covet." Why?

Many commentators rightly say, "There is no suggestion in the text that his wealth was dishonestly acquired." Did Jesus perhaps substitute "do not defraud" for "do not covet" precisely so that the man could *claim* full legal obedience. In terms of *actions*, he is blameless. However, Jesus helps him discern that his *heart* is not in the right place! Why else would he rather go away sad without assurance of eternal life than sell all and follow Jesus? Does he not covet for himself what, according to Jesus, truly belongs to the poor?

How many rich people have claimed that because their wealth was acquired honestly, they have full rights to keep it or use it as they please? How often is the real truth that in their (our?) minds and hearts, they (we?) too have substituted "do not defraud" for "do not covet"? At any rate, Jesus has identified the Achilles' heel of the man's self-acquired "goodness." He is not willing to change masters and invest all he has for God's kingdom. As a result, he walks away with his earthly wealth and a heavy heart. He could have followed Jesus. He could have entered God's kingdom with the promise of a hundredfold return on his investment (10:28-30). But he did not.

Rich People and the Kingdom 10:23-27

Jesus accepted the man's language on *inheriting eternal life* (10:17, 21). But in responding to the issue with his disciples, he changes the vocabulary to *entering God's kingdom/reign* (but cf. 10:30). These are closely related concepts. Yet *eternal life* language has a personal and future ring to it. By shifting to *kingdom of God,* Jesus focuses on participation in the fulfillment of God's purposes, present and future, personally and in concert with others who follow Jesus. In Jesus' ministry, God's reign is already being proclaimed and established. Jesus is inviting people to repent (= change their life's orientation) and believe (= step out in obedience to) the good news (1:14-15). The disciples do not catch Jesus' shift to kingdom-of-God language. They substitute their own designation, to *be saved* (10:26). Jesus lets their term stand as well.

One man has just said no! and walked away sad. Now Jesus says that it is hard for anyone with great wealth to enter God's kingdom. The perplexity of the disciples likely stems from their assumption that wealth is a sign of God's favor (cf. Deut. 28:1-14): "If even the wealthy can hardly enter God's kingdom, who can?" "No one," says Jesus, "not on their own. Salvation is something only God can accomplish" (10:26-27, paraphrased). But does that not erase the difference between those who are rich and those who are not? Yes and no. Reading this text in the light of the preceding, we summarize the basis and conditions for salvation as follows:

• If it would depend on goodness, none can be saved. Only God is good (10:18).

• If it would depend on law-keeping, it would also be impossible; every attempt to be right before the law falls short somewhere (v. 21).

• If it would depend on giving away all that one has, it would be very hard, especially for the rich (vv. 23-25).

• In fact, it depends on what God alone can do (v. 27), or in the language of other NT texts, it depends on grace.

• Yet for grace to be effective, one must receive it. One must let go of whatever holds our hearts, and one must follow Jesus (v. 21); that is particularly hard for rich (or self-sufficient) people to do.

The hyperbole that Jesus uses in verse 25 should be accepted for what it is. It is hyperbole, designed to claim for rich people what verse 27 claims for *all* people. The rich simply cannot enter God's kingdom, nor can anyone else—not until God does what only God can do, and that is to save.

Aramaic scholars have tried to change the camel into a rope (the two Aramaic words are almost identical). Imaginative interpreters have invented a small gate in the Jerusalem wall called the "Needle's Eye." Both of these are misguided attempts to make something Jesus calls *impossible* into something that just might be (barely) possible. But that completely misses the point of the text. Rich and poor are equally incapable of "being saved" apart from God's doing. The point of the text is that rich people have a particularly hard time accepting that.

Gaining True Riches 10:28-31

The disciples witnessed Jesus' dialogue with the rich man (10:17-22). They have just been instructed on the requirements for entry into God's kingdom (for being saved). Now Peter speaks out on behalf of them all: *We have left everything and followed you.* Perhaps he is insecure and wants assurance, hoping Jesus will respond with words of agreement and affirmation; or perhaps he is implying a question, "So what do we get as a result?"

Jesus neither affirms nor denies Peter's claim. Nor does his response speak a word exclusively to the Twelve. As he has frequently done, he makes a general statement applicable to all who truly give up earthly things to follow Jesus. The list of things to be given up is impressive: home, siblings, parents, children, land. Jesus' promise to those who give up these for Jesus and the gospel (the good news that God's kingdom has arrived, 1:14-15) is equally impressive. He promises a hundredfold return on the investment!

Gerhard Lohfink (1984:41) suggests that this list is not a random list of things normally considered valuable; nor is the promised return to be understood as a guarantee that in the end nothing is ever really given up. This list, understood in first-century terms, is a list of life's essentials:

• *Home* is not just where I happen to live now, nor is it a large financial investment. Home is *where I belong.*

• *Brothers and sisters* represent not merely siblings, but my clan, my people. They represent those *to whom I belong.*

• *Mother and father* stand not merely for "parents," but my connection to my ancestry, to father Abraham, to the people of God. They represent *who I am.*

• *Children* stand for more than merely those to whom I've given birth. They count as evidence of God's blessing, and they are a potential source of support in old age. They represent *my security.*

• *Fields* are not merely economic potential and meaningful work. Fields are "land," "the Promised Land." They represent God's promises; they represent *the visible inheritance*.

When these things are given up for Jesus' sake, the disciple is promised a new place to belong, new people to whom to belong, a new identity independent of physical ancestry, new guarantees of God's sustaining care and of a final inheritance. This text is not about getting all the same things back again, plus astronomical interest. It is about having our real needs met in ways that are ultimately far more secure than any physical conditions could ever be.

Jesus is referring to the new identity, new family, and new destiny that disciples share with each other in the kingdom of God. Mark sees this text as a challenge for the church community to provide that sense of identity, care, and support for those who are called brothers and sisters (cf. 3:34-35). This application to the disciple/church community is what is implied in the words *now in this age* (10:30).

That Jesus here is talking about true riches rather than multiplied earthly riches explains the absence of "fathers." In listing the rewards, the list of things given up is repeated verbatim, except that there is no hundredfold return on the fathers. This text functions as Mark's equivalent to Jesus' instruction in Matthew, "Call no one your father on earth, for you have one Father, the one in heaven" (Matt. 23:9). For the first-century Jew, "Father" represented the authoritative leader who alone was responsible for the ordering and the well-being of the household. Jesus redefines family as *my brother and sister and mother* (3:34). Lohfink remarks, "Patriarchal domination is no longer permissible in the new family, but only motherliness, fraternity, and childlikeness before God the Father" (1984:49).

Jesus does not guarantee an easy life. He promises an identity, a support system, and security in abundance, sufficient even for times of persecution. He also guarantees that no matter what may lie along the discipleship road, it leads to eternal life.

Thus these closely linked text units (10:17-22, 23-27, and 28-31) end as they begin. A rich man has asked how to gain eternal life. In Jesus' answer, he has clarified that there is no way humans can achieve it, either by goodness or by obedience. It is God's gift to those who have said yes to Jesus and expressed it by investing everything for his sake and the gospel's (10:29).

Jesus' final paradoxical statement about the first being last and the last being first (10:31) is designed to challenge the disciples and the readers to focus on God's perspective, not on human perspectives.

The rich are not the ones closest to heaven (as the disciples have supposed, v. 24). On the contrary, they might well be the farthest away.
Those who are facing hardship for the sake of God's kingdom can be
reassured that God has not forgotten them and left them somewhere
near the back of the line. They may well be among those who are
nearest to their final eternal reward.

Jesus' Third Passion-Resurrection Prediction 10:32-34

Jesus' third passion-resurrection prediction (cf. 8:31; 9:31) is the
most detailed. It is introduced by a puzzling description of some people being *amazed,* and *those following* Jesus being *afraid.* It is possible that the first group is the disciples and the second the crowd
(NIV). More likely, however, Mark is saying that people in general are
amazed (finally meeting this man about whom they have heard so
much?), but that Jesus' own followers (the disciples) are afraid
(NRSV).

Why were the disciples afraid? In this text they (like the reader) discover for the first time that the destination of this journey is
Jerusalem. Previously they have experienced with Jesus the opposition of those *from Jerusalem* (3:22; 7:1). Now as they approach the
stronghold of Jesus' enemies, they fear that his recurring predictions
of death just might actually come true. Taking the Twelve aside, Jesus
confirms their fears. In Jerusalem, the Son of Man (= Jesus himself)
will be betrayed, condemned, insulted, flogged, and killed *[Son of
Man].* As always, the promise of the resurrection is the final word.

That the *Gentiles* will be involved in Jesus' martyrdom is new
information here. For the disciples, that can only mean the Roman
occupying power. Would it perhaps dawn on them at this point that
Jesus' word about cross-carrying might in fact be an allusion to a literal cross, a crucifixion? (cf. 8:34).

The Misguided Request of James and John 10:35-40

Each time Jesus predicts his passion and resurrection, the disciples
respond as though they have not heard him, have not understood
him, do not believe him, or simply reject what he has said (cf. 8:32;
9:32-35). This time James and John (cf. 9:38, notes) are the ones
who come to Jesus with their misguided request. They want positions
of glory. They are prepared to let Jesus be the greatest in the kingdom, but they want to be second and third. The last time the disciples
argued with each other about who was greatest, they at least were
embarrassed that Jesus knew it (9:34). This time two of them

unabashedly appeal directly to Jesus to make them greatest. Not surprisingly, the others are angry when they learn of it (10:41).

Jesus' answer is a provocative, indirect, and ultimately ironic response. What emerges clearly is that the request by James and John is misguided. It is misguided because it assumes that identification with Jesus, involving leadership in his cause (cf. 10:42), is characterized by power and honor and glory. Instead, it is characterized by a cup, a baptism, and a cross. There is glory on the other side of the cross, but James and John want a shortcut to that glory.

James and John glibly pronounce their readiness to accept whatever *cup* and *baptism* might stand for (after all, they do want those seats in glory). Jesus assures them they will experience the cup and the baptism, but then he does not promise them the special seats in glory they have requested. He says only that God is the one who assigns those seats. There are indeed seats in glory, and they will be occupied, but by whom? That is left open for now (see below).

What is *the cup* and *the baptism*? And who will sit in the seats of honor? If we restrict ourselves to OT and first-century Jewish backgrounds, we would likely conclude that *cup* stands for "whatever God has planned," whether that is the overflowing cup of blessing (Ps. 23:5) or the bitter cup of suffering (Isa. 51:17). To drink the cup is to submit to God's will. Baptism may have been used in the first century as a metaphor for times of suffering and distress (cf. Luke 12:50).

As readers of Mark's Gospel, we find more in these references. Jesus' baptism was his inauguration into ministry, and the accompanying voice defined that ministry in terms of service and sacrifice, to the point of giving his life (cf. 1:11, notes). Looking ahead in the narrative, we also find references to Jesus' cup. In the upper room, Jesus will link the cup to his coming sacrificial death (14:23-25); in Gethsemane, he will struggle to accept that he must drink the cup. What a glib promise James and John make when they say they can easily do the same!

In the light of the rest of the NT, Christian readers find even more meaning in Mark's words. Baptism is an act of full identification with the death and resurrection of Jesus (Rom. 6:3-4). The cup shared regularly in Christian communion represents participation in the death of Jesus and celebration of the new life which Jesus' death made possible (1 Cor. 10:16-17; 11:23-26).

Baptism and the cup, at whatever level one reads, represent the way of the cross. James and John glibly commit themselves to go that way. Here is where the irony of the text appears. Jesus is the only one who will faithfully go the way of the cross, at least on this journey. As the nails go into his hands and the ironic enthronement in glory takes place (*The King of the Jews!* 15:26), we are informed that two people have been assigned places *on his right* and *on his left* (15:27; phrases exactly as in 10:40!). If James and John are truly willing to be baptized with Jesus' baptism and to drink his cup, they will faithfully complete the way of the cross. Then they might be there in positions of glory as Jesus is enthroned!

Yet Jesus predicts the ultimate faithfulness of these disciples (10:39). Someday they will share in his baptism and cup. That is not narrated in Mark's Gospel, but this text and others predict that it will happen on the other side of Jesus' resurrection. Some Markan scholars interpret the ending of Mark's Gospel as projecting failure for Jesus' disciples, not faithfulness. This text makes that view incorrect. Mark's narrative ends without *reporting* the ultimate return of the disciples [*Textual Criticism of Mark*], but not without *predicting* it. Mark's resurrection narrative projects renewal for the disciples who fail, not apostasy (cf. notes on 14:28 and 16:7-8; for alternative views, see Fowler; Kelber; Weeden).

Jesus Teaches About Authority and Service 10:41-45

When the disciples learn of the request by James and John, they respond with anger. Are they indignant that James and John are so unscrupulous, or maybe frustrated at not beating James and John with a similar request? Jesus does not address their anger. He deals with their power-mongering and glory-seeking. Presumably the other disciples have the same tendencies as James and John.

Jesus refers to Gentile political rulers, no doubt thinking of the hierarchical power structures characterizing the Roman empire. Mark 10:42 might refer to those whom people *recognize* as rulers, implying that they are indeed the real rulers (NRSV). But the Greek can also be read differently; it might mean those who are mistakenly *thought to be* the rulers! (*regarded as rulers,* NIV). Is Jesus claiming that real power is not in the hands of those who seem to wield it?

Not many days hence, a helpless victim on a cross will have the title *King of the Jews* nailed above his head. The Gentiles will put it there as an act of mockery, but ironically they will be pronouncing the paradoxical truth. On a cross, Jesus is taking his throne. In weakness, God is unleashing power.

In Jesus' final word of instruction to the disciples before arriving in Jerusalem, Jesus teaches about the true power structures of God's kingdom: service is greatness; to be slave is to be first; he himself will go so far as to give his life for all the rest. Soon these kingdom values will be seen in action. Soon Jesus finishes his journey to the cross.

Jesus' reference to his death as a *ransom for many* has been interpreted in various ways. Clearly Jesus' death is being defined as for the benefit of others; *many* is an idiom that can mean *all the others*. Yet a full doctrine of substitutionary atonement can hardly be claimed for this verse. The word *ransom* (*lutron*) emphasizes liberation more than substitution. Exactly how Jesus' death brings about the liberation of others is not carefully spelled out here.

I have been impressed, however, with the many (sometimes subtle) allusions to substitution found in Mark's Gospel. The voice of God at Jesus' baptism alludes to the sacrifice of Isaac (1:11). Jesus identifies himself with the Passover lamb (14:24). Jesus is handed over precisely because Barabbas is released (15:15). Jesus has *saved others* because he does not *save himself* (15:31). Because of such allusions to substitution, we should not underestimate that element in Jesus' own clear statement of why he gives up his life on behalf of others (10:45).

Bartimaeus Becomes a Seeing Follower 10:46-52

After passing through Jericho, Jesus is only a half-day's journey from his destination, Jerusalem. A blind man, too persistent to be hushed by the crowd, catches Jesus' attention. In response to his faith-filled request, Jesus heals him, and the journey continues. If that were all that this story means, it would still be significant. It reveals Jesus as the compassionate healer; it counts as one more piece of evidence that God's reign is drawing near (Isa. 35:5).

Yet there is so much more. The names and titles used, the specific actions of Bartimaeus, and the location of the incident at the end of the discipleship journey—these all contribute to the richness of this narrative's meaning and function.

The Names

Bartimaeus means "Son of Honor." This is the only time Mark supplies the name of a person Jesus heals, and the sentence in which he does so is worded in an unusual way. Mark refers to *the Son of Timaeus, Bartimaeus* (lit., 10:46). Most English translations (including NRSV) reverse this, making it sound as though Mark is translating the word *Bar* for people who do not know that it means "Son." In reality, Mark is highlighting the meaning of the name more than the identity of the man.

Moreover, Mark sets in stark contrast the meaning of the name and the occupation of the man. A son of honor is begging beside the road! This man, living daily with the shame of his condition, bestows on Jesus titles of honor. Before the narrative is over, we see Bartimaeus, his honor now fully restored, joining Jesus on the way to dishonor and shame. This text is about shame and honor. It suggests that the greatest honor of all is to be allowed to accompany Jesus, no matter where that road will lead.

Jesus, Son of David, blind Bartimaeus cries out (10:47-48, NRSV). Again the Greek word order is reversed to put emphasis on the title: *Son of David, Jesus,* is how the original reads. The title and not the name is repeated in the next verse. *Son of David* was popularly used in the first century to designate the coming Messiah, the one to establish *the coming kingdom* (11:10). Jesus later clarifies that the Messiah is not merely a Son of David but also David's *Lord* (12:35-37). Still, Bartimaeus makes a significant messianic confession, all the more impressive because he acts on his confession by following Jesus on the discipleship journey (10:52).

Before requesting healing, Bartimaeus addresses Jesus as *Rabbouni* (10:51). NRSV tries to capture the honor in the title as *My teacher*. Literally translated, it is *My Great One!* In the only other NT use of the word, Mary Magdalene addresses the resurrected Jesus as *Rabbouni* (John 20:16).

The Specific Actions

Not to be overlooked are Bartimaeus' actions. He begins as a blind man, sitting and begging. Likely he has his cloak spread out on the ground to collect coins from generous or pitying travelers. The NRSV gives the impression later that Bartimaeus *takes off* his coat when he jumps up to go to Jesus (10:50). This is not an accurate impression. The word used (*apoballō*) does not mean "throw off"; it means "cast aside" or "completely abandon." The only other NT occurrence of the word is in Hebrews 10:35, where it clearly means abandon.

How often has blind Bartimaeus cried out to passersby, *Have mercy on me!* (10:48), and then listened for the sound of a coin landing on his spread-out cloak? But when Jesus comes by, these words, *Have mercy on me!* take on a new meaning. They are not a request for alms but for healing and for restoration of honor.

His faith is signaled by his repeated calling, despite the attempts of the crowd to silence him. Jesus responds to his trust and his persistence. Jesus calls to him as well. Bartimaeus hastens to join Jesus, leaving his cloak behind. Suddenly we realize that this is not only a healing narrative; it is a "call story." Jesus calls this man to himself. He responds immediately, leaving everything behind to join Jesus and to follow him (cf. TBC, below).

In response to his obedient faith, Jesus heals Bartimaeus. The narrative ends with the impressive line: *He regained his sight and followed him on the way.* Even before his healing, Bartimaeus has demonstrated insight and faith, a willingness to leave all to come to Jesus. Now that he is healed, he does what Jesus calls every disciple to do; he follows *on the way.*

Note the stark contrast between Bartimaeus and the disciples who have accompanied Jesus from Galilee. To highlight this contrast, Mark records two identical questions, one in the preceding incident and one here. Using exactly the same Greek words, Jesus asks two of his disciples in 10:36 and Bartimaeus in 10:51: *What do you want me to do for you?* James and John ask for positions of honor, seats in glory, prestige, and power, with definitely no suffering. Bartimaeus asks for the miracle of sight; when the miracle is granted, he follows Jesus *on the way* to the cross. Mark's use of *the way* (*hē hodos*) indicates that Bartimaeus' response symbolizes full acceptance of divine priorities (cf. 8:33), and a willingness to identify with Jesus through rejection and death to the glory beyond (cf. 8:35-38). Bartimaeus symbolizes *every* faithful disciple.

Mark has framed this whole discipleship journey section with two miracle stories, both of them about opening blind eyes (8:22-26; 10:46-52). The first happens in two stages, symbolizing that the disciples who could see Jesus as the Messiah, but could not accept the way of the cross, are still in need of another touch. The second one symbolizes what faithful disciples do when their eyes are truly opened: they follow Jesus on the way (Camery-Hoggatt: 163-165, brief but perceptive on Bartimaeus) *[The Discipleship Journey].*

THE TEXT IN BIBLICAL CONTEXT
Good Examples and Bad Examples

In this section, Bartimaeus is presented as a model disciple; he confesses who Jesus is, sees clearly, and follows Jesus on the road to the cross. We do not know whether or not the historical Bartimaeus invested his life in following Jesus; what we know is that the text presents him as a paradigm of faithful discipleship.

The example of Bartimaeus reminds us that Jesus' disciples are often portrayed as less-than-model followers. They seem to learn slowly, they exhibit attitudes and priorities contrary to Jesus' own, and they follow reluctantly (and during Jesus' passion, not at all). The contrast between the reality (Mark's portrait of the disciples) and the ideal (Mark's portrait of Bartimaeus), reminds us that God's ideals are always beyond our reach, though we are never excused if we do not aim to reach them.

God's ideal of obedient following, total allegiance, and undivided commitment is well expressed in Deuteronomy 13:4:

> The LORD your God you shall follow,
> him alone you shall fear,
> his commandments you shall keep,
> his voice you shall obey,
> him you shall serve,
> and to him you shall hold fast.

Perfect conformity to this ideal is called for, but it has never been achieved by anyone, except by Jesus "who in every respect has been tested as we are, yet without sin" (Heb. 4:14). Often in Scripture, characters are portrayed as good examples or bad ones, modeling aspects of the ideal or illustrating the many ways of falling short of it.

The biblical writers often surprise us with their choice of bad examples. We note the "evildoers" against whom God's people are warned and who are regularly portrayed as ripe for God's judgment (e.g., Ps. 10:15-16). Yet the prime bad examples, portrayed as having feet of clay, often are the heroes of faith, the great spokespersons for God, or Israel's fearless leaders! One thinks of Abraham, Moses, and David. They leave a legacy of faithfulness, they are called God's friends (2 Chron. 20:7; Isa. 41:8; James 2:23), God's faithful servants (Heb. 3:5), and people after God's own heart (1 Sam. 13:14). Yet the narratives highlight their failings, their fallibility, and even their terrible crimes. But we can find comfort and encouragement in the fact that God forgave them, restored them, and used them.

As noted above, Mark often portrays the disciples of Jesus as the bad examples. Readers learn about discipleship by observing their failures, by aiming to do better, but also by finding courage in the fact that Jesus never gives up on them.

Often in Scripture, we are encouraged toward more faithful following by good examples. These people undoubtedly had their areas of weakness, but the Scriptures focus on their faith, their courage, and their obedience. One thinks of people like Joseph, Ruth, Esther, and Daniel.

In Mark, the good examples are often the little people, those who appear in the narrative only once, exhibit exceptional insight or faith, and then disappear, leaving behind an image or a symbol of what it means to be truly faithful. Such examples are the healed demoniac from Gerasa in chapter 5, Jairus the synagogue ruler and the full-of-faith woman in chapter 6, and the Syrophoenician woman in chapter 7 (cf. Harder: 110-111). But in Mark, perhaps the premiere good example is Bartimaeus; his example deserves further reflection.

Bartimaeus becomes a symbol of faithful discipleship. He hears the call to discipleship and responds in exact fulfillment of Jesus' demands for disciples as outlined thus far in Mark. The first disciples have left their boats and their nets, their business, their parents, and their co-workers (1:16-20). That was their *everything* (10:28). Jesus has asked the rich man to sell all his possessions and give to the poor (10:21). That would have been his *everything*. Bartimaeus leaves his coins and his cloak, his spot beside the road and his occupation. That is his *everything*.

Jesus asks no more and no less of any would-be disciple. Rich or poor are asked to give up only one thing, *everything*. Those who do, and who then follow up their self-denial by cross-carrying and following Jesus (cf. 8:34), they are disciples indeed. The way Mark has portrayed Bartimaeus, he symbolizes faithful discipleship; indeed, Mark has structured his discipleship journey section with this incident as its highlight *[The Discipleship Journey]*.

The biblical texts often present good and bad examples without any explicit directions to readers as to whether or not the models are to be imitated. However, Paul (esp.) sometimes becomes explicit, affirming (or calling for) appropriate imitation: imitation of other churches (1 Thess. 2:14), of himself (1 Cor. 4:16; 2 Thess. 3:7), of himself and the Lord (1 Thess. 1:6; 1 Cor. 11:1), and even of God (Eph. 5:1). Other writers speak of imitating those who serve diligently (Heb. 6:12) and lead faithfully (13:7). Paul's words concerning the experiences of OT Israel apply also to NT incidents recorded in order to teach faithful discipleship: "These things happened to them to serve as an example, and they were written down to instruct us, on whom the ends of the ages have come" (1 Cor. 10:11).

THE TEXT IN THE LIFE OF THE CHURCH
Hierarchy in the Church
In this section, Jesus rejects greatness through hierarchical leadership in favor of true greatness through service. As modern readers, we

wonder whether the church of Mark's day was struggling with the issues this text addresses (Harder: 99). Did some think the church should be organized hierarchically, with clear lines of authority and power? Were there people in Mark's own church who clamored for seats at Jesus' right and left, but had no room in their theology or lifestyle for servanthood and the cross? Was this perhaps the attitude among some of the church leaders?

Jesus says that the only kind of power that shall characterize the disciple community is the power of servanthood, of slavery, of sacrificing oneself for others. Those who grasp for the accepted power of Gentile (and Jewish) hierarchies, those who lord it over people, who tyrannize those over whom they are placed (cf. Wink: 13-104, on "The Domination System")—they are not truly following, not truly going the way of the cross. They are still thinking human thoughts, not divine thoughts (8:33). They need their blind eyes opened, so that they, like Bartimaeus, can follow Jesus *on the way* (cf. Wink: 105-37, on "God's Domination-Free Order")

L. Doohan refers to hierarchically managed churches as those who delight "in the re-establishment of monarchical power, the rebirth of centralized authority, the dominant influence of career ecclesiastics" (3). Sadly, there are far too many churches of that kind today. As Jesus nears Jerusalem, he teaches some of the harder lessons of true discipleship. Almost two millennia later, they are still among the hardest for the church to learn!

Riches and Selling All

G. Lohfink points out that those who believed in Jesus were required to make one of two possible responses (depending on what Jesus had specifically called them to do). Either they became "sedentary believers" who "remained in their village or town to await the reign of God," or else they were "itinerant followers" who *left everything* (Mark 10:28) to travel with Jesus. These learned from him, ministered in his name, and created the new community that symbolically represented "renewed Israel" (1984:31-5).

While Lohfink's distinction is historically correct, the distinction can also be misunderstood, resulting in a perspective that Lohfink (and more importantly Jesus) never intended. Too often the church has set up double standards for discipleship: high standards of commitment and self-sacrifice for those who would take their faith seriously, especially for those who dedicate their lives to Christian ministry; and lower standards deemed satisfactory for "normal" Christian living. Some traditions define "counsels of perfection" or demand special vows of those who would be involved in Christian ministries (Lohfink, 1998:212-6).

The Bible, however, never sets up double standards. Some interpreters (wrongly, I think) treat the so-called qualifications for elders in the pastoral epistles as the biblical "separate standard," applicable only for leaders. Many denominations (perhaps inadvertently) set up dual standards in their bylaws, adopting policies that exclude some people from particular ministries because something in their past permanently disqualifies them. They are good enough to be normal Christians, but not to lead in the church.

As discussed in connection with Mark 1:16-20, Jesus' call to discipleship is a call to say, "Yes, at any cost." This is true for *every* person, for those who are then in fact called from their nets or families and for those sent home to testify of their new life in Christ and of his coming reign. Mark 10:28-31 (notes) helps us see what it means to *leave all* even when some remain "sedentary" and some become "itinerant" in the service of Christ. God's call and the reward offered for those who heed it are valid for all believers, even though the outworking of the call may look different in different circumstances.

Jesus' specific demand of the rich man in this chapter was to *sell what you own, and give the money to the poor* (10:21). From the rest of the NT, it is clear that this specific requirement is not laid on all who hear Jesus' call. But it is equally clear that no Christian truly possesses anything; we are stewards of what God entrusts to us. Serious discipleship involves a readiness to relinquish and/or invest all we have in ways consistent with our kingdom perspective and Christian calling.

In various situations, Christians have relinquished all claim to private possession, selling their goods so they could live communally and/or give generously. It happened in Jerusalem in the apostolic church (Acts 2:44-45; 4:32—5:6), and it has happened in many times and places since then (e.g., the Hutterites). This does not represent a "higher standard" but rather is one way of exhibiting the radical claim of Jesus on all that we are and have. Whatever form it takes, all Christians are called to share their possessions within the community of believers and to give generously to alleviate the suffering of the poor (cf. J. H. Umble in Swartley/Kraybill: 103-18).

I refer readers to several books I have found helpful in sorting out how Scriptural teaching on economic matters can be faithfully applied today (see Bibliography): Halteman; Swartley/Kraybill, editors; Vincent.

Mark 11:1-25

House of Prayer or Den of Thieves?

PREVIEW

The journey to Jerusalem (8:27—10:52) is over. Now Jesus makes a grand entry into Jerusalem, riding a colt. His entry is filled with paradox and irony. Crowds enthusiastically cheer about a *coming one* and a *coming kingdom*. Little do they know that Jesus will be enthroned as king, and his kingdom will come in power (cf. 9:1) precisely because many of them will become disillusioned with this Jesus and cooperate with those already plotting to get rid of him.

Jesus' journey has a clear destination, the temple. He makes an ominous temple inspection (11:11). With that inspection, a doorway opens to the rest of Mark's Gospel. The temple is mentioned here for the first time. Yet Jesus' relationship to the temple, to its authorities, and to all it stands for, will totally dominate the rest of Mark's Gospel. It can be fairly said, "Jesus died as a result of a conflict with the temple" (Hamerton-Kelly: 1).

After this, everything is temple-centered. Each time Jesus reenters Jerusalem (after spending the night in Bethany), he goes straight to the temple (11:15, 27). There he performs a dramatic "cleansing" (11:15, 16), there he teaches (11:18; 12:35; 14:49), and there he undermines the authority of the religious leaders; he wins every attack against them, sidestepping each of their attacks against him (11:27—12:37). In the temple he publicly affirms a scribe for recognizing that love for God and neighbor is more important than any of the cultic observances visible around them (12:33-34). Over against the temple, Jesus pronounces the temple's doom (13:1-3). Jesus is charged with threatening to destroy and replace the temple (14:58). Finally, at the point of Jesus' death, the temple curtain is ripped open from top to bottom (15:38; cf. Freyne: 59-61).

These are the obvious references. There are many allusions to and symbols of the temple in addition to these: the cursed fig tree (11:14), the removed mountain (11:23), the capstone (12:10), the wasted offerings (12:41-44), the contrasting women who gave (12:42-44; 14:3-9), and so on (T. Geddert, 1989:113-147).

Specific references to the temple begin at 11:11. Yet it has been clear all along that Jesus is not on the same wavelength as the religious leaders and their religious activities. He has claimed the right to forgive sins, independent of any rituals and sacrifices (2:5). Scrupulous purity regulations and cleansing ceremonies (a preoccupation of temple worship) have been foreign to Jesus. He has been in frequent contact, often in direct physical contact, with unclean things and people: a leper (1:41), a man filled with and surrounded by uncleanness (5:1-13), a bleeding woman (5:25-29), a corpse (5:41), a Gentile (7:24-30). Jesus eats freely with sinners (2:15-16) and sharply criticizes those concerned about external purity (7:1-15). Every time people *from Jerusalem* come to check up on Jesus, they prove they are as out of step with him and his views, as he is with them and theirs (3:22; 7:1).

In Jerusalem, Jesus launches his final attack on the ritual-oriented, temple-centered, control-focused leaders who have opposed him. They launch their final attack on Jesus, the one whose authoritative teaching they reject and whose popularity they fear. In the final conflict, who will win? All along the way, Jesus has been giving the paradoxical answer: *they* will, but ultimately *he* will. *They will kill him, and after three days he will rise again* (10:34; cf. 8:31; 9:31).

OUTLINE

Jesus' Triumphal Entry into Jerusalem, 11:1-11

Jesus Curses an Unfruitful Tree, 11:12-14

Jesus Condemns the Unfaithful Temple Authorities, 11:15-19
    11:15-16   Jesus' Action
    11:17   Jesus' Teaching
                A House of Prayer for All Nations, 11:17a
                A Den of Robbers, 11:17b

EXPLANATORY NOTES
Jesus' Triumphal Entry into Jerusalem 11:1-11

It is hard to read Mark without reading Matthew and Luke into it, especially on Sundays of the church year marked by pageantry and celebration, like Palm Sunday. Palm branches decorate our sanctuaries. The OT reading includes Zechariah 9:9-10; Matthew or Luke supply the Gospel reading. "Hosannas" are chanted and sung. We may even dramatize Jesus' triumphal ride into Jerusalem, complete, perhaps, with a donkey (or two). We distance ourselves from the rebuking Pharisees, and we stand back in silence as Jesus weeps for Jerusalem.

Unless it is pointed out, we easily overlook that Mark's text contains no direct reference to Zechariah. In Mark, the branches (if the word *stibas* really means "a branch"; "a leafy twig" is more likely) are not palm branches; the animal is not a donkey; the Pharisees never show up; Jesus does not weep. Possibly the pilgrims in Mark are celebrating Passover festivities more than recognizing Jesus as the coming king. Their cry *Hosanna* (meaning "Lord save") derives from Psalm 118, a text chanted every year as part of the celebrations. Those "coming in the name of the Lord" originally referred to the festival pilgrims (Ps. 118:25-26). *Mark* alludes to the messianic identity of Jesus; it is not clear *the pilgrims* are doing so.

Mark's account of the so-called Triumphal Entry is low-key compared to Matthew's and Luke's. On the surface, it leads nowhere. One is even left with the impression that the crowds have dispersed before they enter the city (11:11). Jesus, perhaps with the disciples, arrives in Jerusalem too late to do anything significant except look around in the temple (11:11; Doohan: 29).

Yet at a deeper symbolic level, Mark's text is loaded. There is irony in the acclamation of the crowds and disciples. Is Jesus entering Jerusalem in victory? Or has he come to die? There is irony in the reference to the coming Davidic kingdom. The crowds have no idea that its coming will be linked closely to the unjust and horrible death of the man they are celebrating today.

There are several allusions to the kingly authority of this Jesus. He rides a previously unridden colt, meaning one not previously used by commoners, one appropriate for his sacred mission (cf. Num. 19:2; Deut. 21:3; 1 Sam. 6:7). By conveying to the animal's owner that *the* **Lord** *needs it*, he enacts a prerogative of the ruling monarch, impressing into official duty the property of private citizens. These features of the text are probably more significant than whether Jesus' instructions to the disciples represent supernatural knowledge or pre-arranged signals.

However little the crowds themselves understand, Mark wants their celebration of the *coming one* (11:9) to serve as an announcement that Malachi's prophecy is being fulfilled. The messenger (John) has prepared the way, now the Lord is coming to his temple, "but who can endure the day of his coming?" (Mal. 3:1-2; cf. Mark 1:2, 11:11, 15-16).

He looked around at everything (11:11). On the surface, the Triumphal Entry ends with an anticlimax. Jesus is celebrated as Messiah on his way into Jerusalem. An hour or two later, he quietly leaves the city with twelve disciples, after making a brief tourist stop in the temple. But there is another level.

In Jeremiah's day, Israel's leaders had vainly hoped their temple would provide immunity for their sins. God performed a temple inspection. "I too am watching, says the LORD." The verdict: You have turned the temple into a "den of robbers in your sight." Hence, the LORD would destroy the temple and cast the people "out of my sight" (Jer. 7:11, 14-15). With that as a background, Jesus' temple inspection in Mark 11:11 takes on a whole new meaning.

Jesus *looks around* (*periblepō*); Mark uses this word to imply seeing into the heart of the matter and preparing to respond accordingly (Bilezikian: 116-7). Jesus is so incensed by what he sees that he is prepared to risk both his popularity and his life in response. The next day he will demonstrate against the abuses going on there (11:15-16) and call the temple a *den of robbers* (11:17). Before the week is over, he will predict its total destruction (13:2). M. Hooker rightly comments on Jesus' advent in Jerusalem:

> Superficially, these chapters seem to be a success story. Jesus rides into Jerusalem and is hailed as king by the crowds; he teaches in the temple, stands up to the authorities, and is applauded by the people. For Mark,

however, they are a story of failure—the failure of Israel and of her leaders to worship and serve God, and her failure to receive his Messiah. (1991:253)

Perhaps reading Luke's reference to Jesus' tears into this text is, in the end, not so far off the mark (Luke 19:41-44).

Jesus Curses an Unfruitful Tree   11:12-14

The next three short units (the material in 11:12-25) are structurally and thematically tied together and may well be given the title "Jesus and the Unfruitful Temple." They will be discussed separately, but the connections between them will clearly emerge in the discussion.

After spending the night in Bethany, Jesus and the Twelve return to Jerusalem. On the way, Jesus does something that must puzzle his disciples, as it has puzzled commentators ever since. He sees a fig tree with leaves but no visible fruit. Approaching the tree, he verifies that it has *nothing but leaves* (11:13). He promptly "curses" it (at least Peter interprets Jesus' words as a curse; v. 21). Mark adds (in defense of the tree?), *It was not the season for figs.* It was two months too early to realistically expect ripe figs, though it would have been possible for early spring green fruit to be on the tree that early.

What are we to make of this? Is Jesus getting edgy? Is he nervous over what he is about to do in Jerusalem? Is he starting to use his powers to destroy rather than save life (cf. 3:4)? Many theories have been proposed, but the views worth serious consideration maintain that the tree stands as a symbol, and that Jesus performs an acted parable. Jesus has spoken and enacted many parables of salvation (4:11, notes). Now he enacts a parable of judgment.

Mark drops hints that this is a parabolic action. Parables call for "hearing ears" (cf. 4:9, 23). The last line of the present incident reads, *And his disciples heard him say it* (11:14b). We wonder, "Do they have hearing ears, ears that understand the meaning of this parable?" This last line says more than that the episode is "To Be Continued." It suggests that here is a need for discernment and interpretation. When the story resumes the next morning (11:20), the first words are *they saw* (v. 20) and *Peter remembered* (v. 21). These three key words, "hear," "see," and "remember," are used 8:14-21 to teach the disciples about discernment. They recur here in a text that calls on the disciples and the readers to discern what is really being said.

If the fig tree symbolizes the judgment of God, on whom does the judgment fall? Readers commonly suggest "Israel" or "the temple." I propose that it is Israel's unfaithful religious leaders who are being symbolized. They are the ones whom Mark pictures as all-leaves, no-fruit (11:17, 20-21, notes; TBC, below; T. Geddert, 1989:125-9, n. 39 on 289) [Israel and Israel's Leaders].

Beyond a doubt, this incident is directly connected to what happens next in the temple. Mark has made another of his famous intercalations, framing one narrative with another [Chiasm and Intercalation], with a structure as diagrammed here:

A • Jesus Curses an Unfruitful Tree. (11:12-14)
  B • Jesus "Cleanses the Temple." (11:15-19)
A' • The Cursed Tree Is Discovered Withered. (11:20-21)

Jesus is not punishing the tree itself; he is making it stand for something else. Similarly, Jesus does not punish the temple itself. The temple itself is doing nothing wrong, nor are the ordinary pilgrims. The temple authorities and other religious leaders are the wrongdoers. According to Mark, they are misusing the temple even when their wrongdoing is elsewhere (11:17, notes). Later Jesus predicts the physical destruction of the temple (13:2), and its doom is directly linked to the misdeeds of the religious leaders (12:40).

Interpreters have great difficulty coming to terms with the seemingly inconceivable and unjust act of Jesus depicted in the fig tree cursing. As a result, they have scoured the text for subtle clues that something is being overlooked. I pass on some of the suggestions that seem worth pondering"

1. W. Cotter (see Bibliography) suggests that the explanatory clause, *for it was not the season for figs,* is not intended to explain why there were no figs, but rather why Jesus did not expect to find any. It "explains" an aspect of the text, but not what immediately precedes it. This is common in Mark. An obvious example is 16:3-4, where the clause *for it was very large* appears to explain the comment immediately preceding it (in Greek): *It was already rolled away.* In fact, however, it explains an earlier comment, on why the women were concerned about the stone. In chapter 16, the NRSV recognizes the "misplaced explanatory clauses" and rewords and repositions them to clarify the meaning to English readers. Suppose we do likewise here:

> Seeing in the distance a fig tree in leaf, he went to see if, contrary to all expectation (since it was not the season for figs), there would be any fruit on it. But sure enough, there were only leaves.

This may not alleviate our concern over the justice of Jesus' action *in relation to the tree*. However, this way Jesus does not come off looking as though he had impossible expectations or did not know anything about the seasons. Thus his "curse" does not come off as a spontaneous outburst of unexpected disappointment but rather as a measured (and symbolic) act. Jesus approaches the tree, not to check out the anticipated fruit, but to confirm his suspicion that there is none. Sure enough, all-show, no-reality. It is a symbolic reenactment of his "temple inspection" the night before (11:11).

Jesus has also approached the temple to confirm his suspicions. He found lots of activity going on, lots of leaves, but no fruit. Jesus responds to the *tree* on his way into Jerusalem. He responds to the *temple* when he arrives. The ultimate meaning and outcome of his response to the temple is foreshadowed in his dealings with the tree.

2. On the question of justice, we might very well be troubled. What did the tree do wrong? Is it a crime to be in step with the seasons? R. Fowler suggests that Mark *intended* to provoke questions of justice and injustice in the reader. This text prepares the reader to keep on asking such questions as the narrative goes on. Where is justice in all this? Is it just or is it unjust—

- when Jesus drives the traders from the temple?
- when Jesus exposes and condemns the religious authorities?
- when Jesus predicts the destruction of the temple?
- when Jesus is brought to trial for all this?
- when the religious and political authorities *seem* to have their way with Jesus?
- when God abandons Jesus on the cross but not in the tomb?

Mark's goal for his narrative is reached when readers ask and answer such questions for themselves (Fowler, 1991:96-7).

3. R. Culpepper suggests part of Mark's meaning is linked to an innocent sounding phrase. Jesus sees the fig tree *in the distance* (lit., *from afar, apo makrothen*). This phrase has been used twice before by Mark (5:6; 8:3), both times (arguably) alluding to Gentiles. Is Jesus looking at the fig tree (temple) and seeing it from a Gentile perspective? That makes sense only at the symbolic level. At the temple Jesus clears out the court of the Gentiles and declares that the temple's real purpose is to be *a house of prayer for all the nations* (11:17). Jesus critiques the religious establishment for exclusiveness, nationalism, and ethnic chauvinism. They have no concern for those still *at a distance* (Culpepper: 178-9).

Jesus Condemns the Unfaithful Temple
Authorities   11:15-19

11:15-16 Jesus' Action

Arriving in Jerusalem, Jesus goes straight to the temple. There he finds *nothing but leaves* (11:13, notes). The outer court (the only part where Gentiles are allowed) is a hubbub of activity. People are exchanging coins so that pilgrims from other lands can pay the temple tax in acceptable currency. Dealers are supplying pilgrims with certified clean sacrificial animals. Specifically mentioned are those who sell doves, those who sell poor people less expensive alternatives to sacrificial lambs (v. 15). The temple court is even being used as a shortcut; the shortest route from the Kidron valley into Jerusalem is right through the temple court (v. 16).

Jesus sees all the activity as *nothing but leaves*. He observes much religious activity. But where is the fruit? Where is prayer? Where in all this commotion and noise is there room or atmosphere for true worship? In the outer court, where Gentiles are welcome to worship alongside Jews, there is no place for *the nations* (v. 17).

Moreover, as we know from other sources, there is also profit-taking. The religious establishment has to certify animals "clean." Thus they can reject any animal that pilgrims present and sell their own to pilgrims at exorbitant prices. They can set the exchange rates on currency unfairly. They can even overcharge for the doves, specifically made available for the poor.

We cannot be sure what upsets Jesus most. Perhaps it is an exclusive Jewish nationalism that has no place for Gentile worship. Perhaps it is profiteering by the officials. Perhaps it is simply the commercialism of it all, crowding out worship. The transactions have deteriorated into money, animals, and techniques. The ceremonial system is running well, but where does he see anyone loving God and neighbor with *heart, mind, soul,* and *strength* (cf. 12:30-33)?

Jesus carries out a dramatic demonstration. He stops the trading, turns over tables and chairs, and blocks off the shortcuts and the merchandise traffic. We may imagine animals running free, birds flapping wildly to escape, coins rolling all over the pavement, and people running around or fleeing in astonishment and confusion.

It is a demonstration, not a large-scale renewal movement. It is not designed to put an end to the sacrificial system. It likely does not put an end to the temple trading, either. We imagine that everything is back to normal in a few hours. But Jesus has made his point, carrying out a dramatic prophetic action, threatening divine judgment on those with whom God is displeased.

11:17 Jesus' Teaching

A House of Prayer for All Nations 11:17a

Jesus uses two OT texts to interpret his action. He quotes Isaiah: *My house shall be called a house of prayer for all the nations* (Mark 11:17a; Isa. 56:7). Isaiah 56 looks forward to the fulfillment of God's eschatological promises: the barriers to worship will be torn down, foreigners will come (56:3), a eunuch will no longer be viewed as a "dry tree" (note well! 56:3; cf. Mark 11:20-21). Those previously excluded are invited into the temple and will find there a place, a name, a spiritual family (Isa. 56:5). They will find joy, acceptance, a place for prayer (56:6-7).

Jesus knows that the temple he has just "cleansed" can never become that eschatological temple. The abuses that have led to Jesus' demonstration will ultimately lead to God's judgment (13:2). A new temple *not made with hands* (cf. 14:58) will become the true house of prayer for all nations (cf. 15:29, 38-39; TBC, below).

A Den of Robbers 11:17b

The temple has not become what it should be. What then has it become? Jesus now quotes another prophet. Jeremiah speaks of Israel's sinful deeds and misguided trust in the inviolability of the temple. The Israelites think their security lies in the temple, but it is destined to be laid waste along with the city and all its unfaithful people (Jer. 7:1-34). In chapters 11–15 of Mark, alert readers detect an astonishing number of allusions to Jeremiah 7; the most important is this quotation: Jesus says that Israel's religious establishment has turned the temple into a *den of robbers* (Mark 11:17b; Jer. 7:11). We know from Jeremiah 7 what this means.

The temple is a den of robbers not primarily because people are being robbed there (though that also happened; see notes), but because the temple authorities retreat to the temple for their security. A robbers' den is the place where robbers retreat for safety. It typically is a cave in the mountains where robbers set up their stronghold, plot further crimes, and guard their loot. It is the place where they think they can escape justice.

Such a robbers' cave is what the temple has become. "Do not trust these deceptive words, 'This is the temple of the LORD, the temple of the LORD,'" said the prophet (Jer. 7:4). The people commit abominations, and sinners stand before God in the temple saying, "We are safe!" (Jer. 7:10). But they are not. The temple is the place where sins are to be dealt with, not covered over. They have perverted the temple. For this, they will be judged and the temple destroyed (cf. Jer. 7:12-15).

According to Mark, Jesus considers the religious leaders a bunch of robbers. By filling the outer court with merchandising, they rob Gentiles of their place of prayer (11:17b). Through excessive profit-taking (in an enforced monopoly), they rob pilgrims, and especially the poor (11:15-17). They rob widows of their houses (12:40). Ultimately, they are robbing God. They steal the honor that belongs to God (12:38-40), and they withhold their love (12:28-34; cf. Jer. 7:30). They are not giving God what belongs to God: themselves (12:17). They themselves produce no fruit for their Lord (11:13), and they steal the produce of the vineyard that has been entrusted to them (12:1-8; cf. T. Geddert, 1989:122).

The unfaithful leaders believe that they are immune from punishment. After all, they have their temple, their ceremonies, their positions of authority. Jesus will call down God's judgment on them (12:40; 13:2). His demonstration in the temple can be called a temple "cleansing." The larger context, however, reveals that the whole temple system is being "disqualified." Jesus' action in the temple prefigures the judgment that will fall on the religious establishment controlling the temple and the religious system it represents (cf. 11:20-21, notes; TBC, below).

11:18-19 Various Reactions

It is amazing how many interpreters read the previous verses as though Jesus were speaking a word of judgment on either the nation or the temple itself. The religious leaders have no such illusions. They know that it is about themselves (11:18). Exactly the same thing happens in 12:12; commentators regularly assume the parable Jesus has just spoken (12:1-9) is about a transfer from Israel to Gentiles. The religious leaders of Israel, and more importantly Mark, know that it is nothing of the sort!

Jesus has been claiming prerogatives tightly held by the priests and the scribes (forgiveness of sin, 2:5; Sabbath regulations, 3:27-28). The religious establishment has been opposing him (3:6, 22; 7:1, 5; and so on). They clearly view him and his claims to authority as a threat to them and theirs. In 11:18 their fear of Jesus is reported and directly linked to Jesus' popularity with the crowds. Mark describes the crowd as *spellbound*, using the same Greek word translated in 1:22 as *astounded*. There the astonished reaction concerned the amazing authority with which Jesus taught. No doubt it is also Jesus' authority that holds the crowd spellbound now; that is precisely the issue the religious leaders address at their earliest opportunity (11:28).

The more allegiance the crowds give to Jesus, the less they give to the religious leaders. All influence, especially religious influence, depends ultimately on the willingness of the people to grant it.

Jesus' action in relation to the temple is directly related to the plot to kill Jesus (11:18). It is a link that will be strong in the coming chapters. As the religious establishment tries to work out a death plan, Jesus and his disciples retire to Bethany for the night (v. 19). The day of dramatic action has ended. But the story of the fig tree is only half told. Its sequel must be linked to the material discussed above.

A Dead Tree and Living Faith 11:20-25

11:20-21 A Dead Tree

The next morning, Jesus and his disciples are returning to Jerusalem and the temple (cf. 11:27; 14:49). On the way they see the fig tree Jesus cursed the day before. He has said only that it will remain fruitless. Amazingly, it is already dried up from the roots. They all *saw, and* Peter *remembered*. Jesus challenges them to understand what it means (11:12-14, notes).

The judgment Jesus has been pronouncing on the religious establishment is symbolically taking effect. It will never bear fruit. In fact, it will not even retain its leaves and branches much longer.

A summary of 11:12-20 is in order:

> Mark has deliberately used the fig tree cursing in order to present the reader with a graphic illustration of the "fruitlessness" of Israel's leadership, the disappointment of Jesus in finding all their religiosity to be "nothing but leaves," and the inevitability of their utter rejection and punishment in consequence of their failure to produce. The framework around the "cleansing" therefore slants the meaning of that event in the direction of disqualification, and that primarily of the religious leadership of Israel. (T. Geddert, 1989:128)

The next section of Mark focuses on what those leaders have been doing wrong and why God's hand of judgment will fall on them and their temple.

11:22-25 Living Faith

The next five verses are loosely tied to what precedes. Verbal threads (faith, prayer, forgiveness) link them to each other. Each builds on the preceding one, and together they have a special relation to the material just covered.

Have Faith 11:22

Peter points out the astonishing effects of Jesus' fig tree cursing. Jesus responds, *Have faith in God.* In context, what does he mean?

1. If you have enough faith, you too can curse trees and they will immediately wither.

2. If you have a genuine, fruit-bearing faith, you need not fear coming under such a curse.

3. When religious establishments are shaken and judged, keep trusting God; your faith is not tied to temples and ceremonies.

We hope the first one is not intended. Probably the second and third capture the correct connection. But there is still another possibility. The words translated *Have faith in God* might also be translated *Hold onto the faithfulness of God* (TJG). In that case it would still be a call for trust in God, but the focus would shift to the character of God, not the quality of human believing. This would impact the meaning of the following two verses.

Verse 22 does *not* mean, "Corporate worship is under condemnation, but private faith still pleases God." Mark nowhere privatizes faith. Instead, he sees a spiritual family replacing an institutional system. In Greek, every occurrence of *you* in the sayings of verses 22, 24-25 is plural. Verse 23, perhaps a proverbial saying, uses the *whoever* . . . form (not retained by NRSV). Its form and meaning make it corporate, like the other statements. This section assumes that the faith expressed, the prayers uttered, and the forgiveness extended, are all *communal* acts.

Remove Mountains 11:23

In this saying, Jesus emphasizes the effectiveness of believing prayer: It can level mountains. This is hyperbole: otherwise, why has no prayer ever resulted in what this saying promises? That the mountain is directly addressed does not mean the power flows from the spoken word. Instead, human faith accesses God's power. God is the one who acts, as implied by the passive verbs: *be removed, be thrown.* The implied condition here, as in all biblical references to effective prayer, is that God wills the results for which we ask.

We remember that Jesus is still walking from Bethany to Jerusalem. I wonder if he gestures up ahead when he refers to *this mountain?* Up ahead, the visual field is dominated by the temple on Mt. Zion. Is Jesus alluding to the coming judgment on the religious leaders and their temple? Many have thought so. Perhaps this nuance should not be excluded, but it would be a mistake to see in this a warrant for praying down judgment on others.

Effective Prayer 11:24

This verse generalizes and confirms the interpretation of verse 23 given above. These verses are not about "name it and claim it." They are about trust in God, who has both the power to respond to our every need and the wisdom to know when our requests should be denied. If we think this verse promises that we can override God's will, forcing God to act by the intensity of our faith, then we have not yet learned to distinguish between literal guarantees and dramatic hyperboles. This verse challenges disciples to make sure their prayers do not go unanswered because they were never uttered, or were uttered with doubting hearts. "The power to perform miracles belongs to God and can be prayed for but not presumed upon" (Dowd: 120).

Some strange interpretations have been proposed by reading too much into the past-tense verb: *Believe that you **have received** it.* I have heard suggestions like these: (1) Your prayer has already been answered, and you just need to notice it; you are already healed, so you just *feel* sick now. (2) What you have requested has already been declared yours in heaven; you just need the right kind of claiming to bring it into your experience.

In generalized statements such as this (v. 24), no great doctrines should be hung on the tense of a Greek verb. In Greek (especially when a Hebrew statement lies behind the text, as here) the tense of the verb often has little to do with the time during which the action takes place. It is unlikely that this promise would mean anything different if the verb were in the future tense: *Believe that you **will receive** it* (a change some Christian scribes introduced into the text).

Forgiving Others 11:25

A doubting heart can make prayer ineffective; so also can an unforgiving heart. This verse suggests that times of prayer should not be filled only with requests. They should be times to examine our own hearts. Have we forgiven others? Have we recognized our own need for God's forgiveness?

The four sayings in 11:22-25 fit well into the larger Markan context. Jesus has condemned a form of religion that focuses on correct coins, certified clean animals, and lots of religious activity, but with no real fruit. The spiritual family that Jesus brings together focuses on trusting and unobstructed relationships with God, and open and reconciled relationships among believers. The true community of Jesus may not decorate itself with a great show of leaves, but on its branches hangs the genuine fruit that Jesus seeks. It may not create impressive ceremonies and rituals in a magnificent temple, but it will be a spiritual family, each brother and sister bound to the other through a common relationship to the one God.

Only here does Mark refer to God as the believers' (plural) *Father* (cf. Matt. 6:9, 14). This text is not about private faith and private prayer; it is about a spiritual family that trusts together, prays together, forgives each other, and celebrates God's forgiveness together.

Verse 26 is not in the best manuscripts *[Textual Criticism of Mark]*.

THE TEXT IN BIBLICAL CONTEXT

Judgment on Institutionalized Religion

I have emphasized that the material above is not ultimately about figs, nor Israel itself, nor even the temple itself. It is about the religious establishment. The point is extremely important, for all that follows in Mark will be affected by this. Indeed, attitudes between Christians and Jews even today depend on seeing this clearly. Christians often assume that "the Jews" killed Jesus and that a Gentile church replaces Israel in the plan of God. Mark does not contribute anything to this misunderstanding. Yet commentators keep reading it into Mark's text.

Israel does not condemn and kill Jesus. Israel is *divided* in its response to Jesus. Some of those who reject Jesus collaborate with Gentiles to kill him. Those who accept Jesus become the nucleus of renewed Israel. Israel is not replaced by Gentiles; faithful Israel is joined by believing Gentiles *[Israel and Israel's Leaders]*. There is no Gentile church in the NT, only an original Jewish church, and then an integrated church.

The fig tree that is cursed is not Israel itself; it is Israel's unfaithful religious establishment, maintained and controlled by religious leaders who have wrong attitudes about their role, their authority, their temple, and their religious ceremonies. The focus on the religious establishment becomes clear when we note the OT allusions contained in the report that the fig tree is found withered. OT prophets often lamented the growing unfaithfulness of Israel, usually locating the problem squarely on the shoulders of the religious leaders.

Consider this example from Hosea 9. I have highlighted words and phrases that are clearly reflected in the present Markan context. The text begins with God reminiscing about and delighting in Israel's faithful past:

> Like the first fruit on the *fig* tree,
> in its first *season*, I saw your ancestors. (Hos. 9:10)

It shifts to God's words of judgment on Israel, which has become unfaithful:

> I will drive them out of my house
> I will love them no more;
> All their officials are rebels.
> Ephraim is stricken,
> Their root is dried up,
> They shall bear no fruit. (Hos. 9:15-16)

The expulsion from the temple in Hosea 9 is linked symbolically to the dried-up fig tree, just as in Mark 11. Just as clearly, the rebellion of the officials is highlighted. It may seem unjust that a tree, a temple, and ordinary pilgrims suffer because of the unfaithfulness of religious leaders. But that only serves to emphasize the greatness of the responsibility laid on their shoulders and the seriousness of their unfaithful performance.

A House of Prayer for All Nations

The quotation of Isaiah 56:7 (Mark 11:17, notes) highlights one of the main abuses perpetrated by the religious leaders, as portrayed in Mark; they have lost sight of God's eschatological ideal (Lohfink, 1998:235). They are content to keep the ceremonial system running. They are concerned to protect the boundaries, not to attract others to the God of Israel.

All three Synoptic writers quote Isaiah 56:7, "My house shall be [called] a house of prayer" (Matt. 21:13; Luke 19:46). Only Mark completes the quotation: "for all nations" (11:17). This does not mean that Mark has a stronger focus on Gentile inclusion than Matthew or Luke. It means Matthew and Luke have registered their focus on "all the nations" in other ways. Matthew includes a great commission (28:18-20), which sends the disciples out to "all nations," and Luke writes an entire volume (Acts) recounting the spread of the gospel to "all the world" (Acts 22:15).

More than once Mark alludes to a temple *not made with hands* that will replace the Jerusalem temple (14:58; 15:29). The physical building *should have* been a place that attracted all the nations. The spiritual temple that will emerge out of Jesus' resurrection will be founded on Jesus and on his apostles and prophets; it will be filled with God's Spirit; it will be holy; it will be home to Jews and Gentiles (Eph. 2:20-22)—everything the Jewish temple has failed to become.

Mark teaches that the community of Jesus will become home to all who are gathered and regathered by the resurrected Jesus (3:33-

35; 10:28-30; 16:7-08). Jesus has welcomed those who are excluded by scrupulous religious authorities ("Preview," above). He has foreshadowed the day when God's grace will flow freely to Gentiles (7:24-30; 8:1-10). The post-resurrection community must carry on that work as it proclaims Jesus' gospel in all the world (13:10).

In Mark 11:15-17 Jesus brings condemnation on those who abuse the Jerusalem temple. Mark, in reporting Jesus' actions and words, is challenging the Christian church to become the kind of temple Isaiah prophesied:

> Foreigners who bind themselves to the LORD to serve him,
> to love the name of the LORD, and to worship him, . . .
> these I will bring to my holy mountain
> and give them joy in my house of prayer, . . .
> for my house will be called a house of prayer for all nations.
> (Isaiah 56:6-7)

THE TEXT IN THE LIFE OF THE CHURCH
When Religion Becomes Mere Ritual

The worship and fellowship experiences I appreciate most are those characterized by informality, spontaneity, variety, friendliness, and broad participation! I am quite the opposite of C. S. Lewis, who once wrote that he could worship with any kind of liturgy, *as long as it was exactly the same every time;* only then was it possible to get past the form and be drawn into the meaning (Lewis, 1964:4-5). The danger in spontaneous worship is that it often lacks artistic beauty and theological depth. The danger with more liturgical forms is that they can become mere ritual.

Many churches make fuller use of rituals and ceremonies than those where I have been most directly involved. At their best, such activities enhance worship; at their worst, they displace true worship. When religious ceremonies are repeated meaninglessly or even mindlessly (cf. Matt. 6:7), they cease to draw worshipers into God's presence and to create the kind of community that practices justice and welcomes the stranger. The "all leaves—no fruit" ceremonial religion that Jesus attacked in Jerusalem had reached that point.

It is easy to get caught up in "religion"—keeping its machinery running and practicing its external forms—while at the same time losing the simplicity of faith, communion with God, and reconciled relationships. Let us not read Mark 11:12-21 as though it were only about *them;* it is about *us.*

C. E. B. Cranfield minces no words when he says:

If we imagine that every denominational tradition and every ecclesiastical vested interest and every bit of ecclesiastical pomp and circumstance are entitled to luxuriate behind the promise that "the gates of Hades shall not prevail against it," we are like those who fondly repeated, "The temple of the LORD, the temple of the LORD, the temple of the LORD are these." (1953:193).

Marketing Faith

A major part of what Jesus objected to in the Jerusalem temple was that a place of prayer had been turned into a booming business! Coins were being exchanged, no doubt at significant profit to those who had the desired currency. Sacrificial animals were being sold, and the market advantage always went to those who needed to certify animals "without blemish" before they could be sacrificed. Possibly the people carrying things through the temple court (11:16) were farmers simply transporting goods from their gardens outside Jerusalem to the city market. They had no thoughts of worship; they were simply taking the shortest route, which just happened to cut through the temple court. Yes, the temple was big business, and at least some people were making a healthy profit from what was happening there (John 2:16; cf. Zech. 14:21).

How tragic when churches resemble big businesses more than places of prayer. It happens in a myriad ways:

• Famous speakers and writers charging exorbitant fees to be key attractions at large fund-raising events.

• Radio and television speakers pleading desperately for funds to keep their ministries going, but padding their pockets on the side.

• Special "yellow pages" promoting "Christian" businesses among church people: the business ethics of the owner are not checked, if only they sign a doctrinal statement and pay for the advertising.

• Building and maintaining great cathedrals and worship centers, thus absorbing ten times the funding for worldwide mission programs.

• Conference-goers staying in the best hotels; they would have been more frugal with their own money, but the church is paying.

• Targeting neighborhoods for evangelism, not because those people are needy, but because demographic research suggests that converts from that area will contribute more to the budget, more quickly resulting in self-supporting church plants.

• Failing to preach about economic justice and the sins of hoarding and self-indulgence, because it would offend the rich in the congregation.

If Jesus were to come and look around at everything (Mark 11:11) in each of our churches, would he see a house of prayer for all nations, nothing but leaves, or worst of all, a den of robbers?

Prayer and Guaranteed Responses

Jesus promised, *Whatever you ask for in prayer, believe that you have received it, and it will be yours* (Mark 11:24). Few statements in Scripture have raised as many questions, provoked as much soul-searching (and finger-pointing), and left faithful prayer warriors as frustrated or disillusioned as this one. The promise that prayer will always result in "getting what we ask for" was surely not meant as an ironclad guarantee that God will never say no. That would make it override the experience of most Christians and also many other scriptural texts.

Part of the problem is that our rational mind-set and our view of Scripture often lead us to extract from a text only its logical content, never suspecting that it is designed mainly for reflection and challenge. Jesus and/or Mark designed this promise as an encouragement to prayer, expectancy, and confidence in God's unlimited power and loving care. We can hardly blame them for saying this if we then *misuse* this promise only as a statement to be harmonized with (or to override) many others, in constructing our "doctrine of prayer."

Many believers have prayed with sincerity and commitment, over long periods of time, for special needs like the recovery of loved ones with terminal diseases. Some report great divine interventions; many have yet to experience any. When there are no great miracles, people often ask, "What went wrong? Were the prayers not uttered correctly? Was there sin in the life of one of the group members? Were we canceling our prayers by not canceling the medical treatments?" How desperately we try to find ways of explaining away the mystery that God does not always choose to intervene, no matter how we pray, despite verses like Mark 11:24.

One "Christian" teacher teaches that God always heals if only the prayers and the pray-ers are right before God, then (apparently) admits to friends, "I know it is not true, but more people are healed if I say that, than if I say it only sometimes works!" God cannot be honored by such deception.

There are no easy explanations why the Scriptures sometimes seem to promise so much, and why the experience of even the most faithful is often so different. But of one thing we can be confident: God is surely not the kind of God who sits back and thinks, "I really would like to do a miracle here, but they just did not use the oil in the right way. They did not claim the answer with the proper degree of confidence. They did not formulate their prayers correctly. There were not quite enough people at the prayer meeting. They stopped praying before the answer broke through. I really would have given them their request, but they just did not quite get their prayers right. Maybe next time!"

Sharyn Dowd's provocative study of Mark 11:22-25 leads her to make the following summarizing statement:

> Prayer is the context for the community's experiences of power, and prayer is the context for the community's experiences of suffering and martyrdom. . . . [Mark's] approach serves the pastoral function of continually bringing the community back to the presence of God, who is the source of their power and the only value worth dying for. The "danger" of the Markan approach to prayer is not that it will be taken too seriously, but that the formative document of a community that experienced both divine power and devastating persecution will be trivialized by a church that experiences neither. (164-5)

Mark 11:27—12:44

Conflict in Jerusalem

PREVIEW

This section consists almost exclusively of conflict stories. Jesus and the religious leaders stand on opposite sides of a great divide. Jesus will emerge the clear winner. Those who lose in the battle of words come back later with swords (14:43,'48-49).

From the start, the religious leaders have opposed Jesus and everything he stands for. They have criticized his contact with sinners (2:16), his lax attitude to spiritual disciplines (2:18), his inappropriate Sabbath behavior (2:24), and his failure to observe cleansing laws (7:1-5). He claims authority in such matters as forgiving sins apart from the sacrificial system (2:5), or regulating Sabbath behavior without appealing to rabbinic interpretations (2:28). So they initiate the death plot (3:6). At stake are their interpretations of the law, their traditions and customs, their rituals and ceremonies. At stake is their own claim to act as God's representatives. At stake is the support of the people, for without that support, their own influence is gone.

Jesus has employed several different strategies in relating to his religious opponents. In an earlier conflict section (2:1—3:6), he took their objections seriously. For the most part, he patiently demonstrated his right to claim what he claimed, to do what he did. After they rejected him (3:6), Jesus' stance became much more aggressive. He did not seek out conflict situations, but when they arose, he took advantage of them. He pointed out the foolishness of his enemies' views, exposed the insincerity of their hearts, and condemned the sinfulness of their ways (3:22-30; 7:1-15).

The conflict now becomes a public event. In the center of Jewish religion, in the presence of the astonished crowds, Jesus and his enemies contest each other. Sometimes *they* initiate the conflict; sometimes *he* does. Always Jesus wins. He sidesteps their traps and springs his traps on them. He handles Scripture more effectively and denounces their ways more devastatingly.

Much of this section directly follows on the provocative action Jesus himself has initiated in the temple. Jesus' "temple cleansing" is really a dramatic demonstration of God's displeasure with the religious leaders. It is an act pronouncing God's judgment on them for "robbing God" and using their temple as a false security. This section clarifies why the religious leaders are doomed to destruction (12:9) along with the temple they are abusing (13:2).

The first two controversies are about authority; both are directly linked to the "temple cleansing" in 11:15-17. In the first (11:27-33), the authorities ask about Jesus' authority to act in this way. In this episode, he refuses a direct answer; but he gives an indirect one in the second episode, the parable of the tenants (12:1-12). Together these texts focus the authority question. By means of the parable and its sequel, Jesus projects both the seriousness and the outcome of the conflict. Each of the conflicting parties rejects the other side's authority claim. The result is that *both sides* lose their lives (12:7-9). Yet in the end, God vindicates Jesus, whose claim to authority is legitimate and whose death is undeserved (12:10-11).

The next two controversies involve traps. The one about taxes springs back on the Pharisees and Herodians, who have set it for Jesus (12:13-17). The one about the resurrection exposes the foolishness of the Sadducees, who posed a problem designed to make Jesus look foolish (12:18-27).

The centerpiece of this section is in the discussion of the great commandments (12:28-34). A scribe, clearly a foil for all the other religious leaders, correctly identifies what really matters. What counts is not legal or ceremonial observance. This text reminds the reader to watch for the theme that has dominated the discipleship journey, the theme of divine perspectives versus human perspectives (8:33).

This section closes with three short episodes. The first is a provocative and puzzling christological debate (12:35-37). The second is a caustic attack on the hypocrisy of the scribes (12:38-40). The third is a story that both praises and laments a poor widow who invests all she has in a temple that is doomed (12:41-44).

OUTLINE

EXPLANATORY NOTES

The Questions About Jesus' Authority 11:27-33

11:27-28 The Enemies' Questions

Jesus is back in the temple, and so are the religious authorities. Jesus' last visit to the temple has consisted of a dramatic demonstration of God's displeasure and a prophetic statement about what the religious leaders are doing wrong (11:17). They have walked out on Jesus to plot his death, and he has retreated to Bethany. In the meantime, they have been seeking ways to condemn Jesus without getting into trouble with the crowds (11:18). He has been teaching his disciples (and Mark teaching his readers) what the "temple cleansing" was really all about (11:11-25). Now they are back together.

Three groups are represented in what may well be an official delegation from the Sanhedrin (cf. 14:53). This council includes chief priests (the most powerful officials representing the priesthood and the ruling Sanhedrin), the scribes (legal experts), and the elders (influential members of the aristocracy). A formidable force confronts Jesus with questions about his credentials.

This is not only about Jesus' human credentials: What kind of training does he have? Has he received appropriate authorization? Does he have permission to act as he did in the temple? This is also about the ultimate source of his authority: Is it merely human, or is it from God? That becomes clear as we listen in on their argument about how to answer Jesus' question (11:31-32).

The question Jesus' enemies ask is twofold: (1) What is the nature of Jesus' authority? Prophetic? Messianic? (2) What is its source? Human? Divine? Perhaps demonic? (cf. 3:22). They challenge Jesus' authority to do *these things* (11:28). Which things do they have in mind? Jesus has been claiming and exercising authority all along: authority to forgive (2:10), to condemn (11:17), to regulate Sabbath observance (2:28), to teach (1:22), to drive out demons (1:27), even to calm storms (4:41). Jesus' action in the temple was his most recent exercise of authority (11:16-17) and therefore probably the most direct occasion for the interrogation. Where does Jesus' authority come from? (11:28; cf. 6:2).

The reader knows that Jesus' authority derives from God's Spirit, which descended *into him* (1:10), and from direct words of divine authorization (1:11; 9:7). But Jesus' opponents are not privy to those events, and they receive no answer from Jesus today.

11:29-30 Jesus' Counterquestion

Jesus' counterquestion concerns John the Baptist's authority. Where did *his* authority come from? This is not just a clever counterquestion. Jesus is linking their response to himself with their response to John. They are rejecting Jesus *because* they have rejected John. If they had truly repented in response to John's message of preparation, they would have recognized and accepted the Messiah. Instead, they rejected *Elijah* and so will also reject the *Son of Man* (cf. 9:12-13, notes).

11:31-33 The Enemies' Dilemma

Jesus' question puts his enemies on the horns of a dilemma. They convict themselves if they concede divine authority to the one they reject. If they concede only human authority, they lose authority with the crowds, the very thing they are trying to uphold! By asking a question they cannot afford to answer, Jesus exposes their hypocrisy. More important to them than truth is their status with the crowds. Any answer (or no answer) is okay, as long as they can keep the people on their side (11:32).

The questions posed by Jesus' enemies remain unanswered. So is the question posed by Jesus—at least it will not be truthfully answered. But there is another important question in this text. It is the one Jesus' enemies assume he will ask if they concede that John came with divine authority: *Why did you not believe him?* This question remains both unasked and, on the surface, unanswered. Yet for Mark's reader, Jesus' unmasking of their hypocrisy (11:33), their self-serving greed (12:1-12), their deception (12:13-17), and so on, all contribute to the true answer. They did not believe John because John called for repentance. John called for prepared hearts, recommitments, new beginnings. The religious leaders were and are unwilling to give up their hypocrisy, power, vested interests, and control. That is why they did not believe John. That is why they need to get rid of Jesus.

Mark's view concerning Jesus' and John's authority has been clear from the start. John is a divinely authorized messenger sent to prepare the way (1:2). Jesus is the Christ. He is the one who "suddenly comes to his temple. . . . But who can endure the day of his coming?" (Mal. 3:1-2). The reader is challenged to adopt Mark's views and to watch what happens as the religious leaders reject those views.

Casual bystanders in the temple would be baffled, not knowing what Jesus is thinking or what the religious leaders are thinking. Would they even recognize that Jesus has just bested his opponents? After all, not one question is answered and some questions are not even asked. Mark's goal is to provoke his *reader* to ask seriously and answer honestly the questions left unanswered here. Mark's reader knows what Jesus' enemies discuss in private and which questions the enemies cannot afford to have Jesus ask. The reader knows the answer to all the questions (those asked and those contemplated), and the reader knows why Jesus' enemies respond as they do.

The irony of this text is that Jesus has once again demonstrated the authority his enemies are challenging. He has evaded their question, embarrassed them, and proved a champion in debate. He has done it all without tricks or deceit. He has demonstrated why the authority they claim is nothing but a sleight of hand, to keep the crowds supporting them. Before God, whom they claim to serve, they have lost authority. They will soon lose their positions as well.

The Parable of the Wicked Tenants 12:1-12

Interpreters have offered a range of opinions on what this parable might have meant in other settings. In some contexts it could be read as a dramatic way of saying, "Crime does not pay; it leads to bigger and bigger crimes until one is trapped and in the end punished!" In the context of a nation chafing under foreign landowners, to whom hardworking tenants are forced to pay huge dividends, it could be a story illustrating valiant rebellion against unjust foreign oppression. Or it could be a story of the *futility* of such valiant rebellion.

In Mark, this parable is about a *beloved Son* (Jesus, cf. 1:11; 9:7) who is killed by wicked tenant farmers (Jesus' religious opponents; 12:12). It is about God's vindication of Jesus. Those who reject Jesus will themselves be killed; Jesus will be raised up (cf. 12:9-11). Thus it is about the disqualification of the current religious leaders and their replacement. Jesus has been authorized as the true leader of God's people.

It is *not* about "unfaithful Israel," and it is not about God rejecting Israel in favor of the Gentiles *[Israel and Israel's Leaders]*. I have never been able to understand why commentators continue to claim it is so, when Mark goes out of his way to make sure we do not interpret it that way.

12:1-9 The Parable Itself

It is impossible to understand Jesus' parable without comparing it to its predecessor, the vineyard parable of Isaiah 5 (cf. Mark 12:1; Isa. 5:1-7). Just as in Isaiah, Jesus' parable begins with a description of the vineyard's origins: the vines are planted, a wall built, a winepress dug, a watchtower constructed.

That is where Jesus departs radically from Isaiah. In Mark 12, the owner leases the vineyard to tenants who are responsible to tend the vineyard and share its proceeds with the absentee owner. In Isaiah, there are no tenant farmers, only the original owner waiting in vain for the healthy crop he has anticipated.

In both parables, the owner fails to enjoy the anticipated crops, but the reasons are quite different. In Isaiah, the vineyard produces only bad crops; in Mark 12, there is a perfectly good crop, but because of the unscrupulous behavior of *the tenants*, none of it reaches the owner. The tenants refuse to give up the owner's share;

they deal violently with the *slaves* who are sent to acquire it; in the end, they are not content to steal the crop. They resort to murdering not only the owner's slaves, but also his *beloved son*. They hope thereby to acquire the vineyard for themselves. But their plan backfires. The owner finally makes an appearance, destroys them, and leases the vineyard to new tenants.

What does the parable mean in Mark? From the content of the parable itself, we learn the following:

1. If God is not getting his due, it is not the fault of Israel; it is the fault of the religious leaders. Commentators rightly point out that the vineyard represents Israel (cf. Isa. 5:7). But most fail to point out that in the parable there is nothing wrong with Israel. The problem is with those who have been entrusted with authority over Israel. Even in Isaiah, much of the blame for Israel's spiritual failure lies with the leaders, "the elders and princes." The LORD tells them, "It is you who have ruined my vineyard" (Isa. 3:14, NIV). In Mark 12, the blame is laid *exclusively* on the tenants/leaders.

2. The present religious leaders are worse than all previous rejecters of God's messengers. Throughout Israel's history (at least according to the NT; cf. Matt. 23:29-39), God's faithful messengers were opposed and often killed. Those presently opposing Jesus are, via this parable, symbolically held responsible for all those acts of treachery against God's messenger, and particularly the final one against God's Son.

3. The religious leaders may think they are securely in control of the vineyard, but in fact, their doom is imminent. They are already plotting Jesus' death. Once they succeed in doing away with him, they will bring God's judgment down on their own heads.

The religious leaders know that Jesus is speaking *against them* (12:12). Why commentators assume he is speaking against Israel is hard to imagine. This is not about replacing the vineyard (Gentiles replacing Jews). This is about replacing *tenants*, the leaders. That much the leaders of Israel clearly understand. Viewing this text in the light of the immediate and broader context, readers of Mark's Gospel understand more.

First, Jesus has supplied an answer to the questions that remained unanswered in 11:28. With what kind of authority does Jesus act? Answer: Divine authority. Where did he get it from? Answer: He was directly sent by God. Jesus is the *beloved Son* (12:6; cf. 1:11; 9:7). His father is the owner of the vineyard. He has come to claim the fruit that the tenants/leaders owe his Father (cf. 11:13).

Second, the supporters of Jesus will become the future tenants of the vineyard. The vineyard is taken from the tenants/leaders who reject the owner's authority by killing the son. It will be given to those who submit to the owner's authority by supporting the Son. Jesus has been training new tenants/leaders ever since he called them in 1:16-20 and appointed them in 3:13-15.

12:10-11 The Vindication of the Son/Stone

There is an abrupt shift of imagery, probably facilitated by a pun on the words "son" and "stone" in the underlying Hebrew. The murdered son becomes the rejected stone. Judgment has already been pronounced on those who rejected the stone (= killed the son; cf. 12:9). Now the stone is exalted; the son is raised up again. It/he becomes the chief *cornerstone* (or *capstone*) of a building. These verses refer to Jesus' resurrection and therefore to the new temple *not made with hands* that will emerge because of Jesus' resurrection (14:58; 15:29). Thus again the judgment to fall on the religious leaders is directly linked to the coming destruction of the Jerusalem temple (and vice versa).

12:12 The Reaction of the Religious Leaders

The religious leaders may or may not have clearly understood that Jesus is making significant christological claims, predicting both his death and resurrection and alluding to the destruction and replacement of the temple (cf. Tolbert: 237-9). But they certainly understand that they are being compared to unfaithful murderous tenants who fall under the judgment of God (TBC, below).

The Question About Paying Taxes 12:13-17
12:13-15a The Enemies' Trap

The conspiracy against Jesus broadens. *They* in 12:12 refers to chief priests, scribes, and elders, the representatives of the Sanhedrin (cf. 11:27). Now *they* send Pharisees and Herodians (cf. 3:6). The coalition consists of virtually all the religious and political leaders in Jerusalem.

They have designed a trap for Jesus. Whichever way he answers, he is in for trouble. With exaggerated flattery, they imagine they can draw him into a straightforward and ultimately damaging answer. The whole prelude to their question is loaded with irony and hypocrisy:

• *Teacher* (as if they are planning to learn from him).

- *We know that you are sincere* (if only they were).
- *You show deference to no one.* (You give straightforward answers to everyone. They will soon wish he did not!)
- *You do not regard people with partiality.* (True, he will embarrass them just as he embarrassed those who sent them!) The literal wording is heavily ironic: *You do not look into the face of people.* (True again: he looks into the heart!)
- *You teach the way of God.* (True, Jesus does teach the way—the word *hodos* is used. Too bad his enemies have rejected *the way* that John has prepared and Jesus is walking.)
- *In accordance with the truth* (something of little interest to those setting their trap for Jesus!).

The question concerns the poll tax imposed by the Romans on every person living in Judea (among other places). To the Jews, this is *their* land and *God's* land. To pay the tax is to concede that the land belongs to Rome. Moreover, the tax has to be paid in Roman coins. These bear the emperor's image, a "graven image" symbolizing Roman civil religion and that the emperor is Lord! Using *these coins* to pay *this tax* is a double abomination. The Jews have chafed under the tax law, but most are paying it. What choice do they have?

Does God's law *permit* paying this tax (TLC, below)? If Jesus says yes, he loses popularity with the crowds (whose enthusiasm for Jesus prevents the religious leaders from acting against him). If Jesus says no, they can lay charges against Jesus before the Romans. Either way, their plot against Jesus moves forward.

12:15b-17 Jesus' Escape

Knowing their hypocrisy, Jesus first exposes it. In response to Jesus' request, someone immediately produces one of the forbidden idolatrous coins. Their trap would have worked better if they had pretended they didn't have any of the detested coins.

Jesus' opponents confirm that the inscription and image on the coin are in honor of the emperor. Then Jesus springs the trap on them. The emperor can have what belongs to him. But what about God? Is God getting what belongs only to God?

The whole point of the previous parable is that the tenants refuse to give the vineyard owner his due. They are robbing God! The ultimate concern of Jesus is not whether the correct number of coins end up in Caesar's treasury. It is whether those entrusted with God's vineyard are faithful tenants.

Caesar's *image* (Greek: *eikōn;* NRSV: *head*) is used elsewhere in the NT to refer to forbidden images (e.g., Rom. 1:23; Rev. 13:14). However, it is also used to refer to Christ being the image of God (e.g., 2 Cor. 4:4; Col. 1:15), to humans being created in the image of God (1 Cor. 11:7), and to believers being changed into the image of God/Christ (Rom. 8:29; Col. 3:10; 2 Cor. 3:18).

Mark's reader, and probably also the original opponents of Jesus, are expected to see in the final part of Jesus' response a challenge to give *themselves* completely to God. If God's image is stamped onto our very being, we owe ourselves fully to God.

Jesus' opponents, instead of giving themselves to God, have robbed God at every turn. They have withheld their love for God and neighbor (12:32-33), substituting for love both legalism and ceremonialism. They have robbed Jewish pilgrims and especially Gentile visitors in the temple (11:15-17). They robbed the poor of their possessions (12:40) and God of the honor that is God's alone (12:38-39). To use the imagery of Jesus' parable, they are stealing the vineyard's fruit (12:3) and trying to steal the vineyard itself (12:7). Then they seek refuge in the temple, turning it into a den of robbers (11:17). They think they can trap Jesus with a question about taxes. Instead, Jesus has sprung the trap on them.

At a historical level, the fall of the temple to the Romans (A.D. 70) will have much to do with Jewish reactions to foreign occupation. Rebellion against Roman taxes and against images of the emperor will both figure prominently. But from Jesus' perspective, the temple will not be destroyed because of Jewish resistance to Rome. It will be destroyed because the religious leaders have resisted God and rejected the Messiah.

The Question About the Resurrection 12:18-27

12:18-23 The Sadducees' Question

The Sadducees come next, one more group of religious leaders, mentioned only here in Mark. They belong to aristocratic priestly families. They have resisted "theological innovations" and consider many of the Pharisees' teachings to be in this category. They have rejected many rabbinic traditions. They believe in neither angels nor the resurrection, considering these to be among the theological innovations not clearly supported by the books of Moses, the only ones they consider authoritative (cf. Acts 23:8).

Their question is designed to make belief in a resurrection look foolish by proposing a dilemma that it might entail. They refer to the ancient law of levirate marriage, whereby the brother of a man who dies without an heir would marry his widow (Gen. 38:8; Deut. 24:5-6). The purpose of the law is to produce an heir to the property of the deceased man. What if a woman is widowed seven times in an unsuccessful attempt to produce heirs for any of the brothers? If there really were such a thing as a resurrection, whose wife would she become in the next life?

12:24-27 Teaching About the Resurrection

Jesus' response critiques the Sadducees on two points. They misconceive the nature of the resurrection life. They also erroneously reject a (properly understood) resurrection life.

Those of us who wish we knew more about that resurrection life might wish this text were considerably longer. What are their misguided images of a resurrection life? What will it really be like? Jesus critiques a conception of a resurrection life that assumes the following:

• That the resurrection life is a simple continuation of this life, with all its relationships intact.
• That offspring would still be needed as designated heirs of men who die childless.

I think it is going beyond the evidence of this text to insist (as some do) that in the resurrection life these things happen:

• Gender distinctions will disappear.
• There will be nothing corresponding to intimate relationships.
• None of the conditions of our prior earthly life will be remembered or be relevant.

We are told too little to insist on any of these. What seems clear is that those raised will not enter into marriages as we know them in this life. Producing offspring to solve inheritance problems will no longer be necessary. That is likely the point on which we will be *like the angels*. The Sadducees would not be persuaded by Jesus' clarification that we will be *like angels*; they do not believe that angels exist.

Jesus' only clear statement about the nature of the future resurrection life is that God is powerful enough to design it. Jesus critiques their doubts that God can work out the logistics of a resurrection life. When asked about the nature of the resurrection life, I would rather say, "God will find a way of working that out!" That is better than advancing a series of options and dilemmas each option would create.

The Sadducees have another problem. They do not properly understand Scripture. Jesus maintains that belief in the resurrection is not a "Pharisaic innovation." It is biblical teaching. While the OT is less clear about a future resurrection life than the NT, there are texts that affirm it (e.g., Dan. 12:2; cf. Ps. 73:26). Jesus bypasses texts that *we* might think would prove the point. He chooses texts that the *Sadducees* would accept as authoritative, in the Pentateuch. His argument may sound strange to our ears, but it was considered appropriate in first-century exegetical discussion. We can set out the chain of logic as follows:

1. God is the God of the living, not of the dead.
2. God is the God of Abraham, Isaac, and Jacob at the time that God speaks to Moses (cf. Exod. 3:6).
3. Therefore, Abraham, Isaac, and Jacob are "alive" at the time God speaks to Moses (follows from # 1 and # 2).
4. But, Abraham, Isaac, and Jacob had died long before.
5. Therefore, Abraham, Isaac, and Jacob must have been resurrected in the meantime (follows from # 3 and # 4).
6. Therefore, there is a resurrection (follows from # 5).

Jesus ends his knockdown argument with a final blow: *You are quite wrong* (lit., *much deceived*)! He has bested all religious leadership groups with his responses to their questions. The next incident reveals that when Mark portrays a group of people as *quite wrong*, that does not mean each individual within the group is wrong.

The Most Important Commandment(s) 12:28-34

12:28-31 Love: The Center of the Law

In this context, a questioner who is not setting a trap, who speaks sincerely and agrees with Jesus' view, is clearly a foil for all the others. In Jesus' interaction with *the scribe,* we find important positive teaching that helps explain what is wrong with all those others whose questions and answers are misguided (cf. 12:34).

Which commandment is the first of all? (12:28b). The question is not about chronology (which was given first?) and not strictly about priority (which is more important than the others?). It has more to do with centrality. Which commandment is at the heart of the law? Which commandment makes the keeping of all the others both possible and meaningful? Which commandment determines the proper application of all the others?

Jesus responds by accepting the scribe's assumption that there is a center to the law. But he also modifies it by clarifying that two commandments are located at the center. The commandments to love

God (Deut. 6:4-5) and neighbor (Lev. 19:18) stand together at the heart of the Torah *[Questioning Jesus]*.

The Hebrew Shema quoted here, *Hear, O Israel: the Lord our God . . .* , was recited regularly in the synagogue. Thus Jesus says, "The center of the law is not some hidden key to be discovered by intricate exegetical maneuvers. The center of the law is the love command(s) repeated regularly in worship."

Some have suggested that there is an implied third great commandment, to *love . . . yourself* (12:31). This, however, misses the point of the passage. The text refers to an active, caring love that invests heart, soul, mind, and strength in the service of God and others. To love others adequately requires a redirection of these energies. Instead of active investment of our energies to serve ourselves, we are called to active investment of them in the service of God and others (cf. 10:43-45). While a healthy self-esteem is compatible with (and perhaps necessary for) a self-giving love of God and others, that is not what this text is teaching.

12:32-33 Love: More Central than the Ceremonies

The scribe agrees with Jesus' answer. He repeats the answer almost verbatim, but then adds, *This is much more important than all whole burnt offerings and sacrifices.* The scribe is making an important distinction. There is a binding moral law, centered in love for God and neighbor. In addition, there is a whole catalog of rules that regulate ceremonies, sacrifices, and rituals. These are much less important (v. 33). Mark expects his readers to add, "That is why Jesus cared so little for those rules and why they were destined to fall away." Jesus' critique of the temple system (11:15-17) is closely linked to the inverted priorities of the religious leaders. They have kept their system running, but have failed to love God and neighbor (TBC, below).

12:34 Not Far from the Kingdom

Jesus declares that the scribe is *not far from the kingdom of God*. Mark's point is that in God's economy, there is something more important than all the technicalities of law-keeping (the preoccupation of Pharisees and many of the scribes). There is something more important than all the sacrifices and ceremonies (the preoccupation of the chief priests, the entire priesthood, and the rest of the scribes). What really matters is the condition of the heart. What matters is the quality of one's relationship to God. What matters is the quality of relationships within the community and with those in need. Love, not legalism or ceremonialism, is the way of God's kingdom.

Why is the scribe declared *not far* from the kingdom? How far is not far? Two points are worth considering. First, nowhere in Mark is anyone ever said to fully enter the kingdom. That experience awaits the kingdom's full consummation. Second, Mark may well be saying that one is positioned *near* God's kingdom when priorities are correctly set. However, life *within* God's kingdom depends not just on *setting* right priorities, but on *living* them out. Jesus is not critiquing this scribe for being *not far* away (= "still outside"). Instead, Jesus is implicitly inviting him (and all others, then and now) to accept and practice the priorities Jesus teaches, thus participating in God's reign.

The Question About David's Son 12:35-37

Jesus has not usually taken the initiative in his debates with his opponents. They have posed the questions (11:28; 12:14-15; 12:23; 12:28), and he has responded. This time Jesus takes the initiative.

Jesus' question implies a critique against *the scribes*. They claim that *the Messiah is the son of David*. Jesus demonstrates from Scripture that the Messiah is in fact David's *Lord*. Jesus quotes Psalm 110:1 (the OT verse most frequently quoted in the NT, to show that Christ is reigning now). Though Jesus credits the statement to David (a point essential to the argument), he also credits it to the Holy Spirit, thereby implying its absolute authority.

Jesus' argument depends on clearly separating between the two appearances of the word *my* in the verse he quotes. The first refers to David, the author, who speaks of *my Lord*. The second refers to God, whom David is quoting: *Sit at my right hand*. It also depends on clearly separating between two occurrences of the word *Lord*. The first refers to God (Yahweh). The second refers to the Messiah (the one who sits at God's right hand). Jesus interprets the verse,

> The LORD [= Yahweh, God] says to my lord [= David's lord, the Messiah], "Sit at my (God's) right hand until I make your enemies your footstool." (Ps. 110:1)

The Messiah is thus David's Lord, sitting at God's right hand until God wins the victory over all the enemies of the Messiah. This much seems clear. But why does Mark include this incident?

Is he denying that the Messiah is also David's son? Probably not, for *Son of David* is an acceptable designation for the Messiah (cf. 10:47-48). More likely he is critiquing the view that the Messiah is

merely David's son and not *also* David's Lord. The Messiah far sur-
passes David's greatness, reigning as king over an entirely different
order (cf. 14:61-62; 15:2, 18, 26, 32).

In this text, Jesus is not directly claiming to *be* the Messiah. Still,
those in Jesus' crowd who wonder whether he is Messiah or not are
surely pondering why Jesus thinks it important to clarify the Messiah's
true nature.

Mark's reader has known since Mark 1:1 that Jesus is the
Messiah. Mark's reader understands that with Jesus' arrival in
Jerusalem, the "Lord" has suddenly come to his temple. And who can
stand? (Mal. 3:1-4; Mark 11:1-11, 31-33, notes). Mark shows that
Jesus demonstrates in the temple (11:15-17), prophesies its doom
(13:2), predicts its replacement by himself and his followers (14:58;
15:29), and pronounces God's judgment on the temple authorities
who reject God and God's Son (12:9). Yet this text (12:35-37) makes
it clear that Jesus himself will not lift up a finger against the temple or
its custodians. The Messiah/Christ waits for *God* to act. Christ will be
victorious, but *God* will give him the victory. Christ sits at God's right
hand until *God* defeats all his enemies. They will be *under [his] feet*
(12:36b; cf. 1 Cor. 15:25) and will see him *seated at the right hand
of the Power* (Mark 14:62); yet throughout this volatile situation,
Jesus himself is a pacifist.

Jesus Denounces the Scribes 12:38-40

What follows is the third consecutive episode directly related to
scribes. In 12:28-34 a scribe is affirmed for correct priorities. In
12:35-37 Jesus critiques a scribal viewpoint. Now Jesus speaks condemnation against some of the scribes' abuses.

Jesus begins with a warning that NRSV gives as *beware of. Be
discerning of* is a more appropriate translation. The element of danger is not completely absent, especially in the claim that the scribes
rob widows of their houses. But Jesus' warning is to be perceptive, in
order not to be fooled! The scribes imagine their long robes will hide
their threadbare pretensions. They think they deserve great respect,
special seats of honor. We remember that not long before, the disciples have been thinking similar thoughts (9:33-34; 10:35-37).

"These impressive-looking scribes," says Jesus, "are hypocrites.
They pray long public prayers, but it is all a sham. They act pious, yet
secretly commit one of the sins most viciously condemned by the
prophets: defrauding the poor." Widow's houses may refer to the property of those for whom they act as legal representatives. Instead of pro-

tecting the rights of their clients, they find ways of robbing them. When the Lord suddenly comes to his temple (Mal. 3:1; see previous section), among those judged will be those oppressing widows (Mal. 3:5).

"Don't be fooled," Jesus warns his hearers, especially his disciples (12:43). "Things are not always as they seem. The scribes are highly respected; they seem to have earned it with their superior piety. Yet underneath a beautiful exterior is hypocrisy and deceit." This theme continues through the next several episodes. "Don't be fooled! Some gifts look impressive, but it is the widow's gift, *worth a penny,* that truly pleases God" (12:41-44). "Don't be fooled! The temple looks impressive and indestructible, but it will soon be a heap of rubble" (13:1-4). "Don't be fooled! Messianic pretenders and apocalyptic deceivers will soon be making extravagant claims, but you must guard yourselves against their deceptions" (13:5-22).

The Widow's Offering 12:41-44

The disciples reenter the picture. Apart from acquiring a colt for Jesus and making a few comments about the cursed fig tree, they have not figured in the narrative since Jesus left Jericho (10:46). But they have been with Jesus in Jerusalem (11:11-12, 19-20, 27) and were presumably expected to learn the same lessons Mark's readers have been learning.

The disciples may have been expressing their admiration for those who put large gifts into the temple treasury. At any rate, Jesus draws attention to someone else, a poor widow, who puts in *all she had to live on* (12:44). The Greek can just as well be translated, *her whole life.* The others give out of their wealth; she gives out of her poverty.

The amount she gives is relatively small. Some have tried to calculate its value and come up with about a tenth the amount a laborer would earn in an hour, perhaps a dollar in our economy. That is all she has. Her sacrifice appears all the more impressive when we realize it consists of *two* coins. She could have kept one, but she gives both. What a model of self-sacrificing devotion to God!

Yet in context, the praise this woman has earned also appears bittersweet. Her piety and personal sacrifice are to be applauded, but what is the cause of her poverty, and what will be done with her gift? Mark has just pictured Jesus condemning religious leaders who reduce widows to poverty (12:38-40). Now Mark creates the impression that this woman's gift aids a religious system in adorning the scribes (12:38) and the temple (13:1), both of which stand poised for God's judgment (12:40; 13:2).

Through no fault of her own, this poor widow who has sacrificed so much, becomes a fitting symbol for a temple and a city that will soon lie in ruins. In the words of the OT's most famous lament, "How lonely sits the city, . . . how like a widow she has become" (Lam. 1:1). Yet for the reader of Mark's Gospel, even this dark cloud has a silver lining. She is also a fitting symbol for the self-sacrificing Jesus who also gives *his whole life* (10:45). For this sacrifice, her story has been remembered.

The story of this widow finds a counterpart in a matching incident in Mark 14:3-9. There another woman sacrifices greatly as she identifies with Jesus and his coming passion. Mark uses these two incidents as bookends around Mark 13; they will help him make the point that Jesus' discourse concerning the future is not a "bizarre apocalyptic tract," as some have called it. Instead, it is a chapter that teaches the impending doom of one temple and the glorious destiny of another *not made with hands* (14:58; for more reflection on 12:41-44 in relation to chap. 13 and 14:3-8, see "Two Women Who Gave," after 14:9, notes; cf. T. Geddert, 1989:134-9).

THE TEXT IN BIBLICAL CONTEXT
Faithful Vineyard; Unfaithful Tenants

In Mark (as in the other Gospels), the ordinary Jewish crowds do not always exhibit only positive responses. Also, their leaders do not without exception prove unfaithful. Jesus recognizes an exception in 12:34, and Mark another in 15:43. Nevertheless, in Mark, as elsewhere in the NT, the responsibility for the rejection of Jesus lies not with Israel as a whole but with their spiritual leaders. Mark's characterizations are consistent on this point (cf. 15:8, notes). The vineyard (God's people) is not without fruit; but the tenants (the religious leaders) are unfaithful stewards and hoard the vineyard's produce *[Israel and Israel's Leaders]*.

I have repeatedly emphasized this because it is so important in interpreting Mark correctly. If we understand Mark 12:1-12 (esp. v. 9) as meaning that Jesus (and Mark) rejects Israel in favor of Gentiles, that will have ripple effects throughout the Gospel (and throughout history). Just to clarify that this is not my viewpoint alone, I quote at length from Larry Hurtado, whose position I fully endorse:

> The subtle but important difference between Jesus' parable [12:3-9] and the similar parable in Isaiah 5:1-7 is that here the emphasis falls upon the *tenants*, who are clearly the leaders of Israel to whom God entrusted the nation. Thus, what we have is an indictment of the religious leadership of

Israel and not of the nation as a whole, except as it is led into disobedience by those attacked here. This is perhaps all the more important in
the light of the sorry history of anti-Jewish feeling that has characterized
too many periods of Christianity. Mark goes so far as to portray the
crowd as favorable to Jesus, making it more difficult for the religious
establishment to take action against him (12:12). Though Mark clearly
approved of the gospel being preached to Gentiles (e.g., 13:10) and was
critical of the religious practices of Judaism (e.g., 7:1-4), he was not anti-
Jewish and must have intended his readers to attribute the rejection of
Jesus by Israel to the stubborn blindness of the Jewish leaders (the tenants) rather than to the people as a whole. (179)

There may have been a larger number of religious leaders positively disposed toward Jesus. If so, Mark has chosen not to highlight
their responses. His purpose is not to distribute praise and blame as
fairly as possible, but to demonstrate that the religious leaders were
ultimately responsible for the rejection of Jesus. In terms of Israel as
a whole, some rejected Jesus and some accepted him. It was precisely
the same with the Gentiles who subsequently heard the good news.

Religious Ceremonies and the Commands of Love

How profound are the insights of the faithful scribe in Mark 12:28-
34! He sees, as his fellow scribes apparently do not, that the law is
not a code of prescriptions and proscriptions; it has a center, and that
center is all about relationships of love. He sees, as the priests in
Jerusalem apparently do not, that the ritual ceremonies of his religion
must take second place to what really counts, an undivided love for
God, and its application in concrete relationships of love with fellow
human beings.

Jesus pronounces him not far from the kingdom. Before the week
is over, Jesus' love for God and neighbor will be demonstrated, as he
gives his life for others. That death, knows Mark, will put an end to
all those burnt offerings and sacrifices that this faithful scribe already
knows to be secondary. As Jesus is crowned on the cross, the kingdom will move even closer to this scribe. If this man will take his stand
with Jesus in obedient discipleship, he will be a full participant in that
kingdom to which he is already so near.

When this scribe declares that the love commands *are much more
important than all whole burnt offerings and sacrifices* (12:28, 33)
he is taking his stand with the OT prophetic tradition. The prophets
often played down ceremonial laws in comparison with the weightier
matters of the law, a broken and contrite heart (Ps. 51:16-17), obedient walking "in the way" (Jer. 7:21-23), steadfast love and the

knowledge of God (Hos. 6:6), doing justice, loving kindness, and walking humbly with God (Mic. 6:8).

Jesus stands in that same tradition. He has declared people forgiven, without any reference to a sacrifice (2:5). He has flouted laws of ceremonial purity (e.g., 1:41; 5:41) and ritual cleansing (7:1-5). He has frequented the temple to demonstrate against its abuses and to teach, but not to participate in any of its rituals. Jesus' own priorities feature neither law nor ceremony; his priority is the pouring out of himself in service and love to God and neighbor (10:45; 14:24, 36).

The centrality of the love commands is maintained throughout the NT. For Paul, love ultimately fulfills the law (Rom. 13:8). Love heads the list of spiritual fruit (Gal. 5:22). Love supersedes in importance all spiritual gifts (1 Cor. 12:31—13:13). For James, the law of love is "the royal law" (2:8). In 1 John, the command to love is both old ("from the beginning," 2:7) and new (proved true in Jesus, 2:8).

When the scribe in Mark 12 values obedient love and right relationships over sacrifices, Mark wants his readers to think back to the "cleansing episode" (11:15-17) that led to most of the conflict in this section of Mark. Jesus claims there that the religious leaders have turned the temple into a *den of robbers*, alluding to Jeremiah's speech attacking worthless religion (Jer. 7:11). Jeremiah sharply critiques those who rely on "burnt offerings and sacrifices" (7:21-22). Rather than these, God wants obedient hearts, says the prophet.

Mark's scribe agrees with Jeremiah's perspective, and of course Jesus does as well. In his teaching in Galilee, Jesus has focused on what goes on in the heart and what comes out of it, not on what sticks to the hands or goes into the mouth (7:2, 15, 18-23). Now in Jerusalem, his focus is on the center of the law, on love for God, on love for neighbor, *not* on all the business of ceremonial religion, animals, coins, doves (11:15-17), burnt offerings, and sacrifices (12:33)—all leaves, no fruit (11:13).

By declaring food laws irrelevant, Jesus has cleansed all foods, as Mark 7:19 tells us. In 11:15-17 Jesus "cleanses" the temple. He views the buying and selling (with its oppression of Gentiles and Diaspora Jews) as violating God's purposes for the temple. In this context "sacrifices" offend God, as the OT prophets declared. Later, the Christian community will learn to live without the Jerusalem temple. Mark speaks of a temple rebuilt in three days (14:58), to be realized in Jesus' resurrection (16:5-7). Christ and the Christian community form the new temple, through and in which worship and forgiveness of sins are mediated (Swartley, 1994:192-4). In this transformation the new wine is truly bursting the old skins (2:22).

In Hebrews 10, the writer celebrates the end of "sacrifices and offerings," citing a litany of ways in which Jesus supersedes and therefore renders obsolete the sacrificial rites of the OT:

• Jesus' final sacrifice is the *reality*, of which the sacrifices required by OT law were *shadows* (10:1-2).

• The annually repeated sacrifices of the OT were unable to perfect the worshipers; by contrast, through a single offering of himself, Jesus forgives and perfects forever the ones being sanctified (10:2, 10, 14, 18).

• The OT sacrifices reminded of sin; through Jesus' sacrifice, they are remembered no more (10:3, 17).

• The sacrifices bring no pleasure to God; Jesus pleases God by carrying out God's will (10:5-8).

• The priest must "stand" and repeatedly offer ineffective sacrifices (10:11); Christ is now "seated" at God's right hand, awaiting the full outworking of his one perfect sacrifice (10:12-13).

• The OT sacrifices were devices to keep the old covenant in effect; Christ's final sacrifice institutes the superior covenant of inner righteousness (10:16-17).

What emerges out of Christ's final sacrifice is a community of people characterized by forgiveness (Heb. 10:18) and sanctification (10:14), confidence (10:19), sincerity, trust, purity (10:22), conviction (10:23), and above all mutual love, deeds of goodness, commitment to corporate worship, and mutual encouragement (10:24-25).

All that became possible because some people were prepared to move beyond OT religious ceremonies and pledge full allegiance to Jesus, the one who pointed to the heart of the law and then practiced it, though it meant sacrificing his own life.

THE TEXT IN THE LIFE OF THE CHURCH

What Belongs to Caesar?

The question about paying taxes to Caesar raises larger issues about the relationship between civil authority and God's ultimate authority over the life of the believer. Some have argued that Mark 12:13-17 clearly holds Christians responsible to obey civil authorities, particularly with respect to paying all required taxes. No matter how immoral a tax may seem, if the state requires it, Christians are obligated to pay it, some say.

However, I believe this conclusion must be challenged on several grounds. First, the question here is *not* about the legitimate authority of civil government in God's plan. This text does not suggest there are two distinct realms: (1) the state (= *the things that are the emperor's,* Mark 12:17a) and (2) God's kingdom (= *the things that are God's,* 10:17b). It is not about nicely divided spheres of responsibility, in which both the state and God's kingdom obligate citizens by their respective but separate demands. The idea of equally authoritative but separate "kingdoms" is not a biblical view. God's authority always stands above all other authority (e.g., Acts 4:19; 5:29).

This text is also not about God *delegating* authority to the state in limited spheres, as though believers must unquestionably submit to all civil laws (and taxes) as an obligation *to God.* This text is about whether one specific tax is lawful. Jesus' final ambiguous answer gives "Caesar" no ultimate authority, either beside God or under God.

There is a second reason why this text cannot be read as though it automatically obligates believers to submit to all civil taxes: it does not address the question whether taxes *must* be paid. It is about whether this particular tax *may* be paid. Mark 12:14 makes this clear. The question is whether it is *lawful* (= *permitted*) in the eyes of God to pay a tax that was a double abomination (notes, above). As much as the Jews dislike the tax, most would rather pay it than suffer the consequences of resisting Rome, assuming of course that it would not be against God's will to pay the tax.

Does God's law forbid the payment of this tax? That is the question of the Pharisees and Herodians, though we remember they are not asking it sincerely. Whether God's law might also permit tax *refusal* in some circumstances is not addressed here.

Mark 12:15 is sometimes thought to take this a step further, as though verse 14 asks whether paying the tax is *permitted,* and then verse 15 asks whether it is *required.* But this misreads verse 15. To ask *Should we pay?* could be taken as a question about obligation. However, in the context it is a question about counsel (the natural reading of the Greek). If Jesus' answer were an unambiguous yes (which it also is not), then it would mean, "If you want to avoid persecution by paying the tax, go ahead, despite the image on the coin and the interpretation of the tax!" A yes from Jesus would *not* mean, "You are not only permitted to pay it; you must pay it." This text does not address the issue of tax withholding as a form of boycott to protest the use of taxes for purposes Christians cannot support. That is even more obvious when we consider two other factors:

1. This text is about graven images and about land claims; the appropriate application of this text would have to be discerned care-

fully where the issues are different from these.

2. Jesus' answer is not an unambiguous yes (= yes, pay the tax). His highly ambiguous answer actually means, "You cannot solve questions about Caesar's claims on you without first settling issues concerning God's claims."

Believers who contemplate "tax withholding" (not tax cheating!) as a form of testimony, protest, and boycott need to think seriously—

• about *the way* it is done (never for personal financial advantage).
• about *why* they are doing it (not to impose a Christian discipleship ethic on a secular, pluralistic government).
• about *consequences* of doing it (is it an effective protest?).

Those who might insist that certain forms of tax resistance are a Christian's *obligation* will find little help from this text in making their case. Those who say that tax resistance is *prohibited* on the basis of this text are surely misreading it (Swartley, 1980:3-4).

Jesus' ambiguous answer to the Pharisees and Herodians suggests that Rome has *some* authority in *some* matters, but God has *final* authority in *all* matters. In its historical context, Jesus' answer was both a compromise position and an uncompromising position. Among influential Jewish leaders, there were some who were inclined to resist Rome's authority at every point. Even violent action against Roman officials was interpreted as an act of zealous faithfulness to God. Tax withholding was advocated by those of this mind. Their view was "Nothing belongs to Caesar!" Among influential Jewish leaders, some also were inclined to submit to Rome's authority wherever possible, making deals, collaborating, keeping the peace. Their view was "Give to Caesar whatever Caesar demands."

Between these extremes is the way of Jesus. Resisting Rome at every turn misinterprets God's kingdom, as though its goal were to overthrow earthly government. Collaborating for the sake of personal benefit also misinterprets God's kingdom, as though its goal were to avoid conflict and to carve out an easy life. Faithfulness to God's reign means living by values different from those of the political rebels but also different from those of the collaborating politicians. Jesus' ultimate answer is "Give to God what is God's, come what may!"

Politically, it looks like a compromise between the available first-century options. But it is in fact the only position ultimately uncompromising. It recognizes only one final authority, the authority of God in whose image we are made (see D. D. Kaufman; T. Peachey).

Mark 13:1-37

The Beginning of the End

PREVIEW

Mark 13 is almost totally about events to occur after Jesus' resurrection. The chapter borrows language from a literary form called *apocalyptic* (with references to signs, great catastrophes, deceivers, final salvation, the return of the Son of Man, and so on). Yet this chapter is quite different from typical apocalyptic writing in the first century. Its main concerns are neither signs nor end-time speculation. It is about such familiar Markan themes as discernment, discipleship, Christology, passion, and the temple.

Mark 13 is not about signs and timetables. It is about discernment, not being fooled by people with timetables and signs. It is about allegiance to Jesus, not believing messianic pretenders, and certainly not pledging allegiance to the doomed temple and the religious system it represents. It is about faithful discipleship in the crises to come and in the unknown waiting period while the Master is absent (13:34-36). It is about faithful mission in the context of persecution. It is about hope: God will protect and save the elect in times of persecution and tribulation. Someday, when the Son of Man appears *with great power and glory* (13:26), the secret kingdom will be secret no longer [*Eschatological Time Frames in Mark 13*].

If these themes are kept central, this chapter does not seem to be an alien intrusion in Mark's Gospel (as commentators often claim). Instead, this chapter is an integral part of Mark's good news and of his challenge to follow Jesus (cf. T. Geddert, 1989).

OUTLINE

Introducing Chapter 13

The Disciples, the Temple, the Sign, and the End, 13:1-4

Discerning the Times, 13:5-23
    13:5-6   Guarding Against Deceivers
    13:7-8   The Beginning of Birth Pains
    13:9-13   Mission in the Context of Persecution
    13:14-18   Events in Judea
    13:19-20   A Great Tribulation
    13:21-23   Guarding Against Deceivers

The Return of the Son of Man, 13:24-27

The Unknown Timing of These Things, 13:28-37
    13:28-29   The Parable of the Fig Tree
    13:30-31   This Generation Will Not Pass Away
    13:32   No One Knows About That Day
    13:33-37   Be Faithful *Because* You Do Not Know When

EXPLANATORY NOTES

Introducing Chapter 13

Mark 13 has proved extremely difficult to interpret. It seems wise to indicate some of the difficulties and also the approach that I take to this chapter before focusing on details of the text.

Interpreters have been divided on such central issues as these:

1. Is a timetable of end-time events presupposed or taught in this discourse, or does the chapter *discourage* readers from working out such a timetable?

2. How many signs does Jesus give in response to the disciples' request for *the sign* (13:4)? There are a range of views:

- There is no valid sign (e.g., Ladd: 322).
- There is exactly one sign (many commentators).
- There is a "baffling multiplicity of signs" (e.g., Cranfield, 1953:196).

3. If there is a sign, what is it, and what does it signify? There are three popular options:

- The *desolating sacrilege* (13:14) signals the imminent fall of the temple.

- The *desolating sacrilege* signals the imminent return of the Son of Man.
- The fall of the temple (13:2) signals the imminent return of the Son of Man (see next point).

4. What is the relationship between the fall of the temple (13:2) and the return of the Son of Man (13:26)? Does the chapter *link* these events or argue *against* linking them? Or is the temple's destruction not even alluded to after 13:4?

5. What does 13:30 mean? *What* things will happen, and before *which* generation passes away?

6. What does 13:32 mean? Is the timing of *the End* totally unknowable, even by Jesus and Mark, or is only the exact day and hour unknown?

On all these points, interpreters are divided. If one assumes that the goal of interpretation is to eliminate ambiguity, it is easy to see why there are so many different interpretations of Mark 13. The chapter contains an astonishing number of ambiguous expressions. Hence, many references and even whole sentences can be read in more than one way. Eliminating the ambiguity involves choices about the "right" meaning. The more choices that need to be made, the greater the chance that interpreters will widely diverge.

My view is that Mark has deliberately created or incorporated virtually all the ambiguity that many interpreters are aiming to eliminate. Interpreting this chapter does not mean getting rid of the ambiguity but understanding why it is there and what role it plays.

In Mark 13:3-4 the disciples ask Jesus for *the sign*, presumably wanting information to help them track a calendar of future events. If one assumes that Jesus obliges them with what they want, then it is reasonable to try to eliminate the ambiguity one finds in Mark 13. Only if one makes that assumption will *the sign* or a list of signs emerge, leading to a calendar of future events.

However, what if Jesus does *not* oblige them? What if Jesus critiques their perspective and teaches that no sign will help them construct an end-time calendar? What if Jesus' entire response to the disciples follows from the assumption that no one knows, that no one *can* know, when the End will come—not Mark the author, and not even Jesus himself (13:32)!?

If no one can know the sequence of end-time events, it follows that no one can know whether the *desolating sacrilege* (13:14) leading to the temple's destruction is the last and final desolating sacrilege, or whether at some future time another desolating sacrilege will stand *where it/he ought not to be* (v. 14). Likewise, we cannot know whether the predicted destruction of the temple is one of the final end-time events, nor whether the turbulent times surrounding the temple's destruction (vv. 14-18) will be part of the final tribulation, nor whether there will be continued opportunity for "mission in the context of persecution" (v. 10) after the temple's destruction, and so on. At some totally unknowable time, *while*, or *right after*, or *long after* the temple is destroyed, the Son of Man will return.

The controlling assumption of Mark 13 is that the timing of the End is totally unknowable. Most of the ambiguity of the chapter *needs* to be there to preserve this unknowability. The ambiguity should not be eliminated but understood.

The Disciples, the Temple, the Sign, and the End 13:1-4

Almost everything in Mark 11–12 features Jesus' relationship to the temple and the religious leaders. His "temple demonstration" (11:15- 17) has led to conflict with the religious leaders there (11:18). Jesus used symbolic actions (11:12-14, 20-21), a parable (12:1-9), subtle allusions (e.g., 11:23; 12:10-11, 33), and overt challenges (e.g., 12:17, 27, 37, 38-40). Thereby he confronted the religious leaders with their hypocrisy and unfaithfulness, prophesied their punishment, and hinted that he and his followers will replace them as the nucleus of the renewed people of God.

It is the religious leaders who are condemned, but the temple is very much at the center of the controversy. The leaders have abused the temple with their trading, by going through empty religious exercises (12:29-33), by finding in the temple their false security, and so on. Their beloved and presumed inviolable temple has become a *den of robbers* (11:17; cf. Jer. 7:11). Jesus maintains that the temple provides no security whatsoever, neither against foreign armies nor against God's judgment.

Jesus has predicted the destruction of the religious leaders (12:9); now he predicts the destruction of the temple. As Jesus and his disciples leave the temple, one of them speaks admiringly of the great temple. Well he might; the unbelievable size and magnificence of the temple is legendary. Yet how inappropriate to rave about the temple, when Jesus has just spent the week condemning what is going on there!

Jesus' question, *Do you **see** these great buildings?* reminds us of all those texts in Mark where the disciples' ability to truly see (and hear) has been questioned. Massive stones and impressive walls fill their vision, but do they really see? Do they see how all that religious activity falls short of God's expectations? Do they see how religious leaders have corrupted and abused what should have been *a house of prayer for all nations* (11:17)?

Jesus has just urged the disciples to see past impressive exteriors. The ones honoring God are not the rich, ostentatiously throwing portions of their wealth into the treasury, but a poor widow, sacrificing out of her poverty (12:41-44). What truly honors God is not a great temple and all its religious activity, but a community of disciples who love God and each other (12:28-31). The disciples gaze with admiration at the huge stones and impressive decorations of the temple; Jesus sees through the exterior to its desecration and doom.

Hence, Jesus utters the prediction that must have shocked his disciples. Every stone of the temple will be thrown down. The OT prophets had predicted previous temple destructions, but never in such unambiguous terms (cf. Jer. 7:14; 26:6; Mic. 3:12).

Jesus' disciples accompany him to the Mount of Olives. From this mountain, prophesied Zechariah, the Lord would establish his kingdom (Zech. 14:4, 9). Now from this mountain, Jesus speaks of the future destiny and final fulfillment of the kingdom he has been proclaiming and establishing since his ministry began. From the Mount of Olives, the entire temple complex is clearly visible.

Perhaps Mark thinks of Ezekiel's prophecy as he narrates Jesus' final exit from the temple. "The glory of the LORD went out from the threshold of the house . . . and . . . stopped on the mountain east of the city" (Ezek. 10:18; 11:23). At any rate, Jesus now sits opposite (or *over against*, Mark 13:3) the temple, and the first four disciples he has called (1:16-20) want to know more. *Privately* (13:3-4), these four will hear Jesus speak about what lies ahead: natural disasters, wars, persecution, great suffering, opportunities for courageous testimony and gospel proclamation, unprecedented tribulation, and finally heavenly portents that signal the return of the Son of Man. Yet as private as this discourse is, Mark makes sure that every reader is included (v. 14). *Everyone* is to take seriously the promises, warnings, and challenges of this discourse (v. 37, NIV).

Verse 4 gives the disciples' *questions,* and verses 5-37 record Jesus' *response.* But does Jesus' response really give the disciples what they want to know? The problems of interpreting this chapter begin here *[Eschatological Time Frames in Mark 13].*

The disciples ask two questions:

1. *Tell us, when will **these things** be?* (the word *these* is plural, *tauta;* NRSV's singular *this* is not correct). This first question explicit-

ly asks about the timing of the temple's impending destruction, and about the timing of *the events that will accompany* this great catastrophe (= *these things*). We do not know what the disciples assume will happen as part of the same complex of events. Do they assume the temple's destruction is part of a series of events leading directly to and including the final Day of the Lord? We do not know. Nor does Jesus explicitly indicate in his response to them which events *he* assumes are connected to the coming destruction of the temple.

2. *What will be the sign that all these things are about to be accomplished?* Since we do not know what the disciples are assuming, we cannot understand their second question, which asks about a sign (*sēmeion*). Are they asking for something that will help them recognize when the temple's destruction is imminent? Or are they asking for a sign indicating that the great final Day of the Lord is about to arrive (since their second question expands beyond the first, referring to *all these things*). We cannot be sure whether the disciples have *the End* in mind at all.

Jesus will not give an explicit answer to their questions *[Questioning Jesus]*. Never again in the entire speech does Jesus refer to the temple (though he likely alludes to it in v. 14). Nor is anything in Jesus' answer ever called a "sign." The word for sign (*sēmeion*) is used *only* in Jesus' warning not to be fooled by those who parade *signs* (v. 22). In the fifth century, Victor of Antioch wrote, "They asked one question; he answers another" (cf. Nineham: 343-4). One might even say, "They asked an unclear answer; Jesus refuses to give a clear answer!"

If we seek Jesus' direct response to a question about *timing*, the best place to look is in verse 32: Nobody knows! That *no one* includes both the speaker (Jesus) and the writer (Mark), through whom this discourse comes to us. If we seek Jesus' response to the question about a *sign*, the best places to look are in v. 22 (with its warning *against* signs) and in verses 33-37. Here we learn that there are no signs, and that discernment and faithfulness are required precisely *because* it is not possible to know when one will be called to give an account of one's service. Faithfulness at *every moment* and not just at the *final moment* is required. Only complete ignorance of the timing can provide adequate motivation for constant readiness. Mark 13 should be interpreted in light of these two assumptions:

The timing of the End cannot be known.
No sign helps to determine it.

Discerning the Times   13:5-23

Jesus' response begins with the word *blepete*, variously translated as *Beware* (NRSV), *Watch out* (NIV), or *See to it* (NASB). Better than all of these is the translation *Be discerning* (or *Be aware*). *Blepete* is the normal word for "look" or "see," here used as an imperative. Throughout his Gospel, Mark has used this word to call for truly discerning vision, seeing what is *really* going on (T. Geddert, 1989:81-87). It is the same word Jesus has used when asking his disciples, *Do you (truly) see these great buildings?* (13:2).

Jesus' first response is a call for discernment. *Blepete* (*see!*) in Mark 13 is the counterpart to *akouete* (*hear!*) in Mark 4. Jesus calls for careful discernment, for eyes that see past the surface details to the true significance. Deceivers will come; do not be deceived. History will bring disasters; do not be fooled into thinking the End has come. Persecution will come; do not overlook opportunities for witness; and so on. This imperative meaning *Be discerning!* occurs four times in Jesus' discourse:

• *Be discerning* when deceivers come (13:5; NRSV: *Beware!*).

• *Be discerning* in times of persecution (v. 9; NRSV: *Beware!*).

• *Be discerning* about all these things I have just said (v. 23; NRSV: *Be alert!*).

• *Be discerning* of the meaning of the following parable and of the opportune moment (the *kairos*) to follow through on its meaning (v. 33; NRSV: *Beware!*).

Blepete is never a call for self-protection (as in *Watch out!*); nor is it a call to recognize *signs* or to figure out a timetable. It is not the *means* of sign-seeking; it is the *alternative* to it (cf. 8:14-21, where discernment is also the alternative to sign-seeking). It is a call to discern which challenges and opportunities will arise in a life of faithful discipleship. It is Jesus' way of saying, "Go into the future with your eyes wide open!"

The last word of this discourse will be another watchword, from a different Greek imperative, *grēgoreite*. Its focus is on faithfulness, not on discernment. This word is used three times in Mark 13:34-37, and elsewhere in Mark only in the Gethsemane account (14:34, 37-38), where the disciples are called to *Keep watch*, meaning *Stay at your post!* Two responsibilities of Jesus' followers are crucial because we cannot know when the End will come—as captured in the first word and the last word of Jesus' speech. These are the two crucial watchwords of Mark 13:

> | *Blepete* | = Be discerning! | (13:5) |
> |-----------|------------------|--------|
> | *Grēgoreite* | = Be faithful! | (13:37) |

13:5-6 Guarding Against Deceivers

Mark 13:5-13 lists a series of situations that will arise in the future. None of them are to be viewed as signs of the end time; they are *but the beginning of birth pains* (v. 8). Deceivers, however, will come along and *claim* that these are sure signs that the End has arrived. They will also make a preposterous claim about themselves, a claim literally translated *I AM* (v. 6). This is the Greek translation for Yahweh (cf. 6:50; 14:62; Exod. 3:14). Perhaps the deceivers are claiming divinity. Alternatively, they may be claiming, "I am Jesus (returned)" or "I am the Messiah (and Jesus was not)." Whatever their claim, the disciples are to stand firm in their allegiance to Jesus, the Messiah, the Son of God. He is the one destined to return as the Son of Man.

It would be a serious mistake to write down "deceivers" at the top of a list of supposed "signs," as some commentators do. They begin listing the signs Jesus cites in answer to the disciples' request for them: (1) deceivers, (2) wars, (3) earthquakes, and so on. This listing is precisely what Mark 13:5-6 *forbids.*

13:7-8 The Beginning of Birth Pains

Wars and rumors or wars (wars near and far) are also not signs signaling the arrival of the End. Then as now, wars provide especially fruitful contexts for apocalyptic speculation. In time of war, especially religious war, speculation thrives as to who will be the Messiah delivering an oppressed people, and who will be the "antichrist" opposing all that is good and right. Neither wars nor the deceivers who capitalize on them are to cause great alarm. War is a fearful thing, but it is not a sign of the end time, says Jesus.

The prohibition Jesus uses, *Do not be alarmed* (13:7), means "Don't get all excited! This is not yet the End!" Earthquakes and famines will also occur, but these too are only *the **beginning** of the birth pangs*, not signs of the End. Such events have always occurred and will continue to occur, from the *beginning* (v. 8) of the post-resurrection age right to its consummation. Mark shares with the rest of the NT the view that the end time (vv. 7, 13) or "the last days" cover the entire period from Jesus' first advent to his second (cf. Heb. 1:2; Acts 2:16-17; 1 Cor. 10:11). Everything that happens after Jesus is resurrected constitutes the end time. The events listed in Mark 13:5-8 belong to that whole time period; they are not to be understood as signs that the End is imminent.

13:9-13 Mission in the Context of Persecution

Verses 9-13 speak of trials faced specifically by believers. This is signaled in verse 9 by the opening address, As for you (TJG). Many interpreters believe Mark's Gospel ends without projecting the renewal of the disciples after their failure during the passion. These verses, however, assume that those who are unfaithful at the time of Jesus' passion will afterward be courageous witnesses for the cause of Christ. Discipleship renewal is offered in the Markan narrative (cf. 14:28). No matter how the silence of the women in 16:8 is interpreted, we know from 14:28 that the disciples are offered a chance to be renewed; we know from this text (13:9-13) and from others (e.g. 9:9; 10:39) that in fact they are renewed after the resurrection.

Though the punctuation of these verses is not quite certain, the NRSV captures the most likely meaning. Here are three references to the handing over (paradidōmi) of Jesus' followers (13:9, 11-12). Jesus uses this same word three times in his own passion-resurrection predictions. In those predictions, Jesus makes it clear that he will be handed over to humans (9:31, by God), that he will be handed over to the Jewish leaders (10:33a, by Judas), and that he will be handed over to Gentiles (10:33b, by the Jewish leaders).

Jesus also predicts for his followers a threefold handing over; it is part of the divine plan and it includes persecution at the hands of both Jews (13:9a) and Gentiles (v. 9b). In such times of persecution, they are explicitly told to keep the following in mind:

• These are opportunities for testimony to (and against) the religious and civil officials (v. 9b).

• Persecution will be a context for worldwide mission (v. 10).

• The Holy Spirit will help them when they are on trial (v. 11). After the promise in 1:8, this is the only reference in Mark's Gospel to the work of the Spirit in believers' lives.

• There is need for endurance, and it will be rewarded with salvation (v. 13).

The predicted persecution and the concurrent evangelizing are located alongside wars, famines, deceivers, and so on; hence, they are not signs of the End. The final phrase, however, calling believers to endure to the End, indicates that persecution will not be located only in this beginning period, but will continue all the way through to the End. It belongs to the whole end-time period, to the beginning stages (cf. 13:7b-8b), and also to the final stages leading to the return of the Son of Man (cf. v. 13b). Jesus' promise, the one who endures *to the end will be saved* (v. 13b), can have various meanings:

1. The end of a particular persecution will bring salvation to those who endure through it.
2. Death will bring salvation to those who endure faithfully until martyred for their faith (cf. 8:35).
3. The Son of Man's return will bring salvation to those suffering persecution at the very End of the age.

Since individual believers cannot be certain whether a given persecution will cost them their lives, nor whether the Son of Man will return in their lifetime, each of these interpretations might apply.

Worldwide mission also belongs to the *whole* post-resurrection period, right up to the End of the age. It belongs to this first period, as shown by its position here in 13:13 and by its connection to the persecutions that characterize this period. There are two ways to take the statement that *The good news must **first** be preached to all nations:*

1. Worldwide evangelization is a divine eschatological necessity. The final return of the Son of Man will be delayed until it is complete, for God has ordained its completion.
2. Or, worldwide evangelization is a central responsibility of Jesus' followers. They are to pursue it energetically, for someday the available time will end.

Mark wants the reader to accept both meanings. The timing of the End is in God's hands alone (13:32); meanwhile, Jesus' followers are to be about the task of bringing the gospel to all nations. Either way, mission fills the whole period, right up to the End. "As long as history goes on," Jesus says, "believers are to be preoccupied with mission in the context of persecution."

We should carefully note the connection between persecution and mission. John's passion opened the door to the ministry of Jesus (1:14). Jesus' ministry and passion prepare disciples to *fish for people* (1:17; 14:27-28). Now, in the post-resurrection period, the disciples' persecution opens new doors enabling others to bring the gospel to the whole world.

Some interpreters only see a dark cloud: "Whenever you go about the task of evangelizing the nations, expect to be persecuted." Mark wants his readers to focus on the silver lining: "Whatever persecutions may come, the gospel cannot be stopped; even when you are on trial, God will speak through you (13:9b, 11), and worldwide mission will go on (v. 10)." Persecution, far from curtailing gospel proclamation, facilitates it. After all, those who proclaim the gospel will surely be taken more seriously if they are willing to suffer and die for their convictions!

The reference to division within families (13:12-13) reminds readers of Jesus' promise that those who give up families for his sake and the gospel will receive "families" back a hundredfold. In the turbulent times ahead, the believer's identity will be with Jesus and the new spiritual family he creates (3:31-35). Jesus' followers will face rejection even by natural siblings, parents, and children (13:12); indeed, they will be hated *by all* (v. 13a). Yet they will never be rejected by the one who has called them to follow and who promises them ultimate salvation if they faithfully endure the difficult times ahead (13b).

None of the events in verses 5-13 are to be understood as signs of the End. They are events that characterize the world in which the believers will live and the mission and destiny of believers in that world. With verse 14, a shift takes place in Mark 13. The text speaks cryptically of events that *might or might not* lead directly to the End.

13:14-18 Events in Judea

Jesus refers in mysterious language to a *desolating sacrilege* (NRSV; NIV: *abomination of desolation*) being set up *where it ought not to be* (13:14). At one level this must refer to something or someone desecrating the Jerusalem temple, for Jesus is referring to events in Judea (v. 14b). If so, after verses 1-2, this is the only reference in this chapter to the temple (and it is not explicit).

What does this mysterious language mean? *Desolating sacrilege* is a phrase known from OT and intertestamental literature. The same Greek words were used to refer to Antiochus Epiphanes' idolatrous sacrifice to Zeus in the Jerusalem temple in 168 B.C.E. (1 Macc. 1:54, 59; Dan. 12:11). This sacrilege led to the Maccabean revolt and the (temporary) deliverance of Israel from Syrian control.

Mark and his readers may be thinking also of a crisis in A.D. 40; the Roman emperor Caligula ordered that his own statue be set up in the temple. That would have been a *desolating sacrilege*—but the Jews protested, the Roman official delayed, and Caligula was persuaded to rescind his order just before he died (Josephus, *Antiq.* 18.8.2-9). Verse 14 might well allude to a similar future sacrilege that would result in a war (A.D. 66-70), bringing disaster on those who do not flee (vv. 14b-18). If the Judeans think they can rebel against Rome and experience another Maccabean miracle, they are mistaken; revolt will lead to doom, not deliverance.

The call to *flee* (13:14b) needs to be understood in that light. Elsewhere in Mark, fleeing signals failure, unfaithfulness, cowardice. That is because it refers to flight from the way of the cross, from Jesus, and from one's mission (14:50, 52; 16:8). In 13:14-15, Jesus calls believers to flee from the place where God's hand of judgment is about to fall on the religious leaders and their temple (cf. 12:9; 13:2; Rev. 12:6).

G. R. Beasley-Murray (14) aptly comments:

> There was no necessity for the disciples to perish through misguided attachment to the doomed city (still less through a confidence in its inviolability); martyrdom for the gospel's sake was another matter.

Jesus counsels flight to the mountains (presumably into hiding places available there). The implication is that when the temple is desecrated, war will break out. Those who mistakenly believe their temple is their security will perish, while those who flee will be saved. The call to flee is thus an act of compassion for those who will listen to Jesus, something the religious leaders have consistently refused to do. The rest of the nation, especially the followers of Jesus, need not perish with them; believers are given an opportunity to get out in time.

> When the judgment falls, all who will trust in themselves, their might, their leaders, their election, or their temple will be judged along with the religious system they represent. All who will take their stand with Jesus will leave the temple and the city to its fate. (T. Geddert, 1989:219)

Incidentally, we now see more clearly why it is important to endure persecution (not *flee* from it) during the period of missionary preaching *prior to* the crisis in Jerusalem (13:9-13). The witness of Jesus' followers is needed so as to proclaim Jesus' message and thus rescue compatriots from the disaster to come.

Those who heed the warnings and flee the crisis will not find things easy. War will erupt so suddenly there will not be time for preparations (13:15-16). It will be especially hard for those who are pregnant or nursing (13:17). If it happens in winter, things will be even more difficult (presumably because cold and rain will inhibit travel).

The text goes on to describe the coming tribulation in truly "apocalyptic" terms (13:19-20)—but first we must backtrack.

Why is this mysterious language used? If verse 14a means what we suggested in the notes above, why is the prophecy given in such cryptic terms? Why no explicit mention of Jerusalem or the temple? Why the admonition *Let the reader understand!* (13:14)?

I have never been quite satisfied with the usual answers:

- It would be politically dangerous to speak more explicitly.
- Or, the reference is not actually to Jerusalem and the temple.
- Or, the reader is expected to know what is meant.
- Or, Mark did not know what is intended.

It seems more likely that verse 14 is to be taken as a deliberately ambiguous reference, designed to make sure the readers do not claim to know more than Mark or Jesus. Neither Jesus nor Mark are intending to take a clear stand on how the desecration and destruction of the temple relate to the End of the age. They do not know. The events surrounding the temple's destruction *might* lead directly to the return of the Son of Man, *and they might not*.

The desolating sacrilege that will appear in the temple in Jerusalem might be the final desecration signaling the imminence of the End. On the other hand, it might be yet another in a series of events that foreshadow another great and final desecration still to come. Jesus does not know when the End will come (v. 32), nor does he know whether or not the temple's destruction is part of the final complex of end events or not (see "Introducing Chapter 13," above).

This explains a grammatical oddity in verse 14. *Sacrilege (bdelugma)* is a neuter noun in Greek. The participle *set up* should also be neuter, but in fact it is masculine. Perhaps Mark is hinting that it is a *person* who will desecrate the temple. He might also be hinting that the desolating sacrilege soon to appear in the Jerusalem temple might not be the final and greatest sacrilege.

Maybe an even greater sacrilege will occur in the future when an antichrist figure ("he") appears. Many have interpreted verse 14 this way, based on comparisons with other NT texts (cf. 2 Thess. 2:3-4). Mark seems to leave open this possibility without either affirming or denying it. If another desolating sacrilege should appear, then *in that context,* the call to *flee* will be a call to disassociate totally from it/him. When the temple is desecrated, flee for war is coming. If history goes on after that war (which it might), then there might well be another desolating sacrilege yet to come, though we cannot be sure. Since we cannot know, we must be discerning! *Let the reader understand!* (13:14).

There might or might not be a time gap between the war described in 13:15-18 and the unprecedented tribulation in 13:19-20. If the events surrounding the temple's destruction constitute the great final tribulation before the End, then there is not a time gap. Yet precisely that identification cannot be made, for Jesus does not know

(v. 32), nor does Mark, nor does the reader.

From *our* perspective, of course, things have become clearer. The Jerusalem temple was desecrated and destroyed in A.D. 70. The Jewish war with Rome ended in disaster for those who clung to their city and their temple, just as Jesus had predicted it would; but the Son of Man did not return then. Mark's current readers now know that *one* of the earlier options has not materialized.

13:19-20 A Great Tribulation

Verse 19 refers to an unprecedented tribulation (*thlipsis*). NRSV speaks of *suffering* happening *in those days*, implying that the reference is merely to the effects of the war mentioned (vv. 14-18). But the text actually says, *Those days will be a tribulation*. A specific tribulation period, one of unprecedented proportions, will characterize *those days*. What is not made specific is which days are meant.

Whenever it comes, whether in connection with the war against Rome or in connection with some future desolating sacrilege, an unprecedented tribulation will precede the End. This great final tribulation will be *shortened* (v. 20) for the sake of God's chosen people. This probably means that God will be in full control of the length and extent of the tribulation. What is left uncertain is whether the tribulation is brought to an end by the returning Son of Man or by some other means prior to that.

We do not know whether there is a time gap projected between the tribulation (vv. 19-20) and the return of the Son of Man (vv. 24-27), just as Mark's first readers could not know whether there would be a time gap between the events of verses 14-18 and the tribulation referred to in verses 19-20. It depends on whether or not the desecration and destruction of the temple and the war in Judea are events associated with the End. That is something neither Jesus nor Mark claimed to know (13:14-18, notes; "Introducing Chapter 13").

Jesus assures his disciples of God's providential care. God will limit the tribulation to what Jesus' followers can bear without losing their faith (for an alternative view of *the elect*, see TLC, below).

13:21-23 Guarding Against Deceivers

In verses 10-13 Jesus clarified that mission in the context of persecution characterizes not only the beginning of this end-time period but *all* of it, right up to *the End*. Now we learn that because of the presence of deceivers, the need for discernment also fills the *whole* time period.

When unprecedented tribulation occurs, deceivers will capitalize on the situation and claim to be able to map out an eschatological timetable. There will be *false messiahs* who will promise a way of deliverance from the tribulation, perhaps claiming to be the returning Jesus. There will be *false prophets* who will speak in support of the false messiahs or make false claims about what will happen next. Such deceivers will produce signs and wonders in attempts to deceive. If they could, they would *lead astray* even true believers (13:22). Jesus calls his followers to be discerning so no one will deceive them (v. 23).

This is the only reference to *signs* since the disciples asked for *the sign* in verse 4. They want a sign; Jesus warns against those who give signs. This chapter is not about signs; it is about the *unavailability* of signs. True, the *desolating sacrilege* is a sign of sorts (though not called one). It is a signal to the discerning that they *must flee* (v. 14). But it is not a sign revealing where history (or present time) is on an eschatological calendar; that is something no one knows (v. 32).

Jesus gives one final word about the time period before the End: *Be discerning!* (v. 23a; NRSV: *Be alert!*). This word has opened the discourse and is also the final word before *the End* is described. Always there will be deceivers claiming to map out the future. Always there will be the necessity of faithfulness and opportunities for witness. Therefore, be discerning, keep watch (*blepete*)! The first major division of Jesus' discourse ends as it began (13:5, 23).

Discernment is necessary because all that the disciples *need* to know, Jesus has already said (v. 23b). They certainly have not been told everything they would *like* to know (e.g., which signs are there? when will all this happen?). But they have been told all that *can* be said.

The Return of the Son of Man 13:24-27

Mark has narrated end events that make the return of the Son of Man imminent. Now he describes that final *coming* in terms well-known from OT references to God coming in ultimate judgment and salvation *[Son of Man]*.

The timing of the Son of Man's return is left completely indeterminate. It will happen *in those days, after that tribulation* (KJV; NRSV: *suffering*). Jesus gives his hearers and Mark gives his readers no clues as to how long *after*. A final unprecedented tribulation (13:19-20) must precede the End, a tribulation that *might* be connected to the Jewish war or *might not* be (13:14-18, notes). Since we cannot know (at least from Mark 13) whether another great tribulation will immediately precede the End, the Son of Man's return must be considered imminent any time after the predicted Jewish-Roman war (the fulfillment of the events predicted in 13:14ff.). Jesus might return immediately thereafter or at any time thereafter. Imminent does not mean it *will* happen soon, but that it *could* happen very soon. Nothing stands in its way; no end-time event *must* precede it.

The returning Son of Man might bring the great tribulation to an end, or else there might be a waiting period, short or long, between the tribulation and the Son of Man's return. We simply cannot know, for a time gap between verse 23 and verse 24 is neither affirmed nor denied. Readiness and faithfulness are called for *because you do not know when* (13:33, 35).

Poetic language borrowing heavily from OT prophetic writings is used to describe the "heavenly convulsion" (13:24-25) that occurs when the Son of Man comes. The heavenly portents are not signs whereby the timing of the Son of Man's coming can be predicted. They are events *accompanying* the great act of salvation (and possibly judgment; cf. 14:62) identified in verses 26-27.

The Son of Man will come *with great power and glory* and will send out angels to gather together the elect, who will share in his power and glory. Thus the believers who have experienced persecution and remained faithful to the end (13:13) experience the glory beyond, just as Jesus' own passion leads to his final vindication by God. Mark gives us few hints as to what will happen after the Son of Man comes (TBC, below).

Verse 26 significantly does not say, "Then *you* will see the Son of Man coming." The verb is indefinite and some pronoun such as "they" needs to be supplied (as in NRSV). The discourse is addressed to four disciples, though intended for all believers (13:3, 14, 37). But when the Son of Man returns, he will return for *whoever* is there to be gathered at that time. All the necessary preliminaries are promised within a generation (13:30), but the End is not necessarily included in that. Again, uncertainty about the timing of the End is carefully preserved.

The Unknown Timing of These Things 13:28-37

Mark now backtracks, not giving us descriptions of what will happen *after* the coming of the Son of Man, but talking about the timing of events that precede the coming of the Son of Man. He gives various kinds of references to timing, but even with their help, we know nothing about the timing of the End itself, except that it is unknowable.

13:28-29 The Parable of the Fig Tree

This parable has sometimes been interpreted as though it encourages the observation of signs and the use of them to predict the timing of the End. But it is far too ambiguous to function that way. Some of the ambiguity stems from the larger Markan context, some from the uncertainty of the Greek, and some simply from the fact that it is a parable. Consider the following difficulties (to list only *some* of them; see also T. Geddert, 1989:247-253).

• Parables in Mark simply do not function unambiguously.

• A fig tree in leaf is not a casual reference to just any tree (as in Luke 21:29); it picks up and reuses symbolism related to another fig tree in leaf that Jesus cursed (11:12-14, 20-21).

• We are not told what is included in *these things* that we are to observe taking place.

• We do not know who or what is *near* when *these things* take place; the Greek leaves this completely unclear.

• We do not know what *near* means: does it mean imminent (nothing must precede its arrival) or guaranteed to be soon?

• We cannot determine (in Greek) whether the word *know* in verse 29 is indicative or imperative. Are we being challenged to discern or guaranteed that we will know?

This parable has two primary messages. One is a general lesson based on the regularity of the seasons. The other is a specific hint as to what believers should discern, beyond the fact that the temple will be destroyed. There are two lessons:

1. When you see springtime events occurring (fig trees gaining leaves), you know that summer is just around the corner. So also, when you see evidences that some of God's promises are being fulfilled, you can be sure the rest will happen as well.

2. One fig tree that had only leaves was cursed because it bore no fruit; that tree stood for the temple and its custodians. Another will arise and prepare for a season of fruit-bearing; that tree stands for the new temple built without hands. So when you see the temple fall, be discerning! This is not an end as much as it is a new beginning.

The first lesson implies we can learn virtually nothing from this parable about the timing of the End. At most we can know that whenever we discern that *these things* have occurred, then something or someone is near.

The second lesson is more instructive; it assures us that God is working out divine purposes. God expects no fruit from the old temple and its leaders; that tree has leaves but will never again bear fruit (11:12-14, 20-21). But God expects a great harvest from a new temple to be raised up in Jesus and his community. The leaves are already there; the summer of fruit-bearing is just around the corner. For Mark, the disqualification and destruction of the physical temple and its custodians is inseparably linked to the vindication of Jesus and the raising up of the new temple, which Jesus and his followers become (cf. 12:9-11).

13:30-31 This Generation Will Not Pass Away

Jesus makes a solemn statement, opening it with *Amen* and following it by a personal guarantee that the statement is more sure than heaven and earth. His solemn statement guarantees,

This generation will not pass away until all these things have taken place.

There have been ceaseless debates as to what *this generation* means and what belongs to *all these things* that it will experience. The most obvious meaning of *generation* is Jesus' contemporaries. Among other suggestions are the following:

- Mark's contemporaries.
- The generation of those observing the greening of the fig tree (v. 28; this is then made to refer to events in *our* day or still future).
- Humanity in general.
- Unbelievers.
- The Jews.

All of these can find some (however little!) biblical support. Yet why not stay with the most natural meaning: Jesus' contemporaries? Because (according to some) the course of history would then show Jesus' prediction to have been in error. Some interpreters are not troubled by the idea that Jesus might have made an incorrect prediction. They argue that the promise itself and not the timing of its fulfillment is the important thing. But most resist this approach. The problem is that many who claim the historical Jesus made only accurate predictions, then end up blaming Mark for putting a "false prophecy" in Jesus' mouth.

It seems to me that there is a better approach. Mark portrays Jesus as consistently refusing to claim knowledge about when the End will come (13:32). Verse 30 incorporates deliberate ambiguity to preserve ignorance concerning the timing. *All these things* will happen within a generation. This includes the events leading up to and accompanying the fall of the Jerusalem temple (13:2). But no one knows how many other events are also included. Above all, Mark's text takes no stand on whether the return of the Son of Man is included or not.

Jesus' solemn prediction in verse 30 should be read this way:

> Within the present generation, all the events that are *guaranteed* to precede the arrival of the Son of Man (including the desecration and destruction of the temple) will be fulfilled. If ordinary history should go on after that (and of this there is no guarantee), then at every minute we must reckon with the possible arrival of the Son of Man. He is *at the very gates* (v. 29).

After the temple falls, there may or may not be further sacrileges and another great tribulation; we cannot know. There may or may not be continued opportunity for mission; we cannot know. We are called to unwavering faithfulness *because* we cannot know (v. 33). For Mark, the End becomes imminent (in the sense described above; cf. v. 24) as soon as the Jerusalem temple is destroyed. That event, prophesies Jesus, will occur within a generation. In fact, it happened in A.D. 70, forty years after the prediction was made.

13:32 No One Knows About That Day

Those who include the Son of Man's return in the prediction of verse 30 often understand verse 32 to be a statement of only "limited ignorance." Jesus and Mark know (according to this view) in which generation the Son of Man will return; the only thing they do not know is the exact day and hour it will occur.

But this overlooks the fact that in verse 32 the two key terms *that Day* and *the Hour* (in Greek) are **names** for the End more than references to its exact timing. No one knows about "the Day of the Lord," and no one knows about "the Hour of fulfillment." We actually need verse 33 to help clarify *what* we do not know. We do not know *when* the End (= *that* Day, or *the Hour*) arrives. We do not know and we cannot know; even Jesus did not know (13:32).

For Mark, the final arrival of *that Day* is foreshadowed when the bridegroom is taken away (cf. 2:20, referring to *that day*). For Mark, the final arrival of *the Hour* is foreshadowed when Jesus is handed over (cf. 14:41, referring to *the Hour*). For those with eyes to see, the passion of Jesus is an act of salvation that makes possible the great and final salvation of God. It is Jesus entering into his glory (10:37-40), from which he will someday emerge in great power and glory (13:26).

13:33-37 Be Faithful *Because* You Do Not Know When

Jesus calls his disciples to be discerning and faithful right up to the End, but they are also called to start immediately. The first test of their faithfulness will come sooner than they think. Jesus now tells a parable about faithful discipleship throughout the entire waiting period, symbolically represented by the four watches of the Roman night: evening (6:00-9:00); midnight (9:00-midnight); cockcrow (midnight-3:00); dawn (3:00-6:00). In any one of these watches, the master might come back. He must not find the doorkeeper sleeping.

The parable of the doorkeeper is preceded and followed by clear statements about its intended meaning. Just before it is Mark's fourth and final use of *blepete* in this chapter (13:5, 9, 23, 33). Within the parable and following it are three occurrences of *grēgoreite* (or cognates; vv. 34-35, 37). Both words can be translated *Watch!* but their meaning is quite different. The first means *Be discerning/aware* (NRSV: *beware*); the second means *Be faithful* (NRSV: *keep awake*) and refers to faithful service during the master's absence. Together, they capture well the meaning of the following parable and this entire chapter (13:5, notes).

Neither of these watchwords is a call to try to figure out when the master will return. The first (*Be discerning!*) calls for discernment into the true meaning of the parable; the second (*Be faithful!*) challenges hearers/readers to respond faithfully to its teaching. Unless the servants are faithfully on duty during *every* moment of the master's absence, he may show up and catch them unprepared, not at their posts, not being faithful servants. The call for alertness (v. 33) and faithfulness (v. 37) is not *in order to* discern the timing of the End, but precisely because we *cannot* know it.

The parable itself speaks of a man on a journey of unknown length. Before leaving, he hands out assignments to the servants, expecting to find them faithfully carrying out their duties when he returns. One assignment is highlighted and developed by referring to the four watches. That is the doorkeeper's task, to be faithfully at the post, awake, alert, guarding. *Watching* stands as a metaphor for uninterrupted faithful service. Enemies may want to make deals with the watcher, or the watcher may grow tired. Danger may arise and with it a temptation to flee or even to deny allegiance to the owner. In fact, all of these *do* happen in the four watches of the night, as Jesus is betrayed, arrested, and tried. In that night, Jesus models faithfulness; all those around him model unfaithfulness.

Mark structures his passion narrative around these four watches:

evening in the upper room, midnight in Gethsemane, cockcrow at the home of the high priest, and dawn at Pilate's courtroom. These are four situations in which those called to be faithful are found sleeping. Only Jesus is faithful as he continues his journey to the cross and models faithfulness in all the watches of the night. His followers must learn from him as they seek to be faithful throughout the time of waiting for the Son of Man to come back. At some unpredictable watch, the master will show up to check on the faithfulness of his servants (T. Geddert, 1987:6-7; TBC, below).

All this would have an enormous impact on a Christian community experiencing persecution, the likely situation of Mark's first readers (for an alternative view, see Juel, 1994:87-88, 146). In moments of crisis, some will be tempted to betray fellow Christians (as Judas did *in the evening,* 14:17-21). Some will be tempted to sleep instead of pray, strike out with sword, or run away in terror (as the disciples do *at midnight,* 14:37-50). Some will be tempted to deny their allegiance to Jesus (as Peter does *when the cock crows,* 14:66-72). Some will be tempted to side with the religious and civil establishment (as all but Jesus do *at dawn,* 15:1-15).

Mark 13 ends with a word that universalizes its call to discernment and faithfulness. Mark looks beyond his own first readers and in effect says, "That includes all of us and any and all who hear or read these words from now until the Son of Man comes again." Jesus says,

> What I say to you [Peter, James, John, and Andrew, v. 3], I say to everyone [including all who will hear the gospel through my followers]: "Watch!" (13:37, NIV)

Everyone in every generation is called to discernment and discipleship in every watch of the night. After all, no one knows which generation of believers will be the one called to be faithfully at their post at the precise moment when the master of the house returns.

THE TEXT IN BIBLICAL CONTEXT

The Prophetic Perspective

Mark 13 reads as a chapter in which both Jesus and Mark reserved judgment on precisely the main question scholars have ever since tried to force them to answer: Is the predicted destruction of the temple a final eschatological event or not?

The predicted temple destruction (and accompanying events) are portrayed in the same eschatological proportions as many OT references to great acts of disaster and/or salvation. Yet no claim is made that this next great act of God will lead directly to the final acts of judgment and salvation. Perhaps it will, or perhaps it will be yet another in a long series of events that keep on *pointing* to those final events.

"Prophetic perspective" is a helpful concept in studying prophetic literature (cf. N. T. Wright). Scholars apply the term to a phenomenon where two time frames are superimposed on each other. Those using the term, however, give it different definitions. For G. B. Caird, it means "prophetic clarity," as he explains:

> The prophets looked to the future with bifocal vision. With their near sight they foresaw imminent historical events which would be brought about by familiar human causes. . . . With their long sight they saw the Day of the Lord. (258)

It is not easy to separate between the long vision and the near vision. Amos links "that Day" (Amos 8:9) with the fall of Samaria. Isaiah links the coming of "Messiah" with the overthrow of Assyria (Isa. 7-11). Habakkuk links "the End" with the destruction of Babylon (Hab. 2:3). Jeremiah, Ezekiel, and Isaiah all link the establishment of God's reign with Israel's return from exile (Jer. 29-31; Ezek. 36; Isa. 49, 51). Haggai speaks of the Lord's house in his day as though it will become the final end-time temple (Hag. 2:6-9).

The historical situations to which each prophet referred have come and gone. Each event somehow pointed to or participated in the fulfillment of God's purposes, but none led to the final eschatological fulfillment the prophets anticipated. Is this prophetic error? Caird says no, since the prophets superimposed the two images *but never lost the ability to distinguish between them* (Caird: 258).

Others have disagreed, suggesting that the prophets were in fact mistaken, but that the prophetic word somehow still stands:

> The prophetic perspective must not be imagined to imply that the prophets were somehow aware that their words would be fulfilled only in the distant future. . . . Their words and predictions were preserved, cherished, and eventually reinterpreted despite their non-fulfillment. (Ambrozic: 220)

Would it not be better to take a middle position between "prophetic clarity" (Caird) and "prophetic error" (Ambrozic)? Why not simply call it "prophetic method"? Imminent historical events foreshadow final events that may or may not find their fulfillment in the immediate future. Statements of imminence should be understood as statements of certainty. If Israel's prophets could pick up and reinterpret previous prophetic words without considering them in error, why could they not intend their own words to be treated in the same way? The prophets had no difficulty renewing prophecies that had once been given and had seemed to go unfulfilled. Since they were convinced God would come in ultimate judgment and salvation, it did not matter that earlier prophets had been uncertain which historical developments would lead to the final judgment and salvation.

One could even view "prophetic perspective" as a literary device. The prophetic texts do not reveal an unintentional mixing of two perspectives, but rather a deliberate ambiguity about the time frames. Consider for example these words from the prophet Ezekiel:

> An end! The end has come upon the four corners of the land. Now the end is upon you, I will let loose my anger upon you. . . . Disaster after disaster! See, it comes. An end has come, the end has come. . . . Your doom has come to you. The time has come, the day is near. . . . Soon now I will pour out my wrath upon you. (7:2-8)

According to this text, is the End already here or only "about to come"? Is the disaster already falling or is it still only a threat? The text paradoxically affirms both the presence and the imminence of the judgment. The text goes on to describe impending disaster, which at almost every point parallels the disasters predicted for Judea in Mark 13, complete with references to those in the field, those in the city, people escaping to the mountains, and so on (Ezek. 7:15-16; cf. Mark 13:14-16).

The prophet Ezekiel seems to have composed a text that deliberately refuses to take a stand on whether the "End" is already present, or whether it is expected in the future. In just this way, Mark 13 predicts both the temple's destruction and the return of the Son of Man, but in such a way that we cannot know whether the two events are linked in time or not.

The Meaning of *the End*

Mark's description of *the End* (13:7, 13) in 13:24-27 is drawn from various OT texts (Isa. 13:10; 34:4; Ezek. 32:7; Joel 2:10). How much of this is intended to be taken literally (by Mark or by the OT authors) cannot be determined. Clearly much of it is hyperbolic poetic language. The reference is to some kind of significant transformation, since it ushers in the final *age to come* (10:30). The biblical writers were not necessarily thinking of a total breakup of the universe, and of the gathering of *the elect* (13:20) to some totally otherworldly nonmaterial "spiritual" heaven.

The gathering from all four directions (13:27b) reflects the Jewish hope that in the end, scattered Jews as well as all nations would come together in the Promised Land. In Mark's context, it suggests a gathering together into the fellowship of those who have followed Jesus. A gathering in the Promised Land (of Israel) is unlikely in Mark's context, since Jesus' followers have been counseled to flee from there, disassociating from those who cling to it (v. 14).

We wish we knew more about what *the coming of the Son of Man* means. It may well allude to both salvation and judgment, though salvation seems more in focus here (in contrast to 8:38 and 14:62). Is the Son of Man coming *into* or *from* the presence of God? In Daniel 7:13 (the text alluded to here), the Son of Man comes *into* the presence of God and there receives authority and a kingdom (Dan. 7:14). If it means the same here, then the elect are gathered so they can join the Son of Man as he comes into God's presence to inherit the now-fulfilled kingdom.

The difference between Mark 13 and Daniel 7 is that in Mark the elect *join* the Son of Man, whereas in Daniel they and their patron angel *are* "like a son of man," receiving "the kingship" (7:13, 27, RSV/NRSV). In Daniel, the title "son of man" may refer to the archangel Michael and to the elect under Michael's protection (12:1; Lederach: 162-8, 253-4). If the reference in Mark 13:26 is to the Son of Man coming to earth *from* God's presence, then the allusion is to the establishment of the final kingdom here on earth (cf. N. T. Wright).

The Four Watches of the Passion Night

The connection between the four watches of 13:35 and the four main events of the night before Jesus' death is signaled by a series of time references in the passion account. The text clearly alludes to three of the four watches: *evening* (13:35) // *in the evening* (14:17); *cockcrow* (13:35) // *the cock crowed* (14:72); *dawn* (13:35, *prōi*) // *morning* (15:1, *prōi*). Only *midnight* (13:35) is not named in the corresponding watch during the night before Jesus' death.

There are, however, converging lines of evidence that Mark regarded the Gethsemane event as the counterpart to *midnight* in the parable of 13:34-36:

1. The parallels between the Gethsemane event and this parable are remarkable. Both texts contain explicit references to "watching-coming-finding-sleeping" (Kelber, 1976:48-49).

2. If Jesus' supper with his disciples was *in the evening* (6:00-

9:00) and Peter's denials at *cockcrow* (12:00-3:00), the Gethsemane experience would be from 9:00 to midnight.

3. Jesus prays three times (14:35-41), each time (it seems) for one hour (v. 37). Then he ends the experience by announcing *the Hour has come* (v. 41).

4. Jews celebrating Passover would connect the arrival of "the hour" (14:41) with "the midnight hour" when God struck down Pharoah and delivered Israel (Exod. 11:29). Jesus is announcing God's new act of deliverance.

All this shows rather clearly that Mark correlates the time in Gethsemane with the second watch of the night.

In each of the watches sketched out in the passion night, there is an explicit contrast between faithfulness (the model of Jesus) and unfaithfulness (represented by those around him). Precisely to highlight that contrast, Mark has designed the correlation between the parable in 13:34-36 and the passion account. Numerous commentators have seen some reflection of the four watches in the passion account. However, there is much more significance to all this than simply an interesting correlation ("Preview" for 14:27—15:15). The passion defines for Mark the meaning of watching in Mark 13. Mark 13 defines for Mark the significance of the passion. For those with eyes to see, Jesus' passion is an eschatological event; it teaches disciples what it means to serve faithfully until the Son of Man returns.

THE TEXT IN THE LIFE OF THE CHURCH
Mark 13 and Popular Eschatology

Mark 13:20 refers to the shortening of the unprecedented tribulation for the sake of *the elect*. Who are *the elect*? One popular view is that these verses refer to a still-future tribulation that Christians will avoid because they will be "raptured." Jews, however (in this view), will suffer the tribulation along with unbelieving Gentiles. For the sake of the Jews (identified as "the elect"), the days of this future tribulation will be shortened. When the Son of Man arrives, these elect (the Jews) will be gathered (13:27) to be where Christian believers have presumably already been taken—according to this view.

People may fabricate such a scheme from other OT and NT texts (though I am skeptical of this cut-and-paste method), but there is nothing to support it in Mark 13. Mark's Christian readers (Jewish and Gentile) surely believe that Mark refers to them all as *the elect*. What has made them *the elect* is their allegiance to the Son of Man, not their ethnicity.

Mark 13 conveys a call to discernment and faithfulness on the part of believers right up to the End. There is no separation between believers and Jews; indeed, at the time of Jesus' prophecy, all believers are Jews. There is no indication that God will give unbelieving Jews extra opportunities to respond; instead, judgment will fall on them. Those who heed Jesus' warning will flee (13:14). There is no "rapture" that whisks away disciples so that they can avoid any of the difficulties predicted here. They will experience difficulties all along the way: wars and rumors of wars (vv. 7-8), persecution (vv. 9-13), and unprecedented tribulation (vv. 19-20). However, they are forewarned so that they can flee before God's judgment falls on those who wrongly believe in the inviolability of the temple and have made it a *den of robbers* (11:17; Jer. 7:11).

Mark 13 does not help Christians to construct an eschatological timetable. Its message is clear: "You cannot know when the End is coming; be ready at all times." Sadly, those who come to Mark 13 with a specific eschatological timetable in mind usually find a way to use the ambiguities of this chapter to make it support their preconceived views. As a result, the call to perpetual readiness and faithful witness is lost (cf. Klaassen, 1999).

After the Temple's Destruction: What Comes Next?

What message does Mark 13 have for modern people reading the text *after* the desolating sacrilege, the destruction of the temple, and the accompanying Roman-Jewish war (A.D. 66-70)? In particular, what eschatological timetable does it predict for *our* future?

If the interpretation in this commentary is correct, then Mark has contemplated three possible scenarios:

1. The events associated with the desolating sacrilege will lead directly to the End.

2. Or, these events will adequately fulfill all prophecies that *have to* precede the End, so that the End can come at any future date.

3. Or, these events will serve as prototypes for future final eschatological events that will lead directly to the End.

Looking back, we know that the return of the Son of Man did not occur during the events surrounding the war between the Jews and Rome, nor in connection with the temple's destruction in A.D. 70. The first scenario Mark considers possible has therefore been eliminated by the passing of time. The other two possibilities remain open.

Option 2 views the events surrounding the temple's destruction (the sacrilege, the tribulation) as the final events that *needed* to happen before the Son of Man's return could be considered truly imminent. Ever since A.D. 70, faithful disciples have been waiting for the one great event that must still happen, the return of the Son of Man. No signs will help predict when that will be.

Option 3 considers the possibility that yet another sacrilege (a final antichrist?) and an unprecedented tribulation (the "great tribulation" of Rev. 7:14?) will occur before the Son of Man's final return.

Mark's text does not permit us to be sure which of these two scenarios will occur. We must reckon with both possibilities. Thus, for all we know, the Son of Man *could* return at any moment, and all the prophecies of Mark 13 will have been completely fulfilled. Or else they will be fulfilled another way: a future antichrist-type figure will appear "where he does not belong" (13:14, NIV, n.) and usher in a great tribulation that leads to the Son of Man's return. For that possibility, we must *be alert* and keep our eyes open (13:5, 9, 23, 33, 35, 37). If that is how Mark 13 will be fulfilled, then when he/it appears, we must be ready to *flee* (= disassociate completely).

Our main preoccupation must continue to be what it has always been, staying faithfully at our posts, and carrying on with the mission to the world in the context of persecution. We seek to be faithful at every moment, *because* we do not know when the End will come [Eschatological Time Frames in Mark 13].

The Value of Eschatological/Apocalyptic Texts

Mark 13:32 refers to the unknown time of the Son of Man's return. It states that no one knows *that Day or the Hour* (TJG). Interpreters often imagine this to be a simple claim that we cannot know on which day of the week or at which hour of the day the Son of Man will return. But 13:32 is much more profound than that. It does declare that we do not know exactly *when,* but it gives much more than a statement about its timing. It also claims, "*That Day* [or the Hour] is of such mystery that we are not able to grasp its character."

Both terms, *that Day* (ekeinē hē hēmera) and *the Hour* (hē hōra), are used technically in Scripture to refer to the same final moment of history, "*the Day* of the Lord" (2 Pet. 3:10), *the Hour* of final fulfillment (e.g., 2 Tim. 1:12; John 5:28-29). In Mark (just as in John), both expressions are *also* used to refer to *that Day* and *the Hour* when Jesus is taken away to be crucified (2:20, 14:41). In effect, Mark is saying, "In the passion of Jesus, we already catch a glimpse of the great and final event that will bring all of history to its God-ordained conclusion."

Profound insight led the church theologian Augustine (of Hippo) to encourage each believer, when contemplating Mark 13:32, to reflect *also* on their own personal end. An inevitable moment, of unknown timing and character, will usher each person into their final destiny with God (Kermode: 127; T. Geddert, 1989:107).

We take apocalyptic texts like Mark 13 with greatest seriousness, not when we turn them into devices for calculating esoteric calendars, but when we let them cause us to reflect on the mysteries of life and death. Then we can invest ourselves in this life according to the values of God's kingdom, and we can live and die in the hope of eternity.

Some Christians have misunderstood and misused these apocalpytic texts. As a result, they see only evil in this world and wait desperately for some miraculous divine intervention to rescue them from it. These texts are functioning as intended when they lead believers to trust God's sovereign care in ambiguous times. Then they can hope for God's future so passionately that necessary sacrifices in this life are readily embraced for Christ's sake.

Jesus called his followers to *watch* (13:34) while waiting for God's final consummation. Watching, however, does not mean calculating timetables and matching newspaper events with the symbols of biblical apocalyptic. Jesus' followers should not claim to know more about the timing of *that Day* than Jesus himself did (13:32). Watching means being on guard against deception, and being faithful in times of testing. The primary purpose of futuristic prophecy is to build hope, to motivate proclamation and service, and to promote faithful discipleship (T. Geddert, 1992:26).

Mark 14:1-26

Preparations for the Passion

PREVIEW

Mark's Gospel has been moving inexorably toward the suffering and death Jesus has predicted for himself, "the passion," as it is called in theological writing. From the very beginning, subtle allusions (e.g., 1:11; 2:20) and narrative comments (e.g., 3:6, 19) have informed readers that there is a plot to do away with Jesus. At the beginning of the discipleship journey (8:31), readers learn along with the disciples that Jesus himself expects to die and rise again. Jesus moves on toward Jerusalem, knowing (and informing his disciples) what will take place there: his death, and beyond it, his resurrection (10:32-34).

Since Jesus' arrival in Jerusalem, the conflict between him and those who reject him has escalated. He condemns them for abusing the temple (11:15-17), rejecting his authority (11:27-33), robbing God (12:1-9), and having wrong priorities (12:33). They seek opportunities to do away with Jesus (11:18; 12:12). Jesus' popularity with the crowd, however, has thus far prevented Jesus' enemies from taking him.

The conflict between Jesus and the religious rulers was held in suspension while Jesus taught his disciples about God's impending judgment on Israel's leaders and their temple. He also foretold crises and opportunities awaiting the disciples, and explained their need for discernment and faithfulness as they evangelize the nations and await the Son of Man's return (13:1-37).

The plot against Jesus now resumes. The religious leaders want to avoid taking Jesus during the coming festival. When the traitor, Judas, makes a deal with them, they throw caution to the wind and arrest Jesus without waiting for the feast days to end. The climactic event begins to unfold. Jesus is arrested, tried, mocked, tortured, and killed. After these are narrated, a brief provocative resurrection account brings Mark's discourse (but not his story) to a close.

The next section, here entitled, "Preparations for the Passion," consists of two subsections, each with three parts. The first subsection I have entitled "Sacrificing Jesus; Sacrificing for Jesus." It features the religious leaders (along with Judas) preparing to engineer the passion, and an unnamed woman identifying with Jesus in his passion. Mark weaves these two events together with his oft-used "intercalation technique" *[Chiasm and Intercalation]*.

A • The Plot to Kill Jesus (14:1-2)
 B • Jesus Is Anointed at Bethany (14:3-9)
A' • Judas Offers to Betray Jesus (14:10-11)

The woman sacrifices greatly to anoint and honor Jesus; Judas sacrifices Jesus in exchange for money.

The second subsection narrates the last meal Jesus eats with his disciples. It is a Passover meal, but it gains new significance as Jesus gives up *himself* as a new means of redemption. Mark has structured his narrative to include preparations for the meal, a dialogue about who will betray Jesus, and Jesus' words of self-sacrifice. The meal happens *in the evening* (14:17), in the first of the four night watches that help define what it means to *watch* faithfully (cf. 13:34-35).

OUTLINE
The Plot to Kill Jesus, 14:1-2

Jesus Is Anointed at Bethany, 14:3-9

Two Women Who Gave, 14:3-9 and 12:41-44

Judas Offers to Betray Jesus, 14:10-11

Preparations for the Passover, 14:12-16

Who Is the Betrayer? 14:17-21

This Is My Body and Blood, 14:22-26

EXPLANATORY NOTES

The story of the anointing woman is flanked by two short episodes related to the plot against Jesus. Her action is thus brought into connection with the passion. Jesus clarifies that connection in his interpretation of what she does for him.

The Plot to Kill Jesus 14:1-2

In two days (the expression also means "the next day") the feast days would begin. Passover was the greatest of all Jewish festivals. Connected to it was the Festival of Unleavened Bread, extending the festival an additional seven days. During Passover, Jerusalem would burst at the seams, swelling to perhaps five times its usual population.

Jesus' enemies want to do away with him as soon as possible, yet they fear repercussions from removing him in the presence of the festival crowds. Their concern is not to preserve the sanctity of the feast, but to prevent rioting by Jesus' many supporters (or enthusiastic fans).

Jesus Is Anointed at Bethany 14:3-9

Meanwhile, Jesus is dining in Bethany, just east of Jerusalem. It is a special meal, as shown by the reference to *reclining* (not *sitting,* as in NRSV). The host is a (former?) leper named Simon. Perhaps Jesus has healed him earlier.

A woman boldly enters the dining room, where presumably only men are dining. To everyone's astonishment, she breaks open a jar of extremely expensive perfumed oil and pours the entire contents of it over Jesus' head. She could have broken the seal and used only a little of the *ointment.* But she lavishes all on Jesus. The costly sacrifice evokes negative responses from some of the guests and positive ones from Jesus.

The objectors express their anger (14:4a) by scolding the woman (v. 5b). Mark does not suggest that the objectors are Jesus' disciples, though some manuscript variants make that claim. The ointment is worth more than what a day laborer could earn in a year. If she had donated it, the woman's critics claim, the proceeds could have been given to the poor. They imply that something *useful* could have been done with that small fortune. Whether they care about the poor is not clarified. It certainly does not honor Jesus to object to the woman's gift in his presence.

Jesus defends the woman, first by silencing the critics (v. 6a), then by interpreting the woman's actions (vv. 6b-9). The woman will be immortalized (v. 9) for a variety of reasons:

1. *She has worked a good/beautiful work* (v. 6b, lit., TJG). Two different words for "good" are at Mark's disposal. One focuses on the rightness of the action, the other on its beauty. The second is used here: the woman did not pause to seek moral justification for her action; she simply expressed her devotion to Jesus. Jesus says it was a beautiful thing. But Jesus says more. He adds interpretations to her actions that the woman may not have considered.

2. *Her timing is right.* The opportunity to minister to Jesus will not last long; this woman has picked the right time to do so. Jesus is not saying, "Forget the poor; they can wait!" Obviously, Jesus cares for the poor (10:21); indeed, every day is the right time to care for them (14:7). Today this woman has given to Jesus, the poorest of the poor. After his passion, she and those like her can give to all the other poor (Pesch, 1977:333). Almsgiving must be more than an occasional religious ritual. Giving to the poor was an expectation during Passover season (cf. John 13:29), and Jesus wants to clarify that a *beautiful work* (*kalon ergon*) must spring from the heart (cf. 7:15).

3. *She has identified with Jesus' death.* Though she may not have intended it that way, Jesus interprets her anointing as *for [his] burial* (14:9). Unlike the twelve disciples, this woman acts in a way that is consistent with Jesus' prediction that he will suffer and die.

4. *She has anticipated the resurrection.* Again, this is not her intention. But Jesus clarifies that she has anointed him *beforehand* (v. 8). It will turn out that this is the only kind of anointing possible. Three other devoted women will attempt to anoint Jesus' body (16:1) afterward, but they arrive too late (16:6). In their planning, they did not anticipate a resurrection.

5. *She has anointed a king.* Mark's readers cannot help but see yet another significance to her action. Jesus has entered Jerusalem as a king (11:9-10). He will be crucified as a king (15:12, 26, 32). Uncomprehending crowds and rejecting opponents alike "proclaim" Jesus as the King, the Messiah, the Anointed One. This woman is the only person in Mark who anoints Jesus!

Mark's reader has known from the start that Jesus is God's anointed one. Now the reader observes the act of anointing. An unnamed woman anoints the Messiah. He is now ready for the passion, where his kingdom will be established. Wherever this gospel is preached, wherever Jesus is called the Christ, this woman's deed, too, is being proclaimed. "By the providence of God, she was the chosen instrument for the ritual from which the Messiah receives his name" (Piper: 177).

Hooker aptly summarizes the message of this text:

> For those who know the end of the story, then, the woman's action epit-
> omizes Jesus' death and resurrection, proclaims his status as king, and
> challenges others to share her devotion to him. (1991:328)

That is the message going forth *wherever the good news is proclaimed in the whole world* (v. 9). The Scriptures give this woman
no name; but by anointing Jesus, she has acted consistent with the
Messiah's name. Because Mark has preserved this story, this
woman's *beautiful deed* has indeed not been forgotten. Her action
was not designed to draw attention to herself, but to her Lord. What
a model she is for those who carry out the worldwide proclamation of
the gospel, as noted in this text!

Mark 13 is preceded by a vignette about a woman who sacrificed
greatly to contribute to the Jerusalem temple (12:41-44). It is followed by this touching account of another woman who brought her
sacrifice to the new temple *not made with hands* (14:58).

Two Women Who Gave 14:3-9 and 12:41-44

The *content* of 14:3-9 is rich with meaning (above). The *context* in
which it is placed adds additional meaning. As indicated above, the
anointing narrative is flanked by two texts dealing with the plot
against Jesus (14:1-2, 10-11; "Preview," above). That structure firm-
ly links this woman's act to Jesus' passion. But Mark has also created a structure linking this woman's act to Mark 13.

Mark 13 is *preceded* by an account of a poor woman who gives
her all in an act of tremendous sacrifice (12:41-44), sadly wasted on
a temple that is promptly declared doomed (13:2). Mark 13 is *followed* by this account of another woman who sacrifices greatly to
honor Jesus, whose impending doom has also been predicted (14:8).

The comparisons and contrasts between these matching events are
striking. The issue of wealth and poverty is clearly addressed in both
texts. Both stories of women who sacrificially give are linked to stories
of men who deceive for selfish gain (cf. 12:38-40; 14:10-11). Both
times the gift could be considered a waste. Yet Jesus and the religious
officials have precisely opposing views on which one really was wasted. Jesus knows that the poor woman's gift, though given to an
impressive and seemingly permanent temple, is in fact wasted on a
structure that is doomed. The "temple" on which the second woman
lavishes her gift may seem far less impressive (or permanent), but it is
destined to survive. Nothing is wasted when invested in this temple!

The widow is a symbol for the self-sacrificing Jesus who also gives *his whole life* (cf. 10:45; 12:44). So is the other woman who pours out all she has (cf. 14:3, 24). Tragically, however, the first woman also symbolizes the doomed temple. The religious leaders have robbed her of her house (12:40); God will now take away theirs (13:2). "How lonely sits the city! . . . How like a widow she has become!" (Lam. 1:1). The second woman, by contrast, symbolizes the temple that God will raise up. Her act of self-sacrifice, like Jesus' own, will be proclaimed throughout the whole world.

Mark has presented the two stories of "Women Who Gave" as a matching pair, forming bookends around Mark 13. Thus we have additional confirmation that Mark 13 is not about the interpretation of signs and the construction of an end-time calendar ("Preview" for 13:1-37). Mark 13 is about God's judgment falling on unfaithful religious leaders and about God raising up Jesus and his followers to be the nucleus of the renewed people of God. It is about identification with Jesus in self-sacrificing discipleship. It is about the proclamation of the gospel in all the world.

Judas Offers to Betray Jesus 14:10-11

Mark does not tell us that Judas' betrayal was motivated by what happened that day in Simon's house. The structural connection, however, hints that his own greed for money has played into his decision to turn traitor. Beyond that, we do not know what has motivated him. The text does not suggest that, by escalating the plot against Jesus, he is trying to provoke him into setting up his kingdom (as some commentators have suggested). Mark's text does not encourage us to give Judas this benefit of the doubt.

The anointing woman has sacrificed a great deal for Jesus. By contrast, Judas is prepared to accept money to turn Jesus over to the chief priests. Thousands of Jews have been buying sacrificial lambs in the days preceding the Passover; now the religious leaders offer to buy one! Thousands of Jews have been handing over their lambs to the priests who would slaughter them; now Judas agrees to hand over Jesus to those who will put him to death.

Preparations for the Passover 14:12-16

The next five verses concern preparations for Jesus' Last Supper with his disciples. According to Mark, this last meal is a bridge event. On one end of the bridge, we see the Jewish Passover. This was an annual reminder and symbolic reenactment of the deliverance of Israel from Egypt, complete with elaborate rituals and careful explanations concerning the meaning of it all. On the other end of the bridge, we see the Christian communion (Lord's Supper, eucharist). The church eats bread and drinks wine in remembrance of Jesus' death, celebrating the covenant created through it.

Both Passover and the Christian communion also have a forward-looking focus. Passover anticipates the great final salvation God will bring in the end time (which Jesus will now claim to fulfill; cf. 14:41, notes). Christian communion anticipates a still future "messianic banquet" (marriage supper of the Lamb, Rev. 19:7), when God's kingdom is fully established in the new heaven and new earth.

Mark's record of Jesus' Last Supper with his disciples contains some features of the Jewish Passover meal and some elements of the Christian communion celebration. Interpreters still wonder,

• What are the original *historical* connections between Jesus' last meal and both of these events (Passover and communion)?

• Did the meal reported here precede the Passover, so that Jesus' death coincides with the slaughtering of the Passover lambs, as in John's Gospel? Or did the meal coincide with the Passover meal, putting Jesus' death a day later, as in Mark's Gospel?

• What are the original "words of institution"? Do they highlight fellowship? celebration of a covenant? forgiveness of sin? substitutionary atonement?

• Did Jesus instruct his followers to reenact this meal, even though Mark does not say so?

Historical critics have not reached consensus on these questions. They have also challenged Mark's statement concerning the timing of Passover in relation to the Feast of Unleavened Bread (14:12). Though I provide a brief synopsis of the debate in TBC below, our understanding of Mark's message does not depend on solving these problems. The comments to follow will focus on the meaning of these events *as narrated by Mark*.

Mark 14:12-16 indicates that the meal Jesus is about to share with his disciples is a Passover meal. Mark's record of the meal itself (14:17-26) highlights only a few of the traditional features of a Jewish Passover meal.

Passover is supposed to be celebrated only within Jerusalem (Deut. 16:5-6). Since Jesus and his disciples have been staying in Bethany, they need to find a place in the city for observing Passover. Participants have to stay in the city till the next morning; the Mount of Olives is defined as within the ritual boundaries of the city (cf.

14:26). Jesus plays the role of head of the household, the one responsible for leading the Passover celebration. His disciples offer to help (v. 12) only to discover that much has already been arranged.

The first part of 14:13 reads almost exactly like 11:1b-2a, where Jesus also sends two disciples to make arrangements. In 11:2-7 they get a colt for Jesus' ride into Jerusalem; in 14:13-16 they find a furnished room suitable for the Passover meal. In both texts, Jesus' authority is highlighted: in 11:3 Jesus calls himself *Lord* (notes), and in 14:14 he refers to *my guest room* (14:14). Jesus lays claim to a room in which momentous events are about to take place.

We are left uncertain here (as in 11:1-6) whether Mark is highlighting Jesus' foreknowledge or suggesting that signals have previously been arranged. Nor can we tell in this case whether Jesus wants the arrangements kept secret, using the secret signal of the *man* carrying the *jar of water* (like a woman; men usually carried water bags), leading to silent following rather than open negotiations. Jesus may have wanted to delay his imminent arrest until after this last meal with his disciples.

What is clear is that Jesus has everything under control. He will go to his death, not because something has gone wrong but because he obediently walks along the road God mapped out for him. There is an interesting (but unprovable) theory that the upper room is in the home of John Mark (the author of this text), and that John Mark may even be the man carrying the water jar (see 14:51-52, notes).

The disciples follow Jesus' instructions and find the *upstairs* room, *furnished* with a low table and cushions for reclining. There they prepare for the evening meal.

Who Is the Betrayer? 14:17-21

Mark does not dwell on the details of the Passover meal, but rather highlights the betrayal of Jesus *by* a disciple (vv. 17-21) and the contrasting self-giving of Jesus *for* his disciples (vv. 22-26).

All this takes place in the *evening* (opsia, v. 17; cf. 13:35, opse). Mark alludes to the time period from 6:00-9:00 p.m., the first of four night watches. In the parable at the end of Mark 13, the *master of the house* calls *his servants* to faithful discipleship in each of the night watches (13:34-36, RSV). The betrayer's treachery will be one way disciples can be unfaithful. Jesus' self-giving represents the appropriate alternative. The three night watches still to come will reveal other aspects of faithfulness and unfaithfulness (cf. 13:33-37, notes; TBC after 13:37).

Jesus arrives with his disciples. They take their *reclining* positions (obscured by NRSV). Reclining at table is part of the Passover reenactment, for the meal celebrates Israel's freedom, and only free people have the luxury of reclining at table (cf. Exod. 12:11, still in slavery). Other features of the meal receive scant or no mention. Bitter herbs, sauces, unleavened bread, four cups of wine, and the Passover lamb—all symbolize important features of Israel's experience in Egypt and God's great act of deliverance. Mark's concern is to highlight the treachery of the betrayer. By doing so in the context of a covenant meal, he pictures the deed in all its stark horror.

John's Gospel quotes the psalmist, "The one who ate my bread has lifted his heel against me" (John 13:18), referring to the one who is "my bosom friend in whom I trusted" (cf. Ps. 41:9). Though Mark does not include this quotation, he implies its content when Jesus says that the betrayer *is eating with me* (14:18). The betrayer is breaking a bond of fidelity, celebrated in a communal meal.

The distress of the disciples reflects their horror that any one of them could betray Jesus. Each in turn asks, *Surely, not I?* The form of the question shows that they expect a negative response from Jesus. Does it reflect (unwarranted) self-confidence that they cannot possibly be intended? Or does it reflect insecurity, and thus a request for Jesus to assure them that he is not referring to them? Either way, Mark wants each of his readers to reflect on their own loyalty to Jesus.

According to Mark's text, Jesus neither assures them of their loyalty nor explicitly identifies the traitor. Instead, the traitor is again referred to as *one of the Twelve, one who is dipping [bread] into the bowl with me* (v. 20). The word *bread* is added by the NRSV. Actually, they are likely dipping vegetables into the bitter herbs as part of the Passover celebration. Thus the bitterness of Israel's experience in Egypt among abusive strangers is connected with the bitterness of being betrayed by a beloved friend.

Who then is the betrayer? The reader has known since 3:19 that it will be Judas. Mark's text, however, implies that each of the Twelve is left wondering *[Questioning Jesus].* According to Hamerton-Kelly,

> Judas is not marked as the scapegoat by Jesus, and the traitor is not expelled. Each disciple indicates by his questioning that he is not sure of his own loyalty. Thus Mark indicates that none of us can escape responsibility for the death of Jesus by scapegoating Judas. (45)

Only one disciple will hand Jesus over to the enemies, but all of them will become disloyal. Each one contradicts Jesus' own prediction and fiercely pledges allegiance to Jesus, even if it costs them their lives (14:27-31). However, before the night is over, they will turn their backs on Jesus (14:50).

The first major episode of this Passover meal ends with a paradoxical statement by Jesus. The Son of Man's betrayal is twofold:

1. It is the destiny mapped out for him in the plan of God, as evidenced by his own foreknowledge of the betrayal and the testimony of Scripture to its inevitability.

2. It is also an act of human treachery that brings down God's hand of judgment on the betrayer.

The contrast between the divine and the human causation of Jesus' betrayal is highlighted by a pun in the Greek (not preserved in the NRSV). Twice in verse 21 *Son of Man* (God's agent to fulfill God's purposes) is set in direct contrast to *that man* (the human agent who precipitates the passion).

> The implicit contrast is between Jesus, who fulfills Scripture by willing obedience to God's will, and Judas, who fulfills Scripture by willful disobedience. It is a necessary characteristic of divine providence that God can turn evil into good. (Hare: 186-7)

This Is My Body and Blood 14:22-26

Nothing is said in the following verses about the institution of a special meal to be reenacted in the Christian community. It is certain that Mark knows of Christian communion celebrations and likely that his own experiences have influenced his narrative of Jesus' meal with his disciples (TBC, below).

At Passover, household heads explain to their families the meaning of the bitter herbs and sauces, the reason the bread is unleavened, the significance of the lamb, and so on. Jesus, by contrast, does not highlight the *unusual* features of the Passover meal. He lifts out those two elements that are *common* to other celebrative meals, the bread and the wine, and links them to his own coming death. (As Mark's community and later believers reenact this meal, they identify again with all that Jesus' passion means and accomplishes.)

During the meal, Jesus takes bread, says a blessing, and shares the bread with his disciples. NRSV says Jesus blesses *the bread*, but this is not in the text. Jews explicitly blessed *God* for the food, rather than blessing the *food*. The disciples would have expected Jesus to explain the reason why the bread was unleavened (because the Israelites left Egypt in haste). Instead, he identifies the bread with himself (*my body; sōma* can refer to the self, the body, or the flesh). The emphasis seems to be on the breaking and the sharing of the bread. Thus the "breaking" of Jesus (his death) results in benefits that are shared within the disciple community.

Similarly, the cup is shared. Two words are spoken over the cup. The first word is an explanation of its significance: *This is my blood of the covenant, which is poured out for many.* Red wine can easily be taken as a symbol for blood, but what is symbolized by the blood?

Mark seems to be highlighting the celebration of covenant (14:24). For Jews, animal sacrifices (shedding blood) are part of covenant-making; eating together is part of covenant-keeping. In the sharing of the cup (blood), Jesus is here renewing covenant; indeed, he is establishing a *new covenant,* as predicted by Jeremiah (cf. Jer. 31:31-34; 1 Cor. 11:25). Some Christian scribes added the word *new* to the text to make explicit this connection (Mark 14:24, NRSV note). Jesus' death (his shed blood) seals that new covenant. By their identification with that death, the disciples can celebrate that new covenant in their common meals.

Another blessing that derives from Jesus' passion is forgiveness for sin. Though this is less explicitly stated here (cf. Matt. 26:28), the whole fabric of Mark's narrative highlights the fact that Jesus' faithfulness becomes the means of forgiveness and renewal for his unfaithful disciples (TBC, below).

Jesus speaks a second word over the cup: *I will never again drink of the fruit of the vine until that day when I drink it new in the kingdom of God* (14:25). This vow of abstinence does not mean Jesus is not present with the community that celebrates the Lord's Supper. Indeed, for Mark the inauguration of God's kingdom is not delayed until some distant future event. Before the next 24 hours have passed, Jesus will be crowned king. His crown will be of thorns, and his throne will be a cross. But through his death, his kingdom will be established. In one sense, this was Jesus' last meal with his disciples; in another sense, it was the first of many they would celebrate, not only in his name, but in his presence.

Jesus and his disciples leave the upstairs room after singing a final Passover hymn. In keeping with regulations for the Passover, they remain within the ritual boundaries of Jerusalem until morning. They spend the *midnight* watch (9:00-12:00) in a garden on the Mount of Olives, rather than returning to Bethany for the night (13:35; 14:26).

The upper-room watch *in the evening* (cf. 13:35) has featured a stark contrast between the self-giving Jesus and the unscrupulous traitor. One is willing to pour out his whole life for the benefit of others. The other is willing to sell his master for money. Covenant fellowship is broken by the betrayal. It is reestablished through self-giving sacrifice.

The Markan community will face similar choices: pay with your life, or turn others in and go free (perhaps even make some money on the side). The persecuted Christian is to follow the example of Jesus, not the example of Judas. Jesus himself has said,

> Those who want to save their life will lose it,
> and those who lose their life for my sake,
> and for the sake of the Gospel will save it.
> For what will it profit them to gain the whole world
> and forfeit their life? (8:35-36)

If one of the ways of being unfaithful is illustrated *in the evening,* so also is one of the building blocks of discipleship renewal. When Jesus sacrifices himself, his life is *poured out for many.* They will fail, but he will be faithful, and his faithfulness will make it possible for them to be renewed.

THE TEXT IN BIBLICAL CONTEXT
Passover and Lord's Supper

The OT Passover celebration was designed to provide annual opportunities for Israel to reexperience (not just recall) the miracle of deliverance from slavery in Egypt. The sacrificed lamb was understood to be a real substitute for the oldest son, who would otherwise be slain along with the Egyptians' firstborn.

As Jesus transformed Passover into the Christian communion, he (God's firstborn) takes the place of the Passover lamb. He substitutes for the lamb; but more important, he substitutes for humans who are (like Israel's firstborn) destined to death. Jesus becomes the great and final sacrifice that accomplishes deliverance from all bondage to sin and its consequences.

What is the relationship between Jesus' last Passover celebration with his disciples and the Lord's Supper celebrated in the Christian church? Clearly, Mark understands Jesus' last meal with his disciples before his death as the first Lord's Supper (communion, eucharist).

The church had been reenacting this meal for 30-40 years before Mark wrote his Gospel. Their celebrations no doubt influenced the way the traditions were handed down and finally recorded. It is no longer possible to know exactly which words of institution the historical Jesus used. There are differences between the various accounts of the Last Supper in the Gospels and in 1 Corinthians. Scholars are generally of the opinion that Mark's version is as close to the original as we can get, on the basis of available evidence (Jeremias, 1990).

Another uncertainty relates to the timing of Jesus' meal in relation to the Passover celebrations going on in Jerusalem. We are certain that Jesus' passion occurred around Passover time. However, according to John, Jesus is on the cross *at the same time* the Passover lambs are being slaughtered in the temple. That is an important part of how Jesus' death is interpreted in John. According to the Synoptic writers, Jesus eats a Passover meal with his disciples, implying that his death takes place the day *after* the lambs are slaughtered. Scholars are divided on whether John's chronology or the Synoptic writers' chronology, or both, are historically accurate.

Many have claimed that John's Gospel (supposedly the more "theological" Gospel) has deviated from historical accuracy for theological reasons. Now that scholars recognize how theological the Synoptic Gospels are, many have reached the opposite conclusion. The difference between John's account and the Synoptic accounts may arise because of two different calendars in use.

The NT makes two different (but related) theological connections between Jesus' passion and the Passover Feast:

1. Jesus' death is redemptive. It corresponds to the slaughtering of the lambs at Passover.

2. Jesus' last meal (leading to the remembrance meal of the church) is a covenant meal, similar to the Jewish Passover meal.

Both of these features can be highlighted by correlating the timing of one of the sets of corresponding events: Jesus' death and the slaughtering of the lambs (John's Gospel), or Jesus' meal and the eating of the Passover (the Synoptics). The evangelists were more concerned with the *meaning* of Jesus' passion than with an accurate report of its timing. That should also be our greater concern. For a clear summary of the historical debates and some comparisons between Mark's account and those of the other evangelists and Paul, see M. Hooker's work (1991:31-43).

We can interpret Mark's Gospel without settling the historical questions; according to Mark, Jesus' last meal with his disciples is a Passover meal (14:12, 16). That Jesus dies *as* the Passover lamb is correspondingly less emphasized. We need to look to other Markan texts to determine whether Mark teaches that Jesus' death is a substitutionary sacrifice (notes on 10:45; 15:15; next TBC section).

Historical critics struggle also with Mark's statement that the Passover lambs are slaughtered on the first day of the Feast of Unleavened Bread (14:12). Passover lambs are regularly sacrificed on the day *before* the Feast of Unleavened Bread begins. One can perhaps take Mark's statement as evidence that Passover lambs are indeed slaughtered on two different days. Or Mark may be combining two ways of referring to "days." Jews normally marked days from sundown to sundown. Gentiles normally marked them from the time of rising until the time of retiring. A combination of these methods is possible if Mark preserves Jewish reckoning for the correct timing of the feasts, yet speaks colloquially for a Gentile audience.

Passover lambs are slaughtered before sundown. The Feast of Unleavened Bread technically begins on that same day (as Gentiles reckon it), but after the sun has set. Again, the meaning of Mark's texts is not affected by the difficulties in understanding his reference to the timing of the Jewish feasts.

One additional feature of the Passover celebration requires comment. Jesus symbolizes his blood with red wine, then passes it around for all to drink. The idea of "drinking blood" seems unpleasant to us; it would have horrified first-century Jews. Consumption of blood in any form was strictly forbidden, since blood represents the life and belongs to God. The symbolic drinking of blood makes Jesus' claim even more profound. He is sharing his very life, a life totally belonging to God, with his own disciples. The horror of "drinking blood" is partially softened by the fact that wine symbolically substitutes for it. But some horror should remain in the symbolic act, for the horror of Jesus' death can never be fully erased. Those who identify with it, identify both with its horror and with its victory.

Jesus' Substitutionary Death

What are the blessings and what constitutes the victory of Jesus' death? Some of these were discussed in the notes on Mark 14:22-26 (above). While other NT authors highlight Jesus' death as a substitutionary sacrifice more explicitly than Mark (cf. 1 Cor. 5:7; 15:3; 2 Cor. 5:21; Heb. 9:11-14), this theme is not absent from Mark (cf. notes on 10:45; 15:12-15). The wine is drunk, but Jesus' blood is *poured out* (14:24). "Pouring out" is an allusion to sacrificial animals and the sacred pouring of their blood onto the altar; thus the animal's life becomes a substitute for the human's.

How many lambs have been slaughtered that very day (in Mark, just before Jesus' Last Supper) as symbolic substitutes for the "first-

born" thus "passed over" (Exod. 12:12-13)? Next year it will be done
all over again (for a positive portrayal of this important event to
Jewish faith, see Fredricksen: 42-50). Jesus, God's beloved Son (cf.
Mark 1:11), pours out his lifeblood "once for all" (Rom. 6:10), and it
is sufficient *for many* (Mark 14:24; as in 10:45, Rom. 5:15, and
other texts, for *many* really means "the many" or "all").

Jesus' death is thus defined as both redemptive (liberating) and
substitutionary (Jesus obtains redemption for us; we do not do it for
ourselves). Jesus does not save himself; that is why he can save others (Mark 15:31) and why he himself is ultimately saved (cf. 8:35).
The Christian community thus celebrates the new life that Jesus'
death and resurrection make possible. It does not focus on endlessly
repeated ceremonies; it focuses on loving relationships instead of
burnt offerings and sacrifices (12:33). It celebrates a "new covenant"
in Christ's blood (Jer. 31:31-33; Luke 22:20; 1 Cor. 11:25; Heb.
9:15). In the imagery of the seer, Christ's robe is "dipped" in the
same blood in which our robes are washed white (Rev. 19:13; 7:14;
"Jesus and His Sacrificial Death," TLC for Mark 15:16-47).

THE TEXT IN THE LIFE OF THE CHURCH
Lord's Supper, Sacrifice, and the Presence of Christ

Throughout history, the church has struggled to understand just how
the communion elements relate to the sacrifice of Jesus. Theological
literature on the Lord's Supper often seems intent on analyzing to
death the mystery of our participation with Christ and each other,
which we celebrate in communion. Scholars try to split fine hairs in
defining what really happens at communion. All this sometimes
serves to block anything meaningful from happening, especially when
churches divide over precisely that one celebration designed to show
our unity with each other in Christ and our common participation in
his self-sacrifice on our behalf.

Some traditions view the communion celebration as a renewed
sacrificing of Jesus and real participation in the self-sacrificing Jesus
(though not as a repetition of his once-for-all atoning sacrifice at
Calvary). This emphasis is usually accompanied by a concern for a
priesthood authorized to lead sacramentally in the sacrifice of Jesus
and mediate the participation of communicants in it. This view, usually associated with the Catholic church, is not limited to this tradition.

Luther, at least in his earlier writings, was reacting to the Catholic
view. He deemphasized the sacrificial aspect of the Lord's Supper,
maintaining that Jesus' sacrifice is not being renewed, and communi-

cants are not performing a "complementary sacrifice" to appropriate Christ's sacrifice. Furthermore, no human can usurp Christ's priesthood by offering Christ on behalf of others, nor should the taking of communion be viewed as somehow meritorious on the part of the participant.

Though Luther retained the Catholic idea of Christ's real presence in the eucharist (even in the elements), he denied that the elements were transformed into Christ's actual blood and body (transubstantiation). He also criticized the Catholic church for denying the reality of God's grace and the sufficiency of Christ's sacrifice as an atonement for sin. Luther later reintroduced some sacrifice language into his understanding of communion but insisted that "we do not offer Christ as a sacrifice; . . . we offer ourselves as a sacrifice along with Christ" (via Aulén, 1958:85).

Other mainline denominations, with the exception of the Orthodox church and perhaps Anglicanism, usually feel more comfortable in the Lutheran camp than the Catholic. Evangelicals, by contrast, typically deny (at least in theory) that anything "really happens" at communion. It is a mere reminder of what God has already done through Christ. Jesus is not in any real sense "present" in the act of celebrating; he is merely "represented." Little wonder that celebration of communion in many evangelicals groups is a relatively insignificant church tradition.

Most Christian groups recognize that Jesus is in some sense *present* and in some sense *absent* in the communion celebration (cf. Jesus' "vow of abstinence," Mark 14:25, notes). We look back, reenacting and reappropriating the benefits of Jesus' death, thus making these *present* again in our experience. But we are also keenly aware of our Lord's *absence*, as we look forward in faith to that day when Jesus' presence will be our unbroken experience in God's kingdom.

It is a contribution of believers churches to emphasize one aspect of communion often missed in the discussions alluded to above. We not only look back and remember; we not only look forward and anticipate. We also look around. Jesus is indeed present at communion, but not simply in the elements or in the remembering. He is chiefly present, as he promised, in the *gathering* (Matt. 18:19-20). The church is not a collection of individuals mystically bound by common participation in a sacrament; instead, the church is a real, living, and interrelating family (Mark 3:34-35).

This family experiences the presence of Jesus in every gathering, and especially so when we gather to relive and reenact our mutual participation in the "body" of Christ (the church), symbolized by the

sharing of the one loaf and communion cup (cf. 1 Cor. 10:16-17).
Thus communion requires no sacred food, no sacred place, no sacred
officiating person, and no sacred occasion. Where believers gather in
unity to celebrate their oneness in Christ, there communion is rightly
experienced in the presence of Jesus who died and rose to make it all
possible. There our covenant with Christ and with each other is regularly renewed.

For additional reading, see G. Aulén, *Eucharist and Sacrifice;*
E. Epp et al., *The Celebration of the Lord's Supper;* J. D. Rempel,
The Lord's Supper in Anabaptism; and E. Kreider, *Communion
Shapes Character.*

Mark 14:27—15:15

The Trials of Jesus and the Disciples

PREVIEW

The evening before Jesus' final suffering and death, his passion, he shared a covenant meal with his disciples (14:17-26). During the meal, Jesus announced the presence of a traitor in their ranks. Also during the meal, he used bread and wine to symbolize his own person, given for his disciples, his lifeblood poured out in violent death to redeem *the many*. The contrast is a stark one: Judas selling the righteous one for personal gain; Jesus giving up his life on behalf of the guilty. Mark locates these events *in the evening* (14:17), connecting it with the first night watch (13:35; 6:00-9:00 p.m.).

In the present section, the three remaining night watches are narrated: *midnight* in Gethsemane (9:00-12:00); *cockcrow* in the courtyard of the high priest (12:00-3:00); *dawn* at Pilate's palace (3:00-6:00). In each of the night watches, Mark features a contrast: Jesus models faithfulness; those around him fail in every way. Through it all, Mark's readers learn the meaning of discipleship; they learn the meaning of "watching" throughout the night of waiting for the owner of the house to come back (13:33-37).

Yet this next section will do more than present pictures of faithfulness (Jesus) and of failure (disciples, especially Peter; a mysterious naked young man; Jewish religious leaders; a Roman politician). It will also give glimpses of the ultimate solution to human failure. Beyond failure is forgiveness and renewal for those who turn back (repent).

The hints have begun already in the first night watch. *In the evening* Jesus has offered his lifeblood for *the many*. Now as *midnight* approaches, he invites the disciples to be reunited with him again after their coming failure (14:28). *At cockcrow* Jesus is condemned, the innocent in place of the guilty, and Peter weeps the repentant tears that signal his recognition of sin (14:64, 72). *At dawn* the substitutionary aspect of Jesus' death is enacted. Jesus, the innocent one, goes to his death; Barabbas, the guilty one, goes free.

Throughout this section, we observe contrasts. Jesus predicts accurately, the disciples predict inaccurately (14:27-31). Jesus prays, the disciples sleep (14:35-41). Jesus openly confesses truth (14:62); Judas hides deception with a kiss (14:45) and Peter with lies and oaths (14:68-71). The crowd is armed with swords and clubs (14:48); Jesus trusts God and obeys the Scriptures (14:27, 49). Jesus willingly accompanies his enemies (14:46); his followers flee into the night (14:50-52). Jesus confesses his true identity though his physical life is at stake (14:62-64); Peter denies his true identity though his salvation is at stake (14:71; 8:35). Pilate is swayed by the crowds (15:15) and the crowds by their leaders (15:11); Jesus submits only to his Father's will (14:36).

On the surface it is all a terrible miscarriage of justice. At a deeper level, it is a tragic miscalculation by religious leaders and politicians. They are desperate to hold on to their authority; as a result, they ultimately lose their positions, their temple, their city, and their land. At a still deeper level, God is working out redemptive purposes.

Only Jesus recognizes that with the arrival of his captors *the Hour* has come (14:41). It is more than his hour of suffering; it is the Hour of fulfillment (14:41; 13:32). At the end of this section, all the preliminary events are over. Jesus is led away to be mocked as a false king, crucified as the Jewish king, and raised up by God as King of kings.

OUTLINE

Predictions of Failure, Renewal, Faithfulness, 14:27-31
    14:27-28   Jesus Predicts Failure and Renewal
    14:29-31   Peter and the Other Disciples Vow
                    Faithfulness

Jesus at Prayer: The Disciples Asleep, 14:32-42

The Arrest of Jesus, 14:43-49

The Disciples' Desertion, 14:50

The Fleeing and Naked Young Man, 14:51-52

Jesus on Trial Before the Sanhedrin, 14:53-65
    14:53-55   Two Trials Begin
    14:56-61a   Jesus and the Temple(s)
    14:61b-65 The Identity of Jesus

Peter on Trial in the Courtyard, 14:66-72

Jesus and Pilate, 15:1-5
    15:1   Jesus Is Handed Over to Pilate
    15:2-5   Pilate Questions Jesus

Jesus or Barabbas, 15:6-15
    15:6-8   A Crowd Comes with a Request
    15:9-11   Pilate Offers to Release Jesus
    15:12-15   Release Barabbas! Crucify Jesus!

EXPLANATORY NOTES

Predictions of Failure, Renewal, Faithfulness 14:27-31

After singing the final Passover hymn (14:26), Jesus and his disciples (except Judas) go to the Mount of Olives; thus Judas is absent when Jesus invites his followers to renew their discipleship after their coming failure and his coming resurrection. While they are (apparently) still on their way to their "garden" destination (so identified only in John 18:1), Jesus engages Peter and the other disciples in what Gundry calls "a contest of predictive ability" (844).

14:27-28 Jesus Predicts Failure and Renewal

Jesus predicts four events, and Mark presents them in a chiasm [Chiasm and Intercalation]:

    A • The disciples will become deserters (14:27a).
     B • He himself will be struck down (v. 27b).
     B' • He himself will be raised up (v. 28a).
    A' • The disciples will be invited to follow again (v. 28b).

The ultimate renewal of the disciples is not guaranteed by this prediction, but it is offered. Even if the disciples hear no more about the meaning and fulfillment of Jesus' resurrection promises, they know where to find Jesus, if they repent of their coming failure (cf. 16:8). We know from other records that they do in fact return to faithfulness after the resurrection. Mark's Gospel, though not reporting that renewal, presumes that it will take place (cf. 9:9; 10:39; 13:9-13; and so on).

Jesus' prediction of the disciples' failure uses the word *skandalizō,* meaning *you will be caused to stumble* (lit.). *Become deserters* in NRSV is too specific, but it does describe how the disciples stumble as they fulfill Jesus' prophecy (14:50; see Swartley and Girard in Swartley, 2000:229-32, 310-1). A variety of factors lead to their stumbling. Their failure is part of the plan of God so that Scripture will be fulfilled (14:27). It results from the weakness of their human *flesh* (14:38). It is also the result of Satan's strong temptations to avoid suffering and the cross (cf. 8:32-33). The disciples will be held accountable for their failure, though it is predicted and inevitable. The one who is faithful in all the watches of the night will atone for their failure ("Preview," above; 10:45; 13:35; 14:24).

Jesus predicts his death by using the image of a shepherd, an apt one; he has been leading his disciples all along the way (8:34), and will lead them again, beyond the resurrection (14:28; 16:7). Verse 27 is a quotation from Zechariah, where God is the one who strikes the faithful shepherd, so that the sheep will be scattered and thus be refined and renewed to faithfulness (Zech. 13:7, 9). Mark's text contains the same emphases; after Jesus' death, he will be raised again; then he, the shepherd, will again lead the sheep that have been scattered (14:28). Human hands will kill Jesus, but God's hand will also be in it (cf. 14:21).

Jesus predicts a post-resurrection reunion: *I will go before you to Galilee* (14:28; cf. 16:7). The context of this prediction indicates that *Galilee* stands for discipleship renewal. A renewed meeting in Galilee will be the disciples' second chance, after failure. In Galilee, Jesus will renew his call to discipleship (cf. 1:14-20) and promise again to make them *fishers for people* (cf. 1:17). This time, in the power of the resurrection, they will faithfully follow on the way of the cross and will carry out their mission in the context of persecution (13:9-13). Galilee stands for renewal; the journey to Jerusalem stands for discipleship. The disciples have *physically* walked that road already; but only Jesus has *truly* walked the way of the cross. After the resurrection, the disciples will repeat the journey, this time faithfully following the resurrected Jesus (16:7, notes).

At the beginning of Mark's Gospel, John's passion becomes the occasion for Jesus' own faithful ministry to begin; so here, Jesus' passion will lead to the disciples' faithfulness and ministry (14:28). When *they* are called to lay down their lives (13:9, 11-13), the baton of ministry will be passed on to others. The Gospel message is not stopped by the silencing of one of its messengers. It is destined to reach all nations (13:10; 14:9), whatever setbacks may be along the way. That is how the secret kingdom works.

14:29-31 *Peter and the Other Disciples Vow Faithfulness*

Jesus and his disciples agree on one thing: come what may, in the end Jesus will still be leading and they will be following. However, Jesus has predicted that the way leading to final faithfulness is through failure and renewal. The disciples (especially Peter) claim that there will be no desertion, not even if faithfulness costs them their lives.

When Jesus first explicitly predicts that he will be rejected, killed, and raised again (8:31), Peter contradicts Jesus. He cannot face the thought that Jesus would be taken from them. Here Peter contradicts Jesus again. He is not content to accept the promise of a final renewal; he vows that there will not be a separation.

The way 14:29 is worded in Greek, Peter is actually agreeing with Jesus that *all* the others will *become deserters;* only he will not. In effect, he says to Jesus, "Your prophecy about the others will be fulfilled, but you are wrong about me; I am the great exception." Peter's great pride will lead to his great fall (Hamerton-Kelly: 28). Jesus' even more explicit predictions (the threefold denial, the cockcrow) are again met with contradiction. Peter first and then also the others rashly promise loyalty, even to death, if necessary (14:30-31).

This dialogue, on the way from the upper room to the garden of Gethsemane, forms the transition from the events of the first watch (*in the evening*) to those of the second (*at midnight*; 13:35). It is another Markan hinge transition ("Preview" for 8:27—9:1). The exchange links to material preceding and following; it forms an intercalation both ways.

Looking *backward*, we see a pattern:

A • Jesus announces the presence of the betrayer (14:17-21).
  B • Jesus sacrifices himself on behalf of the many (14:22-26).
A' • Jesus predicts the desertion of the disciples (14:27-31).

Looking *forward*, we see another pattern:

A • Jesus predicts the desertion of the disciples (14:27-31).
  B • Jesus submits to the Father's will and is taken (14:32-49).
A' • All the disciples desert Jesus (14:50-52).

Both ways, Mark uses the failure of the disciples as a bracket around the faithfulness of Jesus. His faithfulness, in the end, will be the reason those returning to him can be forgiven, renewed, and brought back on the road of discipleship and mission. That is the main point of this transitional incident.

Jesus at Prayer: The Disciples Asleep 14:32-42

Jesus arrives at *Gethsemane,* likely a grove of olive trees at the foot of the *Mount of Olives.* Eight disciples, as we learn from the larger context, are asked to sit while Jesus prays. Jesus singles out three disciples for special experiences (14:32-33; cf. 5:37; 9:2), the same ones Mark recognizes for special failure (8:32-33; 9:38; 10:35). Peter, James, and John accompany Jesus further into the garden. Jesus instructs them to *keep awake* (vv. 34, 37-38). *Keep awake* translates *grēgoreō,* used in Mark only in this text and three times in the doorkeeper parable (13:34-35, 37, *be on the watch/keep awake*). Mark carefully coordinates these two texts; three times in each, Jesus gives the command to *keep awake.* Three times Jesus' disciples fail to do so. The vocabulary of "watching-coming-finding-sleeping" is identical in both texts (see 13:33-37, notes).

To watch (*keep awake*) means to identify with Jesus, remain loyal to him, follow his instructions, and follow him even on the road to the cross. That is what it means to be the faithful doorkeeper in every watch of the night until *the Hour* comes (cf. 13:32, 35; 14:41).

In Gethsemane, the disciples were supposed to express loyalty to Jesus by keeping literally awake (13:34, 37-38), praying (v. 38), and standing or kneeling with Jesus during his time of distress, agitation, and grief (vv. 33-35). They were to show loyalty by calling God *Abba* (v. 36) and submitting to God's will as Jesus does (v. 36). They were to gain spiritual strength to overpower weak flesh (v. 38). If the disciples were loyal, they would keep their eyes wide open (v. 40), seeing beyond suffering and death to the coming of God's reign.

Jesus prays that *the hour* of his passion (13:35b) and *this cup* of God's wrath (v. 36a) might be removed. He knows God can make the hour pass away, that God can remove the cup (v. 36a). But Jesus discerns that God has chosen for him to drink the cup and to experience the hour of suffering (v. 41; cf. 13:11). He discerns that the hour of his passion is *the Hour* of eschatological fulfillment (v. 41). God is working out divine purposes. God's kingdom is being established. If it must be by way of violent death, Jesus is ready.

The disciples, having slept through the crisis, are not ready. They will *come into the time of trial* (v. 38), and on trial they will fail. They will give in to the weakness of the flesh. Their eyes have been heavy (v. 40); they will see nothing beyond enemies and swords and danger. Despite self-confident promises (cf. 14:31; 10:39), they will flee—and thus fulfill the prediction Jesus has just made (14:27-31).

Some words in this text require comment. They are loaded with special meanings in the context of Mark and the rest of Scripture.

Abba, Father, says Jesus (v. 36), here for the only time in any of the Gospels. It reminds us of the story of Isaac and Abraham. As Abraham takes "his son whom he loves" (Gen. 22:2; cf. Mark 1:11), the young boy asks, "Daddy (Abba), where is the lamb for the sacrifice?" At the time, Isaac is carrying the wood intended for the sacrifice of his own life (Gen. 22:7). "God himself will provide the lamb," assures his father (22:8, 13). In Gethsemane, Jesus discerns that this time no substitute will be found for the beloved Son. He, too, is destined to carry the wood. On it, he is destined to lose his life.

Jesus says *to* **Peter,** "**Simon,** *are you asleep?*" (v. 37). Jesus has given Simon a new name, *Peter* (*rock,* 3:15). Since then, the narrator has consistently called him Peter. Here, the only time Jesus addresses him with any name at all (except for calling him *Satan!* 8:33), he uses the old name. Far from being the pillar of solid rock that he should have been, *Simon* leads the others into failure.

Enough! Apechei (v. 41) is difficult to translate. It could mean *Enough* (enough sleep). It could mean *It has come* (the Hour; or the End, as in some manuscripts). It could be a term for a receipt (paid in full). If this last meaning is accepted, then Mark interprets Jesus as saying, "The deed is done. Judas has been paid; I have been bought. I am the sacrificial lamb and will now be led out for slaughter."

Jesus agonizes in prayer for *one hour* (v. 37); then he prays for two more periods/hours. The Passover meal has taken place *in the evening* (6:00-9:00; 14:17, notes); the time of prayer in Gethsemane covers the next three hours, the second watch of the night (9:00-12:00). We have already noted the contrasts between Jesus' faithfulness and the disciples' unfaithfulness. This text contributes to our understanding of watching in the unknown waiting period before the Son of Man returns (13:33-37). Watching has nothing to do with observing signs or knowing when. It has to do with faithfulness, loyalty, prayer, obedience, and the way of the cross.

The second night watch (9:00-12:00) ends at midnight and thus is called *midnight* (*mesonuktion,* 13:35). Those celebrating Passover are remembering how at midnight God struck the Egyptians and delivered Israel (Exod. 11:4); they look forward to a greater deliverance still to come. Indeed, many believed that during the celebration of a Passover feast, God's Messiah would come to deliver Israel again. Now the midnight hour strikes. All over Jerusalem, pilgrims are retiring for the night with a resigned comment, "Maybe next year." Jesus has discerned that *The hour has come!* (14:41). It is the midnight hour, *the Hour* of fulfillment.

Mark uses the expression *that day* to refer both to Jesus' passion (2:20) and to the final *Day* of the Lord (13:32); he also uses the expression *the hour* for both of these (14:41; 13:32). Not even the Son knows when *that Day* and *the Hour* will arrive (13:32-33). But in Gethsemane, Jesus discerns that this day and this *hour* mark the time of eschatological fulfillment. But what irony! The hour of God's triumph is the hour in which God's Son is handed over to sinners (Judas, religious leaders, Roman soldiers).

The Arrest of Jesus 14:43-49

Both Jesus and his disciples are now set on courses with predictable outcomes. He has watched; they have slept. He has prayed; they have not. He trusts God; they trust in the flesh. The captors arrive. Naturally the disciples strike out and flee; they have not been faithful to their discipleship obligations. Naturally Jesus willingly embraces his fate, for he has yielded to and discerned his Father's plans. (T. Geddert, 1989:100)

Mark first identifies Judas as the traitor when he lists *the Twelve* (3:19). When Judas makes his move to betray Jesus, he is again called *one of the Twelve* (14:10), and again at the Passover meal (14:20). Now as Judas appears for the last time in Mark, he is once more called *one of the Twelve* (v. 43). Could there be any more effective way of magnifying the horror of what he does? One of the Twelve brings an armed crowd to arrest Jesus. One of the Twelve betrays Jesus with a *kiss*. This is an inside job, done by one whom Jesus has specifically chosen to be with him. Thus Mark highlights the possibility of a disciple ultimately falling from faithfulness.

The armed crowd is delegated by the religious groups most often mentioned as Jesus' enemies: *the chief priests, the scribes, and the elders.* That they are armed with swords in addition to clubs suggests that at least some of them are Roman soldiers. Presumably Jesus is not easily recognized, especially in the dark; Judas' signal helps them identify Jesus. More significantly, the *kiss* highlights how terrible the betrayal is. Jesus' "bosom friend" (cf. 14:18, notes) turns against him; he betrays him with an *affectionate kiss* (14:44-45, TJG; *affectionate* is implied in the Greek word).

Jesus is seized, but it is not an orderly arrest based on proper authorization. In the scuffle, a *sword* strikes a *slave of the high priest* and severs his *ear*. Mark's narrative leaves uncertain whether or not it is one of the disciples who wields the sword (cf. John 18:10-11; Luke 22:51). The struggle is unnecessary, for Jesus comes willingly. Indeed, his willingness is expressed in a half-taunting question: *Why didn't you simply take me when I was teaching in the temple?* (Mark 13:48-49, abridged). The reader knows the answer; they were afraid of the crowds (11:18; 12:12; 14:2). The religious leaders rely on an armed crowd under cover of darkness to take a man who comes willingly.

Have you come out with swords and clubs to arrest me as though I were a bandit? Jesus asks them (v. 48). The word for *bandit* is *lēstēs*, also translated *insurrectionist* or *robber*. Do they really think Jesus is one of those? Mark uses the same word on two other occasions. In 15:27, Mark reports that two bandits/insurrectionists are crucified, one on either side of Jesus.

The other occurrence is the most fascinating. *Jesus* uses it to describe the very persons who have just sent this mob to get him! When Jesus says the temple has become a *den of robbers* (lit., *a bandit's den,* 11:17), the same word (*lēstēs*) is used to describe the religious authorities who are abusing the temple. The high priests, the scribes, and the elders—these are the real bandits, the real insurrectionists, robbing God and using mob action against God's Son in a futile attempt to steal God's vineyard (12:7-8). Does this armed mob think that Jesus is one of *them?*

"Yet Scripture must be fulfilled," Jesus says. As absurd as it is to send an armed mob to seize an unarmed and willing pacifist, it has to happen, for Scripture has predicted it. No specific text is named, but it may well be a reference to the text Jesus himself has just quoted, Zechariah 13:7 (Mark 14:27).

The Disciples' Desertion 14:50

When Jesus is taken, the disciples flee the scene. These men, in whom Jesus has invested so much, who have vowed only three hours earlier they would die with Jesus, now flee in the crisis. They have proved their prediction false, and Jesus' prediction true (14:27-31)!

Jesus has specifically commissioned the Twelve to be *with him* (3:14). He planned a special meal *with them* (14:14). He arrived in the upstairs room *with the Twelve* (14:17). He announced the betrayer as one eating *with him* (14:18), dipping *with him* in the bowl (14:20). In Gethsemane, Jesus takes his three closest disciples *with him* (14:33). They are there, but are they really with him?

Judas certainly is not with him. The text says he comes *with the armed crowd* (14:43). Nor is Peter, for soon he will sit *with the* high priest's servants/*guards* (14:54) and *deny* that he was *with Jesus* (14:67). Though he has *followed at a distance* a few steps farther than others (14:54), it is not the following expected of a disciple. It represents the curiosity of an overconfident Peter, of one torn between his unconquerable fear and his passionate loyalty.

The other disciples abandon Jesus in Gethsemane; they are *with Jesus* no longer. In a sense, they never were. They have left (*aphiēmi*) everything to follow Jesus; now they leave (*aphiēmi*) him (14:50).

Judas disappears from the Markan narrative at 14:45. His betraying kiss is his last act. At 14:50, ten more disciples disappear from the narrative when they run away. At 14:72, Peter disappears after he breaks down and cries. No mention is made of any of them again until a young man at the tomb announces that they can now go to Galilee to meet the resurrected Jesus (16:7).

The Fleeing and Naked Young Man 14:51-52

Just at the point where the failure of Jesus' closest disciples is narrated in all its predictability and yet its horror, Mark favors his readers with a riddle. A young man, previously unmentioned, naked but for a linen cloth, has apparently been following Jesus. Some people (presumably the armed crowd) attempt to take him, but are left holding only the linen cloth. The naked man flees. This is not the time for comic relief; what then is the meaning of this odd text?

If Mark were a careless author, we might say he just forgot to tell the part of the story that would explain its purpose. But Mark is a subtle author, one who uses symbols with abandon and great effect. He likes to pose riddles (cf. 6:52). There is *no obvious* meaning, so Mark must have hoped his readers would ponder some of the less obvious possibilities.

From earliest times, interpreters have tried their hand at solving this riddle. Some look to the OT for clues, some to contextual clues in Mark. Many look to 16:5, the only other place in Mark where this word *young man* (*neaniskos*) is used; there a young man clothed in white (the color of bleached linen, 9:3; Rev. 19:14) proclaims the resurrection. With all these options, suggestions have ranged broadly:

1. It fulfills an OT prophecy (e.g., Amos 2:16; Gen. 39:12).
2. It symbolizes the shame of the disciples' flight (Mark 14:50).

3. It shows the extent of the disciples' failure: they have left all to follow; now they leave all to flee.

4. It symbolizes Jesus' passion, the shame he faces in his death, and the glory of his resurrection (cf. 16:5; 9:3).

5. It symbolizes Christian baptism: a believer is naked while receiving baptism to identify with Jesus' death, and clothed afterward as one rises to resurrection life (cf. 16:5; Rom. 6:4-5).

Some have thought they could identify the young man as the rich man in Mark 10:17, or as an angel (cf. 16:5), or as John Mark himself!

This last suggestion is one of the oldest and one of the most plausible, I think. There are even circumstantial historical clues that make the theory plausible. If John Mark has written this Gospel, and if the early church later met in his home (cf. Acts 12:12-13), then it is possible that Jesus and his disciples ate their Passover meal at the home where the author of this Gospel lived (14:15). John Mark could well have followed Jesus to the garden, or even more likely, followed Judas and his mob, who first came to the house and then, noting Jesus' absence, headed for the garden. Some scholars dismiss this view as a misguided attempt to turn John Mark into an eyewitness, something neither he nor the earliest church traditions ever claimed he was.

However, there is a more appropriate motivation for taking these suggestions seriously. We need to remember that this John Mark is the young man who abandoned his mission work when the going got tough (cf. Acts 13:13; 15:38; for an alternative view, see Swartley, 1981). Later Barnabas brought him back into the mission (Acts 15:39), and Paul finally accepted him again (2 Tim. 4:11).

Mark's point is not, "I was an eyewitness" but rather "I ran away, too!" There is an amazing three-way correlation between John Mark the author, Simon Peter the primary source, and the astonishingly strong emphasis in this Gospel on discipleship failure and renewal. Peter and Mark both understood this theme well.

Even if John Mark was not *historically* present in the garden, even if his home was not the one used for the Passover meal, I still suspect that John Mark is putting his signature on the canvas with this mysterious notation at 14:51-52. Just at the point where all the disciples fail Jesus, Mark adds,

> I know about that! I have been there! My failure was no less shameful! But I too heard the invitation to meet Jesus again in Galilee (cf. 14:28). These fleeing apostles came back, I came back, and so can you!

If that is what Mark means at 14:51-52, then there is a sense in which he is also represented in the young man who announces the resurrection at 16:5. Clothed *in a white robe*, there is no shame now; he is proclaiming a crucified Jesus who has risen; that is exactly what Mark has been doing now for almost 14 chapters!

In the Passover liturgy, celebrants speak of what God did for *us* (not simply our ancestors) when God brought *us* out of Egypt (cf. Deut. 26:8). When we ask each other in our celebrations of Easter, "Were you there when they crucified my Lord?" we can say we were. We were there to help condemn him to death. We were there to hammer in the nails. In the same way, John Mark can say, "*I was there!* I ran away with all the others in the garden; but I have also been to the tomb, and now I confess, He has been raised!"

Jesus on Trial Before the Sanhedrin 14:53-65

Many details recorded from here to the end of Mark's Gospel are judged "historically improbable" by a host of critical scholars, either because they seem incompatible with what we "know" about first-century practices, or because they are difficult to harmonize with the other Gospels. My own sense is that claims of "historical impossibility" and "inconsistency" are often exaggerated; I see no reason to reject Mark's account as "historically inaccurate" (cf. Hooker, 1991; Gundry; Rivkin; Barrett).

We can certainly be confident that Mark's narrative is not carelessly put together; it is meticulously crafted, complete with irony, double meanings, foreshadowing, and other literary subtleties. We need to seek to understand Mark's message by examining what Mark actually wrote, not by comparing Mark's text with what some critics believe "really happened."

Mark's narrative of Jesus' trial before the Sanhedrin and Peter's "trial" in the courtyard are thoroughly wrapped together *[Chiasm and Intercalation]*:

Jesus Before the Court (14:53)
    Peter in the Courtyard (14:54)
Jesus on Trial (14:55-65)
    Peter on Trial (14:66-72)
Jesus' Trial Concluded (15:1)

Jesus' trial and Peter's are two sides of one coin. Jesus models faithfulness on trial, Peter models unfaithfulness. The rooster crows, ending the third watch of the night (12:00-3:00 a.m., *cockcrow*,

13:35). Mark has favored his reader with yet another remarkable picture of what it means, and does not mean, to be faithful in every watch of the night as disciples wait for the Master's return (cf. 13:34-37).

14:53-55 Two Trials Begin

A Sanhedrin gathering during the middle of Passover night would be highly unusual, possibly illegal, and surely hard to arrange at the last minute. A report of such a trial highlights the resolve of the religious leadership to bring their plot against Jesus to a swift end.

As Jesus is ushered into the high priest's house, Peter sneaks into the courtyard. He has *followed . . . at a distance.* At the literal level, it implies ambivalent cowardice. Peter does not want to be seen, but he does not want to miss seeing, either. At a deeper level, it is a commentary on his discipleship. Where there is no true self-sacrifice and no allegiance to Jesus, physical following is not enough. Peter is no longer truly following; he is merely trailing along behind Jesus.

Hoping to remain unobtrusive, Peter warms himself along with others at the fire. Jesus is in the courtroom; Peter is in the courtyard. Both are on trial. As both sets of proceedings unfold, Mark's reader delights in the intriguing ironies, but at the same time is shocked by what is occurring.

Jesus' trial is narrated first. The two main themes are the temple and Jesus' messianic identity. In neither case is the court going after truth; it has decided beforehand that the trial must lead to a guilty verdict and a death sentence. The challenge is to find a way to reach these. Even before reporting the proceedings, Mark tells his reader that no valid testimony against Jesus is found (v. 55b).

14:56-61a Jesus and the Temple(s)

Mark's presentation magnifies the ineptitude of the conspirators. They cannot even get two liars to say the same thing! (v. 56; cf. Deut. 17:6; 19:15). In the end, the high priest presses Jesus to defend himself against charges that cannot be laid, because the required two agreeing testimonies cannot be faked (v. 60)!

Ironically, the lie reported in the text (v. 58) is not far from the truth. Liars claim Jesus threatened to destroy the temple *made with hands* and three days later build another *not made with hands.* Jesus did explicitly predict the destruction of the Jerusalem temple (13:2) and implicitly the construction of another one (cf. 12:10-11), though it is not clear how Jesus' enemies could know that. There is some truth in the false witnesses' lie.

But there is also falsehood in it. Nowhere does Jesus claim that *he himself* will act either to destroy or to rebuild. The destruction of the temple will not be an act of retaliation by Jesus; it will be an act of judgment by God Almighty. The rebuilding of another temple will be no achievement of Jesus; it will be his vindication by God (cf. 12:9-12, 36). In the end, the charge of the false witnesses is revealed to be a lie; Jesus will destroy no temple and build none. God will destroy the Jerusalem temple and will raise up Jesus and his community as a new temple (cf. 1 Cor. 3:16-17). Both of these events will be God's response to what the religious leaders are doing at this very moment, rejecting Jesus.

What contrast is implied in *made with hands* versus *not made with hands* (v. 58)?

- Made by humans versus made by God?
- Made on earth versus made in heaven?
- Physical versus spiritual?
- Historical versus eschatological?
- Natural versus miraculous?
- Idolatrous versus pure?

It could be any and all of these, but the last one is most likely what Mark intends. In the OT, idols are often described as the work of *human hands* (cf. Ps. 115:4; Isa. 46:6). Jesus has referred to the temple in Jerusalem as a *den of robbers*. Mark's text here goes even further: it is an idol, a weak caricature, a humanly devised substitute for the "holy place" it was intended to be.

Those who are here rejecting Jesus are sealing their own fate and guaranteeing the coming destruction of the Jerusalem temple. *In three days* (by means of the resurrection), God will turn the rejected stone into a cornerstone (12:10). A new temple, God's renewed people, will be raised up; this temple is destined to survive and grow, even after the temple in Jerusalem is a pile of stones (13:2). It will be a divine creation, with an eternal destiny (cf. Heb. 9:11; 2 Cor. 5:1).

That is what Mark's reader is hearing. If we move back into Jesus' courtroom, we find fumbling officials and lying witnesses ironically speaking half truths while trying to get their lies straight. As a contribution to Mark's theology, their charge is loaded with ironic truth. As a contribution to the court case, it leads nowhere. The lies do not produce a valid charge. Although given an opportunity, Jesus has nothing to respond to (14:60-61). Mark likely views Jesus' silence as a fulfillment of Scripture (cf. Ps. 39:9; Isa. 53:7).

14:61b-65 The Identity of Jesus

A promise to build a temple (though Jesus does not confirm that he made this promise) would be understood as a messianic claim, explaining the shift of topics from temple to Christology. The high priest directly asks Jesus for his identity, using the main Markan titles for Jesus (1:1): *Are you the Christ, the Son of the Blessed One?* In typical Jewish fashion, *Blessed One* is used for God. The NRSV, by translating *Christos* here (and in 8:29) as *Messiah*, obscures the fact that this is the same word it translates as *Christ* in 1:1.

To the high priest's direct question, Jesus supplies (as he hardly ever does) a direct answer: *I Am [Questioning Jesus].* He immediately adds a composite quote from Psalm 110:1 and Daniel 7:13. In doing so, he predicts the Son of Man's (= his own) future exaltation and coming role as judge *[Son of Man].* Someday Jesus' present accusers will be facing *him* in *his* courtroom (v. 62). Then the truth will emerge (TBC, below).

The christological titles used here are worth pondering. First, it is noteworthy that Jesus directly responds to the question as to whether he is *Christ* and *Son of God*. According to my count, Jesus directly answers only two of the many questions posed to him in Mark's Gospel *[Questioning Jesus].* In 12:28-31, Jesus is asked about the greatest commandment, and he answers by giving the greatest *two.* Here he is asked whether he claims to be the *Christ* and the *Son of God* (= *Messiah* and *Son of the Blessed One*). He confirms that he is, and then also refers to himself as *Son of Man* and as *I Am.*

At this point, the high priest charges Jesus with blasphemy. Some scholars who look for historical explanations are baffled; where is the blasphemy? Claiming to be Messiah is technically not blasphemy, nor (the critics add) does it become blasphemy by adding the explanatory title, *Son of God.* Moreover, they argue, by calling God *the Power* (14:62; cf. the high priest calling God *the Blessed One*, v. 61), Jesus has technically avoided naming God. Finally, Jesus has spoken of *the Son of Man* without explicitly claiming he is referring to himself. So where is the blasphemy?

Three responses are in order. First, Mark is not picturing a fair trial. If Jesus is falsely accused of blasphemy here, that would not be the only illegal act committed by his accusers.

Second, the word *blasphemy* can be used more broadly for "deriding" or "speaking badly" (as in 15:29). Of course, Jesus did not do this either, but his accusers might have claimed he did. This kind of blasphemy is, of course, certainly not a capital crime, but that might well be Mark's point; the whole procedure is illegal and unfair!

Third, Jesus could have given an affirmative answer to the high priest's direct question in a variety of ways. He chose to do it (according to Mark) with an expression that in effect becomes another christological claim, one that makes Jesus equal with God. He directly names the divine name when he answers *I Am* (*Egō eimi,* the Greek translation for Yahweh, Exod. 3:14). It is not the first time in Mark that Jesus has said *I Am* (*Egō eimi*) and laid a claim to divinity (cf. 6:50). The reader of the Gospel is expected to hear Jesus' answer as the highest christological claim of all. He is both Christ and Son of God, yes, and he also claims divinity for himself. That, from the perspective of the Sanhedrin, constitutes blasphemy. Jesus is sentenced to death, not because his claims are misunderstood, but because they are understood and rejected.

The first and the last words Jesus' enemies speak in Jesus' presence (in Mark) are worth setting in parallel:

> Why does this fellow speak in this way?
>   It is blasphemy!
> Who can forgive sins but God alone? (2:7)

> Why do we still need witnesses?
>   You have heard his blasphemy!
> What is your decision? (14:64)

Each time two questions expressing their own deliberations surround their declaration that Jesus is blaspheming! Jesus claims authority to forgive (2:7) and authority to condemn (14:64). The irony is that, by rejecting Jesus' claims, the religious leaders are themselves blaspheming God's representative. They thus commit the very crime of which they judge *him* to be guilty!

The court decides that Jesus deserves death (v. 64). The mock trial is over; they had decided the outcome before it began (v. 55). When morning comes, they attempt to secure an official death penalty from Pilate, the Roman prefect. Some cannot resist abusing the prisoner; they spit, they smite, they beat, and they mock (v. 65).

Jesus knew this would happen. He announced it all ahead of time: the rejection, the arrest, the abuse, the death sentence (8:31; 10:33-34). How ironic that he is now mocked and condemned as a false prophet precisely as all these prophecies are coming true (v. 65). Indeed, another prophecy of Jesus is being fulfilled at this very moment (cf. 14:30). It is happening in a parallel trial taking place in the courtyard below.

Peter on Trial in the Courtyard 14:66-72

Peter fulfills Jesus' prophecy to the letter. The first denial occurs when a servant girl claims Peter has been associated with Jesus. Peter tries to evade the issue by claiming not to know what she is talking about. The cock crows (vv. 66-68).

She persists in her opinion: *This man is one of them*. This time Peter denies the claim in the presence of the group. Bystanders, believing the girl's opinion, claim that Peter's Galilean origin (clothing? accent?) proves his association with Jesus. This time Peter resorts to curses and oaths in denying it for the third time: *I do not know this man you are talking about* (vv. 69-71).

Peter is not cursing Jesus; he is calling curses upon himself. The oath is Peter's attempt to make his lie believable. By swearing it, Peter invokes the language of a lawcourt. How little he realizes that he is in fact on trial, not only in the high priest's courtyard, but in the court where the Son of Man presides (cf. 8:38). By denying his association with Jesus, Peter condemns himself before God.

Both Jesus and Peter have been on trial for their lives. "At the same time that Jesus is confessing who he is, Peter is denying who he is by refusing to confess that he knows who Jesus is" (Fowler, 1991:144). *I do not know this man*, claims Peter, as he blurts out his self-serving lie. At least he intends it as a lie. Yet truer words were never spoken! Peter truly does *not* know this Jesus. (Camery-Hoggatt: 172).

Three times Peter has slept instead of praying in Gethsemane. Three times Peter has denied Jesus instead of courageously confessing him in the high priest's courtyard. He has failed to perform because he has failed to prepare! But the story is not over. The cock crows the second time, fulfilling yet another prophecy of Jesus. The cockcrow signals the coming morning and functions to wake up Peter to what he has done. He remembers and weeps, the only report of tears in Mark's Gospel. They come from the Rock, Peter, who breaks down after his terrible failure. If it is not yet full repentance, at least it is horror at what he has done, and that is the first step.

The cockcrow is also a Markan code word. It marks the end of the third night watch (midnight—3:00 a.m.; 13:35). As in earlier watches, this watch features a vivid contrast between faithful Jesus and the unfaithful ones around him. As in each of the other watches, Jesus emerges as the one who will provide redemption for the guilty.

Here Jesus is falsely charged with the crime of which others are guilty. He will die in place of those who deserve the death penalty.

They can be forgiven if they heed the invitation of the stricken shepherd after he is raised up again. To Peter, whose failure is the most dramatic, Jesus offers a special invitation to meet the risen Jesus in Galilee (cf. 16:7). Peter, who deserves to lose his life for trying to save it, will be saved by the one who saves his own life because he is willing to lose it (8:35).

How relevant this will be for the Markan community! In times of persecution, a question like "Are you not one of them?" asked by the wrong person, might well be the signal that one's life is at stake. What does it mean to "watch" in the end time? Mark says it means ultimate allegiance to Jesus, following his example, being willing even to die with him. To deny him is to risk losing all.

Jesus and Pilate 15:1-5

Chapter 15 opens with *As soon as it was morning.* The Greek word for morning, *prōi*, is variously translated: *in the morning, early,* or *at dawn.* The significance of this word is that it is the technical term for the fourth watch of the Roman night, the exact term used in 13:35. All four watches of the Roman night have been clocked off in Mark's account of the Passover night (cf. 14:17, 41, 72).

In this fourth watch, *at dawn* (3:00-6:00 a.m.; cf. 13:35; 15:1), Jesus is sent from the Jewish court to Pilate, the Roman governor. All his supporters are now gone. Those called to be *with him* (15:50, notes) have all fled. Only Jesus continues on the way of the cross. Surrounding him now are the religious leaders, his sworn enemies. They have already judged him worthy of death. Before the next three hours pass, Jesus is surrounded by Gentile rulers (particularly Pilate), by a raucous crowd clamoring for his death, and by mocking soldiers, ironically proclaiming Jesus' true identity as *the King of the Jews.* Jesus is on the way to his enthronement, on the cross at Golgatha.

15:1 Jesus Is Handed Over to Pilate

The first verse of this section is somewhat unclear. It appears to summarize the council's decision already reached at 14:64. Perhaps Mark has deliberately structured the text to highlight the contrast between Jesus and Peter in the *third* night watch (cf. 13:35), and the contrast between Jesus and all his enemies (Jewish and Gentile) in the *fourth* (cf. notes, above). At any rate, the day dawns, and Jesus finds himself quickly shuttled off to Pilate's temporary Jerusalem residence (he came from Caesarea for the festival season).

15:2-5 *Pilate Questions Jesus*

A blasphemy charge would be of no interest to Pilate. Instead, Jesus' affirmation that he is *the Christ* forms the basis of the charge. Jesus is claiming to be the Jewish king. Understood in a coercive political sense (not the way Jesus meant it!), this would interest Pilate. Insurrection against the Roman imperial power is a capital offense. This new charge might secure from Pilate the death sentence the Sanhedrin is seeking.

What irony! If Jesus will not take up Israel's throne and attack the Romans, the Sanhedrin will judge his messianic claim to be blasphemy. But to secure a death penalty, they pretend he is about to take up Israel's throne and attack the Romans (cf. Lane: 550-1).

Mark's brief report of the Roman trial begins with the action already under way. *Are you the King of the Jews?* asks Pilate. *King of the Jews* features prominently in the story of Jesus' death, but is used only by people who do not really believe Jesus is a king (15:2, 9, 12, 18, 26, 32). Is Jesus then a king, or is he not? According to the NIV, Jesus answers Pilate, *Yes, it is as you say.* According to the Greek text, that is not what Jesus says. The NRSV comes closer with its translation: *You say so.* Perhaps even that comes too close to registering Jesus' answer as a yes. Jesus is evading the question. He does not affirm that he is the sort of nationalistic, ethnic, and political monarch Pilate and the religious leaders are thinking of. Neither does he deny that God's anointing has made him *King* in the secret kingdom he is proclaiming and establishing (1:15; 4:11).

The religious leaders bring various charges against Jesus, left unspecified in Mark's text (15:3-4). Pilate correctly discerns that this is not about Jesus' guilt or innocence. It is about the *jealousy* of the priestly rulers, presumably because Jesus is much more popular with the crowds than they are (v. 10). The charges themselves impress Pilate much less than Jesus' confident silence in the face of his accusers (v. 5).

Jesus or Barabbas? 15:6-15

15:6-8 *A Crowd Comes with a Request*

A motley crowd of Passover pilgrims interrupts the trial (likely outdoors, 15:8). They have come to solicit from Pilate his usual Passover amnesty, the release of a prisoner (15:6). We assume that this is a crowd of people supporting Israelite liberation movements in general, or else Barabbas in particular. Why would they want a convicted criminal on the loose unless that person, though judged an "insurrectionist" by Rome, was a "prospective liberator" to them? At any rate, Mark's text creates the impression that this is a pro-revolution, pro-Barabbas crowd. He introduces Pilate's custom as the reason they have come (v. 6), and then refers to Barabbas and a recent uprising (v. 7) before reporting the crowd's request (v. 8).

15:9-11 Pilate Offers to Release Jesus

This crowd has not come for the purpose of securing Jesus' crucifixion. Indeed, the idea of offering Jesus as a substitute for Barabbas occurs to Pilate after the crowd arrives (v. 9). Before their arrival, the crowd cannot even have known that Jesus has been arrested and tried by the Sanhedrin. There is no way this text can be read as though Mark is spreading the blame for Jesus' rejection and death on "Israel as a whole" (as commentators often suggest).

Mark's sustained focus on the guilt of the religious leaders is highlighted in this text as well. When the plot to have Jesus killed shows signs of unraveling, the religious leaders scramble to persuade the crowd to stick with their original plan, rather than shift their support to Jesus. Such a ploy would never have worked with the crowds among whom Jesus has been so popular that the religious leaders were prevented from moving against Jesus (11:18; 12:12; 14:2). It works with this pro-Barabbas, pro-revolution crowd. In calling for Jesus' crucifixion, they are asking Pilate to hang Jesus on the cross where (no doubt) Barabbas would have hung.

The irony of it all is that Jesus will hang between two insurrectionists (15:27), as though he were one of them (14:48, notes). Yet the only reason he is there is because he is *not* one of them. Barabbas is one of them; that is why the crowd wants Barabbas released. Jesus refuses to take up military force; he refuses to be a coercive political Messiah; he refuses to lift a sword against Rome. For that, he must die!

15:12-15 Release Barabbas! Crucify Jesus!

Thus Pilate's attempt to secure Jesus' release backfires. Since he has offered Jesus' release as his Passover favor, he can hardly backtrack and claim that Jesus must be released after all for lack of a sustainable charge against him. The chief priests get what they want. The other crowds, those supporting Jesus, had prevented them from acting. This crowd supports violent revolution and turns out to be just what the leading priests need to put pressure on Pilate. Pilate and the religious leaders know Jesus is innocent. This crowd does not care;

they are prepared to sacrifice an innocent man to gain the release of Barabbas. Anyhow, as supporters of violent revolution, they have no use for a pacifist.

The sinners have their day (cf. 14:41). Pilate wants to satisfy the crowd, which wants to satisfy the religious leaders, who want to satisfy themselves. All are guilty, Jew and Gentile, leader and misled follower. The religious leaders who engineer the death plot represent all who abuse positions of religious and political power for personal advantage. Pilate represents all who give in to the pressure of others instead of standing alone for what is right. The crowd represents all whose ethnocentric nationalism keeps them blind to the way of God.

All of them represent those who have been confronted with Jesus' claims and have rejected them. Barabbas represents all who ultimately deserve a guilty verdict, disciples and enemies, Jews and Gentiles, but who are set free because an innocent one was crucified.

Suddenly the function of this text becomes clear to the reader. Jesus' death is being portrayed as substitutionary. The innocent one will die in place of the guilty; the one who saves life dies for the one who has taken life. The innocent victim of Roman injustice dies so that the one who attacks it with the sword may live.

God has handed Jesus over into human hands (9:31), into sinners' hands (14:41). These sinners keep handing Jesus along to others, Judas to the crowd making the arrest (14:44), the crowd to the religious leaders (10:33; 14:10-11), the religious leaders to Pilate (10:33; 15:1), and finally Pilate to the executioners (15:15). At Passover, thousands of lambs are handed over by "sinners" to those who represent them before God. In an act of ultimate irony, God hands over the sacrificial Lamb to humans, to sinners, to executioners. They will do to him whatever they wish (9:12-13). God will respond, not only by raising Jesus again, but by calling back to faithfulness those who have fled and failed, calling to repentance and faith all who will respond (cf. 14:28; 15:39; 13:11).

THE TEXT IN BIBLICAL CONTEXT
You Will See the Son of Man

Mark's statement about the exaltation and coming of the Son of Man (14:62) is a composite quotation from Psalm 110:1 and Daniel 7:13. Psalm 110:1, already quoted at 12:36, refers to the Messiah being not merely David's son, but David's Lord as well. Daniel 7:13 speaks of a Son of Man who is given authority, glory and sovereign power, worship, and an eternal kingdom (Dan. 7:13-14). The court clearly understands the significance of Jesus' claims for himself.

But when, according to Jesus (in Mark), will this Son of Man be *seen?* Scholars are not in agreement whether Jesus is referring to his resurrection or his parousia (final appearance). The "seating at God's right hand" most naturally refers to the vindication and exaltation of Jesus accomplished through the resurrection. Yet the claim that this will be *seen* by those rejecting Jesus and especially the correspondence in language between this text and 13:26 (*coming with the clouds*) suggests that the parousia is intended.

Probably Mark's view is that what the resurrection already accomplishes will be publicly manifested at the parousia. That is when they will *see* the one they are presently condemning to death (cf. Rev. 1:7). When they do, the Son of Man (= Jesus) will be the one with the authority.

Jesus is ready to be misjudged by this earthly court because he knows their decision will be reversed in a higher court (cf. Rom. 2:15-16). After Jesus is vindicated, those who accuse him now will go to trial. Indeed, even now while Jesus is on trial, he is passing judgment on his accusers.

That, at any rate, is what the reader is expected to understand. How much of this is understood by the Sanhedrin cannot be determined. But they understand enough to correctly conclude that Jesus' claim to authority and theirs are not compatible. If they want to preserve their authority, they need to be rid of Jesus. The irony is that precisely by rejecting his authority, they lose theirs. Jesus, by submitting to their misused authority now, is granted authority, glory and sovereign power hereafter.

King Jesus

Pilate's question to Jesus, *Are you the King of the Jews?* (15:2), comes as a surprise to the reader of this Gospel. Jesus has been called many things in this Gospel: *Christ, Son of God, Rabbi, Son of Man* (though only by Jesus himself), *Teacher, Lord, Son of David.* Yet never has he been called *King.* In the first 14 chapters of Mark, the word *king* is used only with reference to Herod (6:14, 22, 25-27) and those before whom Jesus' disciples will bear witness (13:9). In chapter 15, *King* often appears with reference to Jesus, but always in jest, never by anyone who truly believes Jesus is a king.

Most first-century Jews linked together the titles *Messiah* (anointed one) and *Son of David* (heir to David's throne). They expected God would send the "coming one" to be king on David's throne (10:47-48; 11:9-10, notes).

In the OT, the monarchy was a reluctant concession by God to Israel's clamoring "to be like other nations" (at least in one strand of tradition; cf. 1 Sam. 8:20). God permitted them to have a king, and even participated in installing the king (1 Sam. 10:17-24). But God also warned them of the dire economic, military, and spiritual consequences of their choice (1 Sam. 8:11-18). God made it clear that their choice represented a rejection, not of the previous leaders of the people (judges, prophets, and priests) but of God, the one true King (1 Sam. 8:7).

When Jesus enters Jerusalem on a colt (Mark 11:1-11), he presents himself as Israel's "coming king" (cf. Zech. 9:9-10), though he does so with actions, not words. He enters Jerusalem as the one commissioned by God to bring peace/shalom. He comes as the one delegated to bring God's kingly rule. The crowds shout,

> Blessed is the one who comes in the Name of the Lord!
> Blessed is the coming kingdom of our ancestor David. (11:9-10)

Their words are right; yet their understanding of the coming Davidic king may be more like what Jesus refused to affirm than like the one he would not deny (see 15:2, notes).

King of Peace

Israel's hope was that some day a great king would come, a Son of David, who would surpass even Solomon. This one would come as God's Anointed One. He would come with God's authority and would embody the kingly rule of God. He would bring the long-awaited peace/shalom that God's kingly rule promised (Isa. 52:7).

Throughout his ministry, Jesus has brought God's *shalom* to the hurting, the marginalized, the demonized, the foreigner. For this, the rulers and kings of this world rejected and condemned him. They mocked him as a king, and they crucified him with the title *The King of the Jews* above his head (15:26; cf. 1 Cor. 2:8).

At Jesus' baptism, the voice of God has addressed Jesus and said, *You are my Son* (Mark 1:11), alluding to a psalm that celebrates the enthronement of the king. The psalmist prophesied Jesus' fate:

> The kings of the earth set themselves,
>   and the rulers take counsel together
>   against the LORD and his anointed. . . .
> He who sits in the heavens laughs;
>   the LORD has them in derision.
> Then he will speak to them in his wrath,

and terrify them in his fury, saying,
"I have set my king on Zion, my holy hill." (Ps. 2:2-6)

Yes, the "kings" and "rulers" are laughing now, but God will have the last laugh. Yet one can hardly speak of laughter when the King of peace is being mocked by those who hold earthly power, when the Shalom-bringer suffers a violent death, when many of those who have been awaiting God's Messiah, now stand ripe for God's judgment as a result of rejecting him.

Nevertheless, God will use the terrible miscarriage of justice that is happening to establish that kingdom of peace for which Jesus has been sent to live and to die.

Early Christian preaching (cf. Acts 2:36) and hymnody (cf. Phil. 2:9-11) alike highlighted the way God vindicated Jesus, reversing both the injustice done to him and his own self-chosen emptying. Though injustice was done to him, Jesus establishes a reign of justice (Ps. 72:1; Isa. 11:4-5). Though "the kings of the earth" and "the rulers" (Ps. 2:2) plotted to take his life, he establishes God's reign, the gospel of peace (Isa. 52:7).

THE TEXT IN THE LIFE OF THE CHURCH
Who Killed Jesus?

Because of the long sorry history of so-called "Christian" anti-Semitism, it is necessary to point out that Mark contributes nothing to fostering it. There is not a hint in the entire book of Mark, least of all in this text, that Mark wants to lay blame on "Israel as a whole" for rejecting Jesus.

On the Jewish side, the blame is squarely laid on the shoulders of the religious leaders who have rejected Jesus (and not all of them did) [Israel and Israel's Leaders]. The role of the crowds is regularly an inhibiting role; they prevent the authorities from carrying out their plot against Jesus. Only the crowd in 15:8, a crowd that supports violent insurrection against Rome, shares with the religious leaders the blame for rejecting Jesus. Yet even here Mark insists that it is the religious leaders who exert influence on the crowd to call for Barabbas' release and Jesus' crucifixion (15:11).

Mark does not maximize the Jewish role and minimize the Gentile role in Jesus' crucifixion (as some think Matthew does). Jews and Gentiles who reject Jesus share the blame for doing so. Pilate is ultimately responsible for his decision about the crucifixion. The fact that Pilate considers Jesus innocent makes him *more* guilty rather than *less*. To crucify an innocent man by mistake is serious enough; to do so deliberately is worse. The bottom line is that the religious leaders, the crowd supporting violent resistance against Rome, and Pilate—these all play a crucial role in the final result.

Other Gospel writers are perhaps less clear on this than Mark. Those texts that seem to lay blame on "Israel as a whole" (e.g., Matt. 27:25) must, however, be read and applied with care. First of all, it is one thing if a Jew says, "We did it! Our religion, our leaders, and our people did it! We rejected Jesus." It is something quite different if Gentiles say ever after, "They did it!" (cf. Boomershine: 167).

Yet there is more to be said. According to Matthew, a crowd of people wanting Jesus killed (a crowd that perhaps *intends* to represent *all* Israel) claims a willingness to be held responsible. Does that mean that anyone other than those making the claim are *in fact* responsible? They claim their "children" will share their blame. Does that make their children *in fact* guilty? Matthew would agree that this crowd brings guilt on their own heads. I do not believe Matthew would agree that their descendants ever after share in that guilt.

Even the Mosaic law limited the consequences of sin to three or four generations, but promised God's blessings to go on to a thousand generations (Exod. 20:5-6). Let us never forget that the forgiveness available through Christ's death is God's offer to *all* who, through their sinful choices and actions, call down judgment on themselves.

> In front of Pilate's judgment seat, Israel brought down a curse upon itself. But God did not accept this self-cursing. God did not turn the cross into a sign of cursing, but into a sign of forgiveness and newness of life, indeed of his covenant renewal with Israel. (Lohfink, 1998:308, trans. TJG)

Moreover, those in Israel who *did* reject Jesus experienced God's judgment when the Romans destroyed Jerusalem and its temple (at least Mark makes the connection). In that tragedy, many innocent suffered along with the guilty (cf. Exod. 20:5-6). It is totally indefensible to claim that some kind of corporate responsibility for Jesus' crucifixion lies with ethnic Jews throughout history—except in one respect.

There is a sense in which corporate responsibility for Jesus' death lies with every human; each of us must confess to complicity in the evils of this world for which Jesus died. In that respect, the Jews are not automatically innocent any more than any other group or individual. The good news is that God, who *could* hold our sins against us, uses Christ's death as the means of offering us forgiveness.

Cross-Carrying and Jesus' Crucifixion

Jesus has been condemned to die. He now goes willingly the way of the cross, submitting to the tortures of his executioners, submitting ultimately to the will of his Father (14:36). Is this the path he has chosen?

Yes and No. Jesus has indeed chosen the path of obedience at all cost; when the cost turns out to be a violent and unjust death, he does not revise his commitment; he follows through on it. Yet Mark's Gospel does not present Jesus directly choosing death over life. The very thought of his imminent death fills him with horror. Mark describes him as *distressed and agitated* (14:33). Jesus says he is *deeply grieved* (14:34). D. Senior speaks of the paradox that Jesus maintains a willingness to die without willing his own death:

> In Mark's account, Jesus does not choose death; he is intent on his mission of preparing for the coming rule of God. But because that rule means transformation of the human heart and of the social structures the heart ultimately constructs, the messianic mission of Jesus ran headlong into opposition and rejection. Thus while death is not sought, it is clearly foreseen in the Gospel.

> This inner connection between the ministry of Jesus and his condemnation to death gives the cross an *active* meaning in Mark's Gospel. . . . The Passion is, in a very true sense, the *consequence* of Jesus' ministry. . . . The cross, therefore, is an *active* symbol because it is the ultimate expression of Jesus' commitment to give life to others. The cross is "taken up," not merely endured. Jesus is not a mere victim with death imposed. Jesus chose the way that lead to the cross. (140)

In the same way, followers of Jesus take up their crosses, not because they harbor a morbid death wish, nor because they are heroic sufferers. They "carry a cross" by choosing the way of God's kingdom, by choosing to live their lives for God and for others, come what may. If an unjust death or even an unjust life is a consequence, they say with Jesus, *Not what I want, but what you want* (14:36) *[The Meaning of Cross-Carrying]*.

Mark 15:16-47

The Coronation of the King (the Crucifixion)

PREVIEW
Jesus will now be mocked and killed. The reader is torn between delight in an inherently ironic text and horror at what it reports. Jesus is *acclaimed* as King and *rejected* as King in almost every event and word.

* Roman soldiers bow down to Israel's King, honoring him with royal robes and pledging their loyalty. *Hail! King of the Jews!* is their ironic cry (15:16-20).
* Pilate announces that Israel is now ruled by King Jesus. Jesus has taken his throne; let all the world know! *The King of the Jews!* is his ironic label for the crucified Messiah (15:26).
* Two insurrectionists are privileged to take their places, one at Jesus' right and one at his left in his glory! For this honor, the disciples of Jesus have competed (10:37), but in the decisive moment, they are not there to claim their prize (15:27).
* Those who pass by proclaim the gospel: Jesus has lived to save others; now he dies to do the same. To accomplish his mission, he must remain on the cross: *He cannot save himself.* They mock, but they speak truth (15:31).

Jesus suffers deeply, but Mark highlights the mockery more than the physical pain. No one comes to Jesus' aid—not the disciples, who have abandoned him in the crisis; not Elijah, "the patron saint of hopeless causes"; not God, to whom Jesus cries in despair. Jesus' enemies have their way. God has determined that they shall "succeed." Jesus' submission to their schemes has made it possible. After Jesus' enemies "succeed," it is time for the tables to begin to turn.

We learn that some women are present to witness the crucifixion. They are with Jesus to the end, as they have been with him from the beginning. From out of nowhere comes an accomplice to arrange the burial. The women become official witnesses that Jesus "suffered under Pontius Pilate, was crucified, died, and buried" (Apostles' Creed). But it is premature to construct a Christian creed on the basis of Mark 15. Without Mark 16, there is not yet good news. Good Friday and Easter Sunday need each other. Good Friday would be Horror Friday if God did not act decisively to vindicate the rejected King. Easter Sunday would be just a myth of an empty tomb if it were not preceded by the unimaginable torment of Friday. Mark's Gospel indeed proclaims a resurrection, but it will be the resurrection of Jesus, *who was crucified*. That terrible and wonderful story Mark now tells.

OUTLINE
The Soldiers Mock Jesus, 15:16-20

The Crucifixion, 15:21-28
15:21	Simon Carries the Cross
15:22-25	The Crucifixion Itself
15:26	The King of the Jews
15:27	Fellow Criminals

Mockers Mouth the Gospel, 15:29-32
15:29-30	Mockery by Those Passing By
15:31-32a	Mockery by the Chief Priests and Scribes
15:32b	Mockery by the Criminals

The Suffering of Jesus, 15:33-36
15:33	The Darkness
15:34	The Cry of Despair
15:35-36	Let Us See Whether Elijah Will Come

Jesus' Death and Its Meaning, 15:37-39
15:37	Jesus' Death
15:38	The Torn Temple Curtain
15:39	This Man Is God's Son

The Faithful Discipleship of the Women, 15:40-41

The Burial of Jesus, 15:42-47

EXPLANATORY NOTES
The Soldiers Mock Jesus 15:16-20

The Jewish and Roman trials are over; their outcomes are the same. An innocent man is condemned to death on trumped-up charges. Truth and justice are sacrificed on the altars of envy, power, and popularity.

Jesus has already been sentenced and flogged and is now in the hands of his executioners (15:15). The soldiers know what they have to do. This disconcertingly silent sufferer is not the first Jewish nationalist they must execute. They will make of him, as they always do, a public spectacle. He will carry his cross through the streets and hang on it in torment. It will serve as a deterrent to other would-be rebels against Rome. Rome has exposed the pretensions of others claiming to be Israel's kings. Now they will do it to Jesus.

Before the hard work, a little amusement. Jesus is moved indoors, and the rest of the troops are summoned (there may have been as many as 600 soldiers). The coronation of a king is not a private affair. People must be present to watch and cheer and do homage.

A *purple* robe replaces Jesus' clothing. It may well be a soldier's robe, a mocking substitute for royal garments. A *crown* of *thorns* is ceremoniously placed on his head. If the thorns point inward, it is part of the torture. If they point outward, the crown may be designed to imitate the so-called radiant crown honoring the Roman sun-god. We are not told.

Hail! King of the Jews! they shout out in laughter, or perhaps solemnly utter with pretend "fear" and "trembling." Instead of handing him a scepter, they hit him with a reed. Instead of kissing his feet, they spit in his face. Then they kneel in reverence before this foreign King, who is destined to be greater than the emperor of Rome.

They have been *mocking him*, Mark informs us in grand understatement, when it is all over.

> It is theologically and ironically fitting that the Messiah should be rejected in just this way by the ranking officials of Judaism, should be subjected to just this sort of mock coronation, should die in just this fashion at the hands of Roman soldiers, with real brigands on either side. As a scenario it is the perfect burlesque of the truth it caricatures. (Camery-Hoggatt: 175)

The soldiers must get back to work. Jesus loses his kingly robe and is reclothed for the procession to Golgatha. He follows his executioners out into the street. They represent the imperial power. He takes up his cross and follows them (cf. 8:34 and following TBC) *[The Meaning of Cross-Carrying]*.

The Crucifixion 15:21-28

15:21 Simon Carries the Cross

Out in the street, a man named Simon is pulled over by the soldiers. Perhaps his children are named here because they are known to the Markan community. Jesus' cross is transferred to Simon's shoulder. This is Rome exercising its self-proclaimed right to compel anyone to enter into the service of the empire, even if only temporarily. At the level of the story line, it is just physical help with a heavy load, perhaps needed because Jesus' earlier flogging has taken its toll on his strength (15:15). At the level of Mark's discourse, much more is going on.

Jesus has literally carried his cross only from Pilate's headquarters into the Jerusalem streets. Symbolically, he has been carrying it all the way from Caesarea Philippi. Jesus has been teaching the way of cross-carrying ever since he introduced the metaphor (8:34). The cross symbolizes discipleship as submission to God's rule. Jesus' own cross becomes the symbol of his own submission to God's demands, even unto death. To the Roman soldiers, Simon is no more and no less than an unwilling and temporary slave conscripted by Rome. To Mark's readers, Simon symbolizes followers of Jesus, willing to take up the cross and follow him all the way to the place of execution *[The Meaning of Cross-Carrying]*.

15:22-25 The Crucifixion Itself

The procession makes its way to Golgatha. That is where the criminals will be attached to the cross they have carried and then fastened to the poles mounted at the top of the hill for use with other executions, too. Golgatha means *skull*, so-named because of its bald shape, but no doubt also because of its gruesome associations with death.

The soldiers offer Jesus wine and a painkilling drug. He refuses, signaling his willingness to drink God's cup to the dregs. Jesus will not artificially dull the pain if God has willed his suffering. His refusal is also consistent with his forward-looking vow. He will not again drink the fruit of the vine until he can do so as an act of celebration in God's kingdom (14:25).

The crucifixion itself is merely reported (v. 24a). At this point, Mark's narrative provides no description, betrays no emotion, declares no explicit theological truths. These emerge in the narrative that follows. Everything is reported factually, but Mark loads it with symbols, irony, and double messages. The surface is hard and horrible; the subsurface streams of meaning run deep.

Victims of crucifixion usually would hang naked and exposed; but in Judea, in deference to Jewish scruples, a loincloth was often used. Mark reports that the soldiers cast lots for the clothes, an allusion to Psalm 22:18 (TBC, below).

Mark has used the four watches of the Roman night as a framework for teaching about faithful discipleship (cf. 13:35; 15:1, notes). Now we observe a continuation of this three-hour time blocking through the *day* of the crucifixion:

• The death sentence, the flogging, the mock coronation, and the procession to Golgatha take place from 6:00-9:00 a.m. (v. 25).

• The crucifixion and the mockery of Jesus on the cross take place from 9:00 a.m. till noon (v. 33).

• Darkness covers the land from noon through 3:00 p.m. (v. 33).

• His death and burial take place as Sabbath nears (3:00-6:00 p.m.).

The night watches were loaded with symbolic meaning; the references to the daylight hours also influence the narrative. The daytime reports create the impression of a prolonged and therefore all the more horrible suffering. They present time itself moving inexorably toward its God-ordained conclusion.

15:26 The King of the Jews

Jesus' "crime" is that he is Israel's Messiah, the Anointed One. He is *King of the Jews*. His entire mission is to proclaim and to bring God's reign. Now his "crime" is announced to all the world through the inscription hung over his head. Mark thereby makes one of his most profound theological statements: *The King of the Jews,* announces the inscription. "That title has at last found its authentic place of proclamation—fastened on the cross of Jesus" (Senior: 118).

Christ/Messiah and *cross* did not fit together for Peter (8:32), nor for the other disciples, whose fear grew as Jesus' teaching became clearer (10:32-34). When the combination of *Messiah* and *cross* became inevitable, the disciples abandoned the Messiah rather than embracing the cross. King and cross is a combination that Israel's leaders rejected and Roman soldiers mocked. "Christ crucified [is] a stumbling block to Jews and foolishness to Gentiles," Paul said (1 Cor. 1:23). Mark agrees. Jesus hangs in shame, the title of honor written over him. Mark is preaching again.

15:27 Fellow Criminals

Two disciples begged for honored positions at Jesus' left and right in the glory to come (10:37). Jesus is now passing through suffering on the way to that glory. Where are the disciples who have vowed they could drink his cup and be baptized with his baptism (10:38-39)? How will they share the glory beyond the cross if they reject the only way to get to it? Their place is symbolically taken by two others. These are not friends willing to follow Jesus to death (14:31). They are people who deserve the fate he shares with them. They are suffering the consequences of their rebellion against Rome; Jesus suffers the consequences of all human rebellion against God.

There is no verse 28. Some early Christian scribe took Luke's reference (22:37) to Isaiah 53:12 and included it in Mark's text as well: "He was counted among the lawless." It is not in the best manuscripts and has been rightly omitted from NRSV.

Mockers Mouth the Gospel 15:29-32

Three separate groups of people mock Jesus as he hangs between the criminals.

15:29-30 Mockery by Those Passing By

Crucifixions were staged in plain sight, to deter lawbreakers. Those passing by on the road are the first to mock Jesus. Mark says they blaspheme Jesus (*blasphēmeō*, NRSV: *deride*). In Greek, *blaspheme* can be used in the technical sense of speaking evil of God or in the nontechnical sense of verbal abuse. Mark may well expect his readers to ponder this word. The mockers certainly are verbally abusing Jesus; but since Jesus has claimed divinity as God's Son, even calling himself I AM (cf. 14:62-64, notes), the mockers are also speaking evil of God.

The mockers shake their heads, a gesture of contempt explicitly noted as an aspect of mockery in the OT (Ps. 22:7; Lam. 2:15). They are making fun of the one who has (purportedly) claimed he would destroy their temple and rebuild it again. Anyone who can do that can surely come down from the cross and thus save himself (TBC, below)!

They assume that staying on the cross, he will die; coming down, he will be saved. That is good reasoning if people set their minds on *human things*. Those who think *divine things* part ways with such human logic (8:33). They say with Jesus, *Those who want to save their life will lose it, and those who lose their life for my sake, and for the sake of the gospel, will save it* (8:35). Jesus could come down from the cross, but he would thereby lose his life. By staying on the cross, by submitting to his Father's will, he saves it.

15:31-32a Mockery by the Chief Priests and Scribes

Those who have manipulated justice to rid themselves of Jesus, show up to take delight in their accomplishment. They cannot resist joining the mockery, reminding each other, *He saved others: he cannot save himself*. No doubt they truly believe both parts of that statement. Jesus truly had *saved* people (*save* can mean "heal, rescue, preserve," and so on); that is what has made him famous. There he hangs now, helpless, unable to do anything for himself. Obviously he cannot come down, or else he would. *He saved others: he cannot save himself*. What a paradox!

Perhaps the greatest paradox is that Mark agrees with the mockers! They mean their words in jest, believing them true because they do *not* know what Jesus can truly do! Mark's interpretation of their words is much more profound; he believes them true because he *does* know what Jesus can do!

Indeed, Jesus has saved others. Mark's entire Gospel is about the saving work of Jesus. He has healed and rescued; he has forgiven sins, given new life, restored hope, and rebuilt lives; he has taken hopeless victims and sent them home as missionaries proclaiming God's mercy. He has saved others in much more profound ways than the religious leaders will ever acknowledge. No, he cannot save himself, not if he is to stay on the road of obedience. God has willed for him to drink this cup, to be baptized with this baptism (10:39), and Jesus has chosen to submit to his Father (14:36). He cannot come down! Ultimately, he can save others only *because* he does not save himself. If he would save himself by fleeing God's plan, there could be no salvation for others!

The mockers may have mouthed the gospel message. They have not believed it, understood it, or accepted the one who fulfills it. Yet their mocking words become the ironic paradox that interprets the meaning of Jesus' death for those with eyes to see and ears to hear.

Passersby have mocked Jesus for his temple claims: Temple-builders can surely come down from a cross! Now the religious leaders mock Jesus for his messianic claims: *Come down*, King of Israel, so that we may *see and believe!* The two key issues at Jesus' trial are hurled at Jesus on the cross. If Jesus really were Messiah and king, why not prove it? His enemies would gladly believe, if only there were some proof! This is not the first time Jesus refuses to give them the objective proofs they want (cf. 8:11-13).

They want a king and a kingdom that are glorious, self-evident, undeniably visible. Jesus proclaims a secret kingdom, one that has to be believed to be seen. For them, a Messiah on the cross cannot possibly be believed. For Mark, *only* a Messiah on the cross can be believed. And those who *believe* will also *see!*

15:32b Mockery by the Criminals

Mark's oft-recurring pattern of three is fulfilled with the report that the criminals crucified with Jesus also mocked him—the third mockery. The content of their mockery is not given. Even those physically closest to him abandon him in death. His desolation is complete.

The Suffering of Jesus 15:33-36

15:33 The Darkness

The darkness at noon is a symbol of God's judgment (Amos 8:9) and of the fulfillment of God's eschatological promises (Mark 13:24; TBC, below). For Mark, the darkness is not a portent that invokes fear or faith. It is a commentary on the meaning of Jesus' death. It speaks of God's judgment on all humanity, falling now on Jesus; and it speaks of the judgment yet to fall on those who have rejected him.

15:34 The Cry of Despair

Mark says nothing about the three hours between noon and 3:00 p.m. Presumably, silence reigns with the darkness. At 3:00 p.m. the silence is pierced and the darkness lifted. With a loud cry, Jesus quotes Psalm 22:1. Mark first records Jesus' words in Aramaic, then translates them for his reader: *My God, My God, why have you forsaken me?* It is necessary to quote Aramaic to make sense of the crowd's misunderstanding. The words *my God* sound somewhat like *Elijah* in Aramaic (*elōi;* even more so in Heb.: *'eli*).

The irony is that the bystanders misunderstand *the Aramaic!* That means that no one but the *reader* understands Jesus' final words (his first since leaving Pilate's judgment hall). Fowler claims that in Mark's account the only genuine witness to the crucifixion of Jesus is the *reader* (1991:109). We see, we hear, we try to understand.

It is clear that Jesus feels totally abandoned, even by God. For Mark, this is the ultimate expression of losing one's life for the sake of the gospel (8:35). It is full and complete identification with humanity, a final revelation of the depths of human sin, and undeniable evidence that the ways of God are beyond understanding. Yet Mark has given enough allusions to the other half of the story; the reader cannot attribute total despair to the dying Jesus. Jesus himself is confident of a coming resurrection; it will be God's answer to this cry of despair. Jesus has abandoned himself to the will of God; God will do something *amazing in our eyes* (12:11; on the use of Ps. 22, see TLC, below).

15:35-36 Let Us See Whether Elijah Will Come

Those around Jesus misunderstand his cry and imagine he is calling for Elijah's help. Elijah had helped others in distress and was translated to heaven without dying (2 Kings 2:11). Many believed he was still available and ready to help in extreme cases. If Jesus is unable to come down (as their mockery has claimed), perhaps Elijah will rescue him. Their mocking continues.

For Mark, there is more to this. Elijah has already come. He came not to rescue Jesus from the cross, but to prepare *the way* that leads to it (9:11-13; 1:2, 14). This makes no sense to those who (like the disciples, 8:32-33) cannot accept a suffering forerunner or a suffering Messiah. It also does not make sense to those who now see a suffering Messiah but do not recognize him.

It is not clear how the offer of sour wine here links to the discussion about Elijah. Perhaps someone thinks that if Elijah will not rescue Jesus, a thirst-quencher will at least be a small comfort. Or are they trying to prolong the agony? One more possibility is that this is yet another act of mockery. The psalmist lamented,

Insults have broken my heart,
  so that I am in despair.
I looked for pity, but there was none;
  and for comforters, but I found none.
They gave me poison for food,
  and for my thirst they gave me vinegar to drink. (Ps. 69:20-21)

The sour wine may well have been that *vinegar* (15:36, NIV). Jesus is being mocked in the comments about Elijah and is now being insulted through the offer of wine vinegar. Mark does not tell us whether Jesus takes the vinegar. What is clear is that God does not remove the cup of suffering from Jesus (14:36). The end has come.

Jesus' Death and Its Meaning 15:37-39

15:37 Jesus' Death

In Luke, Jesus commits himself obediently into the hands of God and breathes his last (Luke 23:46). In John, Jesus cries out triumphantly, "It is finished," then bows his head and dies (John 19:30; cf. Hooker, 1991:377). In Mark (as in Matthew), by contrast, Jesus dies with a loud inarticulate cry on his lips. His victory over death is important to Mark. So also is his finished salvation work. But in Mark these are not proclaimed from the lips of the dying Jesus. They have been prophesied beforehand and will be reported later. The portrait Mark gives of Jesus' death is focused directly on the starkness of the suffering and on the agony of death.

> Readers of Mark's story become spectators of the event—hostile, indifferent, or irresistibly drawn into the dramatic action. Some find it utter foolishness to make so much fuss over the death of one man when there is so much suffering in the world. Others are awed by the power of God and the wisdom of God. (1 Cor 1:24; Hare: 214)

15:38 The Torn Temple Curtain

Mark alludes to the meaning of Jesus' death in the two events he reports immediately after the announcement that he has died. The temple curtain is torn from top to bottom (v. 38); the centurion at the cross confesses that Jesus is *God's Son* (v. 39). As so often, Mark "explains" the meaning of something, but leaves a good bit of work to the interpreter. We have to explain the explanation.

Does the *curtain* (KJV: *veil*) somehow stand for the whole temple and/or its functions? Is it torn as a sign of something being destroyed or something being revealed? Is the main point that a barrier is being removed? If so, is it to let something in or out? How is the tearing of the curtain linked to Jesus' death cry and expiration? How is it linked to the centurion's confession? With all these unanswered questions, there is room for considerable speculation.

I have encountered 35 proposals for interpreting the torn temple veil (T. Geddert, 1989:141-3). Among them, at least these five can be well-defended by the content and/or the context of Mark 15:38:

1. The *veil* over Jesus' divine sonship is removed (for those with eyes to see, Jesus' death reveals that he is truly God's Son; cf. v. 39).

2. Jesus' death renders obsolete a whole range of ceremonial and sacrificial exercises centered in the temple (cf. 14:23-24).

3. The coming destruction of the temple, now inevitable because

Jesus has been rejected, is already symbolically beginning (cf. 13:2).

4. Through death, Jesus enters into God's presence, having accomplished the sacrifice that atones for all human sin (he fulfills the meaning of the Day of Atonement; cf. 14:24; Heb. 9:1-15).

5. Through Jesus' death, Gentiles have access into the very presence of God (cf. v. 39).

All of these and others can also be found in NT texts outside of Mark's Gospel.

15:39 This Man Is God's Son

We cannot assume that the Roman centurion who has crucified Jesus knowingly makes a full Christian confession. In Greek (with no definite article), it is not even clear whether he claims Jesus is "Son of God" or "a son of a god." Moreover, he may be speaking ironically, just as the Jewish leaders and Roman soldiers have done, who have called Jesus *the Messiah, the King of Israel"* (vv. 18, 32; Fowler, 1991:208).

For Mark, however, a profound proclamation is here being made. Just as *King of the Jews* finds its proper place mounted over the cross (v. 26), so the confession that Jesus is *God's Son* is appropriately linked to his death. Mark has taken his two key titles for Jesus (*Christ* and *Son of God,* as in 1:1) and wrapped them around the last half of the Gospel, where the road to the cross is announced, taught, and traveled. The pattern looks like this *[Chiasm and Intercalation]*:

> A • "You are the Christ" (8:29).
> > B • The Way of the Cross: "He began to teach them that the Son of Man must undergo great suffering" (8:31). "Jesus gave a loud cry and breathed his last" (15:37).
> A' • "This man was God's Son" (15:39)

The centurion is responding to the death of Jesus, not to the tearing of the temple curtain. From his location, facing Jesus (v. 39), he has no way of knowing about an event in the temple. The centurion is *not* responding to some great portent, persuading him with objective proofs. He is responding as one who discerns truth in the face of the crucified Jesus.

Mark's text says the centurion is responding to something he *sees* in Jesus' death. Some manuscripts also refer to him *hearing* something: *When the centurion . . . heard his cry and saw . . .* (NIV). If this is what Mark originally wrote, it is even clearer that Mark alludes to one of his recurring themes. It is necessary to have *seeing eyes* and

hearing ears to discern the secret of God's kingdom (cf. 4:11-12)
[Messianic Secret].

Some hear Jesus' cry and think he is calling Elijah. Some see his
suffering and think it proves him a fake. If we take up our positions
facing the crucified Messiah, says Mark, then the discerning eye and
the discerning ear will lead us also to affirm: *This was God's Son.*

If verse 39 refers directly to verse 37, why does verse 38 intervene? Though the centurion does not see the tearing of the temple
curtain, its *symbolic meaning* is what makes his confession possible
[Chiasm and Intercalation]. Virtually all of the suggested interpretations of verse 38 contribute to our understanding of verse 39. The
centurion's confession symbolizes the faith and salvation now available through Jesus' death.

In death, Jesus is revealed as God's Son, the one who accomplishes the final sacrifice. As a result, anyone can come to God, even
Gentiles. They may never have participated in a Jewish ritual or set
foot in the courts of the temple. Jesus' death makes that unimportant.
The temple is doomed anyway. This Jesus will become the new temple in which all may find God.

The Faithful Discipleship of the Women 15:40-41

Verse 40 comes as a total surprise. A number of women have followed Jesus all the way to the cross. We must assume they were not
at the Passover meal or in Gethsemane, for Jesus predicted the failure of all who were (14:27), and Mark reports that his prophecy was
fulfilled (14:50). But the women are there at the cross.

Who are the women who observe the mockery, the suffering, the
death, and the centurion's confession? Mark gives us the names and
a few details about three of them. Other texts provide a few more
details (or possible connections). Non-Markan sources tell us that
Jesus has expelled demons from *Mary Magdalene* (Luke 8:2; Mark's
longer ending, 16:9). Nonbiblical sources claim she has been a har-
lot. *Mary the mother of James and Joses* might be Mary the mother of Jesus (cf. Mark 6:3). If she is, why is she not identified that way?
Perhaps it is because her identity as Jesus' physical mother is of less
significance to Mark than her faithful discipleship as one of many
brothers, sisters, and mothers in Jesus' new family (15:41; 3:35,
notes). Salome may be the mother of James and John (cf. Matt.
27:56).

These women play two important roles. First, *they are simply
there.* They may not do or say anything, but being there makes them

at least a symbol of following all the way to the cross. Second, *they witness what has happened*. Three times in a short space, we are alerted to what these women (or two of them; cf. 15:47) see. They see Jesus' death (15:40). They see where Jesus is laid (15:47). Finally, they see the open and empty tomb and the divine messenger of the resurrection (16:4-6).

Women were not valued as witnesses in a first-century Jewish context (M. Evans: 35). But Mark considers the testimony of two women to be valid. Otherwise, he would not portray them as witnesses of Jesus' death, his burial, and his resurrection.

Verse 41 comes as another surprise. Mark's narrative, up to this point, led us to suppose that Jesus walked the road from Caesarea Philippi to Jerusalem *in the company of twelve men*. Now we learn that there are many women in the group as well, including these three. Moreover, a description of their relationship to Jesus stands as a stark contrast to the Twelve. The women have followed him in Galilee; they have served him; they have walked the discipleship road with him; they have accompanied him all the way to the cross. Why do we learn of their existence only now, when the journey is over?

Mark has been teaching about discipleship. His narrative strategy has been to contrast faithful Jesus with the unfaithful Twelve. They serve as foils for Jesus. The Twelve ask for inappropriate favors; they fight, misunderstand Jesus' teaching, and in general have trouble keeping in step with their leader. In the contrast between Jesus and his chosen Twelve, the reader is learning about the ways of God (8:33). Mark's strategy would be less effective if he were constantly pointing out the times they do *not* fail, and reminding readers of those more faithful.

There is another reason Mark treats the unfaithful Twelve as one group and now treats the faithful women as another group. In his resurrection report (16:7-8), Mark will use these two groups to develop the themes of faithfulness and unfaithfulness, failure and renewal. The men who have been following Jesus have failed in many ways. Before Mark's narrative closes, these women, who have likewise been following, will fail as well.

The two groups represent two different kinds of failure. Mark's resurrection message is that there is forgiveness and renewal for both kinds, for a failure to follow on the road to the cross, and for a failure to proclaim the resurrection. There is an offer of renewal for those who fail before Jesus' death; the same offer applies for those who do so after his resurrection (see 16:7-8, notes).

The Burial of Jesus 15:42-47

This section closes with a detailed report of Jesus' burial. As evening
approaches, a man named *Joseph* facilitates the burial of Jesus. He
is a prominent council member, possibly of the Sanhedrin. He is a
pious man; Mark comments that he is *waiting expectantly for the
kingdom of God.* Mark does not suggest that he is a secret believer.

Why does he get involved? Perhaps it is simply an act of piety.
The Jews placed high value on such acts. A body hanging overnight,
especially over the Sabbath, and even more so at Passover time,
would be viewed as a desecration of the land. Joseph *went boldly* to
obtain Pilate's permission for the burial, a courageous act if he feared
the repercussions of Pilate viewing him as a sympathizer.

Mark says Pilate carefully verified Jesus' death with the centurion,
thus providing another proof that Jesus has truly died. Mark narrates
the burial in detail, with special emphasis on the rock rolled against
the door of the tomb. Finally, Mark refers to two followers of Jesus
who can function as official witnesses. Mary Magdalene and Mary see
his death, and now they see the location of the grave. It remains for
them to see what happens on Sunday morning.

THE TEXT IN BIBLICAL CONTEXT

OT Allusions in Mark's Crucifixion Narrative

As Jesus hangs on the cross, he quotes Psalm 22:1: "My God, my
God, why have you forsaken me?" (15:34). This is the only OT quotation in Mark's narrative of Jesus' crucifixion and death, and it is
often called Jesus' "cry of despair." But did Jesus really die in despair?

There are many other allusions to OT texts and themes. Some of
them add important nuances to Mark's meaning, and others help us
determine what to make of the one clear quotation.

The text alludes to Psalm 22 more than once before Jesus quotes
it directly in his cry (15:34). In 15:24, the soldiers gamble for Jesus
clothes, an allusion to Psalm 22:18: "They divide my clothes among
themselves, and for my clothing they cast lots." In 15:29, the shaking heads of the mocking passersby remind us of Psalm 22:7: "All
who see me mock at me; they make mouths at me, they shake their
heads." There are more subtle allusions as well.

What this means is that more of Psalm 22 is in Mark's mind than
just the first verse quoted in Mark 15:34. F. Matera (1982:40) has
compiled the following parallels between Psalm 22 and Mark 15:

Mark 15	**Psalm 22**
garments, v. 24	garments, v. 18
two thieves bracket Jesus, 27	bulls, lions, dogs encircle me, 12-13, 16
wag their heads, 29	wag their heads, 7
cannot save himself, 31	let God save him, 8
reviled, 32	scorned, 6
great cry, 34	great cry, 1
centurion's cry; universal salvation, 39	universal salvation, 27-31

These numerous parallels lend considerable credibility to the idea that Mark is picturing Jesus as identifying with all of Psalm 22, and not just with the words he directly quotes. The Psalm as a whole is not an unmitigated expression of despair (laments never are); it speaks also of trust, of praise, of God's faithfulness, sovereignty, and ultimate victory. Jesus dies with words of despair on his lips, but the cross does not put an end to hope (cf. N. T. Wright).

At present, Jesus' experience corresponds to the first verse of the Psalm: *My God, My God, why have you forsaken me?* But Jesus has not given up his hope in God any more than the psalmist, who says:

"Commit your cause to the LORD. . . .
 let him rescue the one in whom he delights!" (Ps. 22:8)
He did not hide his face from me,
 but heard when I cried to him. (v. 24b)
For dominion belongs to the LORD. (v. 28a)
I shall live for him. (v. 29c)

Mockers who shake their heads remind us also of Lamentations 2:15: "All who pass along the way . . . wag their heads." The reference in Lamentations is to mockers deriding those who have lost their beloved city Jerusalem and its glorious temple. How ironic that the mockers in Mark 15:29 are deriding Jesus for his prediction of another temple's destruction! Little do they know that before three days have passed, the "temple" they are presently mocking will be raised up again. Little do they know that, by the time this generation passes (cf. 13:30), their own beloved temple will be a heap of rubble (13:2). Then it will be *their* turn to endure *others'* mocking.

Amos 8 also contributes to Mark's understanding of Jesus' passion. Darkness covers the land for three hours while Jesus hangs on the cross (Mark 15:33), symbolizing judgment. The prophet Amos prophesied a day when God's hand of judgment would fall: "On that day, . . . I will make the sun go down at noon, and darken the earth in broad daylight" (Amos 8:9). The expression "that day" is often a loaded term in the OT, referring not to some unspecified future day, but to a particular momentous Day, the great and terrible Day of the Lord, the Day of the Lord's final judgment and salvation.

Mark's reference to the darkness at noon links the day of crucifixion to the great Day of the Son of Man's return, when *the sun will be darkened, and the moon will not give its light* (13:24). By alluding to Amos 8:9, both in connection with Jesus' death (15:33) and in connection with the Son of Man's return (13:24), Mark links these events together. Someday Jesus will emerge as the final victor and will come in salvation and judgment (13:26; 14:62).

Mark provides another fascinating connection to Amos 8: "On that day, . . . I will turn your feasts into mourning" (8:9a-10a). Mark alludes to this text when quoting Jesus' words about the removal of the bridegroom: *They will fast on that day* (2:20). The day when God's judgment falls is a day of darkness, of mourning, of fasting. But it is also a day of eschatological fulfillment. So Mark picks up the expression *That Day* and uses it also for the day of the Son of Man's return. No one knows about *That Day* (cf. 13:32); but those with eyes to see are learning about it as they pierce the darkness surrounding Jesus' death.

Jesus and Pacifism

The English word *pacifism* is derived from the Latin word meaning "to make peace." The Christ hymn of Colossians 1:15-20 declares that in Christ, God was "*making peace* through the blood of his cross" (Col. 1:20). God is thus pacifist in the sense of being the ultimate peacemaker, for "while we were enemies, we were reconciled to God through the death of his Son" (Rom. 5:10).

The NT teaches two paradoxical truths in relation to Christ's pacifism at the cross. On one hand, it was a unique act, accomplished on our behalf, "for our sins" (1 Cor. 15:3). On the other hand, it was an exemplary act, modeling for believers the stance they too are expected to take in response to an aggressive enemy (Matt. 5:39; Rom. 12:17).

Peter combines both perspectives when he counsels believers how to respond to situations of aggression against themselves:

> If you endure when you do right and suffer for it, you have God's approval. For to this you have been called, because Christ also suffered for you, leaving you an example, so that you should follow in his steps. . . . When he was abused, he did not return abuse; when he suffered, he did not threaten; but he entrusted himself to the one who judges justly. He himself bore our sins. . . . (1 Pet. 2:21, 23-24)

Christ's atoning sacrifice is *in our place;* he did for us what we could not do for ourselves. Yet his willingness to suffer unjustly at the hand of the aggressor is *our model;* what he did, we are called to do as well (cf. E. Waltner: 91-5, 107-9).

Mark, along with other NT writers, portrays Jesus as the willing sufferer, the Suffering Servant (Isa. 52:13—53:12). This Servant is silent when accused, courageously faces unjust persecution, and submits to an unjust death, though he could have fled or fought.

R. Beck describes Mark and his intentions:

> The conflict is a violent one, ending in a legally disguised murder. Meanwhile the protagonist is an acclaimed nonviolent hero. . . . Without withdrawing his resistance, the protagonist, Jesus, refuses to adopt the violent methods of his opponents. (17-18)

D. Senior comments, "The true identity of Jesus as God's Son is manifested not in acts of marvelous power but in an event seemingly devoid of any power, his passion and death" (144). Paul counts this aspect of Christ's crucifixion as God's paradoxical wise foolishness and strong weakness (1 Cor. 1:25).

Those who follow in Christ's footsteps, willingly suffering wrong rather than overpowering the persecutors, will be mocked and abused along with Christ. But through their peacemaking, they will join with Christ, who modeled cross-bearing and required it of those who would follow him. "The fundamental issue of the gospel, therefore, is the right use of power, the same issue that gnaws at our world today" (Senior: 150).

THE TEXT IN THE LIFE OF THE CHURCH
Jesus and His Sacrificial Death

Robert Hamerton-Kelly sets in contrast what he calls the "circle of violence" and the "spiral of grace" (127). Violence begets violence, but grace has the power to break the cycle and lift us out of its jaws of death.

From a human perspective, Christ's death could almost be interpreted within the "circle of violence." If it stands out among other undeserved deaths, it does so because the victim was unusually innocent and his suffering unusually great. Sadly, there have been times when those claiming to represent Christ have acted violently in his name, even retaliating centuries later against the descendants of those who committed their crimes against Jesus. We have not always allowed ourselves to be lifted out of the circle of violence into the spiral of grace.

From a divine perspective, Christ's death is anything but a perpetuation of the cycle of scapegoating and violence. Indeed, Christ's death was designed to break the vicious circle, to end sacrificial deaths, to create a community ready to suffer injustice, rather than perpetuating violence against anyone.

Christ's death is neither a senseless death, nor just one more substitutionary sacrifice. It is presented in Scripture as the only death that ultimately accomplishes that toward which all the other sacrificial deaths merely pointed. In Jesus' death, God's grace is doubly manifest; God is the one who both *provides* the final sacrifice and who *accepts* it as an atoning sacrifice for sin.

Exactly how did the death of Jesus provide forgiveness of human sin and effect reconciliation with God? That question has challenged the best theological minds for two thousand years. Four classical theories of the atonement have been formulated and defended:

1. *The Dramatic Theory.* Jesus' death and resurrection together provide a final victory over all the powers that rally themselves against humans, whether these be the powers of law, of sin, of death, or of the devil. All are defeated through Christ's resurrection victory, since by means of it Jesus is exalted as Lord over all the powers that conspired to bring about his death (cf. Col. 2:15). Gustaf Aulén (and according to him, Martin Luther) are classical spokespersons for this view.

2. *The Satisfaction Theory.* God's righteous anger against sinners needed to be appeased. That anger could be "propitiated" only if an innocent victim paid the price on behalf of the guilty. Christ did this on our behalf; as a result, God holds our sin against us no longer (cf. Rom. 5:6-11). Anselm has traditionally been associated with this view.

3. *The Ransom Theory.* The "price for sin" was not ultimately paid to God, but to God's enemy, Satan. Through human sin, humans were delivered over to the dominion of Satan; it took Christ's death to buy back our freedom. This theory is often combined with the view that God tricked the devil, offering Jesus in place of the sinners, then snatching Jesus away again through the resurrection. The devil has lost his prey and has nothing in return! (cf. Col. 1:13-14). Many of the early Greek Fathers held this view.

4. *The Moral Influence Theory.* The cross motivates people to change their lives. It shows how far God was willing to go to become a sacrifice on our behalf (cf. 1 John 4:10-11), and thus gives us a model and an incentive to express love more deeply. Abelard and later many humanists defended this view.

The second view has dominated much of Western theologizing; yet there have always been representatives of the other views. The first theory often dominates in cultural contexts where animism and demonism have had a strong influence. The fourth often dominates where orthodox faith is set aside for a more humanist version. Yet it is clear from the NT that none of the four can be fully set aside without losing part of the richness of the varied NT portraits.

In addition to the four classical views, a fifth was introduced in the twentieth century. In a complicated but provocative re-fashioning of the language of atonement, René Girard has argued that Jesus came to put an end to the vicious cycle of vengeance and scapegoating. In primitive religions (for Girard, including OT religion), these deep-seated tendencies in human relationships are ceremonially reenacted through the vicarious deaths of sacrificial animals (and of humans, in some religions). This institutionalized scapegoating perpetuates violence. Jesus, however, by pursuing nonviolence and by dying as a surrogate victim, becomes the ultimate Scapegoat, ending forever the "mechanics of violence" perpetuated by those who put him to death.

Robert Hamerton-Kelly's provocative study of Mark, *The Gospel and the Sacred*, uses Girard's theory as a framework for reading Mark, thereby disclosing important insights into Jesus' own commitment to nonviolence and to self-sacrificial (though by no means passive) response to violence and injustice. Followers of Jesus are committed to the same radical stance in relation to violence, especially when it is perpetuated in the name of religion.

The paradox of Mark (and of all NT theology) is that the "victim" in a terrible undeserved death becomes the victor over death. In place of temple-centered sacrifices, a new temple (the resurrected Jesus and the community of his followers) becomes the locus of true worship, where reconciled relationships with God and with fellow humans are celebrated without perpetuating cycles of violence.

We must remember that all theories of atonement through Christ are abstractions; all of the above views are based on at least some valid biblical metaphors and images. In the end, any view that reduces the mystery of the atonement to a rational theory falls short of the NT emphasis. For historical and theological treatments of this issue, consult the works of G. Aulén, 1966; J. Driver; T. Finger; J. Green and M. Baker; and W. Swartley (ed.), 2000 (cf. "Jesus' Substitutionary Death," in TBC for 14:1-26).

Mark 16:1-8

Resurrection . . .
A New Beginning

PREVIEW

Mark's Gospel (as originally written) contains only eight more verses
[Textual Criticism of Mark]. English Bibles regularly print additional
material, especially the 12 verses usually called the "Longer Ending"
(16:9-20). These additional verses came to be attached to Mark in the
third or fourth century; they are absent from the best early manuscripts, and many of the church fathers recognized them as later addi-
tions. Some Bibles print additional early endings; most translations do
well by offering a footnote that indicates significant diversity in the
manuscript tradition; yet most of them do not clearly say that the
additional endings were not written by Mark.

Because Mark includes no appearances of the resurrected Jesus,
no great commission, and no ascension report, his Gospel has often
been judged incomplete. Many have argued that Mark *intended* to
write more but was prevented (perhaps by martyrdom) from doing so.
Some have argued he did in fact write more, but the real ending was
lost. The various additional endings in the manuscript tradition were
probably attached to Mark to bring this Gospel to a "proper" conclusion. Some judge Mark's Gospel as "incomplete" simply because the
other (later) evangelists wrote more.

All four Gospels include resurrection reports. Luke continues with
reports of resurrection appearances, a reference to the future worldwide mission, and a report of Jesus' ascension into heaven. Of these

three additional events, Matthew includes only the first two and John only the first. One may illustrate this as follows:

Resurrection Reports	Resurrection Appearances	Worldwide Mission	Ascension of Jesus
Mark ++++++ > |	|	|	
John +++++++++++++++++++ > |		|	
Matthew ++++++++++++++++++++++++++++++++ > |			
Luke +++ >			

Given this diversity, which is the *right* place to end a Gospel? Obviously, there is no consistent pattern; if Mark wrote first, there *could not* have been a pattern when he wrote. Mark knows the story continues with resurrection appearances (cf. 14:28), a commission to preach the Gospel to the whole world (cf. 13:10), and Jesus' ascension to God's right hand (cf. 12:10-11, 36). Mark has simply chosen not to *report* these as part of his conclusion, whereas other Gospel writers reported *some*, but not necessarily *all* of them. There is no basis here for finding fault with Mark.

Often readers have protested, "Even Matthew and Luke must have known that Mark 16:8 could not end a Gospel; both felt a need to complete the story." That is strange reasoning. We should rather say, "If Matthew and Luke felt no constraints to end their narratives where Mark did, nor even where each other did, then Mark, who wrote before them, surely had the freedom to end elsewhere than where Matthew and Luke did."

Our task is to make sense of Mark's ending as we have it (16:8). It is a provocative ending, perhaps a troubling ending. There are good reasons, however, to suppose that it is the ending Mark intended. Carefully interpreted, it contains both a profound promise and a great challenge. It can even be called a brilliant ending, well suited to the kind of Gospel Mark has written.

Mark ends his narrative by introducing the post-resurrection period with a resurrection report, an invitation, and a challenge. Mark's Gospel opens with the words *The beginning of the good news* (1:1). It ends with an invitation to Jesus' disciples and Mark's readers to make *that* beginning *their* new beginning.

OUTLINE

The Resurrection, 16:1-6

16:1-2   Three Women Prepare to Anoint the Body
16:3-4   Who Will Roll Away the Stone?
16:5   The Young Man

16:6   The Resurrection Announcement

The Invitation to Galilee, 16:7

The Silence of the Women, 16:8

The Ending of Mark's Gospel (and Remarks on 16:9-20)

EXPLANATORY NOTES
The Resurrection 16:1-6
16:1-2 Three Women Prepare to Anoint the Body

Saturday evening at sundown (when the Sabbath ended), three women buy spices, intending a Sunday morning anointing (not embalming) of Jesus' body. (On the identity of these women, see notes for 15:40.) They want to honor the deceased by applying aromatic oils to his body. Little do they suspect that they will arrive too late to fulfill their intentions. Another woman has discerned the times and anointed Jesus' body beforehand (14:8).

They make their way to the tomb *very early* Sunday morning, *when the sun had risen*. By the time they arrive, another "sun" will also have risen. There is no pun in the Greek text (where *sun* and *Son* do not sound alike), but there may well be an allusion to the prophecy of Malachi that "the sun of righteousness shall rise, with healing in its wings" (Mal. 4:2). This chapter will be about the risen one offering healing, restoration, renewal, salvation.

16:3-4 Who Will Roll Away the Stone?

The narrative implies that the stone covering the tomb's entrance is too large for these three women to roll back by themselves. Yet just as their preparations for anointing have been in vain, so also are their concerns about who will roll back the stone. They arrive to find it already removed from the entrance.

16:5 The Young Man

Their next surprise comes when they enter the tomb. Instead of finding Jesus' body, they find *a young man* (*neaniskos*) seated at the right side (of where Jesus' body has been lying, presumably).

Who is this young man? Modern readers who know the other Gospels are inclined to suppose it is an angel. The alarm (terror/astonishment) of the women suggests they also took him to be an angel. Mark's reference to the white robe and the message from

heaven may also be clues that he wants readers to assume an angelic visitation. Humans must pass on the resurrection message (16:8),
but they must first hear it proclaimed by God's messenger.

Why then does Mark not tell us this is an angel? Here he does not
even use the normal Greek word for messenger, *angellos*, that can
apply to human and/or angelic messengers.

Mark calls this young man a *neaniskos* (young man). Mark uses
that word only here and in 14:51-52, where we read of a mysterious
young man who has followed Jesus into Gethsemane. Then, when
the captors come, he disappears naked into the night. We have suggested that the naked young man stands symbolically for all who fail
Jesus in the crisis; it might especially symbolize (or even refer to) John
Mark himself (14:51-52, notes).

Something comparable is happening in 16:5. Mark wants his
readers to see in this *neaniskos* an actual messenger from God who
really does sit in the tomb and proclaim the resurrection news. But he
also wants the reader to see in this *neaniskos* a symbol of *all* who will
announce the resurrection news. They may have run away when the
going got tough (14:50-52), but they have been invited back to
become faithful disciples and courageous messengers of the good
news of the resurrection. If 14:51-52 (see notes) refers at least symbolically to Mark himself, then Mark is now saying, "I know what I am
talking about. I failed, too. But Jesus invited me back, and I too am
proclaiming the good news."

16:6 The Resurrection Announcement

God's messenger first "corrects" the women's reaction. They
were wrong about the anointing and about the stone; now they are
wrong in being alarmed! This is not the time for terror, he says, *Jesus
. . . has been raised!*

The messenger comments on their search for *Jesus of Nazareth,
who was crucified*. We must read his message carefully! He does not
say that Jesus of Nazareth is no more; he has been replaced by the
Christ of faith. He does not say that the crucified one is no more; he
has been replaced by the resurrected one. Many have understood the
resurrection that way, but that is not Mark's view.

For Mark, *Jesus of Nazareth . . . has been raised*. Jesus of
Nazareth is *going ahead . . . to Galilee*. Jesus of Nazareth is the risen
one. There is no Christ of faith who is not Jesus of Nazareth. Nor is
there a risen one who is not the crucified one. The crucified one, now
raised, has left the tomb and precedes the disciples into Galilee. They
will see the crucified one there, now that he has been raised.

Those with eyes to see and ears to hear will discern that in the raising up of the crucified one, another decisive victory for God's secret kingdom has taken place (cf. 4:11). The rejected one has become the victor. God has vindicated the rejected Messiah King.

He has been raised (NRSV) is a better translation than *he has risen* (NIV), for God (not Jesus himself) caused the resurrection. The Greek construction is called a divine passive: God did it! God has answered Jesus' cry of dereliction (15:34). God raised up the stone that the builders rejected (12:10). The new temple is being raised up on the third day (14:57; 15:29).

The women are invited to inspect the place where Jesus' body had been lying. They have seen the open tomb and the divine messenger. They have heard the resurrection announcement. Now they are invited to certify that the body is gone. These women are already official witnesses to Jesus death (15:40) and his burial (14:47). Now they become official witnesses of the empty tomb. But who will testify, as in the other Gospels, "We have seen the Lord"? That is the crucial question around which the rest of the narrative revolves.

The Invitation to Galilee 16:7

Mark's narrative ends with the messenger commissioning the women to tell the disciples about the resurrection, and also with a report that fear prevented them from doing as they were told. What are we to make of that?

Before interpreting these verses, we need to distinguish clearly between "interpreting a narrative" and "reconstructing what actually happened." If our goal were to reconstruct what actually happened, we would set Mark's narrative alongside all other available resurrection narratives. We would compare and contrast; we would reconstruct the original events as well as possible. In doing so, we would discover that some apparent discrepancies are hard to reconcile. Sometimes one record supplies just the information we need to make sense of a comment in another one. J. Wenham's fascinating book *Easter Enigma* deals with the resurrection narratives in this way.

To interpret a narrative is something quite different. It does not involve historical judgments about what "really happened," but rather literary judgments about what the author is seeking to communicate.

It is appropriate for us to ponder such questions as these: Did Jesus appear to Mary Magdalene and to other women? Did any of them report the resurrection message and/or a resurrection appearance to disciples of Jesus? Did Jesus appear to Peter and to other disciples? Did they meet in Galilee? Such questions ask about what actually happened. Those who believe the reports in the other Gospels will answer yes to all of these questions. But in doing so, they have not interpreted Mark 16:7-8.

If we ask what *Mark believed* about all these questions, we have to do some guessing. No doubt he knew many of the traditions recorded in Luke and Matthew, since his text seems to anticipate them. Presumably Mark would say yes to most or all of the above questions. Yet this still does not constitute an interpretation of Mark 16:7-8.

We begin to interpret Mark's ending only if we ask what *Mark's Gospel* teaches or implies about these questions. From Mark's text, we know that the disciples are renewed after the resurrection. Mark's narrative projects a whole series of discipleship activities they will be engaged in after the resurrection (all of them presupposing that they returned to faithfulness after their failure). For example, they will drink the cup Jesus drinks and be baptized with his baptism (suffer in submission to God's will; 10:39). They will report what they experienced when Jesus was transfigured (9:9). They will be persecuted by both Jews and Gentiles for their faith and for their gospel proclamation (13:9-13).

If we know that they have returned to faithfulness, then we know some other things as well: Mark's narrative teaches that the renewal of their discipleship *depends on* following Jesus again to (and in) Galilee (14:28). It teaches that the purpose of that post-resurrection journey is to *see* Jesus in Galilee (16:7).

We can therefore conclude that a post-resurrection meeting between the previously unfaithful disciples and the risen Jesus is assumed in the Markan text. We can be less sure that Mark assumes the women's initial fear is overcome so that they report to the disciples as commanded. That the historical women actually relay the message can easily be demonstrated outside of Mark, but that is not part of Mark's message. Mark's text makes clear that even if they never tell, the disciples will be without excuse.

Here is where Mark 14:27-28 is so important. Jesus tells his disciples about a coming post-resurrection meeting before he dies, and even before they fail! He tells them that they will abandon him on the road to the cross, but that they will follow again, after the resurrection. They will not be abandoned because of their failure; they are invited to return again and meet the risen Jesus in Galilee. All this helps us read Mark 16:7-8 with "Markan glasses."

There are multiple levels of communication in Mark 16:7. Mark is telling his readers what the divine messenger tells the women that

Jesus has already told the disciples. If we want to hear what Mark is telling his readers (that is the goal of interpreting the narrative), we shall have to listen carefully to what the divine messenger tells the women and how it relates to what Jesus has already told the disciples.

The women have heard and seen; now they are instructed to go and tell. The sequel to Jesus' death has already occurred; Jesus has been raised. Now the sequel to the disciples' failure can occur; they can be renewed.

The Greek text of Mark 16:7 can legitimately be interpreted two different ways, as an *indirect* quote (as in NRSV) or as a *direct* quote (as in NIV):

> Go, tell his disciples and Peter that he is going ahead of you to Galilee; there you will see him, just as he told you. (NRSV)

> Go, tell his disciples and Peter, "He is going ahead of you into Galilee. There you will see him, just as he told you." (NIV)

What is the difference? In the NRSV, *you* (all three times) refers to the *women* (and presumably the men along with them). In the NIV, *you* (all three times) refers to the *men only*. To make this clear, let us imagine that the women do in fact go to the other disciples and obey the command of the messenger. What will they say?

> He is going ahead of *us* to Galilee; there *we* will see him, just as he told *us*. (based on NRSV, emphasis added)

> He is going ahead of *you* to Galilee; there *you* will see him, just as he told *you*. (based on NIV, emphasis added)

What is the role of the women, according to the NIV translation? They are to be a communication link, to carry the message to *the disciples and Peter*. The disciples who have run away are not at the tomb. They do not hear the announcement, nor do they know that the resurrection has happened. The women are there; they know; it is up to them to tell the disciples. If they do, the disciples may or may not go. But the responsibility of the women is to make sure the other disciples know they are invited. Taken this way, some commentators go on to say, "If they do not go, the disciples will not even find out about the resurrection. There will be no meeting in Galilee, no resurrection appearances, no discipleship renewal."

However (in NIV), the disciples do not need to hear the resurrection message from the women in order to be invited to Galilee; they have already been invited (14:28). Nor do they need to hear from the women that the resurrection has now occurred. They only need to believe Jesus. Over and over, Jesus has predicted that after three days he will rise (8:31; and so on). If the disciples want to meet the risen Jesus, they can do so whether the women report their experience or not.

If we read the text as interpreted by the NRSV, the women's role is not only to pass on a message to the men. *The women themselves* are being invited to go to Galilee *along with the others* and meet the risen Jesus there. Mark 16:7 is not about the men only; it is also about the women. It is about the commission *they* have been given to proclaim the message; and it is about the invitation *they* have been given to meet Jesus. Together with 16:8, it is also about their response. We shall see that they do not go and tell; they flee and are silent.

We need to be reminded that these women have accompanied Jesus in Galilee and traveled with him to Jerusalem. They are part of the group all along (15:41). If that is not clear in our minds, it is because Mark has not told us about the women until after he has finished telling us the story of the Twelve, right up to their failure in the crisis (14:43-44, 50, 72). The women are introduced later, when Mark reports that they did *not* fail Jesus. They are there from the beginning and follow all the way to the cross (15:40-41). (Their failure is reported in the final verse of Mark's Gospel.)

The difference between the women and the men is that the women are not present when Jesus tells his disciples on the way to Gethsemane that they will all desert him (the women did not). They are not there when he predicts the post-resurrection meeting in Galilee. But now they know. They, too, have been informed. They are to go to the disciples who have failed and remind them, so that they might return to Galilee as a reunited group to meet Jesus. All of this is implied in the NRSV text of 16:7.

The NRSV wording has an interesting implication that should not be missed. The final *you* (16:7; or the final "us" if we look at the way the women's message would be worded in their own report) makes it clear that Jesus' precrucifixion message of failure and renewal (14:28), though originally delivered only to Eleven (after Judas left), is a valid message for *all disciples*. All disciples fail (not only the Eleven); all disciples can be renewed (not only the Eleven). No failure by the women has yet been reported, but there is one more verse to consider. The messenger at the tomb is here informing *more* disciples of a meeting to which *all* are invited. Jesus himself had extended the invitation earlier when he spoke representatively to the Eleven.

The men have failed, the women have not (thus far). The men needed to be told about the meeting in Galilee *before* their failure (otherwise they might never know). The women who remain faithful hear about the meeting when the messenger at the tomb restates the invitation. All are invited, no matter how far they have fallen. That is why Peter is singled out for special mention: *even Peter* (as the two Greek words should likely be translated). All can be renewed. They must go, and if they will go, they will see Jesus. If they see him, they will be able to follow him again.

All along, we have been speaking of the *invitation* to Galilee. The texts says, *There you will see him* (v. 7). This is stronger than an invitation; it is a guarantee by the messenger that the meeting *will* occur; it is more like a summons! The grammarians say it is a future indicative used as an imperative: Jesus' followers are summoned to Galilee; they *must* see the resurrected Jesus. Their future discipleship depends on it!

The Silence of the Women 16:8

If Mark had ended with 16:7, it would have been a provocative and challenging ending, but not a troubling one. By including 16:8, it becomes a troubling one as well; at least that is how many experience it.

The women have heard the resurrection message. They have been instructed to go and tell. What do they do with their commission? They flee in terror and say nothing. Their response has seemed so troubling that some commentators have concluded Mark must have originally written more, or at least intended to do so. Either that, or they twist and turn Mark's final verse into an act of obedience. The women do not leave in terror (they claim), but in reverent awe. They do not flee, but hasten to obey. They are not silent about the resurrection message; they are just so intent on obeying that they do not take time to chat with people along the way. In the end, such interpreters make the verse say virtually the opposite of what Mark has intended. This strategy is neither necessary nor legitimate.

Mark is telling his readers that the women responded *wrongly*. As understandable as their actions and responses are, they were wrong all through Mark 16. They prepared in vain for an anointing that could not happen. They worried for nothing about a stone that was gone before they arrived. They responded to the messenger with alarm, and he promptly told them not to be alarmed. He gave them a message to tell, and they did not tell it. They did not leave in respectful silence; they fled in terror, disobeying the messenger by keeping the resurrection message to themselves.

The final reference is to their fear; in Mark, where there is fear, there is not yet faith (cf. 4:40). "The proper action of faith is to . . . conquer the fear which hinders an obedient following of Christ" (Swartz: 272). The women have been faithful all the way to the cross and to the tomb; but entrusted with the resurrection message, their faith fails.

If we did not have 16:7, we would not know what to do with 16:8. But now the women are in the same position as the men. Both groups have failed. Both have heard the resurrection message *before* they fail. Both know that if they want to be renewed in their discipleship, they must be obedient, they must go to Galilee, they must meet the risen Jesus.

As readers, we are tempted to stand in judgment over the women. How could they? How could they hear the glorious message of the resurrected Jesus, hear that he has sent out an invitation to meet him in Galilee, hear that there is forgiveness for failure, reinstatement after desertion, a welcome back after cowardly denial—how can they hear such a message and remain silent? But as soon as we pass judgment on the women, we sense Mark turning to us, as Nathan did to David: "You are the one" (cf. 2 Sam. 12:7). We too, having now read through to the end of Mark's narrative, have been entrusted with the message of the resurrection. How can we keep silent?

All through Mark's Gospel we have been taught to fix our eyes, not on the Twelve, not on the women, but on Jesus. Jesus is our model. Disciples may start well, with flashes of insight and success, but there will be many moments of blindness and failure. If we keep our eyes fixed on the men who followed Jesus, we can justify all sorts of failures. If we keep our eyes on the women, we can justify our silence about the resurrection message. Mark invites us, challenges us, to fix our eyes on Jesus, who has gone on ahead of us. We must follow him, obey him, go where he goes. Then we too will meet the risen Jesus. Then our failure will be forgiven and our courage renewed. We will take up our crosses in discipleship and proclaim the gospel in mission. "Followership is never easy, never perfect, and never ending" (Malbon, 1983:48).

Perhaps we prefer a "happy ending." Mark could have reported the renewal of the disciples, their joy in seeing Jesus, maybe even their enthusiastic reception of a great commission. But Mark has chosen to finish with a challenge instead of a happy ending. He confronts the reader with choices and opportunities, rather than an excuse to close the covers and say, "I'm glad it ended well!"

The Ending of Mark's Gospel (and Remarks on 16:9-20)

Many interpreters have struggled with Mark's ending. It therefore is appropriate to examine what options are available if we want to "continue the Gospel."

We can stand still at the empty tomb and contemplate our options.

I have often pondered the pace of Mark's narrative. The first half almost flits from episode to episode, though it invites careful reflection on the impact of the way the parts are linked in a larger structure (cf. "Overview" of Part 1).

At the midpoint of Mark, Jesus begins a journey to Jerusalem. The pace changes. No longer is Jesus hastening in and out of Galilee, in and out of synagogues and homes and boats and deserts. He marches steadily towards Jerusalem. At Jerusalem, the pace changes again as each day of Jesus' final week is carefully recounted. As the evening of Passover arrives, the pace changes once more: three-hour blocks of time are counted off all through the night and then all through the following day (see 15:25, notes).

At the tomb, the narrative reaches a standstill. The reader is brought along with the women to the tomb, enters with them, sees what they see, and hears what they hear. The reader is reminded of the Galilean reunion and hears the commission to go and tell. But then the women suddenly flee. The reader is left standing there at the empty tomb. Where does the narrative go from here?

We long for more until we realize that there will only be more if *we* continue the story. We can go to Galilee to meet Jesus. We can go and tell the good news. Or we can stand there afraid and inactive, even fleeing in terror. How the story continues depends on whether we will do as the (remaining) Eleven do, or as the women do, or as the divine messenger instructs. "It is up to the listener to determine how the story will end," says T. Boomershine (188). M. Hooker agrees: "If you want to see Jesus, then follow where he leads. This is the end of Mark's story, because it is the beginning of discipleship" (1991:394; cf. Fowler, 1991:224).

We can look past the end of the narrative to the continuation of the story.

If we respond appropriately to Mark's resurrection challenge, we realize that the end of the *narration* is not the end of the *story.* The last thing Mark *narrates* is a resurrection report, but Mark's Gospel refers to lots of post-resurrection events, in which readers are called to participate. All of Mark 13 and various other texts in Mark (e.g., 9:9; 10:39; 12:9-11, 36; 14:28) discuss events beyond the resurrection that are a part of Mark's projected story.

Mark's Gospel is a book about beginnings! The first word of Mark's Gospel is *beginning* (*The beginning of the good news,* 1:1). Mark's entire Gospel is about how the good news *began.* It began with Jesus proclaiming and bringing God's reign. It began with Jesus going the way of the cross, all the way to the bitter end, and being vindicated by God. Now that Jesus has died and been raised, now that he has reached the glory beyond the cross, this beginning is over. Jesus' beginning makes possible a new beginning for Jesus' disciples, the women, and Mark's readers. All are invited to walk the discipleship road. The narrative ends; the story goes on.

Yet if 16:8 marks the end of the beginning, it also marks the beginning of the end. Mark 13 is about the period of time preceding and leading up to the final glorious return as the Son of Man. Jesus' resurrection marks the beginning of that end. It marks the beginning of that time period when Jesus' followers engage in "mission in the context of persecution" (13:9-13). It is the time to watch and wait, discern and serve (chap. 13), until some unknown future time, when the Son of Man's appearance signals the arrival of the End (13:24-27).

We can complete the loop by going from 16:8 back to 1:1.

Several authors have suggested that when the disciples are invited back to Galilee to begin again, the *readers* are invited back to chapter 1 to begin again. Now that we know how the Gospel ends, there are many new insights to be gained by reading the earlier parts in the light of the whole. Throughout this commentary, I have tried to be sensitive to the "chronological reading experience," indicating what "the reader knows up to this point." But I have also tried to take into account the deeper meanings, the irony, and the foreshadowing that can be recognized when individual texts are seen in the light of the whole.

Hamerton-Kelly refers to "circular" and "spiral" readings of the Gospel:

> The last sentence leaves the reader with a pregnant silence; the first sentence breaks into the reader's silence without warning, without a verb and without an article before *archē* (beginning), as if in telegraphic style. The theme of both passages is [this]: one who goes before to prepare the way.

. . . If Mark is circular, then the journey away from Jerusalem, following the risen Christ to Galilee, will lead us back to Jerusalem through the adventures, conflicts, suffering, and triumphs that the Gospel recounts. . . . Once we have read of the cross and opened ourselves to the hope of the resurrection, the text is changed for us. The poetic of the Gospel, therefore, is not the circle but the spiral. Each time we follow Jesus into the Galilee of another reading, we have been changed by the power of the cross and the hope of the resurrection mediated by the text we have just read. (62)

We can let someone else "finish" Mark's Gospel for him (16:9-20).

The verses usually called Mark 16:9-20 did not originally belong to Mark's Gospel. They are missing from the earliest manuscripts and were written and added to Mark at a later date (cf. "Preview," above). Because older English versions of the Bible give no indication of this, many of us grew up assuming that Mark ends with these verses. As in John, we see a resurrection appearance to Mary Magdalene. As in Luke, we see an appearance to two people traveling in the country. As in all the Gospels, we see an appearance to the eleven disciples and a report that they have trouble believing. As in Matthew, we hear a commission to preach the Gospel in all the world. As in Luke, we hear a report of the ascension.

Happily, most Bibles published today clearly indicate that verses 9-20 are not original; sadly, most readers ignore such notes. They read right past 16:8 and thus miss completely the ending that Mark has intended. Some readers who take note of the poor manuscript support for 16:9-20 are troubled, not knowing what to do with "unauthentic verses" printed in their Bibles. Perhaps they do not know what to do with a Gospel that they feel seems incomplete without these verses.

Some early Christian copyist probably thought Mark was incomplete, and attempted to make up for what was "missing"! The "longer ending" (there are others; see below) was likely created primarily by excerpting from the other Gospels. It fits poorly onto what Mark wrote. The transition from verse 8 (Mark's ending) to verse 9 is very awkward. The language and the themes of these 12 verses are quite different from what Mark wrote. Most noteworthy is the reference to visible evidences designed to lead people to faith, a perspective that fits into Luke much better than into Mark.

Mark 16:9-20 is not part of Mark. But that does not necessarily mean it cannot be part of NT Scripture. One justification for including these verses in the canon is that they were probably attached to

Mark's Gospel by the time final decisions were being made about the limits of the NT canon. Ultimately, it makes little difference whether these verses are included in the canon or not: *virtually everything they contain is found elsewhere in the NT*, except for the promise that Jesus' followers will be protected when handling snakes (cf. Acts 28:3-6) and drinking poison. But whether 16:9-20 is considered canonical or not, it was not written by Mark and should not be drawn into discussions about "Mark's message" in general, or Mark's resurrection message in particular. (See the essay on textual criticism for comments on Mark 16:9-20 *[Textual Criticism of Mark].*)

We can choose from other available "endings" to Mark.

There are various "Markan endings" to be found in the manuscript tradition, besides the "longer ending" discussed above. One well-preserved one has been printed in some NRSV Bibles:

> And all that had been commanded them they told briefly to those around Peter. And afterward Jesus himself sent out through them, from east to west, the sacred and imperishable proclamation of eternal salvation.

This "shorter ending" was probably written explicitly to continue where Mark left off. But it is a rather unsatisfactory continuation; at least the first line seems designed to contradict what Mark wrote.

The grand conclusion of this shorter ending is not inconsistent with Mark's story. Mark too believes that Jesus sent out the "sacred and imperishable proclamation of eternal salvation" (he calls it *good news*; cf. 14:9; 13:10). Since Mark believes the message will be proclaimed *in the whole world* (14:9) and *to all nations* (13:10), he would not quarrel with the formulation *from east to west*. But even if Mark agrees with most of this ending, he has preferred a different one.

Mark prefers not to round it all off with a report that Jesus and his disciples got the whole job done. He prefers to leave an unfinished story. Whether the original disciples and the initially silent women ever do meet Jesus in Galilee and proclaim the resurrection message—that is *their* story. Whether we as readers meet Jesus in Galilee or not, whether we are silent or courageously proclaim the good news—that is *our* story.

THE TEXT IN BIBLICAL CONTEXT
Resurrection in the NT

The resurrection of Jesus is central to the meaning of biblical faith. References to its historical factuality, theological meaning, and eschatological significance are pervasive throughout the NT. As Paul says, "If Christ has not been raised, [our] faith is futile" (1 Cor. 15:17).

Explicit references to a coming resurrection are rare in the OT (cf. Dan. 12:2). However, numerous passages affirm that when God's people (or specifically God's chosen Servant) suffer unjustly, God will not abandon them. Instead, God will vindicate them and restore them to honor (cf. Ps. 16:10-11; 17:15; 73:24-26; Isa. 53:10-12). The NT interprets such texts as intimations of the resurrection first experienced by Jesus and ultimately to be experienced by those who will be raised with him.

The primary evidence for Christ's resurrection in the NT is the testimony of Scripture and of those who met the risen Christ (e.g., 1 Cor. 15:3-8). Among the Gospel writers, Matthew seems to put the most emphasis on *proving* the historical factuality of Jesus' resurrection (Matt. 28:1-15). Mark's emphasis, as indicated above, is that Jesus' resurrection provides a new beginning for disciples who fail (Mark 16:7).

Luke's resurrection message seems to emphasize that the risen Jesus can be experienced in the daily life of believers and especially in the gathered community (Luke 24:31-32). For John, Jesus' resurrection is inseparable from his "glorification" on the cross, a sign that the End has already begun, that eternal life is already available, that judgment has already been pronounced on the world (12:23-32).

Paul's "resurrection theology" is perhaps the broadest in the NT:

1. The resurrection "proves" who Jesus really is, God's Son (Rom. 1:3-4) and head of the church (Eph. 1:19-20).

2. The resurrection "completes" the crucifixion and makes salvation possible (Rom. 5:10; 1 Cor. 15:12-19).

3. The resurrection provides motivation and power for Christian living (Rom. 6:4, 8-12).

4. Christ's resurrection gives Christians hope for their own future resurrection because they "belong to Christ" (1 Cor. 6:14; 15:20, 23).

4. The resurrection makes an ongoing relationship with Jesus possible (Phil. 3:10; Col. 3:1-4).

In all this, it is essential to hold the "historical Jesus" and the "risen Christ" together. It is the crucified one who was raised (Mark 16:6). What Jesus "began to do and to teach" (Acts 1:3), he now continues to do and teach as the resurrected one and Lord of the church. "His divine power has given us everything needed for life and godliness" (2 Pet. 1:3) in this "time between the times" (cf. 1 Cor. 10:11), as we live in the light of Christ's resurrection and in the anticipation of our own.

THE TEXT IN THE LIFE OF THE CHURCH
Meeting Jesus in Galilee

Who is invited/summoned to the Galilean meeting with the resurrected Jesus? All disciples are. The men who failed Jesus before the
crucifixion represent those who fail and are unsure of the way back.
Mark 16:7 provides assurance that the invitation is still valid for them.
The women who witnessed the crucifixion, the burial, and the empty
tomb represent those who continue to follow faithfully, but who fear
to tell, and thereby cast their faithfulness in doubt. Mark 16:7 provides assurance that they, too, are invited. All readers of the Gospel
are invited to meet the resurrected Jesus, regardless of how or how
seriously we too may have failed.

A special notation, *Tell the disciples **and Peter*** (or ***even***
Peter), assures us that the invitation is valid even for those who have
failed most drastically, even for those who have denied that they are
among Jesus' disciples (cf. 14:71).

The ten who ran away in Gethsemane, Peter, the women, and
now also the readers—all are told, "In order to *see*, one must first
obey." This is not about objective proofs that compel belief. It is about
opportunities to find reasons for faith in a life of obedience to an invitation, in a life of following the risen Jesus. Obedience precedes "seeing." That is how it has been throughout Mark's Gospel. *Following*
Jesus is the prerequisite to truly *seeing* him.

Mark ends his Gospel, not by telling the reader what happens in
Galilee, but by telling them what must happen in Galilee. It is not
about literal journeys back and forth between Galilee and Jerusalem,
but about a life of following Jesus.

Certainly the original disciples were expected to travel literally to
Galilee and there see the resurrected Jesus. But for them, just as for
us, Galilee is also a symbol. It is a symbol of the place where their discipleship began, where they heard Jesus' summons to leave all, and
where they made a good beginning. Galilee is where they struggled
to understand the secret coming of the kingdom, and where they saw
powerful evidences of its advance. There they were first commissioned to go out as missionaries. There they faced Jesus' rebukes
when they understood so little. There in Galilee the discipleship journey had begun; it was therefore the logical place for it to start over
again after the resurrection.

Meeting Jesus in Galilee is all about hearing Jesus' call once more.
It is about being with Jesus, being sent out by Jesus, and learning
from Jesus. It is about following Jesus along the road, taking up a

cross and heading for Jerusalem, persecution, possible martyrdom, and ultimately glory. To that, all are invited!

Throughout the first two millennia of church history, countless believers have heeded the call to "meet Jesus in Galilee." Many have suffered greatly for their faithful discipleship, their courageous witness, and their willingness to be out of step with this world in order to remain in step with Jesus. Others have been martyred. All have made sacrifices for Christ's sake.

Mark's Gospel contains no glib promises of an easy life for Jesus' followers. But along with the rest of Scripture, Mark assures believers that a hundredfold reward and eternal life await those who respond to Jesus' call (10:28-31).

Paul aptly calls us to a "watchful discipleship," so central to Mark's Gospel: "Therefore, my beloved, be steadfast, immovable, always excelling in the work of the Lord, because you know that in the Lord your labor is not in vain" (1 Cor. 15:58; cf. C. Lehn's, *I Heard Good News Today*).

Outline of Mark

PART 1: MINISTRY IN AND AROUND GALILEE
Mark 1:1—8:26

**From a Religious System
to a Family of Disciples**

Parables: For Those with Ears to Hear

Victories over Storms and Satan, Sickness and Death 4:35—5:43

The Rejected Prophets 6:1-29

House of Prayer or Den of Thieves?   11:1-25

Jesus' Triumphal Entry into Jerusalem	11:1-11
Jesus Curses an Unfruitful Tree	11:12-14
Jesus Condemns the Unfaithful Temple Authorities	11:15-19
Jesus' Action	11:15-16
Jesus' Teaching	11:17
A House of Prayer for All Nations	11:17a
A Den of Robbers	11:17b
Various Reactions	11:18-19
A Dead Tree and Living Faith	11:20-25
A Dead Tree	11:20-21
Living Faith	11:22-25
Have Faith	11:22
Remove Mountains	11:23
Effective Prayer	11:24
Forgiving Others	11:25

Conflict in Jerusalem   11:27— 12:44

The Questions About Jesus' Authority	11:27-33
The Enemies' Questions	11:27-28
Jesus' Counterquestion	11:29-30
The Enemies' Dilemma	11:31-33
The Parable of the Wicked Tenants	12:1-12
The Parable Itself	12:1-9
The Vindication of the Son/Stone	12:10-11
The Reaction of the Religious Leaders	12:12
The Question About Paying Taxes	12:13-17
The Enemies' Trap	12:13-15a
Jesus' Escape	12:15b-17
The Question About the Resurrection	12:18-27
The Sadducees' Question	12:18-23
Teaching About the Resurrection	12:24-27
The Most Important Commandment(s)	12:28-34
Love: The Center of the Law	12:28-31
Love: More Central than the Ceremonies	12:32-33
Not Far from the Kingdom	12:34
The Question About David's Son	12:35-37
Jesus Denounces the Scribes	12:38-40
The Widow's Offering	12:41-44

Essays

CHIASM AND INTERCALATION The technique of *chiasm* (sometimes called chiasmus) involves structuring a textual unit by surrounding the material at the center with matching elements. A chiasm can be as simple as an A-B-A' pattern, where A and A' represent matching elements (like bookends) around B. It can be as complex as A-B-C-D-E-D'-C'-B'-A'; the letters of the alphabet label matching elements. The elements that are matched can be words and phrases, similar actions, related themes, and so on.

A simple chiasm occurs when one episode is reported in two parts, one before and one after another episode. Mark has many examples of this. Thus the story of Jesus' mother and brothers coming to "take charge of Jesus" is told in two parts, the first part before the section on Jesus and Beelzebub, and the second after it. The pattern can be diagrammed:

A • Jesus and His Family (3:20-21)
 B • Jesus and Beelzebub (3:22-30)
A' • Jesus and His Family (3:31-35)

In this abbreviated form, the structure is sometimes called a "framing technique" or a "sandwich technique" or "intercalation." The chiasm becomes more elaborate if the material in B also proves to be framed around material closer to its center, as is the case with the Beelzebub controversy.

Many other examples of this simple chiasm (intercalation) appear in Mark, such as these:

"The Purpose of the Parables" (4:10-13), framed by the Sower Parable (4:1-9) and its "interpretation" (4:14-20).
"The Hemorrhaging Woman" incident (5:24b-34), framed by the two halves of "The Raising of Jairus' Daughter" (5:21-24a and 5:35-43).
"The Death of John the Baptist" (6:14-29), framed by "The Disciples' Mission" (6:7-13) and their mission report to Jesus (6:30).
"The Cleansing of the Temple" (11:15-19), framed by "The Cursing of the Fig Tree" (11:12-14) and the discovery that it has withered (11:20-21).

"Jesus' Anointing for Burial" (14:3-9), framed by schemes to kill Jesus (14:1-2) and Judas's offer to betray him (14:10-11).

"The Trial of Peter" (his denials; 14:66-72), framed by the two trials of Jesus (14:55-65; 15:1-5).

"The Crucifixion of Jesus" (15:21-25), framed by the mock coronation (15:16-20) and the announcement that the crucified Jesus is "King of the Jews" (15:26).

"The Tearing of the Temple Veil" (15:38), framed by the report of Jesus' death (15:37) and the report of its effect on the centurion (15:39).

Sometimes the intercalation preserves the order in which events actually occurred in history. Even if it does, however, we should watch for additional significance in the structure. Often the intercalation is not dictated by any historical circumstances. The intercalation is an invitation to examine what the two interwoven incidents have in common and to observe any clues as to how they help interpret each other.

Much more elaborate chiastic structures are to be found in the material in 2:1—3:6 (notes) and in 7:31—8:26 (notes). Elaborate chiasms usually put the focus on the element(s) at the middle, hinting that a theme is being developed there that sheds light on the significance of the rest of the material. As in simple intercalation, matching elements of a more elaborate chiasm should be carefully compared. Often similar features provide clues that are significant in interpreting the material.

Modern readers may be skeptical that chiasms are really there (or at least that an author deliberately constructed them). Our bias against chiasm stems from our unfamiliarity with the technique and from the fact that we (perhaps) see no real purpose in it. However, in a day where headings, subheadings, and paragraph divisions were *not* used to mark the progress of the narrative, it made sense to construct the narrative itself in a way that aided in its interpretation (by using chiasm or some other such device). Chiasms create a focus on the material at its middle, often suggesting that the central episode is a key to understanding the entire passage. In smaller chiasms (intercalation), often the framework around the center provides interpretive clues as to how the center should be understood. Chiasms also served to help people memorize material (more important in an oral culture than one focused on writing and reading). There is some evidence that a chiasm was viewed as having an almost mystical power (Stock, 1984).

Chiasms are not always clear: Is it our creative imagination? Or is it really there? Are the parallels coincidental or deliberately constructed? The danger of overlooking chiastic structures is that then we ignore an author's deliberate clues as to how material should be interpreted. The danger of finding too many chiasms is that we focus on incidental or even coincidental elements.

M. P. Scott has proposed a chiasm for the whole Gospel of Mark, finding ten sets of matching elements, concentrically constructed around the center located at 9:7, *This is my Son . . . ; listen to him.* He is convinced that the author has deliberately constructed this elaborate chiasm. Other commentators are not convinced. Some fairly elaborate chiasms have been proposed for which the arguments seem convincing, as explained in "The Structure of 2:1—3:6" and "Mark's Teaching Pattern in 7:31—8:26." This commentary refers to many other smaller chiasms and intercalations.

THE DISCIPLESHIP JOURNEY The journey Jesus makes with his disciples to Jerusalem begins and ends with references to *the way* (*hē hodos;* 8:27; 10:52). *The way* symbolizes discipleship. *On the way* the disciples of Jesus misunderstand him, oppose him, argue about greatness, and compete for seats of honor. Though they are literally *on the way* with Jesus, they are hardly acting as true followers. As the journey ends, a model of faithful discipleship is portrayed, Bartimaeus, who is healed of blindness and follows Jesus *on the way* (10:52). He symbolizes what the disciples should have been doing all along.

In the previews for 8:27—9:1 and 9:2—10:16, diagrams show how Mark has structured the material from 8:22 through 10:52. The entire journey to Jerusalem is about Christology, discipleship, and the healing of the disciples' blindness.

At the beginning of the journey, Peter confesses Jesus as the Messiah (8:29). But he immediately shows that he has not fathomed the full meaning of the confession he has made. He opposes Jesus' teaching about the coming passion. He, like the others, needs the journey to Jerusalem in order to learn to think divine thoughts instead of human thoughts (8:33).

At the end of the journey, Bartimaeus confesses Jesus as the Messiah (10:47-48). Peter's confession is perhaps more technically complete, but he incorrectly understands it. Bartimaeus' confession may be more vague and incomplete, but he understands correctly and acts upon it.

Confessing Jesus as the Christ must flow into a life of faithful discipleship. Otherwise, the confession counts for nothing. But for Mark, both a correct Christology and faithful discipleship are inseparably tied to a third theme, discernment, "hearing ears and seeing eyes" (4:12). Because the kingdom comes secretly (4:11), because the Messiah comes incognito (4:41), only those whose eyes are truly opened in the context of faithful discipleship will be ready to join Jesus on the road to glory by way of the cross.

At the beginning of the journey, the healing of the blind man from Bethsaida (8:22-26) symbolizes what has been happening and still needs to happen to the disciples of Jesus. They are still partly blind, seeing *people as trees walking* (8:24); they need another touch before they will be able to see *everything clearly* (8:25).

At the end of the journey, Bartimaeus is healed of blindness. His full healing is clearly indicated by his willingness to follow Jesus on the road of discipleship. The healing of Bartimaeus does not symbolize what *has happened* to the disciples on this journey. It symbolizes rather what *is possible* for disciples, what must yet happen.

Discipleship involves more than mouthing correct confessions; it is a journey of faithful following. It involves giving up everything to join Jesus; it involves true following, not merely physical journeying; it involves perseverance on the road to the cross.

Teaching true discipleship was Jesus' goal on the journey to Jerusalem and it is Mark's goal in narrating that journey for his readers. Bartimaeus is presented as a "good example." The disciples are sometimes portrayed as "bad examples" (TBC for 10:17-52). But Mark's goal is that both types of example become motivators for us as we keep our eyes fixed on the ideal, and as we renew courage and hope when we fall short. In reality, all disciples are "fallible followers" (Malbon, 1983:47-48), always needing to be challenged, to be forgiven, and to be allowed new beginnings.

ESCHATOLOGICAL TIME FRAMES IN MARK 13 In the preview to Mark 13, I listed some issues for which interpreters give divergent answers. I suggested that the interpreter's goal should not be to eliminate the ambiguities of Mark 13, but to understand why they are there. If *unknowability* of the timing of the End is the controlling assumption of Mark 13, then there may be events that, for all Mark knows, *may or may not* be end-time events.

Let me try to lay out Mark's understanding of end-time events. Some events are *not* part of *the End,* and some *are* part of *the End.* But there is another category of events which *may or may not* be part of *the End.* Mark does not know. Jesus did not know. According to Mark's Gospel, *no one* can know until the events occur and God's undisclosed plan emerges.

The events listed in Mark 13:5-27 seem to fall into three categories:

1. *Beginning events:* These events are *not* directly related to the End. They happen before the final end-time events start to unfold. People claiming such events as signals that the End has come are deceivers (13:5-6).

2. *Events that belong to the beginning **and/or** the End:* These events are not clearly linked to the End, but they are also not clearly separated from the End. The ambiguity is deliberate because no one can know whether these events will lead directly to the End or not.

3. *End-time events:* These are of two kinds. First, they include events on earth that must happen *before* the End can come. Second, there are events in the heavens and the Son of Man's return.

Which events fall into which categories? Here are my suggestions:

1. *Beginning Events*, events that *do not* belong to the End (13:5-13).
   - The need for discernment because deceivers wrongly claim that the things listed below are end-time events (vv. 5-6).
   - Catastrophes, such as wars, earthquakes, famines (vv. 7-8).
   - Mission in the context of persecution (vv. 9-13). Mission and persecution are beginning events (as shown by the position of vv. 9-13) and also events that occur right up to the End (as shown by the content of the verses themselves (note *first,* v. 10; *to the end,* v. 13).
2. *Events that belong to the Beginning **and/or** the End* (13:14-18).
   - *Desolating sacrilege, . . . where it ought not to be* (v. 14a; a cryptic reference to events at the temple and possibly to a future antichrist).
   - War causing great woes (vv. 14b-18; war in Judea possibly prefiguring another great tribulation).
3. *End-Time Events*, events leading directly to *the End* and those constituting the End. These include various kinds of events:
   Events on Earth (vv. 9-13, 19-23).
   - Mission in the context of persecution (vv. 9-13).
   - The greatest tribulation ever (vv. 19-20).
   - The need for discernment because deceivers claim this is the End itself (vv. 21-23).
   Events in the Heavens (vv. 24-25).
   - Sun and moon darkened.
   - Stars falling, and so on.
   Return of the Son of Man (vv. 26-27).

The crucial question is this: Do the events of 13:14-18 belong to the *beginning* events, or to the *end-time* events, or to *both*? Theoretically, there are three possibilities, each with many defenders:

View 1. Verses 14-18 belong to the *beginning events, not* to the *end-time events.* On this view, these verses refer to events in and around Jerusalem only, including a sacrilege there, and the war that results from it (and presumably results in the destruction of the temple; cf. v. 2). These events cause distress for people who are counseled to flee but may have a hard time doing so. The events from verse 19 onward are later end-time events.

View 2. Verses 14-18 belong to the *end-time events, not* to the *beginning events.* On this view, the sacrilege and war in Judea are predicted to lead directly to the final tribulation and the return of the Son of Man. In this view, Jesus and/or Mark has produced an end-time scenario that the passing of time has proved to be false.

View 3. Verses 14-18 are *end-time events,* but belong to *the beginning* of the unknown waiting period before the end. On this view, all necessary end-time events, except the return of the Son of Man, occur during the time of the desolating sacrilege and war in Judea (around A.D. 70). The only event predicted to occur at a totally unknown time after that is the return of the Son of Man. We still await this final end-time event, but we should expect no premonitory signs indicating that its coming is either near or far away. The Son of Man's arrival is permanently imminent; disciples are to fill the entire waiting time with mission, discernment, and faithful discipleship.

Where are there implied time gaps in the sequence of events referred to in Mark 13? Which events are referred to by *all these things* that will occur within *this generation* (vv. 4, 30)? Was the prophecy mistaken or not? Which end-time events, in the teaching of Mark 13, are still in the future from **our** perspective? All these questions would be answered differently, depending on which of the three views one accepts (outlined above).

*Which is the **correct** view?* All of the above views have been vigorously defended. A minority of scholars have said, "We simply do not know." However, most of these have said this because they consider Mark 13 too unclear to allow for a definite decision. My view is that Mark 13 *teaches* us to say, "We simply cannot know." Mark's goal was to *prevent* readers from choosing one of the three options and rejecting the other two.

If we could ask Jesus (as portrayed in Mark 13) which of the three views is correct, he would respond, "It might be view 1 or 2 or 3; we will have to wait and see!" View 2 can certainly no longer be considered a possible option (since the End did not come directly after A.D. 70, when the Jerusalem temple was destroyed), but it was still one of the options possible at the time the prophecy was uttered (and recorded).

I think this is the most satisfactory explanation for what we actually find in Mark 13. The chapter is full of ambiguous statements. There are references to *these things* and *all these things,* without clarity about which things are meant (as in vv. 4, 30). There are references to *those days,* without clarifying which days (as in vv. 19, 24). There are grammatical oddities like neuter nouns referred to with masculine participles (v. 14). There are ambiguous statements possible only in Greek (where subjects of verbs can be left unspecified, as in v. 29).

There is backtracking: instead of moving progressively forward in time, the text keeps jumping back, leaving us uncertain which period of time is meant (e.g., 13:28-29 refer to events prior to v. 26; v. 30 might refer to events prior to v. 24; v. 37 refers to a time period before v. 24; and so on). In addition, there are cryptic references and calls for the reader to understand, but with no hints given (cf. v. 14).

What do we do with all these uncertainties? The typical approach is to eliminate them. Ambiguous statements are studied, one of the possible meanings is adopted, the other possibilities are "proved wrong." Uncertainties are eliminated in order to determine what Jesus (or Mark) must have meant. In the end, one of the three views outlined above is accepted; the other two are rejected.

I am convinced that the ambiguities and uncertainties were *deliberately put there*. They are there so that Mark's (and Jesus') uncertainty about end-time events could be preserved, and so that readers would not claim to know more than Jesus did (cf. v. 32).

Let me say this another way. The disciples want to know when the temple will fall and which sign will signal it (and the accompanying events). They may or may not believe that the fall of the temple signals the End of the age. Jesus does *not* supply what the disciples want. His view is that sign-seeking (here and everywhere else in Mark) is inappropriate. Instead, he clarifies for them that there are hard times ahead calling for discernment, faithful discipleship, and mission. The destruction of the temple will also come about, accompanied by difficult times for people in Judea. A great tribulation will precede the final return of the Son of Man.

What Jesus does *not* know is when the End will come (v. 32). Will the events in Judea lead directly to the End? Will they fulfill the necessary preconditions so that the Son of Man can return at any time? Or will they merely prefigure another set of events that will take place at the end of time? Since Jesus does not know, the chapter appears as it does; it does not tell the reader when the End will come. We do violence to Mark 13 by trying to eliminate the ambiguities.

I have heard people suggest that all this sounds far too complex and improbable to be either Mark's view or Jesus' view. But what if we take 13:32-33 as the basic assumption behind all of Mark 13? No one knows when (v. 32). That is why constant discernment and faithfulness are necessary (v. 33). If that is the assumption that controls all of Mark 13, the whole chapter should reflect the following points:

1. Jesus does not know when the End will come.
2. Mark does not know when the End will come.
3. The reader cannot know when the End will come.
4. No signs can help us predict when the End will come.
5. Coming catastrophes may or may not lead directly to the End; we don't know.
6. Discernment and faithfulness are *always* necessary precisely *because* we cannot know when the End will come.
7. Mark 13 teaches disciples what it means to be discerning, faithful disciples in various kinds of situations that will occur before the end, but Mark does not claim to know when the End will occur.

That is exactly what we find in Mark 13, complete with all the ambiguities that *must* be there to preserve the uncertainties that verses 32-33 affirm.

Two more comments. *First,* I am persuaded that the whole time frame of Mark 13 looks a lot less complicated if we manage to put ourselves into the time frame of Jesus; he is looking *forward* to all of the events recorded there. We look *backward,* and it messes up our perspective. Just one example: I have heard people say that there cannot be a time gap between verses 18 and 19 because *those days* mentioned in verse 19 have to refer back to the same days that have been described as *then* in 14b. We look back in time to *those days,* which refer all the way back to *then.* But Jesus was *looking forward.* For him, *then* in verse 14b was a *future* date. To look beyond that future date (v. 14b) to *those days* beyond it (v. 19) creates a reference that can easily be separated in time from the events referred to in verse 14b.

Second, we do not know when Mark was writing. My own view is that it was likely before the destruction of the temple or soon enough after it that view 2 above was still thought to be one of the possible scenarios. That way, the three scenarios considered possibilities by Jesus (according to Mark) would still be possibilities at the time Mark wrote. If Mark was writing well after A.D. 70, then he himself would know that *View 2* (see above) is no longer possible. In that case, he has preserved all three possibilities (in the mouth of Jesus), though he himself knew that only the first and third could still come about. This is possible, but unlikely, in my view.

Mark 13 is a chapter about which many have thought deeply, and even more have written! It is not an easy chapter to interpret. The perspective I have attempted to lay out here and in the commentary itself is the one that has helped me make most sense of what is clear in Mark 13 and what is unclear. My hope is that those who have worked through this short essay are in a better position to understand the interpretation in the commentary itself and therefore also better able to judge whether it does justice to Jesus' very important but very challenging discourse on the future.

ISRAEL AND ISRAEL'S LEADERS (MARK AND ANTI-SEMITISM)

Regrettably, most commentaries on Mark (and on the other Gospels) contain comments such as "Israel rejected Jesus." Such statements are not accurate (especially for Mark's Gospel) and can easily polarize attitudes to contemporary Israel (anti-Semitism, on one hand; uncritical support for Israel, on the other).

At various points in this commentary, I have pointed out the danger of a careless reading of Mark's Gospel in terms of its references to Israel (see esp. comments on 12:1-12; TBC for 11:1-25 and for 11:27—12:44; TLC for 14:27—15:15). Israel was and is divided in its response to Jesus; exactly the same is true for Gentiles. To create the Christian church, Israel was not replaced by Gentiles. Indeed, in NT times (and in NT theology) there is no such thing as a "Gentile church." There is only a church composed of those within Israel who *did* believe and those Gentiles who responded to the invitation to join them.

Did all Israel's *leaders* reject Jesus? Mark never claims they all did. He says the whole Sanhedrin (*council*) condemned Jesus (14:64b; 15:1). Yet Mark acknowledges that there are exceptions among the religious leaders (cf.

esp. 12:28-34). He reports that Joseph of Arimathea, a member of *the council*, asks for the body of Jesus (15:43; Luke 23:50-51 says Joseph did not agree to the council's action). When Mark portrays religious leaders acting *as a group*, they are always opposed to Jesus. It is part of Mark's characterization. When this commentary refers to *scribes* or *Pharisees* (or other religious groups), these comments refer to Mark's characterization of them. No claim is implied that all or even most of the historical Pharisees or scribes were exactly as Mark characterizes the groups.

Many of Israel's first-century leaders were serious about their faith, eager to please God, and diligent in obeying God's law. But many were excessively legalistic, rejected Jesus, and ultimately plotted to have him put to death. Mark and other Gospel writers use titles like *scribes* and *Pharisees* to refer to these, without implying that they were all the same. See also references to various groups of religious leaders in S. Freyne (44) and M. J. Cook (81-83).

KINGDOM OF GOD IN MARK God's kingdom (*hē basileia tou theou*) is named for the first time in 1:15. Its nearness (or arrival) is introduced as the main theme of Jesus' proclamation in Galilee. Yet Mark narrates the entire Galilean ministry with hardly a reference to it (4:11, notes). References to God's kingdom increase in the second half of Mark, where readers are called to discern what is involved in thinking *divine things* rather than *human things* (cf. 8:33).

In Mark, secrecy surrounds God's kingdom (cf. 4:11). God's kingdom comes *secretly*. It is being established, but its coming is discerned only by those with eyes to see and ears to hear. It is discerned particularly by those who can "see" that Jesus is on his throne as he hangs on a cross with the words *King of the Jews* mounted above his head. As do other NT writers, Mark presents God's reign as present and future, "already" and "not yet," under attack now but destined eventually to be fully victorious, secretly coming now but publicly manifest at the end of the age.

I often use the expression "God's reign" rather than "God's kingdom." I am persuaded that Mark, along with most biblical writers, conceives of God's kingdom as God's "active reigning" rather than as some kind of literal kingdom (with boundaries of time and space). God's active reigning cannot be consigned to heaven, or to the future, or to the church, or to any political system, or to the human heart, or to any other narrowly defined sphere (cf. H. Snyder; TLC for 4:1-34).

God's reign is God's active involvement in creation and in history; it is God fulfilling divine purposes. In the Lord's Prayer we are taught to pray, "Your kingdom come!" The meaning of this line is given in the next: "Your will be done on earth as it is in heaven" (Matt. 6:10). God's kingdom is in the process of coming as God's purposes are accomplished in the world, particularly in and through God's people.

According to Mark, God's reign is established as Jesus does the works of God, calls disciples, works in them and through them, and leads them in the way of the cross, and so on. It involves living by God's values rather than human values. The message of God's reign is like a seed taking root in fertile soil (hearts) and growing up to produce a harvest that pleases God. God's reign does not announce its coming with trumpets or establish itself by force. It grows up *within* a hostile environment; it does not use aggression *against* that hostile environment. Those with eyes to see will discern that, even in seeming defeats, it is advancing.

God's reign, though secret, is not private. It is not something established only in the recesses of the individual heart. It is established as followers of Jesus join God's work in the world, as they gather around Jesus, do his works, and proclaim the message of God's reign. Those with "seeing eyes" recognize that in Jesus the kingdom of God has indeed come with power (cf. 9:1, notes). At the end of the age, all secrecy concerning God's reign will be removed when the Son of Man returns in great power and glory.

THE MEANING OF CROSS-CARRYING (ANOTHER VIEW) What would Jesus' call to *take up the cross* (8:34) have meant to someone reading Mark's Gospel for the first time? It would surely be a puzzling statement for someone who does not know how the story will end. Jesus has just predicted his own death at the hands of the elders, chief priests, and scribes; no reader would suspect that this would be by crucifixion. The Jews did not crucify, and there has been no hint to this point that the Romans will be involved in Jesus' coming passion.

As the reader continues through the Gospel, the meaning of Jesus' reference to cross-carrying gradually emerges. At 10:33-34, the reader learns that the religious leaders will hand Jesus over to Gentiles, who will carry out the death penalty. Suspicion might grow that it will be by crucifixion. Far later in the story, at 15:14, a crowd urges Pilate to crucify Jesus. Suddenly, in the space of ten verses, the whole drama unfolds. Jesus is condemned to crucifixion. He (presumably) begins to carry his cross (though Mark is not quite clear about this); the cross is then transferred to a certain Simon's back (who presumably now carries the cross behind Jesus). A few verses later, Jesus suffers the agony of crucifixion. Jesus has thus modeled cross-carrying, and in a symbolic way, so has Simon. But these events hardly explain how cross-carrying can be part of the definition of discipleship. One needs to read the Gospel at a deeper level to understand that.

Along *the way* from Caesarea Philippi to Golgotha, Jesus is teaching his disciples (and Mark is teaching his readers) about discipleship, and therefore about cross-carrying. Voluntary cross-carrying (cf. 8:34) involves giving up everything and trusting God to make it worthwhile (10:28-31). It involves a willingness to lay down one's life for others (10:45). It involves total submission of personal will to God's will at all costs (14:36). It involves identification with Jesus as he is tried, mocked, tortured, and crucified (15:21). Thus, even from Mark's text, cross-bearing is associated with a range of different attitudes and actions.

If one examines the rest of the NT, that range is even broader (see TBC for 8:27—9:1 for a summary of NT associations with the idea of the cross and cross-bearing). No wonder Christians are often unclear what it means to take up the cross. If you ask the average Christian what Jesus meant when he said to carry the cross, expect a wide range of answers: martyrdom (or willingness to face it), suffering for Christ (or willingness to do so), acceptance of the Gospel and/or the proclamation of it, denial of self and/or sinful desires, rejection of legalism, commitment to reconciliation, pacifism, and so on. Perhaps more common (and less likely correct) than all of the above is the idea that "the cross I have to bear" is any inconvenience, however insignificant, that I happen to find irritating.

One of my former colleagues used to say, "When a question generates seven possible answers, change the question." That is what M. P. Green does in a provocative article "The Meaning of Cross-bearing." The following thoughts partly reproduce and partly expand on suggestions he makes.

Instead of asking, "What does cross-bearing mean in the context of the NT?" what if we ask, "What could cross-bearing have meant to the disciples at the time Jesus first used the expression to define discipleship?" The answer would be something they could have understood at the time, before learning that Jesus would die on a cross and before reading any NT theology!

Green points out that only the Romans crucified. Thus the disciples would not have understood Jesus' predicted rejection and death at the hands of Jewish leaders as a prediction of crucifixion. Further, the Romans crucified primarily for insurrection, for rebellion against the imperial power. By making victims carry their crosses, Rome was making a public statement that it does not pay to rebel against the imperial power. Victims carried their crosses behind the centurion, symbolizing submission to the power against which they had previously rebelled. The death march was to function as a deterrent to other would-be insurrectionists.

As a metaphor for discipleship, cross-bearing might carry with it elements of shame, disgrace, suffering, and so on. But more directly, it would relate to prior rebellion, now come to an end. Disciples have ceased to rebel against God's imperial power (God's reign). The cross-bearer is in a position of submission and is making a public statement that rebellion against God is now over.

In the application of the metaphor, Jesus potentially plays two roles. He is the first and premiere cross-bearer; he models true submission, and others follow after. He is also the one who plays the role of the centurion, the one whom would-be disciples follow to symbolize their submission to the reign of God, which Jesus represents. Thus cross-carrying fits appropriately between self-denial and following Jesus, as an essential component of discipleship (8:34).

If pushed too far, the metaphor breaks down (as all metaphors do). The disciple is asked to take up the cross as a voluntary act; no insurrectionist would volunteer to do the same! Moreover, the end of the road for disciples is not a cruel death (as it would be for insurrectionists); for the disciples, a self-sacrificing life (come what may) results in glory. The cross is a way of life, not merely a way of death.

If we read 8:34 in the light of the entire NT, its meaning is significantly expanded and includes many of the elements suggested above (suffering, martyrdom, servanthood, Gospel witness, pacifism, and so on). These should not, however, be treated as the meaning of cross-carrying. They specify what it might entail to submit to the reign of God.

MESSIANIC SECRET At the beginning of the twentieth century, a provocative study of Mark by Wilhelm Wrede sparked a long debate about the origin and the meaning of the "messianic secret" in Mark (cf. 8:29-30). In this commentary I have seldom referred to a "messianic secret." I am persuaded that there are other aspects of secrecy in Mark more central than the secrecy surrounding Jesus' messiahship itself. For example, in

Mark there is more emphasis on keeping Jesus' identity as *Son of God* "secret" than his identity as Messiah (e.g., 1:25, 34; 3:11-12). There is also direct teaching about secrecy connected with the coming of God's reign (4:11).

The main function of secrecy in Mark is to preserve Mark's view that true insight comes not from unambiguous open proclamation and objective proofs (cf. 4:11-12; 8:11-12), but by way of discernment in the context of faithful discipleship and in the light of the cross. Thus Jesus' true identity as *Christ* and *Son of God* is linked to the passion (cf. 8:29-31; 15:37-39). Only those with special "eyes and ears" recognize it there. Although *some* secrecy is preserved only until the resurrection (9:9), God's reign continues to be a "secretly coming kingdom" until the end of the age.

I have not found it helpful to construct a comprehensive theory that aims to explain all Markan secrecy, especially not one focused specifically on a "messianic secret." What is needed is sensitivity to the function of secrecy in a wide range of texts and to how each of the "secrecy texts" relates to Mark's emphasis on the need for "seeing eyes" and "hearing ears." That is the approach taken in this commentary.

MIRACLES IN MARK   In Mark, as in the other Gospels, the *deeds of power* (6:2) or so-called "miracles" (the word does not appear in Mark) serve to meet specific human needs, often restoring people to wholeness. They provoke reflection and insight, demonstrate the arrival of God's reign, and testify to the true identity and nature of Jesus. They are not isolated from other aspects of Jesus' ministry (like his teaching) that equally occasion amazement and equally testify to the nature of God's reign and to the person of Jesus.

In Mark, more so than in the other Gospels, there is a tendency to play down the "apologetic value" of Jesus' acts of power. Whereas sometimes they are accomplished in *response* to an act of faith, never do they clearly *lead* people to faith. Especially the first half of Mark's Gospel features many deeds of power. Human responses to them vary. Enemies see them and turn against Jesus, blind to who he is, accusing him of operating in Satan's power, and tempting him with a request for signs. Disciples have trouble *seeing* and *hearing*, but they remain with Jesus; there is hope for them. A few people (often Gentiles) respond with remarkable faith and insight. This is in stark contrast to John's Gospel, where miracles/"signs" regularly lead people to faith.

Mark's Gospel does not endorse the desire for *signs*—not when *signs* are understood as amazing events designed to persuade skeptical people (e.g., 8:11-12). If the word *signs* is taken to mean events whose real meaning cannot be understood apart from special discernment, then Mark does endorse the idea of signs, but in his Gospel the word *signs* is never used to refer to such events.

Mark's Gospel rarely focuses on the sheer power exhibited in "miracles" or on the evidential value of them. The focus is rather on the redemptive effects of the miraculous events, and especially the characteristics of God's reign to which they point.

QUESTIONING JESUS Jesus is often asked direct questions in Mark. Disciples, religious leaders, crowds, demons, and others interrogate him. According to my count, over thirty direct questions are posed to Jesus in Mark. (It is hard to settle on an exact number, since some questions are compound, and occasionally the punctuation of a sentence is uncertain.)

How often does Jesus directly and unambiguously answer a question? According to my count, he does so *only twice*. We will return to these shortly.

If Jesus directly answers only two questions, what does he do with the others? Often (about six times) he gives an indirect answer, as he does when Pilate asks him if Jesus is Israel's king. His response: *You say so* (15:2). In effect, he says, "The words are yours not mine; what you mean and what I would mean if I accepted your words are two different things."

Often (about six times) Jesus simply refuses to answer. He does this to a delegation from the Sanhedrin (11:28-30), to the high priest (14:61), to Pilate (15:4), and to others. Jesus answers when he chooses to, no matter what is at stake. "What better way to channel our thinking than to challenge us with unanswered questions?" (Fowler, 1991:126, cf. 132f.).

Several times Jesus responds in an oblique way so that what is given is not really an answer. This happens, for example, when Jesus' disciples ask who the betrayer is (14:19-20). *It isn't I, is it?* they ask (TJG). *It is one of the Twelve* is Jesus' ambiguous response, forcing each questioner to answer their own question.

Often Jesus responds to a direct question with a counterquestion:

"Why don't your disciples' fast?"
  "How can they fast when the bridegroom is with them?" (2:18-19)
"Why are they doing what is unlawful on the Sabbath?"
  "Have you never read what David did?" (2:24-25)
"Don't you care if we drown?"
  "Why are you so afraid?" (4:38-40)

These are three examples; there are at least 13 more. In addition, there are over 20 occasions where no direct question is asked, but a situation arises and Jesus responds with a question.

All of this has much to do with Markan "secrecy." Jesus tries to lead people to insight; he does not give all the answers. He opens ears and eyes; he does not draw pictures for the deaf and describe the landscape for the blind. He poses riddles, speaks in parables, and critiques blindness; but he seldom tells people what they should have seen and heard. If this is how Mark pictures *Jesus*, is it any wonder that *Mark* also poses riddles and teaches in enigmas, without always explicitly saying what he is getting at?

Observing how Jesus responds to questions in Mark helps us deal with two texts where commentators have struggled greatly. In 4:10 the disciples ask about the Sower Parable. Commentators have castigated Mark for giving a "wrong interpretation." They assume that if the disciples want to know what the sower parable means, then what Jesus says next must be his "answer" (4:10-13, notes). But if Jesus is not in the habit of answering questions directly and unambiguously, it may well be that the disciples want him to explain the parable, and Jesus uses the opportunity to teach them about hearing ears *instead*. The chapter makes much more sense if interpreted that way.

Mark 13 is also illuminated by observing how Jesus deals with questions. At the beginning of the chapter, Jesus' disciples ask what *sign* will help them know how far along God's eschatological timetable history has moved (13:4). Numerous scholars have simply assumed that what Jesus gives next must be what they want, a sign (or signs). But we should be predisposed to assume that if they want a sign, he will probably give them something else. That is precisely what we find (chap. 13, notes).

On (*only!*) two occasions Jesus gives unambiguous direct answers, and even when he does, he immediately supplements his direct answer with more than the questioner(s) have asked about. A scribe wants to know about the greatest commandment; Jesus gives two (12:28-31). The high priest asks if Jesus is *Christ* and *God's Son*; he says he is, but his "answer" says he is more than these. He is also truly divine, and he will some day come as final judge (14:61-62). On these two occasions, Jesus gives direct answers, and then gives his questioners more than they bargained for.

Mark's reader should assume that there are two situations in which we will most likely gain clear and direct answers from Jesus. That is when we truly want to know the answer to these two questions: *Who is Jesus? What is God's will for those who follow Jesus?* That is what Mark's Gospel is all about.

SON OF MAN   *Son of Man* is clearly a favorite self-designation of Jesus. All four Gospels give evidence (though none as clearly as Mark) that *Son of Man* functions primarily in three contexts.

1. When Jesus makes authority claims. In Mark, for example, the *Son of Man* claims authority twice, both times in chapter 2. He claims *authority on earth to forgive sins* (2:10) and to regulate *Sabbath* observance (2:28).

2. When Jesus refers to his own impending passion (8:31; 9:9, 12, 31; 10:33, 45; 14:21, 41).

3. When Jesus predicts the divine vindication that will follow the passion (8:38; 13:26; 14:62).

The pattern is clear: (1) Jesus claims divine authority. (2) This claim is rejected by many, leading to the passion. (3) This claim is confirmed by God, who raises and exalts Jesus.

Scholars are divided on whether the historical Jesus used *Son of Man* in all three of these ways. Some accept that Jesus made the statements, but deny (at least in the case of the third kind) that he was referring to himself.

There have also been major debates about the *significance* of the designation *Son of Man*. Some connect it to Jewish literature that features a coming glorious "Son of Man" as an apocalyptic envoy from God. More recently, an older view has been refined and restated, that it focuses on the lowliness of Jesus' humanity. The title is used in this way by Ezekiel, where "son of man" seems to mean mortal, and is translated that way by NRSV (Lind: 381).

Most persuasive, I think, is the view that Daniel 7 is the primary background. There "one like a son of man" is given authority and a kingdom by the "Ancient of Days" (God; 7:13-14, RSV). This "son of man," possibly the archangel Michael (representing Israel as its patron angel; cf. 12:1; Lederach:

162), is later identified with "the people of the holy ones [watchers, angels] of the Most High" (the faithful remnant of Israel; cf. 7:18, 22, 27).

For a more detailed discussion, the reader is encouraged to carefully examine an article in Morna Hooker's commentary on Mark (1991:88-93) as well as the literature she recommends there for further study of the issue. I am in substantial agreement with the conclusions she reaches:

1. The historical Jesus *did* refer to himself as *Son of Man*, and did so in all of the three ways indicated above (authority claims; predictions of the passion; predictions of future vindication and glory).

2. The Gospel writers clearly treat *Son of Man* as a direct reference to Jesus himself.

3. The most significant OT text providing a background for Jesus' usage of *Son of Man* (at least as presented in Mark) is Daniel 7:13-14, 18.

4. *Son of Man* is not so much a title as it is a role. It represents the faithful remnant of the elect people of God. Jesus represents that faithful remnant, elected by God to suffer *even to death* (Mark 14:34; cf. Rev. 12:11) and be vindicated through resurrection and glorification (cf. Dan. 7:21-22).

Mark, despite having considerable secrecy about Jesus' two main titles, *Christ* and *Son of God,* attaches no secrecy to *Son of Man*. It is possible that Jesus uses *Son of Man* to forestall legal charges: religious leaders cannot charge Jesus with blasphemy if they cannot prove he was talking about himself. But usually it is a neutral designation used to make statements that help the readers and the characters within the narrative understand the true meaning of the main titles for Jesus (cf. the shift from *Christ* to *Son of Man* in such texts as 8:29, 31 and 14:61-62).

One of the unsolved mysteries in NT scholarship is why Christian writers preserved Jesus' own use of *Son of Man,* but virtually never use *Son of Man* themselves when referring to Jesus. Apart from self-designations in the Gospels, we find in the NT only two hints that anyone else ever referred to Jesus that way (Acts 7:56; Rev. 1:13).

TEXTUAL CRITICISM OF MARK Various factors influence minor (and occasionally major) differences between English translations. Sometimes translators simply disagree on the probable meaning of the Greek text, and their disagreements affect their translations. (All translations are to some extent interpretations.) However, sometimes the differences result from uncertainty as to what the original text actually contained.

The science of textual criticism involves the collection and evaluation of all available Greek manuscripts, and then a carefully considered decision as to the most probable original reading. There are some significant differences between the King James Version and all modern translations (the KJV usually contains extra words or even verses). The explanation is simple: when the KJV was produced, text critics had not yet found and used the oldest and best manuscripts of the NT now available. Between the various modern translations, there is far less variation.

Because the division of the text into chapters (in A.D. 1205) and verses (in A.D. 1551) took place before our modern translations were produced, some verses seem "missing" today. No authentic material has in fact been "lost." Instead, verses (or parts of verses) that are now considered inauthentic (added later by copyists) have been identified and appropriately removed. For example, the KJV of Mark 7:16 reads, *If any man [sic] have ears to hear, let him hear.* Probably a Christian scribe incorporated the words of Mark 4:9 or 4:23 into the context of chapter 7. The verse is rightly omitted from modern translations. A second example is the KJV of Mark 11:26: *But if ye do not forgive, neither will your Father which is in heaven forgive your trespasses.* Here the material was probably incorporated from Matthew 6:15, and again is rightly omitted from Mark's text.

Occasionally (as in 3:31-35 and 14:68-72) scribes seem to have tried to "solve problems" by introducing small changes into the text. As a result, contemporary scholars have a hard time discerning how many times Mark's original text referred to sisters in 3:31-35, and to crowings of a rooster in 14:68-72.

Often scribes (sometimes accidentally; sometimes deliberately) added, deleted, or modified a few words or letters, resulting in minor variations in the reading of individual verses. Most times the original reading can be easily discerned. Occasionally there is some uncertainty. I have commented on such minor (and in the last case, major) uncertainties in the notes for 1:1, 40-41; 2:16; 3:14; 6:20, 22; 8:35; 9:29; 14:4, 41; 15:39; and 16:8. Of all the texts listed above, only four texts (in my judgment) are significantly affected by the textual decisions translators have made.

In 1:1 there is some uncertainty whether *Son of God* belongs to the original text. This is clearly one of Mark's two main titles for Jesus, whether or not it is contained in Mark's opening verse. However, Mark's narrative strategy would need to be reevaluated if one concluded that Mark used only one of his main titles (*Christ*) in the opening verse. I believe *both* titles should be included.

In 9:29, some scribe added the words *and fasting* to Jesus' explanation for the disciples' ineffectiveness in driving out a demon. These words should be omitted. Including them does violence to the intended meaning of the text. In the larger context, it is clear that techniques are not what the disciples lack; the problem is that they rely on techniques and their own past successes, rather than relying on the power of God (notes).

In 15:39 the Greek participle *kraxas* (having cried) may or may not be part of the original text. According to NRSV (assuming *kraxas* is not original, perhaps incorporated from Matt. 27:50), the centurion's confession of Jesus as Son of God is the result of discerning what he has seen. According to NIV (assuming *kraxas* is original), it involves discerning what he has seen and heard. Since the manuscript evidence is indecisive, I am inclined to accept the NIV reading; it preserves at this crucial place a theme that Mark has introduced at strategic places throughout the Gospel. "Seeing eyes" and "hearing ears" are needed in order to discern who Jesus really is and what his life, death, and resurrection truly mean.

By far the most significant text-critical problem for interpreters of Mark is the matter of the authentic ending. Interpreters are virtually unanimous that 16:9-20 was not written by Mark. But if so, where did these verses come from? When and why were they attached to Mark? What is their canonical status? Is Mark 16:8 the ending Mark intended? If not, was he prevented from finishing the book, or did he write an ending that has since disappeared?

If Mark intended to end at 16:8, what does this provocative ending mean? In the commentary on 16:1-8, I have proposed answers to these questions. Whether they seem adequate is for the reader to judge (cf. esp. "Preview" and "The Ending of Mark's Gospel," in notes after 16:8).

THREE LESSONS FROM A BOAT   Many commentators have been impressed with how often Mark's Gospel features threefoldness. Some examples are obvious. Three times Jesus asks his disciples to watch with him; three times they sleep (14:32-42). Jesus predicts Peter's threefold denial (14:30), and Mark counts off all three as they are fulfilled (14:68, 70-71). Some events keep on recurring, but three occurrences of them are specifically highlighted. For example, Jesus refers to his coming passion and resurrection often, but clearly the journey to Jerusalem is structured around three explicit passion-resurrection predictions (8:31; 9:31; 10:33-34).

Similarly Jesus and his disciples are often in the boat together and frequently cross the lake. But three specific trips across the Sea of Galilee are highlighted by Mark (4:35-41; 6:45-52; 8:14-21). Many interpreters have seen in these three boat trips a pattern worth contemplating. They have proposed various theories on what pattern Mark wants the readers to notice.

Some see a christological pattern: Jesus' mighty work on the first trip provokes the question, *Who is this?* (4:41). On the second, he identifies himself with the words *It is I* (*I am,* 6:50). On the third, Jesus is (as some interpret the text) the *one loaf in the boat* (8:14) that is shared by Jew and Gentile alike.

Some see a mission pattern: By stilling the storm, Jesus conquers the barrier separating Jew and Gentile (4:35-41). By walking on the water and urging the disciples to understand the feedings, he prepares to bring Jews and Gentiles together (6:45-52). In his own body (the one loaf), he unites Jews and Gentiles, urging disciples to interpret the two feedings as signs of the salvation of both groups (8:14-21).

I have been impressed with another pattern in the boat trips. In the first one (4:35-41), Mark seems to say, "Jesus is Master of all that threatens his followers; even the powers of nature cannot conquer those who find in Jesus their security." Mark follows this up with a qualification in the second one (6:45-52): "But that does not mean Jesus will remove every obstacle in your lives. Sometimes he wants to assure you of his prayers and his presence while you go on battling the waves" (see notes). Then in the third one (8:14-21), Mark qualifies this even further: "Jesus sometimes intervenes, but he will not produce miracles on demand. If you think that in Jesus you will find unambiguous proofs or an easy life, you have misunderstood him" (notes).

Mark's Gospel teaches about the power and authority of Jesus, his readiness to act on behalf of people in need, his mighty works that testify to the coming of the reign of God. But Mark's Gospel also teaches that the way of following Jesus is not always paved with success, glory, or comfort. More often, it involves suffering, deprivation, rejection, even death—and beyond it, glory! The reign of God will be victorious even though it will seem to suffer setbacks along the way. Jesus teaches those lessons not only on the long road to Jerusalem but also on the Sea of Galilee, when the disciples' boat becomes his classroom.

Palestine in New Testament Times

+Means city has uncertain location

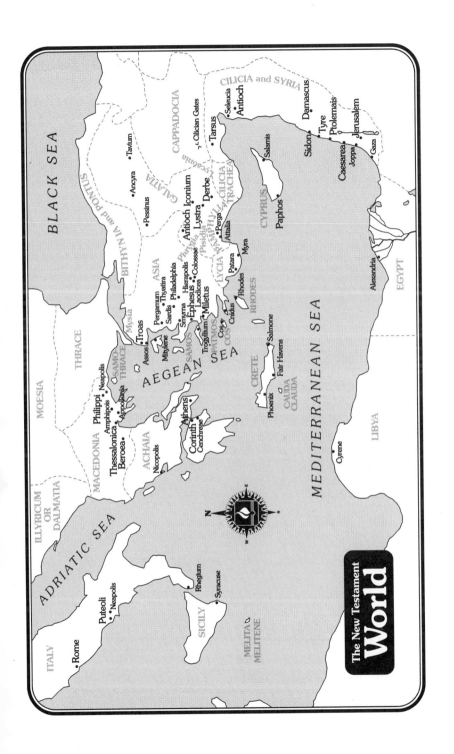

The New Testament World

Bibliography

Achtemeier, Paul
   1962   "Person and Deed: Jesus and the Storm-Tossed Sea."
          Interpretation 16:169-176.
   1975   *Mark*. Philadelphia: Fortress.
   1978   *Invitation to Mark*. Garden City: Doubleday.
   1986   *Mark*. 2d ed. Proclamation Commentaries. Philadelphia:
          Fortress.
Ambrozic, Alosius M.
   1972   *The Hidden Kingdom*. Washington, DC: Catholic Biblical
          Association of America.
Anderson, Hugh
   1976   *The Gospel of Mark*. London: Oliphants.
Anderson, Janice Capel, and Stephen D. Moore, eds.
   1992   *Mark and Method*. Minneapolis: Fortress.
Arnold, Clinton E.
   1992   *Powers of Darkness: Principalities and Powers in Paul's
          Letters*. Downers Grove: InterVarsity.
   1997   *Three Crucial Questions About Spiritual Warfare*. Grand
          Rapids: Baker Bks.
Aulén, Gustaf
   1958   *Eucharist and Sacrifice*. Philadelphia: Muhlenberg Pr.
   1966   *Christus Victor: An Historical Study of the Three Main Types
          of the Idea of the Atonement*. New York: MacMillan.
Bacchiocchi, Samuele
   1977   *From Sabbath to Sunday: A Historical Investigation of the
          Rise of Sunday Observance in Early Christianity*. Rome:
          Pontifical Gregorian Univ. Pr.
Barrett, C. K.
   1968   *Jesus and the Gospel Tradition*. Philadelphia: Fortress.
Beasley-Murray, George
   1957   *A Commentary on Mark 13*. London: MacMillan.
Beck, Robert R.
   1996   *Nonviolent Story: Narrative Conflict Resolution in the Gospel
          of Mark*. Maryknoll, N.Y.: Orbis Books.

Berg, Werner
    1979 *Die Rezeption alttestamentlicher Motive im Neuen Testament—dargestellt an den Seewandelerzählungen.* Freiburg: Hochschul Verlag.

Best, Ernest
    1965 *The Temptation and the Passion: The Markan Soteriology.* New York/London: Cambridge Univ. Pr.
    1981 *Following Jesus: Discipleship in the Gospel of Mark.* Sheffield: JSOT Pr.
    1983 *Mark: The Gospel as Story.* Edinburgh: T & T Clark.
    1986 *Disciples and Discipleship.* Edinburgh: T & T Clark.

Bilezikian, Gilbert G.
    1977 *The Liberated Gospel.* Grand Rapids: Baker Bks.

Blackwell, John
    1986 *The Passion as Story: The Plot of Mark.* Philadelphia: Fortress.

Bonhoeffer, Dietrich
    1954 *Life Together.* New York: Harper & Row.
    1963 *The Cost of Discipleship.* New York: MacMillan.

Bonk, Jonathan J.
    1991 *Missions and Money: Affluence as a Western Missionary Problem.* Maryknoll, N.Y.: Orbis Bks.

Boomershine, Thomas E.
    1988 *Story Journey: An Invitation to the Gospels as Storytelling.* Nashville: Abingdon.

Boyd, Gregory A.
    1997 *God at War: The Bible and Spiritual Conflict.* Downers Grove: InterVarsity.

Brooks, James A.
    1991 *Mark.* Nashville: Broadman.

Brown, Colin
    1985 *That You May Believe: Miracles and Faith—Then and Now.* Grand Rapids: Eerdmans.

Burdon, C.
    1990 *Stumbling on God: Faith and Vision in Mark's Gospel.* Grand Rapids: Eerdmans.

Caird, G. B.
    1980 *The Language and Imagery of the Bible.* Philadelphia: Westminster.

Camery-Hoggatt, Jerry
    1992 *Irony in Mark's Gospel.* Cambridge: C. Univ. Pr.

Carson, D. A., ed.
    1982 *From Sabbath to Lord's Day: A Biblical, Historical, and Theological Investigation.* Grand Rapids: Zondervan.

Clapp, Rodney
    1993 *Families at the Crossroads: Beyond Traditional and Modern Options.* Downers Grove: InterVarsity.

Cole, Robert Alan
    1961 *The Gospel According to St. Mark.* Grand Rapids: Eerdmans.

Collins, Adela Yarbro
    1992 *The Beginning of the Gospel: Probings of Mark in Context.* Minneapolis: Fortress.

Cook, Michael J.
    1978   *Mark's Treatment of the Jewish Leaders*. Leiden: E. J. Brill.
Cotter, Wendy J.
    1986   "For It Was Not the Season for Figs." *Catholic Biblical Quarterly* 48:62-66.
Cranfield, C.E.B.
    1953   "St. Mark 13." *Scottish Journal of Theology* 6:189-196.
    1966   *The Gospel According to St. Mark*. Cambridge: C. Univ. Pr.
Culpepper, R. Alan
    1980   "Mark 11:15-19." *Interpretation* 34:176-181.
De Vaux. *See* Vaux, Roland de.
Dewey, Joanna
    1976   *Disciples of the Way: Mark on Discipleship*. Cincinnati: Women's Div., Bd. of Global Ministries, U. Methodist Church.
    1980   *Markan Public Debate. Literary Technique, Concentric Structure, and Theology in Mark 2:1—3:6*. Chico: Scholars Pr.
Donahue, John R.
    1973   *Are You the Christ?* Missoula: Univ. of Montana.
Doohan, Leonard
    1986   *Mark: Visionary of Early Christianity*. Santa Fe: Bear & Co.
Dowd, Sharyn Echols
    1988   *Power, Prayer, and the Problem of Suffering*. Atlanta: Scholars Pr.
Driver, John
    1986   *Understanding the Atonement for the Mission of the Church*. Scottdale: Herald Pr.
Dyck, Cornelius J., trans. and ed.
    1995   *Spiritual Life in Anabaptism*. Scottdale: Herald Pr.
English, D.
    1992   *The Message of Mark: The Mystery of Faith*. Downers Grove: InterVarsity.
Epp, Edwin W., Henry V. Friesen, and Henry Peters
    1979   *The Celebration of the Lord's Supper*. Newton: Faith & Life Pr.
Evans, Craig A.
    2000   *Mark 8:27—16:20*. Dallas: Nelson/Word. *Also see* Guelich.
Evans, Mary J.
    1983   *Woman in the Bible*. Downers Grove: InterVarsity.
Farrer, Austin M.
    1954   *St. Matthew and St. Mark*. London: A. & C. Black.
Faw, Chalmer.
    1993   *Acts*. BCBC. Scottdale, Pa.: Herald Pr.
Finger, Thomas N.
    1985   *Christian Theology: An Eschatological Approach*. Vol. 1. Scottdale, Pa.: Herald Pr.
Fowler, Robert M.
    1981   *Loaves and Fishes: The Function of the Feeding Stories in the Gospel of Mark*. Chico: Scholars Pr.
    1991   *Let the Reader Understand*. Minneapolis: Augsburg.

France, R. T.
   1990   *Divine Government: God's Kingship in the Gospel of Mark.*
          London: SPCK.
Freyne, Seán
   1988   *Galilee, Jesus, and the Gospels.* Philadelphia: Fortress.
Fredricksen, Paula
   1999   *Jesus of Nazareth, King of the Jews: A Jewish Life and the
          Emergence of Christianity.* New York: Alfred A. Knopf.
Funk, Robert W.
   1973   "The Looking-Glass Tree Is for the Birds." *Interpretation* 27:3-
          9.
Garrett, Susan R.
   1998   *The Temptations of Jesus in Mark's Gospel.* Grand Rapids:
          Eerdmans.
Geddert, Gertrud A.
   1996   "Reaching Out in Faith." In *All Are Witnesses,* ed. D. Friesen.
          Hillsboro: Kindred.
Geddert, Timothy J.
   1986   "We Prayed for Healing—But She Died." *Mennonite Brethren
          Herald,* Sept. 19, 6-8.
   1987   "How Do We Read the Gospels?" *M. B. Herald,* Nov. 13, 6-7.
   1989   *Watchwords: Mark 13 in Markan Eschatology.* Sheffield:
          Sheffield Academic Pr.
   1992   "Apocalyptic Teaching." *Dictionary of Jesus and the Gospels.*
          Ed. Joel B. Green et al. Downers Grove: InterVarsity.
   1996   "Demonization: A Biblical View." *Christian Leader,* Feb., 4-6.
Geisler, Norman L.
   1992   *Miracles and the Modern Mind.* Grand Rapids: Baker Bks.
Girard, René. *See also* Swartley, 2000
   1986   *The Scapegoat.* Baltimore: John Hopkins Univ. Pr.
   1987   *Things Hidden Since the Foundation of the World.* Stanford:
          Stanford Univ. Pr.
Gnilka, Joachim
   1978   *Das Evangelium nach Markus, Mk 1—8, 26.* Zurich: Benziger
          Verlag.
   1979   *Das Evangelium nach Markus, Mk 8, 27—16, 20.* Zurich:
          Benziger Verlag.
Green, Joel B.
   1997   *The Gospel of Luke.* NICNT. Grand Rapids: Eerdmans.
Green, Joel B., ed.
   1995   *Hearing the New Testament: Strategies for Interpretation.*
          Grand Rapids: Eerdmans.
Green, Joel B., and Mark D. Baker
   2000   *Recovering the Scandal of the Cross: The Atonement in the
          New Testament and Contemporary Contexts.* Downers Grove,
          Ill.: InterVarsity.
Green, Michael P.
   1983   "The Meaning of Cross-bearing." *Bibliotheca Sacra* 140:117-
          133.

Guelich, Robert A.
   1989   *Mark 1—8:26*. Dallas: Word. *Also see* Evans, Craig A.
Gundry, Robert H.
   1993   *Mark. A Commentary on His Apology for the Cross*. Grand
          Rapids: Eerdmans.
Halteman, James
   1995   *The Clashing Worlds of Economics and Faith*. Scottdale:
          Herald Pr.
Hamerton-Kelly, Robert G.
   1994   *The Gospel and the Sacred*. Minneapolis: Augsburg Fortress.
Harder, Lydia Harder
   1998   *Obedience, Suspicion and the Gospel of Mark*. Waterloo:
          Wilfrid Laurier Univ. Pr.
Hare, Douglas R. A.
   1996   *Mark*. Louisville: Westminster.
Harrington, Wilfred
   1979   *Mark*. Wilmington: Liturgical Pr., M. Glazier.
Hays, Richard B.
   1996   *The Moral Vision of the New Testament*. San Francisco:
          HarperSF.
Heil, John Paul
   1992   *The Gospel of Mark as a Model for Action*. Mahwah, N.J.:
          Paulist Pr.
Hershberger, Guy Franklin
   1957   Ed. *The Recovery of the Anabaptist Vision*. Scottdale: Herald Pr.
   1958   *The Way of the Cross in Human Relations*. Scottdale: Herald Pr.
Hooker, Morna D.
   1967   *The Son of Man in Mark*. London: SPCK.
   1983   *The Message of Mark*. London: Epworth.
   1991   *The Gospel According to St. Mark*. London: A. & C. Black.
Hoover, Susan Bame
   1995   *Faith the Cow*. Elgin, Ill.: Brethren Pr.
Humphrey, H. M.
   1992   *"He Is Risen!" A New Reading of Mark's Gospel*. Mahwah,
          N.J.: Paulist Pr.
Hurtado, Larry W.
   1989   *Mark*. Peabody, Mass.: Hendrickson.
Iersel, Bastiaan Martinus Franciscus van
   1988   *Reading Mark*. Collegeville: Liturgical Pr.
Janzen, Waldemar
   2000   *Exodus*. BCBC. Scottdale, Pa.: Herald Pr.
Jeremias, Joachim
   1963   *The Parables of Jesus*. New York: Scribner.
   1990   *The Eucharistic Words of Jesus*. London: SCM.
Johnson, Sherman E.
   1972   *The Gospel According to St. Mark*. London: A. & C. Black.
Josephus, Flavius
   1999   *Antiquities of the Jews*. In *Josephus: The Complete Works*.
          Trans. W. Whiston. Nashville: Thomas Nelson.

Juel, Donald H.
  1990   *Mark*. Minneapolis: Augsburg
  1994   *A Master of Surprise: Mark Interpreted*. Minneapolis: Fortress.
  1999   *The Gospel of Mark*. Nashville: Abingdon.
Kaufman, Donald D.
  1989   *What Belongs to Caesar?* Scottdale: Herald Pr.
Kealy, Seán P.
  1982   *Mark's Gospel: A History of Its Interpretation from the Beginning Until 1979*. Mahwah, N.J.: Paulist Pr.
Kee, Howard C.
  1977   *Community of the New Age*. Philadelphia: Westminster.
Kelber, Werner H.
  1974   *The Kingdom in Mark. A New Place and a New Time*. Philadelphia: Fortress.
  1976   Ed. *The Passion in Mark*. Philadelphia: Fortress.
  1979   *Mark's Story of Jesus*. Philadelphia: Fortress.
Kermode, Frank
  1979   *The Genesis of Secrecy. On the Interpretation of Narrative*. Cambridge/London: Harvard Univ. Pr.
Kingsbury, Jack Dean
  1981   *Jesus Christ in Matthew, Mark, and Luke*. Philadelphia: Fortress.
  1983   *The Christology of Mark's Gospel*. Philadelphia: Fortress.
  1989   *Conflict in Mark: Jesus, Authorities, Disciples*. Minneapolis: Fortress.
Klaassen, Walter
  1981   Ed. *Anabaptism in Outline*. CRR. Scottdale: Herald Pr.
  1999   *Armageddon and the Peaceable Kingdom*. Scottdale: Herald Pr.
Klassen, Steve
  2000   *Mark*. Word Wise Curriculum. Winnipeg: Kindred Prodns.
Kraybill, Donald B.
  1978   *The Upside-Down Kingdom*. Scottdale: Herald Pr.
Kreider, Eleanor
  1997   *Communion Shapes Character*. Scottdale: Herald Pr.
Kydd, Ronald A. N.
  1998   *Healing Through the Centuries: Models for Understanding*. Peabody, Mass.: Hendrickson.
Ladd, George Eldon
  1964   *Jesus and the Kingdom: The Eschatology of Biblical Realism*. New York: Harper & Row.
Lane, William L.
  1974   *The Gospel According to Mark*. Grand Rapids: Eerdmans.
Lederach Paul M.
  1994   *Daniel*. BCBC. Scottdale, Pa.: Herald Pr.
Lehn, Cornelia
  1991   *I Heard Good News Today*. Newton: Faith & Life Pr.
Lewis, C. S.
  1964   *Letters to Malcolm: Chiefly on Prayer.* New York: Harcourt, Brace & World.
  1996   *Miracles: A Preliminary Study*. New York: Touchstone.

Lightfoot, Robert H.
   1962   *The Gospel Message of St. Mark*. Oxford: O. Univ. Pr.
Lind, Millard C.
   1996   *Ezekiel*. BCBC. Scottdale: Herald Pr.
Lohfink, Gerhard
   1984   *Jesus and Community*. Minneapolis: Fortress.
   1998   *Braucht Gott die Kirche?* Freiburg: Herder.
McCowen, Alec
   1985   *Personal Mark*. London: Fount.
McKenna, David L.
   1982   *Mark*. Waco: Word.
Mackrell, Gerard Francis
   1987   *The Healing Miracles in Mark's Gospel*. State Mutual Bk &
            Periodical Serv., New York/Middlegreen, U.K.: St. Paul Pubns.
Malbon, Elizabeth Struthers
   1982   "Galilee and Jerusalem: History and Literature in Marcan
            Interpretation." *Catholic Biblical Quarterly* 44:242-55.
   1983   "Fallible Followers: Women and Men in the Gospel of Mark."
            Semeia 28:29-48.
   1986   *Narrative Space and Mythic Meaning in Mark*. San Francisco:
            Harper & Row.
Mann, Christopher S.
   1986   *Mark*. New York: Doubleday.
Mansfield, M. Robert
   1987   *Spirit and Gospel in Mark*. Peabody, Mass.: Hendrickson.
Marcus, Joel
   1992   *The Way of the Lord*. Philadelphia: Westminster.
Marshall, Christopher D.
   1989   *Faith as a Theme in Mark's Narrative*. Cambridge: C. Univ. Pr.
Marshall, I. Howard
   1967   *St. Mark*. Grand Rapids: Eerdmans.
   1977   Ed. *New Testament Interpretation: Essays on Principles and
            Methods*. Grand Rapids: Eerdmans.
Martin, Ralph P.
   1973   *Mark: Evangelist and Theologian*. Grand Rapids: Zondervan.
   1981   *Mark*. Atlanta: John Knox.
Marxsen, Willi
   1969   *Mark the Evangelist: Studies on the Redaction History of the
            Gospel*. Nashville/New York: Abingdon.
Matera, Frank J.
   1982   *The Kingship of Jesus: Composition and Theology in Mark 15*.
            Chico: Scholars Pr.
   1986   *Passion Narratives and Gospel Theologies: Interpreting the
            Synoptics Through Their Passion Stories*. Mahwah, N.J.:
            Paulist Pr.
   1987   *What Are They Saying About Mark?* Mahwah, N.J.: Paulist Pr.
Mauser, Ulrich W.
   1963   *Christ in the Wilderness*. Naperville, Ill.: Allenson.

Meagher, John C.
   1980   *Clumsy Construction in Mark's Gospel.* Lewiston, N.Y.: Edwin
          Mellen.
Meye, Robert P.
   1968   *Jesus and the Twelve: Discipleship and Revelation in Mark's
          Gospel.* Grand Rapids: Eerdmans.
Moltmann, Jürgen
   1990   *The Way of Jesus Christ: Christology in Messianic
          Dimensions.* San Francisco: HarperSF.
Moule, C. F. D.
   1965   *The Gospel According to Mark.* Cambridge: C. Univ. Pr.
Muddiman, J. B.
   1975   "Jesus and Fasting: Mark ii.18-22." In *Jesus aux origines de la
          Christologie,* ed. J. Dupont. Louvain: Leuven Univ. Pr.
Myers, Ched
   1988   *Binding the Strong Man: A Political Reading of Mark's Story
          of Jesus.* Maryknoll, N.Y.: Orbis Bks.
   1996   *"Say to This Mountain': Mark's Story of Discipleship.*
          Maryknoll, N.Y.: Orbis Bks.
Neirynck, F., et al.
   1992   *The Gospel of Mark. A Cumulative Bibliography, 1950-1990.*
          Louvain: Leuven Univ. Pr.
Nineham, D. E.
   1963   *The Gospel of St. Mark.* Middlesex: Penguin Bks.
Osiek, Carolyn, and David L. Balch
   1997   *Families in the New Testament World.* Louisville: John Knox.
Peachey, Titus
   1993   *Silence and Courage: Income Taxes, War and Mennonites
          (1940-1993).* Akron, Pa.: MCC.
Peatman, W.
   1992   *The Beginning of the Gospel. Mark's Story of Jesus.*
          Collegeville: Liturgical Pr.
Peck, M. Scott
   1983   *People of the Lie: The Hope for Healing Human Evil.* New
          York: Simon & Schuster.
Perrin, Norman
   1970   *What Is Redaction Criticism?* London: SPCK.
   1976   *Jesus and the Language of the Kingdom.* Philadelphia: Fortress.
   1977   *The Resurrection According to Matthew, Mark, and Luke.*
          Philadelphia: Fortress.
Pesch, Rudolf
   1976   *Das Markusevangelium I.* Freiburg: Herder.
   1977   *Das Markusevangelium II.* Freiburg: Herder.
Petersen, Norman R.
   1978   *Literary Criticism for New Testament Critics.* Philadelphia:
          Fortress.
Phelan, John E.
   1990   "The Function of Mark's Miracles." *Covenant Quarterly* 48:3-
          14.

442   **Bibliography**

Piper, Otto A.
  1955   "God's Good News: The Passion Story According to Mark."
         Interpretation 9:165-182.
Quesnell, Quintin
  1969   *The Mind of Mark: Interpretation and Method Through the
         Exegesis of Mark 6:52.* Rome: Biblical Institute Pr.
Rempel, John D.
  1993   *The Lord's Supper in Anabaptism.* SAMH. Scottdale: Herald
         Pr.
Rhoads, David, and Donald Michie
  1982   *Mark as Story: An Introduction to the Narrative of a Gospel.*
         Philadelphia: Fortress Pr. 2d ed. with Joanna Dewey.
         Minneapolis: Fortress, 1999.
Richardson, Alan
  1942   *The Miracle-Stories of the Gospels.* London: SCM Pr.
Riedemann, Peter
  1999   *Peter Riedemann's Hutterite Confession of Faith.* Trans. and
         ed. John J. Friesen. CRR. Scottdale, Pa.: Herald Pr.
Rivkin, Ellis
  1984   *What Killed Jesus?* Nashville: Abingdon.
Robbins, Vernon K.
  1984   *Jesus the Teacher: A Socio-Rhetorical Interpretation of Mark.*
         Philadelphia: Fortress. 1992, pbk.
Ryken, Leland
  1984   *The New Testament in Literary Criticism.* New York: Frederick
         Ungar.
Schweizer, Eduard
  1960   *Lordship and Discipleship.* Naperville, Ill.: Allenson.
  1970   *The Good News According to Mark.* Atlanta: John Knox.
Scott, M. Philip
  1985   "Chiastic Structure: A Key to the Interpretation of Mark's
         Gospel." *Biblical Theology Bulletin* 15:531-48.
Senior, Donald
  1984   *The Passion of Jesus in the Gospel of Mark.* Wilmington:
         Liturgical Pr., M. Glazier.
Snyder, Howard
  1991   *Models of the Kingdom.* Nashville: Abingdon.
Stock, Augustine
  1982   *Call to Discipleship: A Literary Study of Mark's Gospel.*
         Wilmington: Liturgical Pr., M. Glazier.
  1984   "Chiastic Awareness and Education in Antiquity." *Biblical
         Theology Bulletin* 14:23-27.
  1985   "Hinge Transitions in Mark's Gospel." *Biblical Theology
         Bulletin* 15:27-31.
  1989   *The Method and Message of Mark.* Wilmington: Liturgical Pr.,
         M. Glazier.
Str.-B.   Strack, H. L., and P. Billerbeck
  1922-61 *Kommentar zum Neuen Testament aus Talmud und
           Midrasch.* 6 vols. in 7. Munich: Beck.

Swartley, Willard M.
  1973 "A Study in Markan Structure: The Influence of Israel's Holy History upon the Structure of the Gospel of Mark." Dissertation, Princeton Theological Seminary.
  1980 *"The Christian and Payment of Taxes Used for War."* Elkhart, Ind.: MBCM. Adapted version in *Sojourners*, Feb. 1979; and in "MCC Peace Section Newsletter," Jan. 1981.
  1981 *Mark: The Way for All Nations.* Scottdale: Herald Pr. Repr., Eugene, Ore.: Wipf & Stock, 1999.
  1983 *Slavery, Sabbath, War, and Women: Case Issues in Biblical Interpretation.* Scottdale: Herald Pr.
  1984 Ed. *Essays on Biblical Interpretation: Anabaptist-Mennonite Perspectives.* Elkhart: Institute of Mennonite Studies.
  1994 *Israel's Scripture Traditions and the Synoptic Gospels: Story Shaping Story.* Peabody, Mass.: Hendrickson.
Swartley, Willard M., ed.
  2000 *Violence Renounced: René Girard, Biblical Studies, and Peacemaking.* With a response by René Girard. Telford, Pa.: Pandora U.S., and Scottdale, Pa.: Herald Pr.
Swartley, Willard M., and Donald B. Kraybill, eds.
  1998 *Building Communities of Compassion.* Scottdale: Herald Pr.
Swartz, Herbert L.
  1988 "Fear and Amazement Responses: A Key to the Concept of Faith in the Gospel of Mark, A Redactional/Literary Study." Unpublished ThD. diss., Univ. of Toronto.
Taylor, Vincent
  1953 *The Gospel According to St. Mark.* London: MacMillan.
Telford, William
  1985 *The Interpretation of Mark.* Philadelphia: Fortress.
Thompson, Mary R
  1989 *The Role of Disbelief in Mark.* Mahwah, N.J.: Paulist Pr.
Tolbert, Mary Ann
  1989 *Sowing the Gospel: Mark's World in Literary-Historical Perspective.* Minineapolis: Fortress.
Turner, C. H.
  1925 "Marcan Usage: Notes, Critical and Exegetical, on the Second Gospel." *Journal of Theological Studies* (OS) 26:145-56.
Vaux, Roland de
  1965 *Ancient Israel: Social Institutions.* New York: McGraw-Hill.
Vincent, Mark.
  1997 *A Christian View of Money: Celebrating God's Generosity.* Scottdale: Herald Pr.
Waltner, Erland, and J. Daryl Charles
  1999 *1-2 Peter, Jude.* BCBC. Scottdale, Pa.: Herald Pr.
Weeden, Theodore J.
  1971 *Mark—Traditions in Conflict.* Philadelphia: Fortress Pr.
  1976 "The Cross as Power in Weakness." In *The Passion in Mark,* ed. W. Kelber. Philadelphia: Fortress.
Wenger, J.C., ed.
  1956 *The Complete Writings of Menno Simons.* Scottdale: Herald Pr.

Wenham, John
  1985   *Easter Enigma: Do the Resurrection Stories Contradict One Another?* Exeter, U.K.: Paternoster.
Williams, James G.
  1985   *Gospel Against Parable.* Decatur, Ga.: Almond Pr.
Williams, R. Rhys
  1987   *Let Each Gospel Speak for Itself.* Mystic, Conn.: Twenty-Third Pubns.
Williamson, Lamar
  1983   *Mark, Interpretation: A Bible Commentary for Teaching and Preaching.* Atlanta: John Knox.
Wink, Walter
  1992   *Engaging the Powers: Discernment and Resistance in a World of Domination.* Minneapolis: Augsburg Fortress.
Wrede, William
  1971   *The Messianic Secret.* Cambridge: James Clarke.
Wright, A.
  1982   "The Widow's Mites: Praise or Lament?—A Matter of Context." *Catholic Biblical Quarterly* 44:256-65.
Wright, N. T.
  1997   *Jesus and the Victory of God.* Minneapolis: Augsburg Fortress.
Yeatts, John R.
  Forthcoming   *Revelation.* BCBC. Scottdale, Pa.: Herald Pr.

Selected Resources

Best, Ernest. *Mark: The Gospel as Story*. Edinburgh: T & T Clark, 1983. In 22 short essays, examines Mark's sources, his purpose and style, many of the Gospel's key themes, the "drama of Mark's Gospel," and its continuing significance. Helpful on the nature of discipleship and the role of Jesus' disciples in Mark.

Dowd, Sharyn Echols. *Power, Prayer, and the Problem of Suffering*. Atlanta: Scholars Press, 1989. Careful study of prayer and suffering in Mark. Interprets 11:22-25. Shows how Mark calls disciples to prayer, faith, and faithfulness, knowing God *can* do miracles but often *does not* miraculously alleviate suffering and persecution.

Garrett, Susan R. *The Temptations of Jesus in Mark's Gospel*. Grand Rapids: Eerdmans, 1998. Readable, helpful study of how Mark portrays temptation and testing in the life of discipleship. Careful, balanced scholarship. Reflection on discipleship.

Geddert, Timothy J. *Watchwords: Mark 13 in Markan Eschatology*. Sheffield: Sheffield Academic Press, 1989. Deals with topics such as sign-seeking, discipleship, persecution, Jesus' relationship to the temple, and especially the meaning and function of Mark 13. More technical than this commentary.

Guelich, Robert A., *Mark 1—8:26*. Craig A. Evans and R. Guelich, *Mark 8:27—16:20*. Dallas: Word, 1989, 2000. Helpful, thorough. For each textual unit: comments verse-by-verse; comments on the form, structure, and setting; explains text; gives bibliography.

Hooker, Morna D. *The Gospel According to St. Mark*. London: A. & C. Black, 1991. Shares fruit of a lifetime of studying Mark. Well-balanced and readable. Draws on a range of interpretive methods.

Hurtado, Larry W. *Mark*. Peabody, Mass.: Hendrickson, 1989. Based on *Good News Bible*. Briefly explains each unit from a fairly conservative perspective. Discusses selected words and phrases. Helpful for a Sunday school teacher.

Juel, Donald H. *The Gospel of Mark.* Nashville: Abingdon, 1999.
Interprets key texts and themes in Mark's Gospel. Helpfully discusses meaning of "interpreting" a Gospel. Readable.

Kelber, Werner. *Mark's Story of Jesus.* Philadelphia: Fortress, 1979.
Reads Mark's story line, teases out hidden meanings, and interprets
their significance in relation to Kelber's view of Mark's historical
context. Provocative, with some debatable viewpoints, such as the
narrative role of the disciples in Mark. Challenges assumptions.

Kingsbury, Jack Dean. *Conflict in Mark: Jesus, Authorities,
Disciples.* Minneapolis: Fortress, 1990. Traces stories of Jesus, the
authorities, and the disciples. Conflict abounds as characters interact and stories interlock. Challenges readers to faithful discipleship,
a lifestyle modeled by Jesus and projected into the future.

Klassen, Steve. *Mark.* Word Wise Curriculum. Winnipeg: Kindred
Productions, 2000. Adult group study guide for 13 weeks. Useful
alongside this commentary.

Matera, Frank J. *What Are They Saying About Mark?* Mahwah,
N.J.: Paulist Press, 1987. Gives students of Mark a survey of the
scholarly landscape, with its astonishing or even troubling diversity.
Wisely claims that radical and negative views of Mark are losing
ground to saner and more positive biblical viewpoints.

Myers, Ched. *'Say to This Mountain:' Mark's Story of Discipleship.*
Maryknoll, N.Y.: Orbis, 1996. A study guide for groups. Like
Binding the Strong Man, focuses on issues of social justice.
Interprets (or even *over*-interprets) Mark's text in its original social
political situation. Challenges readers to radical peacemaking.

Rhoads, David, and Donald Michie. *Mark as Story.* Philadelphia/
Minneapolis: Fortress, 1982; with Joanna Dewey, 1999. Examines Mark's literary techniques, plot development, and characterizations. Less technical than Robert Fowler's *Let the Reader
Understand* (Minneapolis: Augsburg, 1991).

Senior, Donald. *The Passion of Jesus in the Gospel of Mark.*
Wilmington: Liturgical Press, M. Glazier, 1984. Interprets Mark's
account of Jesus' suffering, death, and resurrection in the light of
his whole Gospel. Shows Jesus' passion in its horror, majesty, and
theological depth, with a challenge to faithful discipleship.

Swartley, Willard M. *Mark: The Way for all Nations.* Scottdale:
Herald Press, 1981. Reprint, Eugene, Ore.: Wipf & Stock, 1999.
Inductively observes Mark's composition techniques, key words,
OT allusions, geographical, temporal, and numerical references,
and so on. Readers discover Mark's (sometimes hidden) meaning,
and his missionary emphasis "for all nations."

Index of Ancient Sources

The Author

Timothy J. Geddert (Tim) teaches New Testament at Mennonite Brethren Biblical Seminary, Fresno, California. He and his wife, Gertrud, are active members of Fig Garden Bible Church, where both have been involved in leadership and in preaching. They have six children: two grown sons, a younger daughter, and three young boys. The fact that Tim was able to write this commentary while helping to parent their youngsters is a tribute to the support and patience of his wife, Gertrud, to whom this book is dedicated.

Tim has memorized Mark, written a doctoral dissertation and scholarly monograph on it, and presented scholarly papers on it. He has also taught courses on Mark and preached from it in seminary classes and churches. Now he fulfills one of his personal dreams—to publish his insights into the meaning and challenge of Mark's Gospel in a form accessible to the average Christian reader.

Tim was born and grew up in Saskatchewan, Canada. After graduating from Bethany Bible Institute in Hepburn, Saskatchewan, he completed a B.A. in Philosophy (Saskatoon, 1976) and an M.Div. in Biblical Studies (Fresno, 1978). He then spent five years planting and pastoring a church in Ft. McMurray, Alberta, before earning a Ph.D. in New Testament (Aberdeen, Scotland, 1986).

Tim is married to Gertrud (Andres), who first came to North America from her native Germany to study theology and counseling. They are raising their family bilingually and biculturally. They have shared a joint appointment as church workers in Ingolstadt, Germany (1990-93), and have also lived in Germany while Tim has been on sabbatical leave.

In addition to preaching, teaching, and writing, Tim enjoys a range of activities, including bicycling with his older sons (to eight countries neighboring Germany, and on the West Coast trail from Abbotsford, B.C., to Fresno). He paints houses and church buildings (where he was a member in Scotland, Germany, and California). He travels, sometimes cooks, and has published several cookbooks.

Timothy J. Geddert's monograph on Mark is *Watchwords: Mark 13 in Markan Eschatology* (Sheffield, 1989). Some of his articles related to Mark are listed in the Bibliography (above).